OXFORD STUDIES IN AFRICAN AFFAIRS

General Editors
JOHN D. HARGREAVES *and* GEORGE SHEPPERSON

THE TRADITIONAL HISTORY
OF THE
JIE OF UGANDA

THE
TRADITIONAL HISTORY
OF THE
JIE OF UGANDA

BY

JOHN LAMPHEAR

CLARENDON PRESS · OXFORD
1976

Oxford University Press, Ely House, London W. 1

GLASGOW NEW YORK TORONTO MELBOURNE WELLINGTON
CAPE TOWN IBADAN NAIROBI DAR ES SALAAM LUSAKA ADDIS ABABA
DELHI BOMBAY CALCUTTA MADRAS KARACHI LAHORE DACCA
KUALA LUMPUR SINGAPORE HONG KONG TOKYO

ISBN 0 19 821692 0

© Oxford University Press 1976

Printed in Great Britain by
Cox & Wyman Ltd
London, Fakenham and Reading

To Molly and Kere

Preface

THIS book is the first attempt to reconstruct the pre-colonial history of the Jie of Uganda. It is also the first detailed historical study of any of the Central Paranilotic-speaking peoples of Karamoja District, Uganda, or of the neighbouring areas of north-western Kenya or the southern Sudan.

This reconstruction has been based primarily on Jie oral tradition, systematically collected during a sixteen-month period of field-work from November 1969 to February 1971. As this project was among the first in which one of the more pastorally oriented communities of East Africa has been studied by a professional historian, the rather specialized methodology which elicited the historical data is described in detail. While this work covers many aspects of the Jie historical experience from *c*. 1720 to *c*. 1915, its central theme is that of the development of the Jie political community.

My own interest in the pastoral and semi-pastoral peoples of East Africa developed between 1963 and 1967 when I was working as a teacher in Tanzania. The last two years of that period were spent teaching and working in Masai District, and it was during that time that I became specifically interested in the Paranilotic-speaking peoples. During that same period, I visited Turkana District in north-western Kenya and thereby briefly acquainted myself with a Central Paranilotic-speaking community.

In the autumn of 1967 I enrolled in the African Area Studies course for an M.A. at the School of Oriental and African Studies, London University. During the year of that course, I became intensely interested in the methodology of oral history and read much of the existing literature on Paranilotic-speaking peoples. I was also able to devote a good bit of time to the study of social anthropology, thereby acquiring a methodological outlook which was to prove immensely valuable later on. By the following year, I had decided that I should like to undertake an oral-history project on one of the pastoral or semi-pastoral Paranilotic-speaking peoples of East Africa. At the suggestion of Professor Roland Oliver, who was to supervise my subsequent Ph.D. work, I began to consider a project amongst the Jie. A colleague from SOAS, Mr. John Tosh, was beginning a project amongst the Langi of north-central Uganda, with whom the available data suggested the Jie had had interaction in the past. Moreover, Professor P. H. Gulliver, a social anthropologist and the only scholar of any discipline ever to have studied the Jie, was also at SOAS and I had had the opportunity to study under him during my M.A. course. By the end of 1968 I had definitely decided to undertake field research on Jie oral history, and after a further nine months of preparation, I embarked on my field-work in Uganda in the autumn of 1969.

In the sixteen months spent in Karamoja District, Uganda, and Turkana District, Kenya, nearly 200 formal interviews were carried out. The data thus collected served as the basis for my Ph.D. thesis, 'The Oral History of the Jie of Uganda', which was written between March 1971 and May 1972 in London. This book has drawn heavily on that thesis, although some of the more purely ethnographic and archaeological data contained in the thesis have been omitted here.

One could not hope to carry out the research necessary for a work such as this without the support, advice, and hospitality of many other people. The sixteen months of field-work in East Africa and nine months of my writing-up period were financed by a generous grant from the Foreign Area Fellowship Program of New York. The remainder of my writing-up period was financed by the School of Oriental and African Studies, London University, with an Additional Grants Award.

Throughout every stage of my research, my Ph.D. supervisor, Professor Roland Oliver, gave freely of his advice and guidance. A number of other scholars in Britain, including Professor P. H. Gulliver, Professor A. N. Tucker, Dr. P. Spencer, Professor D. A. Low, Dr. R. G. Abrahams, and Dr. J. Tosh, also gave generously of their time and advice both before and after the completion of my project.

For various help given me in Kampala, my thanks go out to Professor and Mrs. J. B. Webster, Mr. and Mrs. K. Gourlay, and the Hon. Mr. M. Choudry (then Uganda Minister of Water and Mineral Development). I also appreciated the efforts made to facilitate my examinations of Secretariat Minute files on Karamoja by the staff of the Entebbe Archives. For hospitality and support in Nairobi, I am grateful to Dr. and Mrs. A. H. Jacobs, Dr. and Mrs. G. Muriuki, and Professor B. A. Ogot. In Moroto, I gratefully acknowledge the various kindnesses and help of Mr. and Mrs. J. B. Weatherby, Mr. and Mrs. M. Quam, Mr. J. Wilson, and the Revd. and Mrs. B. Herd.

During my auxiliary field-work in Turkana District, I appreciate the support and hospitality of the District Commissioner, Mr. R. A. Riyamy, as well as his subordinate District Officers and Chiefs in whose areas I worked. I also acknowledge the warm and open hospitality accorded me and my wife by the Fathers of St. Patrick Missionary Society and by the Sisters of the Medical Missionaries of Mary, and I would like to especially thank Frs. Anthony Barrett and Leo Trainer, and Sister Bernadette.

In Kotido, Mr. A. M. Owor, A.D.C. for Jie County, not only gave me full co-operation, but also took a genuine interest in my work. Thanks also go to Mr. S. Logire, the Jie County Chief, and to his subordinate sub-county and parish chiefs, among whom Messrs. Samuel Locwei and Robert Loporoit deserve special mention. I am also grateful for the help given me by the chiefs of the Karimojong, Dodos, and Labwor Counties. The staff of the Kotido Police Post gave me valuable support, and special thanks go to C.I.D. Inspector Ernest Amanjiru and P.C. Simon Ojuka. For their hospitality and help which was quite outside their commercial activities, my appreciation goes out to the merchants of Kotido, including Messrs. P. K. Patel, R. K. Patel, J. B. Patel, Ramesh Thakore, and their families. I would like to thank Mrs. Joyce Amanjiru for the friendship and kindness she gave my wife. A very special gratitude must go to Miss Jessie Bryden of the B.C.M.S. mission who not only welcomed us with warm hospitality and provided our housing, but was a real friend as well.

For active scholarly support during my research, I am grateful to Mr. John Weatherby, Mr. John Wilson, Mr. Hamo Sassoon, Professor Bertin Webster, and Dr. Nobuhiro Nagashima. I am also indebted to Col. J. Chidlaw-Roberts, Col. H. Moyes-Bartlett, and Mrs. D. Clark for various help and information given me after the completion of my field research. I also appreciated the advice, suggestions, and comments of Professor Gulliver, Professor Webster, Dr. Tosh, Dr. Jacobs, Dr. Spencer, and Mr. R. Herring which helped me prepare my data for publication.

A considerable debt of gratitude is owed to my research assistants, and especially those who were employed on a full-time basis: James Lodungo, Ernest Korobe, and Mario Longok. These young men cheerfully put in very long hours and endured considerable hardships that often went far beyond what could reasonably be expected of them. An even greater debt is owed to the men, Jie and non-Jie alike, who served as my informants. In almost all instances, these men co-operated to the fullest possible extent with my research, with very little of the suspicion and reluctance with which one might expect a stranger to be received. My thanks also go out to the Jie people as a whole for their acceptance of me and my family amongst them. Very special thanks must be given to the Lokwor clan of Kotido who sponsored my formal initiation into the Ngikosowa age-set, and to Mabuc, who became my Jie father.

Finally, an inestimable debt is owed to Molly, my wife. She endured a myriad of discomforts, the tedious routine of proof-reading and typing, and my own periods of flagging spirits with consistent good grace, and her unfailing support and patience throughout the entire project has aided me in more ways than I could even attempt to mention. My thanks also go to my son, Kere, who in his own stoic way came to accept the excuse he heard so many times during his first year and a half: 'Not now, Daddy is writing.'

Contents

List of Figures

List of Maps

Abbreviations of Sources

THE sources primarily used in this work were the interviews (termed 'historical texts') which I carried out during my period of field-work in Uganda. When citing these interviews, the names of the informants who provided the testimony are given, together with an abbreviated reference to the 'historical text' in which that testimony was given. The 'historical texts' are abbreviated as follows: 'J' for Jie, 'D' for Dodos, 'BK' for Bokora Karimojong, 'MTK' for Matheniko Karimojong, 'TK' for Tome Karimojong, 'MOK' for Mothingo Karimojong, 'L' for Labwor, 'NY' for Nyakwai, 'Y' for Eyan, and 'T' for Turkana; they are followed by the chronological number of the interview. Thus, for example, 'J55' refers to Jie historical text number 55, and 'T15' refers to Turkana historical text number 15.

Journals and periodicals frequently referred to are abbreviated as follows: *JAS* for the *Journal of the African Society*, *JRAI* for the *Journal of the Royal Anthropological Institute*, *GJ* for the *Geographical Journal*, *UJ* for the *Uganda Journal*, and *SNR* for *Sudan Notes and Records*.

Secretariat Minute Papers from the Entebbe Archives are abbreviated E.A., followed by the archival file number. Foreign Office Confidential Prints are abbreviated F.O.C.P., followed by the print number.

Note on Orthography and Pronunciation

I HAVE not followed a scientific orthography in this work and, in general the Central Paranilotic and Lwo words and terms I have used are spelled phonetically. In all cases these phonetic spellings were arrived at only after listening closely to the pronunciation of the word by a number of different informants (usually Jie), and I was invariably aided and advised in determining a spelling by one or more of my research assistants.

I have spelled 'Karimojong' with an 'i', rather than as 'Karamojong' as some previous writers have done, as I am satisfied that most of my Karimojong and Jie informants pronounced the name with a definite 'i' sound. Similarly, I have spelled 'Dodos' with an 's', rather than 'Dodoth' as is sometimes encountered in previous writing. While a 'th' sound is frequently lisped by Central Paranilotic-speakers, it was clear that most of my Jie and all my Dodos informants pronounced the name with a definite 's' sound. Some Dodos added an almost whispered 'o' sound at the end of the name.

It should be noted that the 'ng' sound encountered in so many Central Paranilotic words and names is velar n sound, as in the English 'singer'. The sound 'ch' is represented in both Central Paranilotic and Lwo by 'c'. One exception to this is in the spelling of the area, 'Acholi'. I have included the 'h' here to make a clear distinction between the area and the people who inhabit that area, whose name I spell 'Acoli', in the usual manner.

CHAPTER I

Environment, Settlement Patterns, and Previous Historiography

THE Jie,[1] numbering about 33,000 people, belong to the linguistic group called, by A. N. Tucker, the 'Central Paranilotes'.[2] They live entirely within the boundaries of Jie County in central Karamoja District of Uganda. The county corresponds closely to Najie, the traditional tribal area of the Jie, and encompasses an area of roughly 1,300 square miles.

To the north of the Jie live the Dodos; to the south are the Bokora Karimojong; to the south-east, the Matheniko Karimojong; to the east, down the escarpment in Kenya, are the Turkana; to the west, several of the traditional states of the eastern Acoli; and to the south-west, the Labwor and Nyakwai. The Dodos, the Turkana, and the Karimojong groups are, like the Jie, Paranilotic-speaking, while the western peoples all speak Lwo dialects.

Only to the west and south-west, where the high ground dominated by Mt. Napono (6,420 feet) and the Labwor hills marks the boundaries between the Jie and their Lwo-speaking neighbours, are there natural and easily discernible frontiers. Elsewhere, uninhabited bush-country invariably forms a rather fluid 'no man's land' between the various tribal areas.

Karamoja District and Najie are part of the relatively dry north-eastern plateau of Uganda which drops away steeply on the east, down the Turkana escarpment to the semi-arid plains west of Lake

[1] The Jie call themselves, and are called by their Paranilotic-speaking neighbours, 'Ngijie'. The prefix *Ngi-* can be translated 'the people of' or 'those of' and invariably prefixes all Central Paranilotic group names. In general, the *Ngi-* form will not be used in this work, *except* when referring to generation and age-set groups. The Jie call their country 'Najie' and their language 'Ajie', and I shall use these terms throughout.

[2] The following tribes can be included in this linguistic grouping: Jie, Dodos, Karimojong, Iteso, Eyan, and possibly Lokutio in Uganda; Turkana and Itesyo in Kenya; and Toposa, Dongiro, and Jiye in the Sudan. This group has also been referred to as the 'Karimojong Cluster' and the 'Teso-speaking group'.

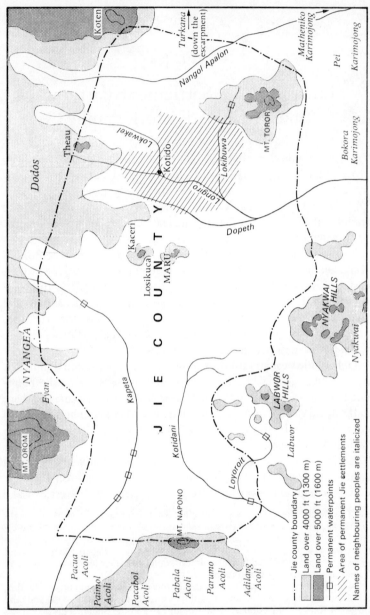

MAP 1. Sketch map of Najie showing main physical features and neighbouring peoples.

Rudolf which form the north-western corner of Kenya. Like much of Karamoja District, Najie is generally flat, but dotted with isolated rock outcroppings and hills. The main elevation is between 3,500 and 4,000 feet, but in the Losilang and Rengen areas of northern Najie the elevation rises to over 4,000 feet, and a string of hills, the highest of which is Theau (4,770), extend northwards into the country of the Dodos. To the east the ground also rises to something over 4,000 feet, dominated by Koten Hill (5,556 feet). In the west are a scattering of isolated hills, including Maru (4,701 feet) and Kaceri or Poet (4,765 feet). Finally, standing in relatively lofty isolation to the south, near the frontier with the Bokora Karimojong, is Mt. Toror, at 6,391 feet, the highest point in Najie.

There are four main river courses, the Nangolapalon and the Dopeth (with its tributaries the Longiro, Lokwakel, and Lokibuwo) flowing southwards towards Lake Bisina (Salisbury), and the Kapeta and the Kotidani flowing westwards to join with the Moroto, and eventually the Nile.

All these river courses remain dry for most of the year, except during the heaviest of the rains, when they are apt to fill up with startling abruptness. With the return of drier weather, they rapidly dry up again, although it is possible to dig water from the river beds at certain points for much of the dry season.

These digging points (*ngakare*) traditionally provided the Jie with most of their dry-season water, and they are still relied on to some extent, although government-constructed bore-holes and dams now provide a more abundant supply and a more certain alternative for some areas. Other sources of dry-season water include natural cisterns in rock outcroppings, and water-holes and wells dug by the Jie, generally in close proximity to their settlements. Most of these sources, however, can be relied on for only a few weeks after the cessation of the rains.

There are two seasons: a wet season, lasting from approximately late March to mid-August; and a dry season, beginning in August and going on to the following March. Although each wet season has its own peculiarities, there are usually heavy rains in April and May, resuming in July and early August, after a drier period in June.[3] This pattern is reflected in the names of Jie months. The time roughly corresponding to April is *Locoto*, which can be translated 'the time of mud', and May is *Titima*, 'the time of tall sorghum'. The periods corresponding to July and August are respectively *Lomodokogwec*

[3] P. H. Gulliver, *The Family Herds* (London, 1955), p. 17.

and *Losuban*, 'the time when the stirring-stick remains dirty (with food)' and 'the time of marriages'—the happiest times of the Jie year.[4]

Rainfall records for Najie are scanty. Records of annual rainfall at Kotido in central Najie for the years between 1947 and 1957 (exclusive of 1950) appear in Dyson-Hudson's *Karimojong Politics*. These show a high of 39·39 inches in 1947 and a low of 19·22 inches in 1953. The average annual rainfall during the ten-year period works out to about 27 inches.[5]

Most of the rainfall in a given year is usually confined to the four wet months, although a few inches are liable to fall as the rainy season builds up and then diminishes. Again the names of Jie months reflect the pattern. The time corresponding to September, when the rains begin to taper off, is *Lopoo*, 'when it gets dry', and January, when the dry season is at its height and rainfall is virtually non-existent, is *Lokwang*, 'the white time', referring to the great clouds of white dust which envelop the landscape.[6]

In six of the ten years recorded by Dyson-Hudson rainfall was less than the 27-inch average, and in four of those years it was less than 23 inches. There was also nearly a 50-per-cent variance between the 1947 high and the 1953 low rainfalls. It is also important to note that much of the first rain each year is lost in run-off, the parched ground being unable to absorb the sudden deluges; and a fierce east wind, which blows up the escarpment from the semi-arid Turkana plains throughout the dry season, does much to intensify the effects of the dry season by rapidly evaporating surface water and blowing away a good bit of loose top-soil. It can be misleading, therefore, to think strictly in terms of a 27-inch average rainfall for Najie.

Not all parts of Najie have the same amounts of rainfall. Kotido and central Najie (where the figures listed by Dyson-Hudson were recorded) would appear to experience the mean rainfall. To the west, however, in the Kaceri and Losikuca area and westwards to Kotidani, the rainfall is considerably higher, probably approaching the 40-inch average of the Labwor Hills, which these areas border.[7]

On the other hand, the eastern part of Najie around Koten Hill

[4] Lotiang (and others), J 27.

[5] N. Dyson-Hudson, *Karimojong Politics* (Oxford, 1966), p. 31. Gulliver, working mainly without records, estimated the average rainfall at about 25 inches. Gulliver, ibid.

[6] Lotiang (and others), J 27.

[7] Rainfall records for the Abim/Alerek area of Labwor for the years between 1947 and 1957 are found in Dyson-Hudson, ibid. There was considerably less fluctuation in annual rainfall here than in the Kotido area.

seems considerably drier than the Kotido area just 25 miles west, and one area of Mt. Toror in southern Najie is reputedly the driest place in all of Uganda, with only negligible rainfall.[8]

Despite this light and erratic rainfall, seed agriculture traditionally plays an important role in Jie economic life. Although widespread and even total crop failures are common, rather extensive plots of cultivated ground surround every Jie homestead, especially near river-banks and low-lying depressions which retain more sub-surface water.[9] Sorghum (*mumwa* in Ajie) is the staple crop and represents by far the greatest percentage of the total cultivation,[10] although finger-millet (*ngakima*) has been increasingly grown in certain western areas of Najie in recent years.

Sorghum is regarded by the Jie as their original crop; it is common to hear Jie elders say 'God created sorghum and cattle on the same day'. *Ngadekele* (a variety of pumpkin) and a type of cucumber are also thought to be of ancient origin, but other crops (still regarded as more or less exotic) including sim-sim, groundnuts, maize, sweet potatoes, cow peas, and tobacco are all thought to have been borrowed from Lwo-speakers, and are only cultivated by the Jie to a minimal extent.[11]

Traditionally, Jie agriculture was almost exclusively the domain of women.[12] The Jie statement that 'sorghum is the cattle of women', recorded by Gulliver,[13] is typical of their outlook.

The yearly agricultural cycle begins several weeks before the advent of the rains with the tilling of the plots surrounding the homestead. These plots belong, in every sense, to the woman who is in charge of their cultivation, and she is the one who bears the

[8] Personal communication with John Tether, Geologist in charge of the Uganda Government Geological Survey of Karamoja.

[9] P. H. Gulliver, 'Jie Agriculture', *UJ* 18 (1954), 65, estimated that in about two out of every five years rainfall is insufficient for a successful harvest.

[10] D. N. McMaster, *A Subsistence Crop Geography of Uganda* (Bude, Cornwall, 1962), p. 55, estimated that in 1958 the acreage devoted to sorghum cultivation in Karamoja District represented one-fifth of the total for all of Uganda.

[11] Lokec (Lomorumoe) and Ariny, J-96.

[12] In the past twenty years, however, many Jie families have adopted ox-drawn ploughs for the initial tilling of garden plots. The ploughs and their teams are invariably driven by men and, in some areas, have completely replaced the traditional lines of women with their short-handled, iron-tipped hoes. It is notable, however, that Jie men rationalize this new activity which has so directly impinged on the women's traditional domain in non-agricultural terms. A man ploughing in his wife's field once told me: 'No, I am not cultivating; I am driving oxen. Could a woman drive oxen? No, only men can do that.'

[13] Gulliver, loc. cit. (1954), 66.

responsibility for providing labour for every phase of the cycle. It is not unusual for the women of one area to band together to work communally on each others' plots at tilling times, but after this initial stage, cultivation is left to the owner of the garden. Usually, she is helped by her daughters, co-wives, or other women from her husband's settlement, and even male members of a settlement may supply occasional labour: an older man perhaps helping a wife to weed, or a small boy taking a turn with his sisters on the bird-scaring platforms as the grain ripens. Young men commonly help with the building of granary baskets at harvest time.

The harvest of the main crop is usually simultaneous with the end of the rains, although a certain amount of grain is often harvested before. It is important that dry weather accompanies the main harvesting so that the sorghum can be properly dried before it is stored in the granaries. It is paradoxical in this country of light rainfall that Jie crops are occasionally ruined by too wet an end to the rainy season, causing the grain to rot in the fields or on the drying floors.

The harvested sorghum is used basically in two ways. A great deal of it provides the main ingredient for a variety of beers brewed throughout the year by the women of a settlement. Most of this beer is consumed on ceremonial occasions in which it often plays an important ritual role. The sorghum is also used to make a soft bread (*atap*) which ideally should provide the staple food at the Jie homesteads for much of the dry season. Cucumbers, pumpkins, greens, and other produce are consumed as they ripen during the wet season as relishes for the *atap*, and a small quantity is often dried for use later in the dry season.

The Jie economy, traditionally as well as at present, was certainly a mixed one, and the Jie cannot be considered 'pastoralists' in the real sense of the word. Nevertheless, because of a tendency on the part of many past writers to present the peoples of Karamoja as 'pastoral', the point seems to need emphasis. Such writers seem to ignore an article written by P. H. Gulliver in 1954 in which he makes it clear that cereal foods are equally as important as animal food in the Jie economy. He also felt that this had been the case for many generations, and indeed that the Jie would starve without their agricultural produce.[14]

---

[14] Gulliver, loc. cit. (1954), 67–8. See also McMaster, op. cit., p. 29, where he states that the recent agricultural advances among the Paranilotic-speaking peoples of Uganda 'are really manifestations of traditional tribal ways, modi-

Gulliver goes on to point out that the disdain with which truly pastoral peoples (pastoralists through choice, such as the Pastoral Maasai) look upon agriculturalists, certainly does not exist amongst the Jie and their neighbours in Karamoja. Rather, there is a distinct Jie tendency to view successful agricultural peoples with respect. It should also be mentioned that the Jie do not shun hunting and gathering activities, as do the truly pastoral societies, but rely on such activities as an integral part of their economy. The importance of their balanced economy to the Jie is frequently reflected in their prayers on ritual occasions:

> (Leader) There are cattle, and they are good.
> (Response) They are!
> (Leader) There is food [crops] and it is good.
> (Response) It is!
> (Leader) Should the cattle die, there are crops.
> (Response) There are!
> (Leader) If the crops do not grow, there are cattle.
> (Response) There are!
> (Leader) Let there be rain so there will be cattle and crops![15]

The economic, sociological, and ritual importance of cattle to the Jie and their Paranilotic-speaking neighbours has been fully attested in the writings of Gulliver and Dyson-Hudson. Although agriculture is of equal importance in the economic sphere, livestock would seem to be of rather more importance in the sociological and ritual spheres: those spheres, significantly, which are dominated by the men.[16] As agriculture was seen to be almost exclusively the domain

---

[15] A Jie ritual observed on 5 May 1970.

[16] The ritual importance of agricultural foods, in the form of beers, has been somewhat overlooked by previous writers. Before my formal initiation into a Jie generation-set, Mabuc Loputuka, my Jie 'father' counselled me in this way: 'A castrated male animal and beer—these are the things a man must provide if he is to be initiated. The animal and the beer, both are part of initiation.' Certainly beer played an important role at a great many of the ritual occasions observed in Najie in 1969–71.

---

fied and burgeoning in new conditions'. Certainly the dramatic modifications of Jie settlement patterns in the past twenty years have been dictated by agricultural, rather than pastoral, considerations. In that span of time the Jie population has doubled, and extreme pressures have been brought to bear on much of the already denuded and over-worked agricultural land in the traditional settlement areas. This has led to large emigrations of Jie westwards to the relatively more fertile land around Kaceri and Losikuca. These emigrants have become intensely agricultural in their outlook, cultivating large fields of sorghum, and even finger-millet and maize.

of women, stock management is almost entirely the domain of men.

Ideally, the livestock of a Jie family is owned in common by a set of full brothers, the more senior exercising the greatest authority over its control. A considerable proportion of the stock is in turn allocated by the brothers to their wives, so that each woman of the family has a certain number of animals to provide food for her and her children. This allocation in no way implies ownership on the part of the women, and the ultimate control of all livestock remains in the hands of the men.[17]

Milk, drunk both fresh and sour, is the main food obtained from the cattle. It is often mixed with blood, obtained by piercing the neck of a living animal with a blocked arrow. Meat is less frequently eaten. Cattle are seldom killed except for a ritual purpose, and even then most of the meat is consumed by initiated men, rather than by women and children. A goat or sheep (or a cow which has died of natural causes) will occasionally be slaughtered for a family's food, but only in time of famine.

The location of Jie herds (traditionally as well as at present) depends on both the time of the year and the security of frontiers bordering on hostile neighbours. Ideally, the bulk of the livestock follows a pattern of transhumance in which it moves from the westernmost to the easternmost extremities of Najie, and back again, in a single year.

The west, with its higher rainfall, tends to be an area of moist savannah woodland with high grass which is only of real use to domestic stock during the early part of the rainy season when the new grass is still short and green. As the western grass grows taller, the Jie herds begin to move eastwards during the height of the rains, taking advantage of the ephemeral grass cover and surface water of the heavily denuded central area and the drier, short-grass, savannah woodland conditions of the east.

As the rains diminish, the herds are driven westwards again, becoming increasingly concentrated on the few permanent water points there, especially along the Kapeta River, as the dry season runs its course.[18] The actual movement of a given herd is determined by its owner, and there is, as might be expected, considerable individual variation from the ideal pattern.

Periods of conflict, moreover, have at many times closed various

---

[17] Gulliver, *Family Herds*, pp. 57–63.
[18] Ibid., p. 18.

areas of Najie to stock movement. At present, for example, much of eastern Najie is unusable because of heavy incursions by Turkana raiding parties. In the past, western, southern, and northern pasture areas have at one time or another been closed to Jie grazing, and at least once the all-important permanent water-points at Kapeta were wrested from their control. At such times, patterns of transhumance must be altered accordingly. Apart from the Kapeta, other dry-season water could be obtained at the foot of the Labwor Hills at Loyoroit, at the deep Lokibuwo wells below Mt. Toror, and usually at Lotisan well near Koten Hill. It was imperative to the survival of their herds that the Jie hold at least one of these water-points.

Ideally, again, a small herd of milch-cows, as well as a flock of small stock and a few donkeys are retained at the permanent settlements to provide food for members of the family who remain there throughout the year. Usually these animals include those of a woman's allocated herd, but obviously the numbers which can be retained depend on the intensity of the dry season. As the dry season progresses and as cows go dry, more and more animals are driven from the permanent settlements to join the main herds ranging the outlying pastures.

The dichotomous division of the herds is reflected in Jie settlement patterns: a Jie family, like its livestock, is usually divided into two parts for most of the year. The women, children, and old people generally remain throughout the year at the permanent settlements clustered within a radius of about 10 miles of Kotido in central Najie. Until the recent westward emigrations took place, it was in this settled area that virtually all agricultural activity went on, and it is here also that most ritual and social activity is focused. Young men and older boys (accompanied at times by girls, and visited by the mature men who own the herds) spend most of their time at the stock-camps which move with the herds in their annual treks across Najie.

The permanent settlements (ere, pl. ngireria, termed 'homesteads' by Gulliver) are very much self-contained villages in miniature. A great deal of time and effort is expended in their construction, and they are hardly ever abandoned except in the face of a severe drought, a widespread famine, hostile incursions by enemies, or as a means of escaping a supernatural misfortune which the members of a homestead believe that particular location has brought them.

In the past, most Jie clans probably occupied a single homestead. This is still true for some of the smaller clans, but it is more usual now for a homestead to accommodate a single extended family (termed simply 'Family' by Gulliver), although it is common to find only part of a large extended family, or, conversely, several small families resident in a single homestead. A typical homestead often contains a hundred or more individuals.

The Jie consider an extended family to be all the agnatic descendants of a common grandfather. This extended family is further broken down into what Gulliver terms 'houses' (the descendants of a common grandmother), and the houses into 'yards' (a wife, and her children, of one of the current adult members of the extended family).

A homestead is completely surrounded by a palisade of interwoven branches. Within the palisade, each 'yard' generally has its own enclosure, so that, from the air, a homestead gives the impression of a series of interlocking circles, all encompassed by a larger circle.[19] The constituent 'houses' of a homestead usually have their own gate, and there are usually several stock enclosures located in the middle of the complex. Dwellings are constructed of mud and wattle, plastered inside with cow-dung, and covered with roofs of 'terraced' thatching. Apart from these dwellings, there are usually wicker granaries, grinding-stones, enclosures for small animals, and perhaps a few small shrines in each yard's enclosure.

The homestead is built with matters of defence very much in mind. The outer palisade is usually seven or eight feet high and extremely difficult to scale or breach. Gates (except the main gate of the central stock enclosure) are never more than three feet high, and require anyone seeking entry to do so on hands and knees. Gates can be shut with large thorn branches, and the low doorways of the window-less dwellings can be closed with wicker doors. Small, partly open huts are built to accommodate young fighting men at positions from which the stock enclosures can be effectively guarded.

A homestead usually forms part of a cluster of homesteads belonging to one clan. Gulliver aptly terms such a cluster a 'clan hamlet'. A homestead is seldom built out of sight of another, and virtually never beyond hailing distance of one.

The temporary stock-camps (*awi*, pl. *ngauyoi*) built by the younger men in charge of the transhumant movements of livestock back and forth across Najie bear little resemblance to the permanent home-steads. The camps tend to be only very temporary, especially during the early parts of the dry season when frequent movement is essential.

---

[19] See Gulliver, *Family Herds*, p. 72–5, for an aerial diagram and the listing of the composite population of a typical Jie *ere*.

Camps are hardly ever more than a series of low rings of thorn to enclose the stock, and perhaps a hastily constructed hut of branches and grass to provide some shelter for the herdsmen. The camps tend to take on a slightly more permanent aspect when, at the end of the dry season, they are concentrated for longer periods around the water-points in the west, but in no case do they ever approach the permanence of the homesteads.

Jie informants indicate that this dichotomous division of families between the permanent homestead and temporary cattle-camp is the traditional settlement pattern which has been in effect since at least the middle of the eighteenth century. Informants do state, however, that in major crises (such as the great rinderpest epidemic of the late nineteenth century) large numbers of Jie were sometimes forced to abandon the settled heartland of Najie to move to outlying areas for a year or two in search of food and water. It would seem, however, that large-scale abandoning of the permanent homesteads was extremely rare, and never entire.[20]

During times of major crisis two additional means of subsistence, hunting and gathering, play especially important roles in Jie economic life.

Jie traditions recall great herds of wild animals ranging in many parts of Najie in the eighteenth and nineteenth centuries, and it is not uncommon even now to see small herds of gazelle, hartebeeste, giraffe, and other game within a few miles of the heart of the settled area. The Jie traditionally hunted smaller animals with throwing-sticks and large animals (including even elephant and rhino) with spears. Snares and other traps were also less frequently employed for big game. Hunts were often co-operatively organized by entire terri-torial divisions (large settlement units, described in Chapter II below), the bag divided among all participants. Game Department regulations and dwindling numbers of animals have curtailed Jie hunting activity in recent years. Although large animals are seldom

---

[20] Gulliver, *Family Herds*, p. 18, indicates that in pre-Colonial times the Jie system of annual transhumance involved the entire population. Gulliver's statements must have been engendered by Jie testimony relating to those rare occasions when a crisis made nearly universal transhumance necessary.

Comments made by H. M. Tufnell, one of the first British officials to visit Najie, indicate that in the early years of this century a larger proportion of the Jie population was transhumant than at present, but that universal transhu-mance was not practised. In his report of 4 Oct. 1911, Tufnell states: '[The Jie] have their permanent villages which they occupy in the rainy season and they only move about in dry weather when water becomes scarce. Even then their villages are never entirely deserted'. E.A. 2119.

hunted any more, young men still organize co-operative hunts for small game.

An extensive variety of wild fruits, roots, tubers, leaves, pods, and barks were (and still are) gathered by Jie of both sexes.[21] Such wild foods provide valuable additions to the diets of Jie resident both at the permanent homesteads and at the cattle-camps.

The importance of wild foods and game meat in Jie subsistence is inversely proportional to the annual yield of cultivated crops and the domestic herds. While hunting and gathering activities go on almost constantly, their importance ranges from merely that of a rather pleasant pastime and a means of collecting additional dietary varia- tion in a 'good' year, to that of a grim economic necessity in years of crop failure or livestock disasters.[22] These activities consistently offer an alternative to the Jie mixed economy subject to the dramatic environmental vicissitudes of Najie.

The Central Paranilotic-speaking peoples of eastern Africa have so far received very little attention from historians. At the time of my arrival in Najie, no systematic historical research had been under- taken among the Jie, or among any of the other Paranilotic-speaking peoples whose territory borders Najie. Even the Lwo-speaking groups neighbouring western Najie had received only cursory historical investigation.

Just before the commencement of my own work, J. B. Webster of Makerere University, directing a team of Makerere research students, had completed a survey of the oral traditions of the Central Paranilotic-speaking Iteso, who live a good distance south- west of Najie, beyond the Nyakwai and Bokora Karimojong; and John Tosh, a colleague from the School of Oriental and African Studies in London, was nearing the completion of a research project among the Langi, western neighbours of the Labwor, whose oral traditions strongly indicated some past connection with Central Paranilotes.

Such projects as Webster's and Tosh's were deviations from the

[21] See J. G. Wilson, 'The Vegetation of Karamoja District, Northern Region, Uganda', *Memoirs of the Research Division*, Uganda Department of Agricul- ture, Ser. 2, no. 5 (1962), for a nearly exhaustive listing of the almost incredible variety of wild foods commonly gathered in Karamoja.

[22] Raiding and commercial activity also can be seen as additional means of subsistence for the Jie. The former is primarily a means of securing livestock, and the latter primarily a means of obtaining agricultural foods. Supplies of *posho* distributed as famine relief by the Government of Uganda in recent years may be seen as a final source of Jie subsistence.

more usual research projects based on oral history which had been previously carried out in East Africa, in which the more strongly centralized (and usually Bantu-speaking) societies had received by far the most attention. Nevertheless, the work of Webster and Tosh, as well as such earlier work as that of Jacobs among the Pastoral Maasai, Ogot's among the Southern Lwo, Were's among the Aba-luiyia, and Muriuki's among the Kikuyu, had shown that rich oral history existed in societies without what should strictly be termed 'state organization', thus verifying Vansina's feeling that 'historical research carried out in depth in societies without state organization might reveal much more of their history than has been commonly supposed to be possible'.[23]

With the notable exception of Jacobs's work with the Pastoral Maasai, however, almost no historical research had been undertaken amongst the more pastorally oriented peoples of East Africa. Because of their segmentary social structures and their age- or generation-set systems, these groups appeared to present rather specialized and difficult problems to historical investigation amongst them.

Many of these groups, including at least four Central Paranilotic-speaking ones, had been studied by social anthropologists, from whose points of view the possibility of effective historical research amongst them seemed remote indeed.[24] Of all these observers, Dyson-Hudson held perhaps the most definite views on the impossibility of serious historical research amongst the Central Paranilotes. He writes: '. . . as far as indirect knowledge [of the past] is concerned the Karimojong themselves are of little explicit help, since they either incapsulate the past into present relationships or release their hold on it altogether'.[25]

In spite of such opinions, a few writers had attempted (largely by the use of oral traditions) to reconstruct at least a skeletal outline of Jie and other Central Paranilotic history, concentrating their attention on the origins of the various Central Paranilotic tribes.

Gulliver, who spent a longer time in Najie and undoubtedly went relatively deeper into Jie oral traditions than any other previous writer, reconstructed a picture in which the proto-Jie are seen to be part of a concentration of peoples which he terms 'the

[23] J. Vansina, *Oral Tradition* (London, 1965), p. 173.
[24] The Jie and the Turkana were studied by P. H. Gulliver, the Karimojong by N. Dyson-Hudson, and the Dodos by E. Marshall Thomas, who, although a journalist rather than a social anthropologist, used a basically anthropological approach to her work.
[25] Dyson-Hudson, op. cit., p. 258.

Karamojong Cluster', originally based on the Magos Hills in what is now Matheniko County in the north-eastern part of the area inhabited by the Karimojong. At the Apule River, not far to the south-west of the Magos Hills, the proto-Jie are supposed to have broken away by force from their 'fathers', the Karimojong, thus earning for themselves the sobriquet 'Ngijie' (the fighting people). Moving back to the north-east, the Jie supposedly established themselves at Koten Hill, some miles north of the Magos Hills, and here a group of them, ultimately to become the Turkana, are said to have broken away peacefully, and descended the escarpment into the Tarash valley. Gulliver estimated that this happened not later than 1750–1800.

According to Gulliver's reconstruction, the departure of the Turkana was followed by the westward exodus from Karamoja of a number of peoples including the ancestors of the Lango and Labwor, as well as ancestral elements of the Iteso. This exodus supposedly allowed the Jie themselves to move westwards from Koten into the area vacated by the emigrants around present Kotido in central Najie. In Gulliver's view,[26] as the Jie moved west, the Dodos split peacefully from the Karimojong (settled still at Apule) and moved northwards to their present area. At approximately the same time, the Toposa (and possibly the Jiye of the Sudan) broke away from the Jie, and also moved north to their present area, at a date which Gulliver estimates at 1800.

This reconstruction of the history of Jie origins has become the 'standard' one, used in virtually all writing since the early 1950s, and during that time it seems to have been critically examined by only one observer. In an unpublished paper, 'Historical Relations Among the Central Nilo-Hamites', presented at Makerere Institute of Social Research in 1968, Nobuhiro Nagashima, a social anthropologist working among the Iteso, undertook to examine and analyse all the oral traditions of Central Paranilotes that had been recorded up to that time. After a thorough examination, Nagashima concluded that the primordial Central Paranilotes were originally based not on the Magos Hills, but further east, down the escarpment in present-

---

[26] Gulliver's reconstruction can be found in 'The Karamojong Cluster', *Africa* (1952); (with Pamela Gulliver) *The Central Nilo-Hamites* (London, 1953); 'The Teso and the Karamojong Cluster', *UJ* 20 (1956). His estimate of 1800 as the date of the Toposa breakaway from the Jie is close to the date of 1780 or 1790 estimated by A. C. Beaton in L. F. Nalder (ed.), *A Tribal Survey of Mongalla Province* (London, 1937), p. 67, and in 'Record of the Toposa Tribe', *SNR* 31 (1950), 131.

day Turkana District in Kenya. Here, he suggests, one group of Turkana remained behind while the rest of the Central Paranilotes climbed the escarpment and, in accordance with Gulliver's view, dispersed to form the various tribal groups.

To Nagashima, the Iteso are definitely seen to have originally been part of the primordial Central Paranilotes, while the Langi are assumed to have been either the vanguard of that group, or perhaps a group directly related to the Jie. Finally, Nagashima concludes, a group which was to become Turkana split from the Jie at Koten and descended the escarpment to join with a pre-existing group—those Turkana who had remained behind when the primordial Central Paranilotes climbed the escarpment in the first place. Despite his reinterpretation of some of the data, Nagashima's reconstruction does not differ very radically from Gulliver's, and indeed many discrepancies between the two centre on simply the order in which various groups broke away from a 'Karamojong Cluster' somewhere in eastern Karamoja.

Where a radically different reconstruction of early Jie history does occur is in the writing of Fr. J. P. Crazzolara. To Crazzolara, the 'aboriginal' inhabitants of north-eastern Uganda were two groups of linguistically related peoples whom he terms the 'Western Lango' and the 'Eastern Lango', the latter being the ancestors of the present Central Paranilotic-speaking peoples. Crazzolara thinks that perhaps seven or eight centuries ago a large-scale Madi invasion swept over much of the territory of the 'Western Lango', most of whom were either absorbed or destroyed, except for a few who probably fell back to the east to join their eastern 'brothers', whose territory extended eastwards from modern Kitgum in Acholi District. This was followed from the mid-sixteenth century by the advent of the Lwo, who imposed their culture and leadership on the now predominantly Madi population in the former 'Western Lango' territory, and created still more pressures on the beleagured western frontier of the 'Eastern Lango'.

Relying on a study of place- and clan-names in north-eastern Uganda, extensive research into Lwo and Madi historical traditions, and a series of conversations with elders living near various Roman Catholic Missions in Karamoja, Crazzolara concludes that the Jie, Dodos, Turkana, and Toposa represent displaced 'Eastern Lango' populations gradually forced back to the east into the heart of Karamoja from their invaded homelands further west. In Karamoja, the various 'Eastern Lango' elements are supposed to have dispersed:

the Dodos and Toposa moving off to the north, the Turkana further east and down the escarpment into Kenya, the Karimojong (who, in Crazzolara's view, represented one of the easternmost of the 'Eastern Lango' groups) southwards from their previous home in northern Karamoja into their present country, and the Jie remaining in the Kotido area of central Najie.[27]

Far from presenting any clear picture of early Jie history, then, previous reconstructions seem diametrically opposed: Gulliver and Nagashima seeing the Jie arrive in Najie from the east, and Crazzolara seeing them arrive from the west. In the light of this, Dyson-Hudson's contention that effective historical research cannot be carried on at all among the peoples of Karamoja would seem to take on additional weight.

And yet, the researches into Jie oral history which produced the data for this book brought to light not only a feasible solution to the problem of Jie origins raised by the work of Gulliver and Crazzolara, but also a whole storehouse of oral tradition bearing on many aspects of Jie history for at least the past 250 years. To understand the methodological approaches which elicited these traditions, it is first necessary briefly to examine the Jie socio-political structure, for it is within this structure that Jie oral history is maintained and passed on from generation to generation.

[27] Fr. J. P. Crazzolara, 'Notes on the Lango–Omiru and on the Labwoor and Nyakwai', *Anthropos*, 55 (1960).

CHAPTER II

Reconstructing Jie History: The Transmission, Dating, and Collection of Oral Traditions

ON all levels of the Jie social structure can be found strongly corporate groups with very real feelings of unique identity, overtly expressed in their individual unitary participation in ritual and other activity. These groups, including major divisions, territorial divisions, and clans, are of key importance to the oral historian because each is the repository of its own oral traditions, perpetuated entirely within that group, either as a whole, or by its constituent parts. It is imperative that the historian be aware of the structure and variations which occur at several levels of that structure, if he is competently to collect and analyse these traditions.

The permanently settled area of Najie is divided into two major divisions,[1] each leading a largely autonomous existence. Numerically and territorially the larger of the major divisions is Lokorwakol (the people of which are called 'Ngikorwakol') which occupies basically the southern and eastern parts of the settled area, while Rengen (sometimes referred to as 'Lokaloding', and the people 'Ngikaloding'), the second major division, occupies the north-west (*see* Map 2). Each major division traditionally organizes its generation-set (*asapanu*) system independently of the other, and appoints its own hereditary fire-makers (*ngikeworok*, s. *ekeworon*) and (until the end of the nineteenth century) its own hereditary war-leaders. Each functions independently in ritual matters, and dry-season grazing and watering patterns are carried out, for the most part, separately. Only in times of dire crisis (usually of a military nature) have the two major divisions traditionally worked in close concert.[2]

---

[1] The major divisions were termed 'political moieties' in my thesis and previous writings. The term 'major divisions' has been adopted for this book at the suggestion of several social anthropologists.

[2] Logwela and Kere, J 125.
There is not the same emblematic association with certain animals by the Jie major divisions as Dyson-Hudson describes (op. cit., pp. 127–32) for the

In their dealings with outsiders, the Jie make little distinction between the major divisions: a man is 'thoroughly Jie' be he from Rengen or Lokorwakol. Within Najie itself, however, the distinction between the major divisions is of much more importance and indeed many of the Jie of Lokorwakol have a tendency to regard themselves as the 'real Jie', and to view the Rengen as an immigrant population descended from non-Jie ancestors.[3] There are also slight dialectical differences between the major divisions, and again Lokorwakol Jie often claim that their dialect is 'proper Ajie', and that the Rengen 'speak like Dodos'.

Each major division is in turn broken down into a number of named territorial divisions[4] which occupy a specific and well-defined area (see Map 2 and Figure 1). River or stream beds usually mark the boundaries between territorial divisions, but even in those few cases where no natural boundary exists, the people of the areas concerned are invariably aware of exactly where one division ends and another begins. There are seven territorial divisions for Lokor-wakol, which (for reasons outlined below) should be listed in the following order: Kotiang, Losilang, Kanawat, Komukuny, Kotido, Panyangara, and Nakapelimoru. Rengen has four territorial divisions which should probably be listed in this order: Lokatap, Kadwoman, Kapelok, and Caicaon.

This definite and universally accepted order in which the territorial

[3] As far as I know, no Rengen hold the opposite view that they, to the exclusion of the Lokorwakol Jie, are the 'real' Jie. However, rather more of my research was carried out in Lokorwakol than in Rengen. Our home was located in the Kotido territorial division of Lokorwakol, and my initiation into a Jie age-set was sponsored by the Lokwor clan of that division. Although I have consistently tried to avoid it, my interpretation of Jie history may have a certain unavoidable Lokorwakol bias.

[4] Gulliver termed these 'districts'. To avoid possible confusion with the modern government use of the term 'district' and to emphasize their territorial nature, I have adopted the term 'territorial division'. Gulliver did not choose to regard Rengen as a separate major division, but classified it simply as a 'district'. Nor does he mention Lokorwakol as a specific unit of Jie society. He does, however, clearly indicate that in many ways the Rengen are quite distinct from the other 'districts'.

Karimojong 'sections'. Both Jie major divisions do have a ritual association with the ratel (ekor) and, unlike the Karimojong, there is a strong prohibition against killing it. One territorial division of the Rengen have a further vague association with rock hyraxes and a certain type of black snake. In no case, however, are the members of any Jie grouping known collectively by the name of their emblematic animal. The food taboos observed by certain Jie clans (see below, p. 24) are again entirely different from the Karimojong emblematic association.

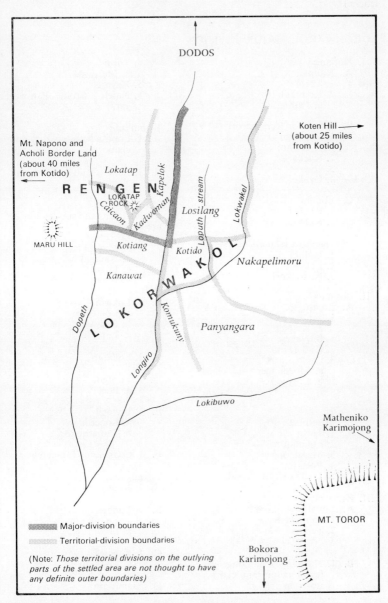

MAP 2. The major divisions and territorial divisions of Najie.

FIG. 1. Jie Territorial Divisions and Clans

(The territorial divisions of each major division are indicated by roman numerals, sub-territories by capital letters, clans by arabic numbers, and sub-clans by small letters.)

LOKORWAKOL MAJOR DIVISION

I. Kotiang
  A. Kadukan
    1. Toroi
    2. Kadukok
      a. Pading

  B. Loonei or Remokwori
    1. Lopongo
      a. Kalooi
    2. Kaekar
    3. Oyarot
    4. Oyakol

  C. Lominit
    1. Kaekar
    2. Kakuloi

  (Independent related clans)
    1. Kulok
    2. Lokwor
    3. Ngadakori

II. Losilang
  A. Lojoo
    1. Jimos
      a. Kalolet
      b. Nayese
    2. Kathewok
    3.
      a. Moruonger ⎤ sub-clans
      b. Locoto   ⎟ of Toroi,
               ⎟ settled in
               ⎦ Lojoo

  B. Mirethiae
    1. Toroi
    2. Lokatap
    3. Mamulope
    4. Poet
    5. Lodera (from Kotido)

III. Kanawat
  A. Lobal or Lokore
    1. Ngikakere
    2. Tesiyo
    3. Nyakwai

  B. 1. Ngikeinyak or Longelep
      (sub-territory and clan)
    2. Lokatap
    3. Tesiyo
      a. Lomampocet

    4. Toroi
      a. Meriwala
    5. Nayese
    6. Natelo (from Panyangara)

IV. Komukuny
  A. 1. Loposa (sub-territory and clan)

  B. 1. Lodera (sub-territory and clan)
    2. Jimos

V. Kotido (clans and sub-territories are the same)
  A. 1. Loser
      a. Mamukinei
      b. Nadipal
      c. Logole
      d. Magos

  B. 1. Lokwor
      a. Lokiding
      b. Lodipoi
      c. Longelel

  C. 1. Lokatap

  D. 1. Losogot
      a. Poet

  E. 1. Lokocil
      a. Loperdu
      b. Tamathokori

  F. 1. Cedmeu or Longerep

VI. Panyangara
  A. 1. Kapuyon or Lokore

  B. 1. Lodoca
      a. Lomukura
      b. Lojom

  C. 1. Loletio
      a. Loperdu

  D. Riamiriam
    1. Sinotoi
      a. Ngikaloding

2. Mamulope
3. Kimula

E. Rikitai
1. Jimos
2. Poet

F. Kadokini (sub-territory and
group of clans from Rengen)

Independent clans not part of a
named sub-territory
1. Ila
2. Natelo
3. Kapwor
4. Gule

VII. Nakapelimoru
A. Wotokau

A₁. Ngerepo group of clans
1. Ngikalogwala
2. Ngikalogwang
3. Nyakwai or Rogom or
Mazula or Palakwa

A₂. Thiokol group of clans
4. Poet
a. Aonyot
5. Kairwata

6. Karewok or Kareu
7. Lokore
8. Nathinyon

B. Kadoca
1. Karewok or Kareu
a. Magos
2. Loriu
a. Lokocil
3. Kalokori
4. Kalobur
5. Lokore

C. Lokokorok
(Oyapua group of clans)
1. Kalobur
a. Oyakwara
b. Ngolemoru
2. Jimos
3. Cakalomun
4. Longerep
5. Nyakwai

D. Potongor
1. Longelep
2. Lokocil
3. Lopao
4. Liwa
5. Lomus
6. Kalia

RENGEN MAJOR DIVISION

I. Lokatap
1. Kalolet or Lodoi or
Ngikalodioki
2. Wotokau
3. Kapalokadong
4. Poet
5. Lunguto
6. Orom
7. Ladoket
8. Kimula

Kadwoman
1. Lokadeli
2. Kapwor
a. Lotubo
b. Ratai
3. Gelangole
4. Cilapus
5. Lomejan

6. Nariwo
7. Lobore

III. Kapelok
1. Ngikalopetum
2. Loperdu or Lodorio
3. Nayese
4. Tesiyo
5. Ladoket

IV. Caicaon
1. Korimunyen
2. Nayese
3. Kimula
4. Lopetae
5. Ngikalogwel
6. Kokoria
7. Kanameriongor
8. Karewok
a. Nabwalin
9. Kwaluro

divisions are listed is demonstrable on a number of important ritual occasions performed on the level of the major divisions. In the ceremonies of *angola* (a blessing of the people in times of stress) and *akiwodokin* (to bless the livestock, or to 'free' them to go to the cattle camps at the onset of the dry season), representative groups of each territorial division pass through an improvised 'gate' in the order given above, so that, for the Lokorwakol, Kotiang goes first and Nakapelimoru last.[5] At rituals where the spearing of oxen takes place, including the inauguration of a new generation-set, the same order holds.

Dyson-Hudson has identified a similar sort of 'rank' among the clans of the Karimojong, and, according to his information, this ranking is determined by the order in which the clans settled in the Karimojong areas. Thus, the first participants in rituals similar to those of the Jie are thought to be 'the clans who long ago were first in the land', while those that follow behind are 'former enemies of the Karimojong who were defeated and absorbed into the society'.[6]

Although rather different in its expression, the Jie rationale for the 'ranking' of their territorial divisions is also based on the seniority of their groups. The rank of the Lokorwakol territorial divisions is traditionally based on the order in which they settled in their present areas from a concentration in Kotiang. Thus, the first group of emigrants from Kotiang are supposed to have settled Losilang, the second group, Kanawat; and so on. For the Rengen, the territorial divisions are ranked in the order in which they settled in the area around Lokatap Rock, the focal point of Lokatap, the senior territorial division.

With the exception of a relatively few ceremonies performed by the major division as a whole, however, most important Jie ritual activity is performed individually by the territorial divisions at their own ritual groves. Most *angola* and *akiwodokin* ceremonies occur at this level, as do rain-making rituals and inauguration of age-sets within the generation systems. Some territorial divisions even have ceremonies unique to themselves, as a further expression of their corporate nature.

---

[5] With the Rengen, the situation is more complex. They seem to have two ritual groves where the ceremonies can take place, and the order of their divisions depends on which ritual grove is used. Invariably, however, Lokatap appears to be ranked first and Caicaon last, no matter which grove is used.

[6] Dyson-Hudson, op. cit., p. 89.

FIG. 2. *Ngitalia* of Four Jie Clans

I. Cedmeu of Kotido
  A. Brides wear aprons made from the tying-straps of the skirt
  B. Brides wear gazelle-skin capes
  C. Married women wear calfskin skirts
  D. Cannot eat bushbuck (*akoloba*)
  E. Perform *lobunat* (in which an ox is smothered with a woman's apron instead of being speared) as finalization of marriage ceremony

II. Jimos of Losilang
  A. Brides wear apron made of small sticks (*ekulungur*)
  B. Married women wear goatskin skirts, trimmed with eland skin
  C. Cannot eat bushbuck
  D. Perform both *lobunat* and *lomalol* finalization of marriage ceremonies

III. Lokwor of Kotiang
  A. Brides wear apron of small sticks
  B. Married women wear gazelle-skin capes after birth of first child
  C. Married women wear hide skirts trimmed with hartebeest skin
  D. Cannot eat bushbuck or squirrel (*loceleku*)
  E. Perform both *lobunat* and *lomalol* ceremonies
  F. Hair of first child not shaved until birth of second

IV. Kalokori of Nakapelimoru
  A. Brides wear apron of leather thongs (*ngarukaneth*)
  B. Married women wear goatskin clothing
  C. Can eat any animal
  D. Perform *lokidori* finalization of marriage ceremony (in which an ox is speared)
  E. Present all the bride-wealth cattle to bride's father at one time (instead of in a number of instalments, in the usual Jie manner)

Each territorial division is subdivided into a number of smaller units which can be termed 'sub-territories'.[7] In some territorial divisions, each sub-territory is inhabited by a single large clan, while in others sub-territories are composed of a number of completely unrelated clans which simply happen to be settled together in one particular area. As one might expect, sub-territories made up of a single clan tend to exhibit a much stronger corporate feeling than those in which a number of different clans are represented.

Indeed, the clan (*ateker*, pl. *ngatekerin*) tends to be the most strongly corporate group in Jie society. The Jie themselves usually define a clan as 'all the people who share one *etal*'.[8] An *etal* (pl.

[7] Gulliver termed them 'settlements'. Jie group terminology tends to be extremely vague: a major division is simply termed 'a part of Najie' (*agule anajie*), a territorial division is termed 'a part of Lokorwakol' (*agule analokorwakol*) or 'a part of Rengen' (*agule anarengen*), and a sub-territory (e.g. Lokore of Kanawat) 'a part of Kanawat' (*agule anakanawat*).

[8] Ajie clan terminology is deplorably vague and confusing. The term *ateker* is used not only to identify that group I am terming 'clan', but is also used in a looser way for 'tribe', and occasionally even 'territorial division'. Thus, to ask a Jie for the name of his *ateker*, the answer 'Jie' or 'Panyangara' is as likely

ngitalia) is an observance or prohibition which often, but by no means always, has to do with marriage observances and clothing regulations for brides and married women. Every clan has a number of *ngitalia*, and rather typical ones of four clans are given as an example in Figure 2.[9] Jie informants almost invariably stated that 'people who share one *etal*' are 'one people', and that marriage within such a group is impossible. Very often, however, unrelated clans will share one or even several *ngitalia* in common: for example, the first three clans listed in Figure 2 share a common prohibition against eating bushbuck, and yet each can intermarry freely with the other two. Thus it is the whole range of *ngitalia* subscribed to by a clan which makes it different from any other, and it is to this unique combination that the Jie refer when they speak of a clan sharing 'one *etal*'.

In fact, most of the larger Jie clans are not exogamous. For these clans, exogamy is required only of their constituent sub-clans (*ngatekerin nguna cicik*), each of which subscribes to a slightly different range of *ngitalia*. In these cases, it is the sub-clan that 'shares one *etal*', but the clan as a whole is still thought of as 'one people'.[10]

There are at least seventy different clans in Najie (*see* Figure 1).[11] Most of these are compact clans living entirely within one territorial division, or even sub-territory. At least fifteen (including some of the largest) are dispersed clans, with branches in two or more territorial divisions, and occasionally in two or more sub-territories of the same

[9] I am grateful to Nobuhiro Nagashima who, while staying with me in Najie in 1970, made me fully aware of the importance of a clan's *ngitalia*. Each clan also has its own distinguishing livestock brand (*alemacar*) which consists of specific patterns burned on the animals' hides, and notches cut into their ears. The general pattern of the brand is also copied in haircuts given to very young children by many clans. Occasionally Jie informants described a clan as 'all the people who share one brand', but more often the brand was merely described as one of the whole range of *ngitalia* subscribed to by a clan.

[10] In a few instances there are groups termed by the Jie 'sub-clans' which are in fact totally unrelated to the clan with which they are associated, and subscribe to an entirely different set of *ngitalia*. In most cases, these 'sub-clans' were alien groups which were 'adopted' by a pre-existing Jie clan. Some territorial divisions also have 'groups of clans', which are usually rather like a loose confederation of clans. Again, these 'groups of clans' were often formed as later-arriving aliens attached themselves to a pre-existing Jie clan or clans.

[11] Crazzolara, loc. cit., 212–13, lists sixty-four Jie 'clans', but many of these are in fact the names of sub-territories, or other locales.

to be elicited as the name of his clan. Sub-clans are merely termed *ngatekerin nguna cicik*, meaning 'small parts of clans'.

territorial division. Almost invariably, members of a dispersed clan consider one branch as the original from which the others split off. In some instances, the various branches each subscribe to a slightly different range of *ngitalia*, but in almost every case, it is the clan as a whole, rather than the individual branches, that remains the exogamous group.

In general, the clan exhibits more corporate unity than any larger group existing in Jie society. Loyalty to one's clan can transcend loyalties to the territorial division or sub-territory. Although in some clans the emphasis may be on the constituent sub-clan or branch, in by far the majority of cases a clan's unity is expressed in the concept of its being 'one people', reinforced (at least theoretically) by its common subscription to 'one *etal*'. The ritual observances which form an important part of a clan's *ngitalia* are usually performed by a clan as a unit, or sometimes by its individual sub-clans or dispersed branches, and certainly there is far more ritual activity at this level than the important, but none the less relatively infrequent, ritual activity performed by sub-territory, territorial division, or major divisions.

Furthermore, it is the clan (or sometimes its constituent parts)[12] that functions as a unit in the performance of ritual activity based on the sub-territory or territorial division. Ceremonies of *angola* and *akiwodokin*, for instance, occur at the level of territorial division more frequently than at the major-division level, and in the performance of the territorial-division ceremonies the clans are the units that pass through the 'gate' in a prescribed order. As was the case with the territorial divisions, there is usually a rather vague feeling that the higher 'ranked' clans in these ceremonies were the first to establish themselves in the given territorial division, and so are ritually more important. The corporate nature of the clan is further underlined by the seating of the adult male members of one clan together in a prescribed portion of their generation-set's seating area at all ritual functions of the territorial division.[13]

In his recent work on the Kikuyu, Godfrey Muriuki has shown

[12] In a few cases it is the sub-clan that functions as a unit in these rituals. For example, the Magos sub-clan of Loser passes through the 'gate' before the other three, which go through as a group toward the end of the order. Most frequently in such cases, it is an 'adopted' sub-clan that has an order different from that of the pre-existing clan to which it is attached.

[13] A fuller treatment of Jie territorial divisions and clans is provided by Gulliver in *The Family Herds*, and additional information on all the various groups in Jie society is contained in the second chapter of my London Ph.D. thesis, 'The Oral History of the Jie of Uganda'.

that that society, very much like the Jie, is a segmentary one, without any sort of control or regulation being exerted over its tribal oral traditions by any single section of the community. Muriuki points out that Kikuyu traditions, therefore, tend to be 'largely free, informal and widely diffused'. Among the Kikuyu, these more popular tribal-wide traditions were often found to be 'vague and unhelpful', and Muriuki accordingly placed a rather stronger reliance on the traditions of clan and lineage.[14]

The picture given by Muriuki of the Kikuyu is in many ways similar to that of the Jie. There are, in fact, very few tribal-wide traditions existing among the Jie. Traditions do occur on the major-division level, but here, as with the popular tribal-wide traditions of the Kikuyu, they are often deplorably vague. In many ways, the most reliable Jie traditions appear to be those perpetuated by the individual clans and even sub-clans. Such traditions are largely concerned with the origin of the group and its settlement in Najie, and, in the case of the dispersed clans, its fragmentation into branches.

Such traditions tend to be of real importance only to the clan itself, and there seems to have been little chance of distortions from external sources creeping into them. In many more centralized African societies where a notion of 'commoner' and 'royal' clans exists, there are also controls exerted to ensure that the traditions of all clans are in accordance with the 'official' version of the ruling clan, which will often tend to rationalize and aggrandize its own position, sometimes at the expense of the 'commoner' clans.

Unlike those more centralized societies, the Jie have no such notion of 'commoner' or 'royal' clans. Rather, the Jie clan system is strongly egalitarian, and little importance is attached to a clan's 'rank' in the performance of *akiwodokin* and *angola* ceremonies. The first groups to participate in these ceremonies may be accorded a certain vague respect on account of their ritual importance, but there is never any feeling of inferiority, based on their lower 'rank', among those groups which follow behind.

The clans that perhaps come closer to being 'royal' clans among the Jie are those of the hereditary fire-makers (*ngikeworok*), genera-tion-set leaders, and war-leaders. Even in these clans little of the exclusiveness and pride of position which is so strong a feature of many more centralized societies could be discerned. Their oral

[14] G. Muriuki, 'A History of the Kikuyu to 1904', unpublished Ph.D. thesis, London University, 1969, p. 15.

tradition hardly ever attempt to aggrandize their importance or even unduly to justify their hereditary functions in society. On the contrary, informants of these clans often tend to minimize their own position, and those from fire-making clans of both major divisions (the Jimos clan of Losilang for Lokowakol, and the Kalolet of Lokatap for the Rengen) have no hesitation in relating their own clan histories which clearly indicate that theirs were not the original fire-making clans.

Although hereditary functionaries must be selected from a rather limited number of kinsmen from a specific clan, it is in line with Jie egalitarianism that the actual successor to an office is elected by the senior elders of the major division as a whole. Once elected, there is invariably a matter-of-fact acceptance by the Jie of the powers invested in such a functionary, but it is again typical of their egalitarian attitudes that even the candidate for the office of fire-maker (the most important ritual functionary in each major division) should possess, above all, the following attributes:

> The person selected as *ekeworon* [fire-maker] must always be a gentle person. He must stay at home quietly and not roam about with the warriors. He must not be proud. He must not be rude. He must not be violent. He must always be kind to all the other people. If a man is not like this, he is not selected.[15]

At the other extreme, the dispersed Poet clan found in many territorial divisions might be considered the nearest thing to a 'commoner' clan in Jie society. The Poet, remnants of a conquered and absorbed non-Jie people, still perform the annual tasks of building the fire-maker's granaries and supplying him with grain as a reflection of their defeat and absorption. However, there was never any hint that the other Jie (including even the fire-making clans, who intermarry with them freely) considered the Poet in any way 'inferior', and the Poet, for their part, never once tried to conceal either their defeats or their service to the fire-maker. In fact many told of their duties with resignation verging on pride:

> After the Jie defeated my people, my ancestors came here to Losilang in the time of the father of my grandfather. We were given the task of helping the fire-makers. It was God's will, and so it became our work to build the entire granary—even to the poles and the roof—and then we filled it with grain to the very top.[16]

---

[15] Lowakori (Anselmo), Locan, and Cokon (Irar), J 90.
[16] Lopeirinyet (Angura), J 87.

It is of prime importance that alien groups are absorbed into Jie society with remarkable speed and ease. In accordance with the general egalitarianism, all clans have the right to regard themselves as 'thoroughly Jie', despite alien origin or the time of their arrival in Najie. I was frequently made aware that this could even apply to me:

> You are a stranger here, from a different tribe. But if you remain here, you will marry Jie girls and you will leave children behind when you die. Perhaps your children would be called the Ulaya [European] clan, but they would be Jie no matter what their name.[17]

In the vast majority of cases, Jie informants, even those of comparatively recent alien origin, had no hesitation in relating their clan histories in full. However most of the distortions which did occur were, in fact, among those clans of alien origin, and most took place early in my research, when I was still largely unknown and some people were suspicious of my investigations. In most cases, informants of these clans were hesitant to reveal their alien origin to a stranger who might not understand that they were now as 'thoroughly Jie' as any other group. These informants would simply refuse to relate any of their clan history at all, saying, 'We don't know' or 'We are Jie. We have always been Jie'.

The testimonies of neighbouring clans and often the range of *ngitalia* and the *angola* order of the clan itself were usually clear indications of alien origin. Some informants from clans of alien origin even cited their own *ngitalia*, as a kind of mnemonic device, in support of their traditions of alien origins: '. . . and so, we Kapwor were descended from those Acoli of Kotidany. Even now we have the Acoli *etal* of slaughtering a hen at marriage time to remind us of our Acoli ancestors.[18]

By the end of my research, virtually every clan's history was in line with traditions told about it by other clans, its own *ngitalia*, and its *angola* order. In the great majority of cases, therefore, high reliance was placed on the oral traditions of the clans themselves. In the relatively few cases where more credibility was given to sources other than the clan's own history, there was fairly clear indication that for some reason the clan's traditions had been distorted.

---

[17] Lokwii (Nakeapan), J 42. I am fairly certain that my son, Kere, who was born in Moroto, but brought to our home in Najie when a week old was considered by many to be in every way a Jie.

[18] Akejan, J 71.

Sub-territories and territorial divisions also have their own oral traditions. Unlike the clan traditions, which tend to be known only in a very restricted area, many traditions concerning sub-territories and territorial divisions are recounted by a major division, or even a tribe, as a whole. As with the clan traditions, I have generally assigned rather more credibility to the traditions of a specific group about itself, which were usually fuller and more factual than the more popular versions told by the rest of the major division or tribe.

For example, the following tradition concerning the immigration to Panyangara from Rengen of a group known as Kadokini is universally known by informants of the entire Lokorwakol major division:

> Long ago the Kadokini came from Rengen. The Rengen had a feast in which a tortoise was slaughtered. When it came time to divide the liver of the tortoise, they found there was not enough to go around, and the leader of the Kadokini was given none. He grew very angry and took his people away to Panyangara. That is why they are now called 'Kadokini' [from *adokini*, to go away in anger]. We don't know when they came here, but our grandfather found them already settled in their present area when they came to Panyangara from Lokibuwo.[19]

The story is a source of great amusement to the people of Lokorwakol, and it is invariably concluded amidst uproarious laughter. It is clearly based on an entirely separate tradition of the Lokatap Rengen in which dissension and subsequent emigration is caused by the unequal division of a hartebeest's liver. Another feature of the story common to many such widely known popular traditions is the strong reliance on the supposed derivation of a group name. Many of these traditions should be treated with great caution.[20]

The Kadokini themselves give a rather different version of their immigration to Panyangara, which states, in part:

> Before the time of [the generation-set] *Ngisiroi*, no one lived here in this part of Panyangara. Even the other Panyangara were down there at Lokibuwo near Toror. Our people lived in Rengen, in the area north-west of Lokatap Rock. Most of our pastures, therefore, were west of the Dopeth River. But each time our people took their cattle west of the river to graze, they were attacked by Dodos and many of their cattle were stolen. Our people grew angry at this, and so they decided they must leave Rengen and come to this part of Panyangara for safety.[21]

[19] Anunu and Cope, J 28.
[20] See Chapter IV, pp. 106–7 below.
[21] Tede (Teko) and others, J 24.

This tradition is clearly a more factual and useful one than the more widely known 'liver of the tortoise' tradition. Naturally enough, the Lokorwakol informants, with little reason to care when the Kadokini moved to Panyangara or exactly what caused them to do so, have invented a pleasing story at the expense of many of the duller elements of reality. It is only to the Kadokini themselves that the story of their emigration from Rengen is important, and as their own tradition demonstrates, they are the only ones who have bothered to preserve that story in full.

In general, then, rather more credibility is given to traditions perpetuated by a group about its own history than to traditions concerning its history related by outside groups, especially in the majority of cases where the traditions of those outside groups tend to corroborate the testimony of the group itself, and where *angola* and *akiwodokin* order tends to support the group's traditions.

Nevertheless, the group traditions often tend to become progressively less reliable, the larger the group. In most cases, this can be attributed to the diverse composition of these larger groups. Sometimes when relating a tradition of their territorial division or major division, informants embellish the tradition with elements of their own clan histories, not strictly applicable to the history of their territorial division or major division as a whole. On the other hand, informants will at other times relate the events of a territorial or major division tradition as though their own ancestors took part in them, even though their own clan histories clearly indicate that such participation would have been impossible.

Traditions relating to the origin of an entire major division, or those few that undertake to explain the origin of the entire tribe, usually tend to be merely 'pleasing stories' of the 'liver of the tortoise' type cited above, from which many important historical elements have been dropped. Moreover, these 'origin' traditions vary from one area to another: many of the informants of Lokorwakol territorial divisions telling of how the Jie came to Najie from Koten Hill in the east (true, in fact, for some, but by no means all, of their clans), and many informants of Rengen territorial divisions telling how the Jie came from the borderland of Acholi in the west (again true for only some clans). Since the Jie, like most other societies, were made up of not one, but a whole variety of peoples who came together to form the present tribal group now known as 'Ngijie',[22]

[22] See below, Chapters III and IV.

it is hardly surprising that this should find reflection even in the vague traditions of the society's larger groups.

Such widely known popular traditions have been termed by Vansina 'tales concerning general history', whereas the more reliable and factual Jie traditions of sub-clan and clan would correspond to his 'tales concerning local history' and 'tales concerning family history'. As Vansina points out, these tales concerning general history tend to be really useful only when treated together with the tales concerning local and family history, 'so as to bring out more clearly the links between them' and in so doing, 'to provide a very accurate check on the traditions relating to general history'.[23]

It is only through a systematic collection of oral traditions on all levels of Jie society, followed by a careful comparison and analysis of them, that a coherent picture emerges. On the one hand, the 'tales concerning local and family history' often contain many of the important historical elements dropped from the 'traditions concerning general history', whereas the more widely known traditions often permit the clan and sub-clan traditions to be seen in some kind of over-all perspective.

Previous observers of Jie and other Central Paranilotic history have not made thorough or systematic collections of the traditions which exist on all the various levels of the social structure. Usually the only traditions bothered with were those relating to 'general history', the most universally known, but the vaguest and in many ways least reliable of all oral history. This has led some, including Gulliver and Crazzolara, to over-generalized and seemingly contradictory reconstructions of Jie and other Central Paranilotic history; while other observers, like Dyson-Hudson, have simply thrown up their arms in despair and concluded that a reliable reconstruction of Central Paranilotic history was impossible. Working only with a few 'tales concerning general history', with little or no reference to the traditions concerning the smaller constituent groups of the Karimojong (as was obviously the case), it is hardly surprising that Dyson-Hudson should write: 'These narratives only partially overlap, do not always agree, are often not mutually known, and so in the end cannot satisfactorily be resolved into one connected account.'[24]

Before turning to a brief examination of the informants themselves, the manner in which interviews were conducted, and other questions

---

[23] Vansina, op. cit., pp. 155–6.
[24] Dyson-Hudson, op. cit., p. 263.

of practical methodology, it is necessary to deal with perhaps the most complex problem confronting an investigator trying to reconstruct the history of the Jie or any other Central Paranilotic-speaking group: that of chronology.

In his book, Dyson-Hudson offers a Karimojong 'origin' tradition of the typically vague 'tales relating to general history' sort in order to show how such narratives, common among the Central Paranilotes, lack any of the chronological awareness which might make them of at least some historical value. He writes: 'If it is chronology that minimally distinguishes history from legend, then clearly this [example, and others like it] cannot be seriously offered as history, for the period of all these events is equally *kanoan nooi*—"in the long, long ago".'[25]

Even in as vague a tradition as that repeated by Dyson-Hudson, however, it is possible to discern at least a relative chronology of the events described. While he is correct in his assertion that these widely known popular traditions usually tend to describe all events as having taken place *kanuana nooi*, most of them are also told in such a way that there is a definite chronological progression from the most remote to the most recent events. Even in the extremely vague example selected by Dyson-Hudson, such a chronological progression is both clearly stated and easily discernible.

Of course, relative chronology is of little use to a historian if he does not have any specific chronological 'pegs' on which to hang at least some events, and so, in general, the widely known traditions are, taken by themselves, of little help.

Most historians who have worked with the more centralized and agricultural peoples of East Africa have found that the 'dynastic generation', based on king lists or 'genealogical generations', based on genealogies of individuals, provide vital tools in the reconstruction of their chronologies. As noted above, however, the Central Paranilotes, with their shallow genealogical memories and their strongly egalitarian society, can provide the investigator with neither the genealogies nor the king lists necessary for the reconstruction of a chronology in any depth. While some Jie informants will speak of an event happening 'in the time of my grandfathers', very often the meaning is 'in the time of the ancestors', and in very few cases could an event be associated with any named ancestor beyond the grandfather. It is impossible, therefore, to use the

[25] Dyson-Hudson, ibid.

'genealogical generation' in the same way and to the same extent that it has been used among some of the more centralized East African societies.

Moreover, oral historians cannot simply assume that the length of genealogical generations is roughly the same in all societies, but rather, as A. H. Jacobs has pointed out, they must always 'be tested against sociological facts of each society in which they are used' to determine accurately their length. In the case of the Pastoral Maasai, for example, Jacobs found the mean length of a generation to be on the order of forty years, whereas both Oliver and Ogot found a mean length of about twenty-seven years for dynastic generations among the Ankole and Luo.[26]

Although the same vast genealogical data as collected by Jacobs over a long period on the Pastoral Maasai has not been gathered for the Jie, every indication is that the mean length of a Jie genealogical generation is closer to that of the Pastoral Maasai than to that of the dynastic generation of the Ankole or Luo. In *The Family Herds*, Gulliver examines in detail the extremely complex process by which a prospective Jie bridegroom amasses the bride-wealth animals necessary for his marriage. Because the numbers of bride-wealth livestock are so considerable, Jie men tend to marry (and father children) relatively late in life. Gulliver observed that 'for a Jie man, marriage before the age of 30 is rare'.[27] This was certainly still true in 1969–71, with most men marrying for the first time in their early or even mid-thirties. In the relatively few cases where I had specific data, the average span of time between the birth of a man and that of his eldest surviving son was on the order of thirty-five years or more. The testimonies of Jie elders indicated that the marriage age was even higher in the past, and they frequently complained that, 'young people are growing up faster nowadays than in the past. Even children (e.g. men in their late twenties) are marrying these days'.

In that the names of individual ancestors beyond the grandfather are not remembered, Jie genealogical memories are shallow. However, like the other Central Paranilotes, the Jie have a system of generation-sets (*asapanu*) based on the genealogical generation, by

[26] A. H. Jacobs, 'A Chronology of the Pastoral Maasai', in *Hadith I*, ed. B. A. Ogot (Nairobi, 1968), p. 20. I am very grateful to Dr. Jacobs for several long discussions he had with me concerning problems of chronological reconstructions among the Paranilotes.

[27] Gulliver, *Family Herds*, p. 242.

which the Jie remember the name of a generation as a whole long after the names of individual members of that generation have been forgotten.

Jacobs has shown that the Pastoral Maasai have two different words for stories relating to events of the past. One of these, *enkiterunoto*, he translates as 'myths', and notes that these stories usually begin with the phrase, 'Now long ago, when sky and earth were still one . . .'. The other Maasai word, *enkatinyi*, which Jacobs translates as 'history or oral traditions', generally begin with such a phrase as, 'Now long ago when the Ilkidotu (or another age-set) were warriors . . .'.[28]

While the Jie and the other Central Paranilotes do not seem to have terms corresponding exactly with the Maasai *enkiterunoto* and *enkatinyi*, many of their more widely known and popular traditions relating to 'general history' begin with the words, *kanuana nooi* (as noted by Dyson-Hudson), or *kolong esek*,[29] 'in the long, long ago'. Many other Jie traditions, especially those relating to 'local or family history', however, begin with such a phrase as, 'in the time of Ngisiroi (or another generation-set) . . .'. Sometimes the Jie reinforce this with reference to their own genealogy (although almost never to a specific ancestor by name) in this way: 'In the time of Ngikok, the generation-set of the father of my grandfather . . .'.

Jacobs, taking some of his inspiration from H. A. Fosbrooke,[30] has shown that by dating based on the last twelve Maasai age-sets it is possible to reconstruct a reliable Maasai chronology going back about 200 years.[31] By the use of a similar tool, the generation-set, it is possible to construct a reliable Jie chronology back to about 1700.

Each Jie major division has its own parallel but autonomous generation-set system, with the Lokorwakol major division invariably taking the lead in initiations. In both major divisions, the generation-set system cuts across the territorial and (pseudo) kinship-based

---

[28] Jacobs, loc. cit., pp. 14–15.

[29] It is difficult to translate these terms exactly. *Kanuan* indicates a very remote time, usually considerably more than 100 years, in the past. *Kolong* usually indicates a time of anything up to about 100 years in the past. *Paaran* and *Ngoon* are the words indicating the recent past: the former, a period of a few years; and the latter, a few weeks or even days.

[30] H. A. Fosbrooke, 'The Maasai Age-group System as a Guide to Tribal Chronology', *African Studies*, 15 (1956).

[31] Jacobs, loc. cit., p. 16. In recent personal communication, Jacobs informed me that he is now in fact able to carry a reliable chronology back to about 1615–25.

social groupings of territorial division and clan. The system largely determines the allocation of ritual and political power within the Jie society. Although the nineteenth century saw a dramatic concentration of such powers in the hands of certain hereditary functionaries, largely exterior to, and partially independent of, the generation-set system, the system has endured, and is even now a major factor in Jie ritual and political life. What is of most concern here, however, is the structure of the system and the dynamics of its operation.

It should perhaps be emphasized that unlike the 'class-systems based on time'[32] of many other societies of eastern Africa, the Jie generation-set system is based primarily not on biological age, but on genealogical generation. The basic and irrevocable principle upon which the Jie system is based is that, simply stated, all the sons of a man must be initiated into the generation-set following his own. Unlike the Karimojong, who, according to Dyson-Hudson, can alter this principle to fit a few very exceptional cases and occasionally initiate a man's sons into the next generation-set but one, the Jie are adamant that the basic principle of their system can never be broken. Despite Dyson-Hudson's implied objections (op. cit., p. 175), Gulliver is certainly correct that Jie males are considered to be 'part' of a generation-set from the moment of birth, even though that generation-set may be as yet unformed. Before my own initiation, Mabuc, my Jie father explained:

> When a child is born, people know immediately what generation-set he is to belong to. A son can be initiated only into that generation-set following his father's. We consider the second generation-set after the father's to be the same as the father's. Could a child be initiated, then, into the same generation-set as his own father? That is foolish. You are to be of Ngitome [generation-set], and so that son of yours who was just born can be only of Ngikoria. That is the way. It goes on and on like that. It doesn't change.[33]

Because it is based on this irrevocable generational principle, there is a tremendous range in the ages of the members of one generation-set and initiations into it must be kept 'open' for a very considerable period of time. At the inauguration of a new generation-set, it is common for many of its first initiates to be mature or even elderly men, and indeed for some men to die of old age before they are

---

[32] The phrase is borrowed from A. Legesse.
[33] Mabuc (Loputuke), J 112.

initiated at all.[34] At the same time, there will be some future members of the generation-set as yet unborn. Furthermore, as Gulliver has noted, a man may well be biologically older than some of his father's younger cousins, who are, nevertheless, initiated into the father's generation-set, and considered 'fathers' by the biologically senior son.[35]

FIG. 3. A Reconstruction of Jie Generation-sets back to Ngisir

(Generation-sets are indicated by roman numerals. The popular nickname is given first, followed by the 'real' name in parentheses. Age-sections are indicated by capital letters, and age-sets by arabic numerals.)

	Approximate date of
GENERATION-SET	*earliest initiations*
I. Ngisir (the decorated ones)	1680
II. Ngipalajam (those of the uncured hides)	1720
(Ngitome?) (those of the elephants)	
A. ? Ngimirio (those of the mice)	
B. ? Ngingatunyo (I) (those of the lions)	
III. Ngikok (those of the soldier-termites)	1760
(Ngikoria?) (those of the ratels)	
A. ? Ngieleki (I) (those of the earrings)*	
IV. Ngisiroi (those of the dik-diks)	1800
(Ngitome?)	
A. Ngimadanga (those of the ticks)	
B. Ngiwapeto (I) (those of the elands)	
1. ? Ngirionomong (those of the black oxen)	
2. ? Ngiyarameri (those of the white-spotted, twisted-horn oxen)	

[34] The Jie system lacks the same strong 'role-phase' concept which is an important facet of other East African class systems based on time, especially those in which biological age plays an important part. Jie initiation implies ritual, rather than biological or social, maturity, so that an uninitiated Jie male can marry, take part in warfare, own livestock and otherwise live a more or less normal life, with the important exception of his participation in ritual affairs.

[35] Much of my description of the Jie generation-set system is based on the work of Gulliver, with special regard to his article, 'The Age Organization of the Jie Tribe', *JRAI* 83 (1953). Although in some instances my own data do not agree with his, my researches into the Jie system would have been incalculably more difficult had Gulliver's work not preceded my own.

In my generation-set, still in the early stages of its formal existence, there was already a range of ages of at least thirty years. At the same time, a number of adolescent boys recently initiated into Ngimugeto, the generation-set of Mabuc, my Jie father, who were biologically younger than any of the members of my own generation-set, had to be treated with great respect and were addressed as 'father'.

V. Ngikokol (those of the black-spotted oxen) 1840
(Ngikoria)
   1. Ngimugeto (I) (those of the topis)
   2. Ngikorio (I) (those of the giraffes)
A.
   1. Ngimuria (I) (those of the klipsringers)
   2. Ngirisai (I) (those of the leopards)
B.
   1. Ngieleki (II)
   2. Ngitukoi (I) (those of the zebras)
   3. Ngitiira (I) (those of the *etiira* trees)

VI. Ngikosowa (I) (those of the buffaloes) 1880–5
(Ngitome)
   1. Ngingatunyo (II)
A.
   1. Ngikwei (those of the jackels)
   2. Ngilobai (those of the hartebeests)
   3. Ngibooko (those of the tortoises)
   4. Ngibeerei (those of the grasshoppers)
   5. Ngiyamanyang (those of the grass-eaters)
B.
   1. Ngidewa (those of the grass-snakes)
   2. Ngiyangamong (those of the light-brown oxen)
   3. Ngikolimoru (those of the plovers)
   4. Ngimoru (those of the mountains)
   5. Ngisuguru (those of the thorns)
   6. Ngitibilanajep (the tongue-breakers)

VII. Ngimugeto (II) 1920–3
(Ngikoria)

A.
   1. Ngirengelim (those of the red feather pom-poms)†
   2. Ngirisai (II)
   3. Ngikorio (II)††
   4. Ngigwete (those of the gazelles)
   5. Ngitukoi (II)
   6. Ngieleki (III)
B.
   1. Ngimuria (II)
   2. Ngitiira (II)
   3. Ngiwapeto (II)
   4. Ngikakerekerei (those of the woodpeckers)

VIII. (Ngitome) 1963
   1. Ngikosowa (II)

* *Ngieleki* in fact refers to a small black seed worn by the Jie as a decoration
behind their ears rather than to an earring as such.

† Gulliver lists Ngirisai as the age-section, with Ngirengelim as a constituent
age-set. Virtually all my informants claimed it was the other way around.
It would seem that Ngimuria is the name of the final age-section, but I am not
certain of this.

†† Some of my informants indicated that Ngigwete were initiated before
Ngikorio II, but as Gulliver was in Najie just after these age-sets were
initiated, I have followed his order here.

While thus primarily based on a generational principle, the generation-sets themselves are, none the less subdivided into groups based largely on coevality. Each generation-set is composed of approximately three 'age-sections', each of which is in turn divided into three or more 'age-sets'.[36] The age-set initiates only during a 'good year', that is, a year in which rainfall is sufficient to grow enough grain to prevent famine and to provide the beer necessary for initiation rituals, and in which there are sufficient numbers of oxen and he-goats to be speared by the initiates. As such years tend to appear both infrequently and sporadically in Najie, there can be no definite statement as to the intervals of time between age-sets. My own age-set, the second of the present Ngitome generation-set, performed its initiations seven years after the initiations of the first age-set, while on the other hand, in the exceptional occurrence of several 'good' years following one upon the other, there can be as little as a year or less between age-sets.

The criterion for initiation into a given age-set by members of one genealogical generation is largely one of biological age. The first age-set of a given generation-set to be initiated tends to be of those oldest uninitiated men who have waited a considerable time for their initiation. Since some of these will be even elderly men, the range of ages of the initiates of this first age-set tends to be rather more considerable than the range in the ages of the members of the following age-sets, whose initiates tend to be men in their early twenties or late teens when the age-set begins its initiation. To the Jie this is the 'proper age of initiation', and although the actual age at which a young Jie man is initiated depends largely on the number of sons and the number of available livestock of his father, most of the age-sets of a generation-set tend to be composed largely of initiates of the 'proper age'. Only at the end of a generation-set, when the Jie are anxious to complete the initiations of the final age-set or two, are younger and younger boys, well below the 'proper age', initiated. Therefore, it is only at the two extremities of a generation-set that there is any very great range in the ages of the initiates of an age-set, whereas the great majority of those of the other age-sets tend to be men 'of the proper age' at initiation.

[36] The terminology was coined by Gulliver. Again, Ajie terms are vague and confusing. Although an 'age-set' is generally termed *anyamet* (pl. *nganyameta*), the same term is usually also used for 'age-section'. On the other hand, *asapanu* is often used loosely to describe not only a generation-set, but an age-section and age-set as well. The terms are reversed in Akarimojong, *anyamet* generally referring to a generation-set, and *asapanu* to an age-set.

The age-sections are usually rather informal groupings of several age-sets, taking their names from the most senior of their constituent age-sets. In Gulliver's words, an age-section emerges when an age-set decides it 'associates more closely with the following junior sets than with the previously initiated senior sets.'[37] The age-sections tend to be the vaguest of all the groupings of the Jie generation-set system, and there is no formal ceremony of any kind to mark their opening or closing.

The opening of a new generation-set is marked by a formal inauguration ceremony at Nayan ritual grove of Lokorwakol, followed a short time later by the inauguration of the parallel Rengen generation-set at their own ritual grove. A hereditary first initiate (considered the leader of the entire generation-set), for the Ngikorwakol drawn from the Toroi of Kotiang, and for Rengen from the Kalolet of Lokatop, is initiated just before the inauguration ceremonies with the spearing of an ox in his own father's kraal. The new generation-set is then considered 'open' and is formally named. Each territorial division, in its prescribed order, then begins the initiation of its own first initiates.

The time of the opening of a new generation-set seems to be determined by a combination of different factors. First, there is usually considerable pressure being exerted by mature and even elderly uninitiated men, anxious to be granted the ritual status they feel should be concomitant with their biological maturity. At the same time, the generation-set of their 'fathers' should have been initiating for a sufficiently long period so that only relatively few of its potential members (in the main, adolescent boys) remain uninitiated. Concurrently, the generation-set of their "grandfathers", who play a key roll in the inauguration and naming of the new generation-set should be at a point where only the most junior of its age-sets are still surviving. Furthermore, those surviving members of the 'grandfathers'' generation-set should be of an age where it is reckoned unlikely that they will produce any additional sons, who would necessarily have to be initiated into the final age-set of the 'fathers'' generation. Finally, when the eldest son of the previous hereditary generation-set leader is of the 'proper age for initiation', the Jie realize that the time for the inauguration of a new generation-set must be at hand.[38]

---

[37] Gulliver, loc. cit. (1953), 152.
[38] If, as the rather limited data suggest, the mean length of time between the birth of a man and his eldest surviving son is between thirty-five and forty

It should be emphasized, though, that it is the combination of these factors that sets the necessary machinery in operation for the inauguration of a new generation-set. Any one of these factors taken by itself would be insufficient to provide the necessary dynamics to set the inauguration process in motion. Mature uninitiated men, for example, may pressure for the inauguration of their generation-set well before the other factors have come into line. Because the total machinery is not yet geared for the inauguration of a new generation-set, some men grow old and some even die before their initiation.

On the other hand, if most of the necessary factors clearly indicate that the time is ripe for the inauguration to take place, one factor may be adjusted somewhat to fit in with the general pattern. For example, when the Ngimugeto generation-set, the fathers of the presently initiating Ngitome (*see* Figure 3), was initiated, considerable pressure had been exerted for a long period by an increasingly large number of mature and elderly potential Ngimugeto. Apparently the members of the 'grandfathers'' generation-set, Ngikokol, had dwindled to a handful of survivors of the most junior age-set, Ngitiira, most of whom were elderly men. In spite of this, Koroc Lokepon, the designated first initiate of the hereditary generation-set leader's clan was still a young boy, below the 'proper age of initiation'. Because all the other factors were in line for an inauguration and the resulting pressures were acute, Koroc was initiated anyway: a boy hardly ten years of age; so young that his father had to help him grasp the spear with which his initiation ox was killed.[39]

Since the survivors of the generation-set of the 'grandfathers' play

[39] Koroc (Lokepon), J 103. However, Koroc's was a rather exceptional case. Koroc's own father had not been the first initiate of his own generation-set, Ngikosowa, although Dila, Koroc's grandfather, had been the first initiate of his. It was Dila's eldest son who had been the first initiate of Ngikosowa, but it would seem that he died fairly early in life without leaving any sons of his own. Thus, the designation of first initiate of Ngimugeto evolved to Koroc, whose father, Kapel, was apparently the second son of Dila. While this may or may not explain why Koroc was not yet of the 'proper age' at the time when all the other necessary factors were in line for the inauguration of Ngimugeto, it clearly shows that it would be a mistake to regard the genealogical generation as the sole criterion determining the span of time between generation-sets.

years, then the span of time between the initiation of a hereditary generation-set leader and his eldest son would also be thirty-five to forty years, if both were initiated at the 'proper age'. His youngest son, if initiated at the proper age, might not be initiated until seventy or seventy-five years after his own initiation.

an important role in the inauguration of the generation-set of the 'grandsons', they choose the names given to the first few age-sets of the new generation. These names are usually the names of already defunct senior age-sets of the 'grandfathers" generation, and often there is a close correspondence between the names of all the age-sets of the alternate generations (*see* Figure 3). In a sense therefore, the 'grandsons" generation-set is seen to replace that of the 'grandfathers'.' As Gulliver has written, in this way a 'spiritual and ritual inheritance is passed on in a continuous line from the grandfather's generation to all levels of the new generation'.[40]

Although Gulliver did not note it, there appears to be evidence that the identity between alternate generation-sets is also expressed by the use of the same name for those alternate generation-sets as a whole. It seems, therefore, that the Jie system is in fact a cyclical one, in which two generation-set names, Ngitome and Ngikoria, invariably recur in alternate order.[41]

Awareness of this cyclical repetition of names came only gradually as lists of past generation-sets were collected from about 200 Jie informants. According to Gulliver's reconstruction of the generation-sets,[42] the generation-set of the 'grandfathers' during my own stay in Najie would have been called Ngikosowa (those of the buffaloes). Although a great many Jie informants also stated that the generation-set was called Ngikosowa, many others claimed its name was Ngitome (those of the elephants). At first this did not cause great concern, as the vagueness of the term *asapanu* often led to confusion; and some informants frequently listed the name of a constituent age-set or age-section, rather than the name of the whole generation-set itself. It did seem odd, however, that so many informants should give Ngitome, which Gulliver listed as merely the third age-set of the generation.

On ritual and other occasions, the 'praise songs' of the 'grandfathers" generation were recorded, one of which began:

Nyamonia a ngikosowa	[In] the forest of buffaloes,
awatar angitome	the elephants were standing there.
Ioye, nyengori.	Oh, the dark grey ones.

[40] Gulliver, loc. cit. (1953), 149.
[41] See Fig. 3. There is less evidence that these names were used for the more remote generation-sets, and so the names are followed by question-marks.
[42] Gulliver, loc. cit. (1953).

and the other:

| Toremo, nyetome, i toremo | Spear the elephant, spear it. |
| Atome ayong. | I am the elephant.[43] |

Why should the praise songs of the 'Buffaloes'' generation be so concerned with elephants, after whom only one constituent age-set was named?

Upon further investigation virtually every informant stated that the 'real' name of Ngikosowa was in fact Ngitome, and before my own initiation I was instructed that the name of my whole generation-set was Ngitome, 'like that of your grandfathers'.' It seemed, therefore, that Ngikosowa was merely a sort of nickname given to the 'grandfathers'' generation-set to distinguish them from all the previous generation-sets (e.g. their 'grandfathers', their 'grandfathers' grandfathers', and so on), who had also been called Ngitome.

The establishment of these facts cleared up some long-outstanding problems with the names of the other generation-sets. The generation-set of the current 'fathers' was listed by Gulliver as Ngimugeto (those of the hartebeests), and indeed many Jie informants also identified it as such. A great many others, however, referred to it as Ngikoria (those of the ratels), a name Gulliver did not list at all. The praise song of the generation-set began 'Iya o, Amia Nyekor ngatuk . . .' ('Oh, the ratel has captured cattle . . .').

Again, Ngimugeto informants seemed about equally divided in referring to the generation of the 'grandfathers' (e.g. the now defunct generation of 'great-grandfathers') as Ngikokol (those of the black-spotted oxen) and, once again, Ngikoria. With further investigation, it became clear that the 'real' name of these alternate generation-sets was, in fact, Ngikoria, and that the names 'Ngikokol' and 'Ngimugeto' were merely the nicknames by which they were distinguished from each other.[44]

---

[43] An additional eight praise songs of the current Ngitome generation-set were also recorded, and every one referred to elephants. In all probability most, if not all, of these songs were also sung by the 'grandfathers' generation.

[44] Frank Stewart of Trinity College, Oxford, working without the benefit of field-work, independently reached very similar conclusions to my own regarding some aspects of the Jie generation-set system. See his unpublished Oxford D. Phil. thesis, 'Fundamentals of Age-Set Systems', 1972.
In personal communication with R. G. Abrahams, I learned that his own researches amongst the Labwor, whose generation-set system certainly has taken some of its inspiration from the Jie one, strongly pointed to a cyclical recurrence of two names, one of which, *Ekoria*, clearly parallels the Jie *Ngikoria*. Although rather different in its operation, the Turkana generation-set system,

The point of greatest interest to an oral historian here is that, despite the cyclical recurrence of two names, Jie informants generally gave the distinguishing nickname of a past generation-set, rather than simply repeating the two 'real' names over and over again. Only those informants who seemed in every way the least well informed did this. Rather, for the majority of informants, the existence of past generation-sets, even those in the distant past, well beyond the recollection of purely genealogical memory, were of sufficient importance and interest that their distinguishing nicknames should invariably be given in preference to their 'real' names.

This is not to say that all of the 200 informants questioned could

---

as described by Gulliver ('Turkana Age Organization', *American Anthropologist*, 60 (1958)) and corroborated by my own research is also a two-name cyclical system. My data on the Dodos system are too sparse to allow for any definitive statement, but again there are pointers to a two-name system.

For the Karimojong, Dyson-Hudson describes a four-name cyclical system. Despite such Karimojong statements as generation-sets 're-enter the place of their grandfathers' and 'they will be named after the animal of their grandfathers', as well as the general close identification between alternate generation-sets, Dyson-Hudson writes that 'the alternate generation-sets do not bear the same inclusive names: that is, the system is a four-group system, not a concealed moiety system' (op. cit., p. 158). However, my own admittedly more modest researches among the Karimojong did tend to indicate that the Karimojong system, like that of the Jie, may well be a 'concealed moiety system' after all. Many of my Karimojong informants claimed that only two of the four names listed by Dyson-Hudson, Ngitukoi and Ngimoru, were the ones which reappeared for alternate generation-sets, and the other two names were simply nicknames by which two of the recent generation-sets were commonly known. The testimony of two Bokora elders is typical: 'The two names, Ngitukoi and Ngimoru, keep following each other, again and again. In the past, generation-sets were often known by other names, such as Ngimirio, Nginyatunyo, or Ngipalajam. But the real name of even these generation-sets was either Ngitukoi or Ngimoru. They were also given a second name—shall we say Ngimirio—by which they were generally known.' (Loyep (John) and Lobanyang (Esero), BK 2).

Certainly the existing generation-set listed by Dyson-Hudson as 'Ngigete' was as often referred to as 'Ngitukoi' as it was 'Ngigete' during my stay in Karamoja. According to Dyson-Hudson's list, Ngitukoi was all but defunct twenty years before my arrival in Karamoja, and it was initially very confusing to find a group of that name. Only after the realization that the Karimojong, like the Jie, might have only a two-name system, did the existence of a vigorous generation-set called Ngitukoi make any sense. It might also explain the existence of several generation-sets before Dyson-Hudson's 'oldest' generation-set, Ngingatunyo, whose names did not correspond to any of the four names he lists. If Dyson-Hudson is correct in his concept of a four-name system, the Karimojong would have a system unique among all the other Central Paranilotic-speaking peoples about whom we have any data. It is also difficult to understand what rationale there would be for a four-name rather than a two-name repetition in a class system based on genealogical generations.

recall the names of all eight generation-sets listed in Figure 3. In fact, only a small minority of informants were able to list all the names, in order, back to Ngisir. It is of great significance, however, that the minority of informants who were able to give the complete list of names invariably did so in exactly the same order despite their living in widely separate areas of Najie. Moreover, those informants were invariably exceptionally good informants in every way, and each was renowned in his own part of Najie as an expert on the things of the past.

The great majority of informants were able to list the generation-sets back to, and including, Ngisiroi (the 'grandfathers' of the most senior surviving elders) with ease, and a great many others were able to carry the list back to Ngikok.[45] On the whole, the average Jie elder seemed to be far more informed concerning the generation-sets of the past than, for example, the constituent clans of his own territorial division, and indeed most seemed to enjoy discussing the generation-sets more than any other subject.

This nearly universal interest in past generation-sets was even clearly demonstrated by a group of elders during an observed ritual function. On this occasion, the elders of Kotido assembled at Nakerwon ritual grove to discuss arrangements for the initiation of the second age-set of the Ngitome generation-set. After preliminary prayers and invocations, the group began an impressively detailed discussion of past generation-sets, with elder after elder arising to recall the various feats of arms and other major events associated with each generation-set. Some elders even mentioned deeds associated with individual age-sets or age-sections of generation-sets as long past as Ngisiroi.[46] Although this was the only occasion on which such a discussion was witnessed, elders testified that such discussions invariably precede the formation of a new age-set, and they must do much to maintain the relatively high universal interest in, and knowledge about, the generation-sets of the past.

It is possible, therefore, to reconstruct a list of generation-sets going back to Ngisir with a reasonable degree of certainty.[47] There

---

[45] A few informants obviously made up names in order to please me or to avoid appearing poorly informed. In most cases these informants became very confused in such renderings. The majority of informants simply stated 'I don't know' if asked to extend the list further back.

[46] A Jie ritual observed on 5 May 1970.

[47] As will be pointed out in Chapter III below, however, 'Ngisir' itself may not refer to a generation-set at all, but rather to an epoch before that specifically recalled in oral tradition.

remains, however, the greater and equally important task of determining whether it is possible to gauge reliably the span of each
generation-set in terms of a fairly specific number of years, and so
establish a chronological foundation for Jie oral history.

One point needs emphasis: it is meaningless to speak of the length
of time that a Jie generation-set is 'open' for initiations. When a new
generation-set begins its initiations, there are invariably a number of
potential members of the previous generation-set as yet uninitiated,
and occasionally still unborn, if any members of the 'grandfathers''
generation are still capable of producing additional sons. The
previous generation-set does not 'close' its initiations when the new
one is inaugurated, but rather there is invariably an overlap period
when age-sets of both generations are initiating separately, but
concurrently. Often, this overlap goes on for many years, although
an effort is usually made to initiate even very young boys of the
'fathers'' generation so that initiations into that generation-set can
be brought to as rapid an end as possible.[48]

As this overlap period can vary considerably from one generation-
set to another, and the initiates of those final age-sets initiated after
the commencement of the following generation-set tend to be only a
small minority of the members of the generation-set as a whole,
and are considered even by the Jie to be 'out of step' with the rest
of their generation-set, it is more expedient to determine the span of
time between the opening of one generation and the opening of the
next, rather than to attempt to determine the span of time during
which one generation-set is 'open' for initiations.

The span of time between Jie generation-sets is, of course, an
approximate, rather than a specific, number of years, quite unlike
the span of other East African class systems based on time in which
class-sets are initiated with the reappearance of certain flowering
plants or other such mnemonic devices. Gulliver estimated that
this span was approximately twenty to thirty years, while for
the Karimojong, Dyson-Hudson estimated twenty-five to thirty
years. It is suggested here that that span is more on the order of

---

[48] Gulliver was not aware of this overlap period, as none was in existence during
his stay in Najie. During my own stay, however, the Ngikakerekerei age-set
of Ngimugeto was initiating concurrently with the initiations of the second
age-set of their 'sons' generation, Ngitome. At that point, Ngitome initiations
had been going on for seven years, and most of the Ngikakerekerei being
initiated were adolescent boys. Despite the repeated hopes of elders that this
would be the last Ngimugeto age-set, a number of even younger potential
Ngimugeto were still uninitiated when I left Najie.

approximately forty years, although obviously some fluctuation must occur.

The most recent Jie generation-set to come into formal existence was Ngitome, which began its initiations in 1963. The year was attested to by all those initiates of the generation-set who had had sufficient primary education to be cognizant of specific years, and by members of Local Government who had recorded it as such. If Gulliver's estimate of twenty to thirty years was correct, then the previous generation-set, Ngimugeto, would have begun its initiations sometime between 1933 and 1943.

While none of the early Ngimugeto initiates had had sufficient education to be aware of the specific year in which the generation-set began its initiations, many were able to indicate almost the precise year in several different ways. From a large number of testimonies, all of which point to roughly the same year, five have been selected here as being particularly reliable, but still representative of the great mass of testimony.

A rather rough approximation of the date in which Ngimugeto initiations began was provided by virtually all Ngimugeto informants who claimed that their generation-set began its initiations at least several years before *Lomee*, 'the disease which killed almost all the goats'. In the 'Calendar of Notable Events in Jie' drawn up by the Jie County Chief, Mr. S. L. Logira, in 1968 to aid census workers and currently on file in the A.D.C.'s office, Kotido, *Lomee* is listed as having taken place in 1926. This is supported by information contained in the Karamoja District Annual Reports and Tour Books, as recorded by Dyson-Hudson: '1926: Almost all goats died of contagious pleuropneumonia.'[49]

A similar, although still only approximate date, was indicated by Timothy Ecak, an elder now about seventy years old, who was one of the first Jie converts to Christianity. After being given some education by B.C.M.S. missionaries, Ecak was appointed evangelist of the Kotido mission. According to Mrs. Doris Clark, Ecak's appointment was in 1933.[50] This is supported by Ecak himself, who began keeping a sort of diary in the year he was appointed. The first entry is the birth of his eldest son who, according to the diary, was born in 1933. Ecak claimed that his son was born 'about ten years

⁴⁹ Op. cit., p. 76. All the Moroto records have subsequently been destroyed. Mr. Logira is himself a Labwor, but his information presumably came both from Jie elders and from the Moroto records, before their destruction.
⁵⁰ D. Clark, *Looking at East Africa* (London, 1953), p. 12.

after the first Ngimugeto speared their oxen', not long after he himself, as a youth of about twenty, was initiated into one of the final
age-sets of the previous generation, Ngikosowa.[51]

Again, the same approximate date for the opening of Ngimugeto
was indicated by Koroc Lokepon, the hereditary first initiate of
Ngimugeto who is, by all possible indications, a man of about sixty
years of age. According to his own testimony and that of virtually
all other informants who were present, he was a young boy about
ten years old when he opened the Ngimugeto generation-set.[52]

A more definite date was indicated in the testimony of Joseph
Lobalong who was seized by the European called 'Topana' at Loyoro
and forced to be an *askari* when he was a young man. Although he
does not know the year, Lobalong recalls that it was 'at the time
when the Germans were fighting in Tanganyika', and that another
youth, Nameu, was seized at the same time. Nameu, now deceased,
ultimately became County Chief of Jie, and a citation awarded him
at his retirement by the Colonial Government, and still in the possession of his son, Korobe, indicates that his service as an *askari* began
in 1914. Lobalong claims that he served as an *askari* for 'about nine
years', and after serving 'about four years' he took part in the
expedition against the Turkana, known as the 'Labur Patrol', in
1918.[53] Approximately five years later, Lobalong claims he was
mustered out and returned home to Najie: although he is not certain, he recalls that the year was 1923. In the same year Lobalong
was initiated into one of the final Ngikosowa age-sets, concurrently
with the initiation of Koroc Lokepon and the other first initiates of
Ngimugeto.[54]

Finally, virtually the same year was indicated by Ansilmo Lowakori who, after a certain amount of Mission education as a youth,
entered Local Government service. Ansilmo's father told him that he
(Ansilmo) was born at the time that their territorial division, Nakapelimoru, was forced to move west out of their own area by the
European called 'Magala' as a punishment for their alleged collabora-
tion with illegal Ethiopian traders. Ansilmo was told by his father

[51] Ecak (Timothy), J 126.
[52] Koroc (Lokepon), J 103. Koroc indicated his age at the time of initiation
by choosing a boy of about nine or ten from a large crowd of children standing near by during the interview.
[53] H. Moyes-Bartlett, *The King's African Rifles* (Aldershot, 1956), p. 441;
and especially R. O. Collins, 'The Turkana Patrol, 1918,' *U.J.* 25 (1961).
J. Barber, *Imperial Frontier* (Nairobi, 1968), p. 182.
[54] Lobalong (Joseph), J 130.

that his birth had taken place while the Nakapelimoru were planting their first sorghum crop in the west. Anxious to learn the date of his birth, Ansilmo consulted records at Moroto before their destruction and learned that the Nakapelimoru were moved west in 1919. Ansilomo's father also told him that Koroc Lokepon and the other first Ngimugeto initiates speared their oxen when that sorghum crop planted in the west was harvested: in other words, the late summer of 1920, and on into the early part of 1921. This was supported by other Nakapelimoru elders who were alive during the western exile, many of whom additionally stated that *Lomee* took place a few years after the Nakapelimoru were allowed to return to their own area.[55]

From these and a great number of supporting testimonies, it seems clear that a date early in the 1920s, and more specifically a date between 1920 and 1923, is indicated for the beginning of the Ngimugeto generation-set. It appears, therefore, that the period of time between the beginning of Ngimugeto and the beginning of the following generation-set, Ngitome, was between forty and forty-three years.

A similar time span seems to have occurred between the beginning of Ngimugeto and the previous generation-set, Ngikosowa. As would be expected, indications of the date of the beginning of Ngikosowa are neither as abundant nor specific as was the case with Ngimugeto. Still, a considerable amount of information concerning the various constituent groups of Ngikosowa both supports the date for the commencement of Ngimugeto and is indicative of a fairly specific date for the commencement of Ngikosowa. Again, the following indications are typical of the great mass of testimony.

Figure 3 shows that Ngikolimoru was the second age-set of the final Ngikosowa age-section, Ngidewa. Informants are agreed that it was initiated just after the battle between the Jie and the Bokora Karimojong at Loreapabong, and Captain T. Grant, the Political Officer of the Turkwell Mission at the time, reported that the battle took place in October 1910.[56] As the majority of initiates of this age-set would have been of the 'proper age of initiation', they would have been born about 1890. In 1970 only a few elderly men of this age-set, all of whom seemed to be in their eighties, still survived.

Again, Nginyamanyang, the last age-set of the middle age-section, Ngikwei (*see* Figure 3), were initiated just before the battle of Caicaon

[55] Lowakori (Ansilmo) and Lokelo (Yeyatum), J 109.
[56] Report of T. Grant, 13 Feb. 1911, E.A. 1049, Part II.

against the Acoli, which 'Karamoja' Bell indicates happened about 1902.[57] The men of this age-set also should have been men of the 'proper age', and so most would have been born about 1880. Only one survivor of the age-set, who fought at Caicaon as a newly initiated youth of about twenty, was located in all of Najie during my stay there.[58]

Many older Jie informants stated that Ngikwei, the age-set which gave its name to the middle age-section (*see* Figure 3) was initiated 'at the time of *Lopid*', the great rinderpest epidemic which, according to Captain Turpin, took place in 1894.[59] As there were obviously no 'good years' immediately following *Lopid*, it is reasonable to assume that the Ngikwei were initiated just before, rather than just after, it took place. Again, members of this age-set would probably have been men of the 'proper age', and if so, born around 1870. This tends to be borne out by the fact that in 1951 Gulliver found only one aged survivor of the age-set in all of Kotido territorial division.

Going further back, the first age-section of the generation-set which, by the Jie system, was also known as Ngikosowa, had only two constituent age-sets: the Ngikosowa themselves (e.g. the first initiates of the whole generation) and Ngingatunyo (*see* Figure 3). Many of the Ngikosowa would have been mature men who had awaited initiation for many years, while the Ngingatunyo would have been composed largely of men of the 'proper age'. In spite of this, Ngikwei, the third age-set, saw fit to associate themselves more closely with the age-sets junior to themselves than with the Ngingatunyo, and so the Ngikwei age-section evolved (*see* Figure 3). Since the rinderpest epidemic was followed by a plague of locusts, a drought, and an outbreak of smallpox, several years must have passed between the initiation of Ngikwei and the following age-set, Ngilobai. Still, Ngikwei chose to associate more closely with Ngilobai than with Ngingatunyo, which strongly indicates that there was an even longer span of time between the initiations of Ngikwei and Ngingatunyo. Indeed, Jie traditions clearly state that another cattle disease, *Loukoi* (probably pleuropneumonia) took place some years before *Lopid*, and if it did not cause the same terrible devastation as *Lopid*, it was nevertheless a heavy blow to the Jie economy. Turpin

---

[57] W. D. M. Bell, *Wanderings of an Elephant Hunter* (London, 1925), p. 63.
[58] This old man, Lobilatum, although physically infirm and totally blind, was still mentally alert and was one of my best informants. He died in October 1970, apparently the last survivor of his age-set.
[59] C. A. Turpin, 'The Occupation of the Turkwel River Area by the Karamojong Tribe', *UJ* 12 (1948), 62. If anything, Turpin's date is probably a bit late.

estimates that *Loukoi* took place about 1887.[60] Although Jie traditions did not specifically mention whether Ngingatunyo was initiated
before or after *Loukoi*, they do mention that they were active at that
time. It can be reasonably deduced that the Ngingatunyo were
initiated sometime before *Loukoi*, and that the outbreak of the
disease prevented further initiations until those of the Ngikwei in
the early 1890s. During the war-leader Loriang's campaigns against the
Bokora in the first decade of the twentieth century, the Ngingatunyo
were one of the most senior age-sets on 'active duty' with the Jie
army, and as such would have been men in their forties at that time,
and by the time of Gulliver's stay in Najie, all the Ngingatunyo (at
least in Kotido) were dead. Both of these facts indicate that a
majority of the Ngingatunyo were probably born in the 1860s and
therefore initiated in the 1880s.

Jie traditions do recall that the first Ngikosowa were initiated
before *Loukoi*, but after *Loongoripoko* (occasionally called *Lopetun*)
another disease which in all probability corresponds to Turpin's
Logipi, which he estimates occurred in 1876.[61] Jie traditions also
recall that the first initiations took place 'before the first *Habaci*
[Ethiopian] traders arrived in Najie'. Informants are further agreed
that these Habaci preceded the *Acumpa* (Swahili) traders by some
years. There is apparently no record of when exactly the first traders
made their appearance in Karamoja, but it is known that when the
first Swahili trader, Jumba Kimameta, arrived in Turkana in 1884,
he found that Ethiopian traders were already active in that area.[62]
It seems likely that Ethiopians had visited northern Karamoja by a
similar date, although as Barber points out, the amount of trade at
that time must have been rather insignificant and restricted.[63]

Clearly, the Ngikosowa began initiations sometime before 1887,
and from all indications a date somewhat earlier in the 1880s is very
likely. A span of thirty-five to forty years, therefore, appears to have

---

[60] Ibid.
[61] Ibid.
[62] See J. Thomson, *Through Masailand* (London, 1885), p. 531, where he
states that when Kimameta entered Turkanaland he found 'natives ornamented
with beads such as are not known among the [Swahili] traders . . .' and he met
people who spoke of a 'great salt lake [Lake Rudolf] on which there were
boats, and said that from that direction they had heard of guns'. See also
L. von Hohnel, *The Discovery of Lakes Rudolf and Stefanie*, Vol. ii (London,
1894), p. 251.
[63] Barber, op. cit., p. 92. Gulliver, in personal communication, also agreed
that it is very likely that the first Ethiopian traders had reached Karamoja
by about 1880.

occurred between the beginning of Ngikosowa initiations and those of Ngimugeto.

While there are no written sources to allow the assignment of a specific date to any event during the time of the previous generation-set, Ngikokol, it is possible to get some idea of when members of some of its constituent age-sets were born by examining their activities at specifically dated events.

For example, current Jie elders in their seventies (their ages calculated from their participation in battles and other events for which definite dates exist in written sources) universally recall that when they were small children in the first decade of this century, Ngitukoi, the penultimate age-set of Ngikokol, were old men (*see* Figure 3). Loriang, the great war-leader, was of this age-set, and it is universally remembered that he was a man in his early seventies at the time of his death in about 1915. By the time of the Ngimugeto initiations which, as has been shown, were in the early 1920s, only a small handful of Ngitukoi, all very aged men, were still alive. From these and a few other indications, the Ngitukoi would have been born in the 1840s, and, if they were initiated at the 'proper age' (which, by their position in the generation-set, they should have been), their initiations would have taken place in the 1860s.

Going further back, Ngimuria, the third age-set of the generation-set, had dwindled to only a few aged survivors by the time of the battle of Tiira, a defensive fight against the Dodos. Informants universally state that it took place a few years before Caicaon, and so, about 1895. At the time of the battle all the surviving Ngimuria were too old and infirm to take part, although it is common in such defensive actions for even rather elderly men to take part in the defence of their homes. It would seem from this that the Ngimuria must have been born in the 1820s, and initiated in the 1840s. As at least two other age-sets of the generation-set were initiated before Ngimuria, it is reasonable to suggest a date in the early 1840s for the beginning of the Ngikokol generation-set; again roughly forty years before the beginning of the following generation-set.

If such an interval of approximately forty years does exist between generation-sets, then the 'fathers' of Ngikokol, the Ngisiroi, would have begun their initiations about 1800, and their 'fathers', Ngikok, would have begun theirs around 1760 (*see* Figure 3). There is a nearly universally known Jie tradition which states that at the time of the inauguration of Ngikok, a devastating cattle raid was launched against a people variously called 'Ngikapwor' or 'Ngiseera' living at the Kotidani River west of Najie. Further traditions recall that after this raid there was a drought of very long duration which caused a terrible famine throughout north-eastern Uganda. As a result, the people of Kotidani, their cattle stolen and their crops withered, moved gradually west through the Labwor Hills[64] to Mt. Otuke where they dispersed, most continuing on to Lango and Acholi, and a few returning to the east.

Traditions collected by Weatherby among the Tepes and by Webster among the Eastern Acoli also recall a prolonged drought which brought on a great famine. Each observer, working independently, deduced that the drought occurred at the end of the eighteenth century, roughly in the 1780s,[65] well within the span of Ngikok initiations, therefore, according to the suggested forty-year interval between Jie generation-sets.

Furthermore, Fr. Crazzolara estimates that 'between the years 1750 and 1800' a considerable number of immigrants from Karamoja pushed into Lango from Mt. Otukei, and both Driberg, and more recently Tosh, have agreed that immigrants were coming into Lango via Mt. Otukei by 1800.[66] Crazzolara's dates correspond almost exactly with the dates suggested here for the span of the Ngikok initiations.

From every indication, therefore, the span of time between Jie generation-sets is, on the average, approximately forty years.[67] Moreover, there is evidence that a similar interval existed between Turkana, and probably Karimojong and Dodos generation-sets, as well.[68]

---

[64] This tradition is supported by Labwor informants.

[65] Personal communication with Weatherby and Webster.

[66] Crazzolara, loc. cit., p. 200. J. H. Driberg, *The Lango* (London, 1923), p. 31, J. Tosh, 'The Background: Environment, Migration and Settlement', p. 19. Chapter I, of the first draft of his London Ph.D. thesis on the history of the Lango.

[67] Fig. 3 shows that fewer and fewer constituent groups of the generation-sets before Ngikokol are remembered by Jie informants. There is probably a tendency for the names of age-sections to be remembered longer than the names of individual age-sets; the constituent groups remembered for the earliest generations are probably age-sections rather than age-sets. Therefore, any kind of precise dating for events taking place during these earliest generations is impossible except in those cases where traditions specifically state that they happened when the generation-set in question was at the beginning or the end of its initiations. In most cases, events of the early generation-sets can be dated only be reference to the whole span of years during which the generation-set in which they occurred was actively initiating.

[68] For indications of this forty-year interval in non-Jie generation-set systems, see my London Ph.D. thesis, especially Appendix 4.

It remains to examine briefly the informants themselves, as well as the practical methodology which enabled the collection of their oral history. With the realization that many important aspects of Jie oral history might best be approached through the traditions of the smaller social groups—the clans and the sub-clans—an attempt was made throughout the latter part of my research to make contact with as many of those groups as possible. As my home near Kotido was roughly at the geographical centre of the permanently settled area of Najie, the most outlying settlements of any territorial division were not more than 20 miles away. It was a fairly easy matter, therefore, to canvass the entire area of permanent settlement, although the lack of motorable tracks meant that some settlements were accessible only on foot. As a result, informants from every territorial division and from most clans were interviewed.

Another problem which was easily solved was to identify the class of Jie from whom the fullest and most reliable traditions might be collected. From the beginning it became increasingly clear that the senior elders, the last survivors of the 'grandfathers'' generation, Ngikosowa, were, as a group, the best potential informants. Naturally there were exceptions to this, and an individual elder's ability to recount oral traditions depended very much on his own particular personality and interests.

Some of the best informants were men, who, by Jie standards, tended to be rather shy and quiet. It was discovered that many such men had not taken as active a part in warfare in their youth as their coevals, and had preferred to remain behind at the permanent settlements with the older people when most youths of their age departed for the harsher, but more adventuresome, life of the cattle camps. Often, such men seemed to have a natural interest in oral history, and from an early age would sit near groups of elders and eavesdrop on their discussions of 'the things of the past'.

On the other hand, many other excellent informants were more flamboyant elders, who, in their youth, had been great warriors whose deeds are still recalled in the Jie war-songs. In many such cases, elders seem to have taken an interest in 'the things of the past' only later in life, sometimes largely because it was expected of them. The senior elders as a group are held by the Jie to be the authorities on oral tradition, and it seems to be a matter of pride with many elders to live up to the expectations of their people. Those elders who are the senior men of their clans and sub-clans are also expected to be the final authorities on the *ngitalia* and the traditions associated with the group.

Furthermore, the more senior elders tend to have much more opportunity to be exposed to oral traditions than any other class of Jie society. They are invariably present at ritual occasions, where oral traditions can play an important part in discussions. They are also the men who, as a group, have a great deal of leisure time, much of which is spent sitting under a favourite tree with kinsmen or neighbours even senior to themselves discussing the 'things of the past'.

In all, seventy-one elderly Ngikosowa were interviewed. These men must have represented a considerable proportion of the survivors of that generation-set in 1969–71. Although some were better than others (and a few were senile), they were, as a group, very good informants. Moreover, most were of such an age that even if they were not able to recount much oral history, they were invariably able to provide oral evidence about events of the early twentieth and late nineteenth centuries in which they themselves took part.

Rather more informants of the 'fathers'' generation-set, Ngimugeto, 114 in all, were interviewed. As a group, the Ngimugeto were not as well informed as the Ngikosowa, but some individual Ngimugeto were among the very best informants. Many of these were older Ngimugeto, rather 'out of step' with their generation-set, and biologically of an age more in correspondence with the surviving Ngikosowa. Others were younger men who, because of their individual personalities or circumstances, took a greater interest in oral traditions than most of their coevals.

For example, Elizeo Lower, although only about fifty-five, proved to be an outstanding informant. Elizeo was born severely crippled in all four limbs, which prevented him from going out to the cattle-camps or participating in raids as a youth, and so invariably he remained behind at the permanent settlements where he developed an avid interest in the traditions he heard being told by the older members of his family. In the same way, Sampson Looru, although rather older than Elizeo, was still considerably younger (both biologically and socially) than most Ngikosowa, and yet he was one of the four or five best informants interviewed. Sampson, an extremely soft-spoken and gentle man had avoided going to the cattle-camps as much as possible as a youth, and had usually remained behind in his father's settlement, where he helped to care for his very aged grandmother, regarded at that time as one of the chief authorities on the oral traditions of her area, and from her he learned many 'things of the past'.[69]

In many cases, Ngimugeto were interviewed in order to collect rather specialized information. In some cases they were clan or sub-clan leaders, the elder Ngikosowa all having died. The current Jie war-leader, the ritual fire-maker of the Rengen, the leader of the Kaceri settlers, and members of the Lokorwakol families which supplied their ritual fire-makers and generation-set leaders were all Ngimugeto.

As a group, however, the Ngimugeto seemed to lack both the inclination and the leisure time to know the oral traditions as fully and as well as the Ngikosowa, as a group, did. Often, Ngimugeto seemed rather intimidated by the existence of a surviving Ngikosowa kinsman, and would advise me to 'Ask my "father" these things. He is the elder here, and he knows these things better than I do'. Also, many younger Ngimugeto were too busy with the daily management of livestock and domestic affairs to be very concerned with oral traditions: 'Am I an elder, do you think, that I can just sit under a tree and talk about these things of the past?'

The other twenty-nine informants interviewed were either of the 'sons'' generation, Ngitome; uninitiated men; non-Jie visiting or living temporarily in Najie; or women. Most of the uninitiated men and Ngitome were relatively older men, 'out of step' with their generation. Only seven women were interviewed, most of them elderly. One of these was among my best informants, while another was among the poorest. The women usually knew the traditions of their husbands' clan better than those of their fathers' clan, and because so many of the *ngitalia* pertain to marriage and women's dress, they seemed to be more familiar with the ranges of *ngitalia* of various clans than most men.

The process of finding suitable informants, never very difficult, became progressively easier as research went on. Soon after my arrival in Najie, a meeting with all the sub-county and parish chiefs was arranged for me by Mr. Logira, the County Chief, and it was largely through them that contact with my first informants was made. These first informants were usually elders well known to the chief of their area as men with considerable knowledge of oral traditions. Because the chiefs were the intermediaries in those meetings,

---

[69] Looru's grandmother must have been rather exceptional, for I never heard of any other Jie woman who was regarded as quite such an authority on oral traditions.

however, many of those first informants seemed convinced that I was in some way connected with the Government, despite attempts by the chiefs and myself to assure them I was not. As many older Jie had a distinct tendency to idealize the time when there was a European administration as one of 'peace and rain', it was occasionally not really to my disadvantage to be considered 'the Government'. Nevertheless, most informants met through the chiefs seemed rather suspicious of the motives of 'the Government' in asking them about their oral traditions.

Early in my research, therefore, I began to work as much as possible without direct help from the intermediary chiefs. Some informants were contacted through my research assistants during visits to their homes. It soon became clear that each area of Najie had certain elders who were considered authorities on oral tradition and that there were several elders who were known virtually throughout Najie as the foremost authorities. A special effort was made to obtain introductions to such elders by others with whom contacts had already been established.

As work progressed, I became a familiar figure in almost every part of Najie, and by the end of the first nine or ten months, much of any earlier suspicion concerning me and my work had died down. Ritual functions were attended on a regular basis, and from the beginning a point was made of associating with the Ngitome generation-set, into which I was ultimately initiated. By the mid-way point in my research, locating suitable informants had become rather a 'snowballing' process, with previous informants suggesting the best informants of a particular clan or sub-clan, and often accompanying me to their homes to make a formal introduction. By the end of my stay in Najie, a few elders were even coming to my home in Kotido to announce, 'You have spoken with all my "brothers"; now I am here to tell you the things I know of the past'.

Most of the data were collected in a series of 132 formal interviews. Each interview was tape-recorded in its entirety and subsequently translated and transcribed almost verbatim with the help of a research assistant. The interview itself generally lasted for about an hour, although a few were only half as long, and others went on for well over two hours. Most informants, especially the older ones, became tired after about one hour and made it obvious that the interview should be concluded. Each interview was preceded by about fifteen to thirty minutes of 'small talk' about the weather, the cattle, the sorghum, recent raids, and so forth. Usually I provided millet beer during this stage of the interview and everyone taking part in the interview drank as we talked. When the informants seemed at ease, the purpose of my work and the tape-recorder were explained.[70] After the interviews, the informants' voices were played back briefly for them, and they were thanked with a small gift of snuff tobacco, and occasionally *posho*, sugar, salt, or other food.

Almost all the interviews were conducted in Ajie through a research assistant who served as interpreter. Perhaps a third of the informants knew Kiswahili reasonably well, and I had informal chats with them before the interviews, and sometimes part of the interview itself would be carried out in Kiswahili. My own knowledge of Ajie was rather slight, though a considerable vocabulary of specialized words used frequently in interviews was built up. By the end of my work, I could converse on a very simple level and could follow the general drift of the testimony, but I never approached a knowledge of the language whereby an informant could be interviewed directly in Ajie.

Three research assistants were employed on a full-time basis during my stay in Najie. Although fewer than ten Jie young men had completed four years of secondary education by 1969, I was fortunate enough to secure two of them as my first two research assistants. The third assistant, who began work during the latter part of my research, had completed a year's secondary education, but had also lived in Kampala for a year where his everyday language had been English. In all cases, the assistants had a high enough standard of English for me to be able to trust their translations implicitly. Interviews were translated sentence by sentence, and my assistant and I usually spent four or five hours in translating and transcribing a single hour of tape. An effort was made to do this within a day or so of the interview so that if any part of the testimony was unclear, an informant could be seen again briefly while the interview was still fresh in everyone's mind. During the interviews themselves, the research assistant would provide a brief summary of an informant's testimony before I asked another question. These summaries became shorter as my own understanding of Ajie increased, and could frequently be dispensed with altogether by the end of my stay in Najie.

---

[70] No informant ever objected to the 'radio that catches the wind' (the tape-recorder), and most were delighted when their voices were played back. It was only if I or a research assistant attempted to jot something down on paper that some informants became nervous. Excerpts from these tape-recordings, amounting to about ten hours of listening time, are being deposited with Indiana University.

Questions asked during the interview were made as general as possible, and I conscientiously tried to avoid any question which could be answered by simply 'yes' or 'no', or which might 'lead' the informant in any way. Before an interview, twenty or forty questions would be written out on a note card to serve as a guide to my questioning, but during the interview deviation from these questions was constant as informants' testimonies indicated new areas of inquiry.

The earlier research projects of Webster in Teso and Tosh in Lango had suggested two radically different outlooks on the number of informants to be interviewed at one time. Among the Iteso, Webster had used the 'group interview', in which as many as a dozen informants were interviewed together; Tosh, on the other hand, interviewed all of his informants singly.

In my own research, both methods were employed. At the beginning, the 'group interview' was used rather more, although five was the maximum number of informants that could be effectively interviewed at one time, and an ideal number was more like three. To interview more than five informants was to invite chaos, and control over the interview was extremely difficult to maintain.[71]

Working with a small group of less than five informants seemed to have several things to recommend it. In the first place, since Jie elders typically came to decisions in council, the best renderings of oral traditions might also be given in a group situation. Sometimes this was the case, in fact, with elders discussing a tradition among themselves before telling it. On the other hand, many group interviews tended to be dominated by one man, more forceful than his companions, who would do almost all the talking and even shout down any of the others who tried to express their own views. Also, in a group situation where men from two or more clans might be represented, there was a tendency for only one group's traditions to be related, as though they applied to all the clans present.

The group interview was often useful when working in a given area for the first time with unknown informants: there was more likelihood of getting at least some useful information from the

[71] The maintenance of order in the interview situation was often a problem. As interviews were usually held under an elder's 'favourite tree' often near a well-worn path between homesteads, considerable groups of women, children, and young men would frequently congregate nearby, joking and talking among themselves. Old men usually had sufficient respect and authority to command silence or to order away noisy spectators, but some of the younger informants did not, and some interviews were nearly ruined by background noise.

group as a whole than from only one poor informant on his own. It was also a good method to use when interviewing very old men who were often too feeble to speak for very long periods on their own.

Second and third interviews with exceptionally good informants, and interviews conducted primarily to collect clan histories or other more specialized information, were better conducted with a single informant, however. In such cases, the informant was usually enough of an authority for simultaneous testimony from other informants to add little to his testimony and possibly to do much to muddle it. Interviews with single informants increased during the second half of my research, so that by the end of my stay in Najie virtually all interviews were with a single informant, or perhaps with a primary informant and a single companion of his choice.

The formal interview was not the only means of collecting information. Ritual occasions proved helpful both in collecting data and in meeting prospective informants. Songs, especially war-songs and generation-set praise songs, heard on these ritual and more formal occasions (as well as during the formal interviews) provided a considerable amount of useful historical information. Except for about five brief trips, my wife and I remained in Karamoja for our entire sixteen months in Uganda. Even a day-trip out of Najie to Moroto for necessary petrol and food supplies was not undertaken more frequently than every two or three weeks. As a result, we became very familiar figures, especially in our 'home area' of Kotido, and so informal visits to the homesteads of neighbouring elders with whom we became friendly provided another source of useful information.

Throughout the project, two auxiliary disciplines, social anthropology and archaeology, provided additional tools of great help in the collection of oral historical information. Social anthropology provided methodological tools to arrive at an understanding of Jie social organization and the generation-set system. Other information was collected by the examination of a large number of archaeological sites in northern Karamoja, many of which played important roles in Jie traditional history. I was helped and advised throughout my investigations by Hamo Sassoon, as well as by Charles Nelson and Larry Robbins, all professional archaeologists, and by John Wilson, John Weatherby, and Alan Jacobs, all amateur archaeologists with great practical experience in East Africa.

In addition to the 132 Jie interviews, a series of sixty-three formal interviews were conducted among neighbouring peoples in order to collect data corroborative to Jie traditions. None of these tribes had been studied in depth by a historian at the time of my arrival, although during my research Bertin Webster began a project among the Eastern Acoli kingdoms which produced invaluable data. Simultaneously John Weatherby was conducting research among the 'Fringe Cushitic'-speaking Tepes of southern Karamoja and John Wilson had finished a study of the remnants of the Iworopom in the same area; a certain amount of rather indirect comparative material was provided by both these investigators. Nevertheless, the histories of all the peoples actually neighbouring on Najie, with the exception of the Eastern Acoli, remained a mystery. Since so much of Jie history was that of their interaction with neighbouring peoples, it was necessary to form a clearer picture of the histories of those neighbours about whom so little was known. As J. E. G. Sutton has written, 'If we try to study tribes or groups in isolation, we will end up . . . with tribalist histories full of biases and antiquarianism'.[72]

The sixty-three non-Jie interviews, therefore, helped to place Jie oral traditions into some kind of more general perspective.[73] Because of the similarity in dialects, my Jie research assistants were able to serve as interpreters in all but the Nyakwai, Labwor, and Marille interviews, although temporary assistants (usually secondary-school students) from each area were hired to help with translations, and to serve as guides and intermediaries.

In general, both Jie and non-Jie informants whom I interviewed proved to be far better informants than I had any reason to hope they would be, as the excerpts quoted from many of their testimonies in the following chapters will, I hope, at least partially demonstrate. At the expense of over-generalizing, it could be said that the most important attribute almost universally shared by informants was honesty. There was seldom any discernible attempt by informants to fabricate information on the spur of the moment to 'please' me. In most cases, if informants did not know any traditions pertaining to a certain question, they would frankly say so.

[72] J. E. G. Sutton, 'The Settlement of East Africa', in *Zamani* (Nairobi, 1969), p. 96.
[73] Those interviews are broken down as follows: 20 Turkana interviews, with 50 different informants; 13 Dodos interviews, with 30 informants; 11 Labwor, with 25 informants; 9 Bokora Karimojong, with 17 informants; 4 Matheniko Karimojong, with 7 informants; 1 Mothingo Karimojong, with 1 informant; 2 Ngitome Karimojong, with 2 informants; 2 Nyakwai, with 5 informants; 1 Merille, with 3 informants; and 1 Eyan, with 1 informant.

CHAPTER III

The Background to the Jie Genesis

As we have seen, previously published accounts present irreconcilably dissimilar pictures of the origin of the Jie and other Central Parani-lotes, Gulliver and Nagashima concluding that the Jie entered Najie from the south-east and Crazzolara believing that they arrived from the west.

While both interpretations are based on kernels of historical fact, both are oversimplified and misleading. A careful collection and analysis of Jie oral tradition shows that they, like countless other peoples, African and non-African, cannot be thought of as having had any one single 'origin'. Far from being a matter of a more or less definable political entity moving from point *A* to point *B*, the Jie genesis is in fact the story of amalgamation and close inter-relationship between a great variety of peoples. To understand this complex story, it is necessary to examine the various groups which (to borrow Ogot's phrase) 'have mingled in the crucible of history'[1] to form the present Jie people. The story has its begin-nings in the distant past, long before any of the present Central Paranilotic political communities had begun to come into formal existence, with the expansions outwards from a concentration in eastern Karamoja of certain Paranilotic elements in the early eighteenth century. Oral tradition, therefore, is of only limited help in the examination of groups which pre-existed the formation of the present Central Paranilotic societies, and so one is forced to rely on additional means to secure a clear glimpse back through the haze of time.

Long before any of the Central Paranilotic-speaking groups were to occupy their present homelands, those lands were inhabited by others. Although a great deal remains to be done, sufficient archaeo-logical investigation has already been carried out to show that thriving Stone Age cultures once existed in many parts of Karamoja. Although representative of a culture which once extended throughout much of eastern and southern Africa, and by no means central to the

[1] B. A. Ogot, *History of the Southern Luo* (Nairobi, 1967), p. 53.

distribution of that culture, the type site of the Second Intermediate 'Magosian' Culture is located at a water-hole in the Magos Hills.[2] Microlithic tools, ostrich-eggshell beads and stone balls similar to the Magosian type have been found at other sites in Karamoja, and both Wilson and Weatherby have found large numbers of bored stones (probably digging-stick weights) of the type associated with Magosi, although radio-carbon dates are so far entirely lacking.

No sites with definite Magosian associations have been located in Najie, but again, very little professional archaeological research has so far been done. His archaeological survey of the Kotido area in 1970 led Charles Nelson to suggest that there have been four discernible groups of inhabitants in Najie. While his 'Group I' was represented by 'Later Stone Age hunters and gatherers, having no pottery, agricultural equipment or stock', he does not suggest any connection between them and the Magosian or any other earlier culture.[3] Similarly, other sites in Najie have been located by Wilson, Sassoon, and myself.

Many of these sites are located near natural rock cisterns, and while some were found in or near rock shelters, others were in the open. Typical features of these sites are microlithic tools: backed blades, crescents, awls, and various bladelets, some no more than 2 cm. in length. They are often accompanied by larger scrapers, ostrich-eggshell beads, stone mullers, and occasionally stone axes.

Also found at these sites, and presumably associated with the microlithic tools, are sherds of very thin pottery with a 'deep-grooved' design. Although substantial variations occur, the pottery invariably betrays an extremely high degree of skill and artistry. Of the design, Sassoon has written: 'the grooving is so extremely regular and perfect that one is constantly thinking that the pot must have been turned on a wheel'.[4] Rock slides, circles of flat stones set into the ground, 'ubao-boards' cut into stones (usually of four rows, very occasionally of two),[5] deep-basin grinding stones, and rock paintings are also frequently found at, or very near, these sites. While the rock paintings

[2] See S. Cole, *The Prehistory of East Africa* (New York, 1965), pp. 201–7.

[3] C. Nelson, 'Report on Archaeological Survey of the Kotido Area, April 1970', a supplement to *Uganda Monuments Section Monthly Report, April 1970.*

[4] H. Sassoon, *Uganda Monuments Section Monthly Report, April 1970*, p. 2. L. H. Robbins, in 'The Archaeology of Turkana District', an unpublished paper presented at Nairobi, 1970, pp. 12–13, quite reasonably urges a cautious approach to this pottery until some radio-carbon dates have been secured.

[5] Other holes cut into rocks in various parts of Najie were clearly not 'ubao-boards', and were probably used either for crushing wild fruits or for shaping iron cow-bells.

may well be associated with the artefacts of the Late Stone Age, it is much less certain whether the *'ubao*-boards', grinding stones, and stone circles belong to the Late Stone Age culture, or to later Iron Age cultures which have superimposed them on pre-existing sites.[6]

Wilson and Weatherby have found rock paintings (often of giraffes or elephants in dark red or white) at several Karamoja sites, while Sassoon has located faint paintings which appear to include a set of concentric circles at Kalobur in Najie, and Wilson has found a set of very finely done miniature animals (possibly sheep) at the same site. Weatherby, basing his ideas on hints in Tepes oral tradition, has suggested[7] that in many cases the paintings had a deep religious significance to the cultures that produced them, and were not merely the scribblings of idle hunters, or an attempt to 'bewitch' the animal depicted, as has so often been conjectured.

Weatherby's ideas gain support from the discovery of a set of paintings near Madang on the Jie–Dodos frontier by Wilson and myself early in 1971. Although faint, and in some cases partially worn away, the paintings appear to have been mainly of geometric symbols, with the possible exception of what seems to be a human figure drawing a bow. The unique feature of the site, however, is a considerable number of stones set into a series of concentric semi-circles all facing in towards the rockface on which the symbols are painted. The effect is one of a large open-air amphitheatre with all attention focused on the paintings. A natural rock platform which extends out over the paintings could well have been employed as a kind of 'stage' or 'altar'.

This Late Stone Age culture with its microlithic tools, symbolic rock paintings, and fine 'deep-grooved' pottery appears to correspond with Nelson's 'Group II' inhabitants of Najie: 'A group using LSA tools, but with pottery and possibly stock'.[8] The identification of this culture with any group in oral tradition, however, remains more of a problem.

John Wilson, who has spent many years studying the remnants of the Oropom people in southern Karamoja, has argued that the Oropom may well have been the very early inhabitants of a vast part

---

[6] Notes on a number of the archaeological sites investigated in Karamoja are contained in my London Ph.D. thesis, especially in Appendix 5.

[7] In personal communication. His ideas are presumably also contained in the Ph.D. thesis on the oral history of the Tepes which he has recently completed at Makerere University.

[8] Nelson, ibid. I believe that by 'stock', Nelson is referring only to small stock: sheep and goats.

of East Africa including most of the territory now inhabited by the
Central Paranilotes.[9] From the physiognomy of surviving individuals,
Wilson suggests that the Oropom may have been a Bushmanoid
group, and from his own impressive archaeological investigations
and on Oropom oral traditions he has collected, he concludes that
the Oropom possessed a remarkably sophisticated Late Stone Age
culture, of which the 'deep-grooved' pottery was a product. Wilson
further holds that much of what is now central and northern Karamoja was subsequently occupied by a Kalenjin-speaking group of
pastoralists, akin to the present-day Merille and Pokot.

While many of Wilson's ideas deserve careful and serious attention,
there is absolutely no hint of any previous Oropom occupation of
Najie in Jie oral tradition. While Oropom and/or other Bushmanoid
groups may well have been the original inhabitants of Najie, their
presence would have been of so remote a date that there is no
recollection of it in the oral traditions of the Jie, and most of the
other Central Paranilotic groups. There is, on the other hand, some
indication of the presence of early Kalenjin groups in these traditions
and, indeed, as Wilson has noted, their former occupation seems
attested to by the survival of a number of Kalenjin place names.

However, the clearest recollections in Jie traditional history of a
pre-existing population, possibly associated with the Late Stone Age
sites, almost invariably refer to a group which came to be called
'Ngikuliak'. It is highly probable that this group originally spoke
what Tucker has termed a 'Fringe Cushitic' language,[10] and
was related to the other Fringe Cushitic-speakers in Karamoja:
the Tepes (or Sorat), the Nyangea, and the Teuso (or Ik). It seems
likely that the Ngikuliak formed a central link in a more or less
unbroken chain of Fringe Cushitic groups which extended the whole
length of Karamoja, from the Tepes on Mt. Moroto in the south,
to the Teuso on Mt. Mogilla in the north.

The oral traditions of all the present Central Paranilotic groups
in Karamoja definitely recall that the Fringe Cushitic-speakers were
earlier inhabitants of their present areas:

The Nyangea did not come here to this land with the Dodos. They
were already living here when we arrived. Nor did the Teuso come

[9] J. G. Wilson, 'Preliminary Observations on the Oropom People of Karamoja . . .', *UJ* 34 2 (1970), 125–45.
[10] See A. N. Tucker, 'Fringe Cushitic', *SOAS Bulletin*, 30. 3 (1967). I would
like to express my appreciation to Professor Tucker for the considerable time
he has spent helping me to understand many of the linguistic aspects of the
non-Bantu languages of East Africa.

from anywhere else, but have always lived at Morungole where the Dodos found them. They were trappers and traded game-meat and gourds to the Dodos for goats. They collected honey and grew small gardens.[11]

The Ngikuliak are magic. If any misfortune befalls them, it will also befall the Jie. That is because they are the oldest people in Najie. God put them here. Orwakol [the leader of one group of Paranilotic-speaking Jie] found them here when he came. They were the first.[12]

God created the Tepes on their mountain, Moroto. When the Karimojong came here to this land, the Tepes were already on the mountains—Moroto, Napak, and Kadam.[13]

While there is general agreement in most Jie traditions that the Ngikuliak were a pre-Jie group, there is less agreement concerning their original linguistic affiliation. Some informants claimed that they spoke a Paranilotic language, 'something like Ajie, but with stammers and terrible sounds',[14] while many others expressed a belief that the Ngikuliak were in fact originally Fringe Cushitic-speaking: 'The Ngikuliak were the same as the "Ngiruwatwol" [People of the decorated calabashes, i.e. Teuso]. They originally spoke the Ngiruwatwol language. They were both trappers, both "Wa-Dorobo".'[15]

The Ngikuliak appear to have lost their original language at a fairly early date, considerably before the formation of a distinct political entity called 'Jie'. It is not surprising, therefore, that some informants should be unaware of any tradition suggesting that the Ngikuliak were once linguistically akin to the Teuso. Indeed the Ngikuliak, far more than the Tepes or Teuso, have been almost completely absorbed into Paranilotic society, and so in some ways

---

[11] Yosia Akure (and others),D 2.
[12] Akuremeri (and others), J 7.
[13] Emanikor and Lodum, MTK 1.
[14] Nakade (Peter), J 57.
[15] Apalodokoro (and others), J 23. Although Apalodokoro used the Kiswahili term 'Wa-Dorobo' to describe the Ngikuliak and Teuso, he most certainly did not mean to imply any specific relationship between the Ngikuliak and the Okiek peoples. Rather, he was merely expressing the fact that all were similar in that they were trappers.

C. M. Turnbull ('The Ik: Alias the Teuso', *UJ* 31 (1967)) has collected a Teuso story of creation 'remarkably similar to the Dorobo' and notes that some Teuso elders call themselves 'Wandorobo'. Despite this and the fact that the attitude of the Jie and the other Central Paranilotes towards the Fringe Cushitic-speakers is expressed in a way uncannily similar to the way the Pastoral Maasai regard the Okiek, any definite association between the two groups of trappers has certainly not been established.

it is difficult to reconstruct a clear picture of them as they existed before the eighteenth-century Jie genesis.

Nevertheless, it is important to try to reconstruct at least some picture of the Ngikuliak as they existed before that time. Two compact Jie clans and one dispersed one (the Ngikuliak themselves and the Ngadakori of Kotiang, and the dispersed Lokwor of Kotiang and Kotido (*see* Figure 1)) seem to be descended mainly from Ngikuliak ancestors, and the Ngikuliak were to form considerable symbiotic relationships with the Jie to provide an all-important refuge for impoverished Jie during much of the eighteenth and especially the late nineteenth centuries.

In 1969–71 only a few families who still referred to themselves as 'Ngikuliak' existed in Najie. There was a marked tendency for these remnants to depict themselves as 'thoroughly Jie' to all inquiries, although their truly Paranilotic neighbours referred to their alien origin in a very definite (and often contemptuous) way. Undoubtedly some of the traditions of originally Paranilotic-speaking clans concerning the way of life of the Ngikuliak must be treated with caution, as they sometimes embody the misconception so often perpetuated by Paranilotic-speaking peoples about those pre-existing groups that they come to dominate.[16] Many such Jie traditions present a picture of the Ngikuliak as 'worthless people' who 'lived in the forests like baboons'. However, some Ngikuliak informants (including Lomare, the senior elder of one of the remnant families, and a famous diviner) were able to overcome their suspicions and provided invaluable information which, when taken together with information contained in some of the more reliable Jie traditions, provided at least some glimpse of the Ngikuliak as they existed before the advent of the Paranilotic-speakers.

As in the Jie traditions, Ngikuliak informants claimed that their ancestors were the original inhabitants of Najie, and, while no specific relationship with the Teuso or any other Fringe Cushitic-speaking group was ever admitted, it was stated that their ancestors once spoke another language, totally unlike Ajie.[17] Both Ngikuliak and

[16] In 'Okiek History', soon to be published as Chapter I of the forthcoming volume, *Aspects of Pre-Colonial History of Kenya* (B. A. Ogot, ed.), R. H. Blackburn, who has recently done extensive field-work among Okiek groups in Kenya, lists a number of such misconceptions regarding the Okiek, a number of which are precisely the same as those perpetuated by the Jie about the Ngikuliak. I am grateful to Mr. Blackburn for supplying me with off-prints of his chapter.

[17] The former Ngikuliak language now appears to be entirely forgotten, except for the survival of a few Ngikuliak place-names (most of them onomato-

Jie informants agreed that they, like the other Fringe Cushitic-speakers, were a hill people, and although they appear to have had some settlements on the plains, their real homes were on the isolated hills and mountains of Najie, as a song recalls:

I	Ara Maru nyekosia,	I	Maru [mountain] was ours,
	Iye ya.		Iye ya.
	Nyemoru kata Loceno		Mountain of Loceno.
	Nyemoru kata Awangaki		Mountain of Awangaki
II	Ara Toror nyekosia	II	Toror [mountain] was ours,
	(refrain)		(refrain)
III	Ara Kotidani nyekosia	III	Kotidani [hill] was ours,
	(refrain)		(refrain)[18]

The mountain considered by the Ngikuliak as their original home is Maru, west of the Dopeth River, and outside of what was to become the permanently settled area of Najie (*see* Map 1). Archaeological investigations at Maru (and a near-by rock outcropping called Nasokodomoru), and at Kalobur in the western part of Nakapelimoru territorial division, which is also recalled as a former Ngikuliak settlement, have revealed extensive settlement sites containing the typical Late Stone Age artefacts mentioned above. Lomare, the most knowledgeable informant of the Ngikuliak interviewed, stated that in the past his people made stone tools, and expressed the opinion that his female ancestors made the 'deep-grooved' pottery. Certainly clay pipe-bowls found at Maru and at other sites, which could definitely be associated with the Ngikuliak, bore designs of an artistry which closely matched that of the 'deep-grooved' pottery.[19] Unlike any Jie informant, Lomare seemed well acquainted with the rock

---

[18] Nyaramoe, Lokong (Israel), and a group of women, J 37. An exceptionally large number of Ngikuliak songs is remembered. Most, like this one, are sung in Ajie, although some contain a few non-Ajie words. Some Jie informants (rather grudgingly) admitted that the Ngikuliak were able to compose very pretty songs, and apparently some tunes of Ngikuliak origin have been used for more recent Jie-composed lyrics. The 'Loceno' and 'Awangaki' of this song were Ngikuliak leaders.

[19] Most of the Jie informants who were asked to identify the makers of the 'deep-grooved' pottery were unable to do so. Those who did almost invariably named the Ngikuliak, but of course this may have been because they naturally supposed that as the pottery was not Jie, it must therefore have been made by the only non-Paranilotic group which Jie tradition clearly remembers as having been previous occupants of Najie.

---

poeic), and a single word, *pidic*, recalled in both Jie and Ngikuliak traditions. The word, meaning 'to put something away or out of sight', is quite unlike the Ajie *kiwa*. Lokiru, John Weatherby's Tepes research assistant, has expressed his belief that it is a Teuso word.

paintings at Kalobur, and described an additional set at Maru, claiming that they were the work of his Ngikuliak ancestors and were a means of identifying various Ngikuliak camp-sites.[20]

The Ngikuliak informants agreed with Jie traditions that gathering played an important part in their economic life, and named wild roots, *ngacupeno*, *ngielo*, and *ngaboye* as most important. They further indicated, however, that trapping was not traditionally as important as many of the Jie traditions made out, but that hunting did play some role in their economic life. Hunting and gathering activities were augmented by cultivation. Although Jie informants spoke scornfully of their 'tiny gardens', and the Ngikuliak themselves readily admitted that the later-arriving Paranilotes had superior agricultural techniques, the Ngikuliak seem to have developed an agricultural system well suited to their life in the hills, including a system of terracing, still evident on the steep western slopes of Maru. Gardens were tilled with sharpened digging sticks (*ngabothanin*), and both men and women took an active part in all phases of cultivation.[21]

Their main crop, and the one considered their original, was finger-millet (*ngakima*). Its discovery is supposed to have taken place in this way:

> Long ago the Ngikuliak cultivated no food, but collected only that which grew in the bush. Then one day some people noticed a few grains of finger-millet near the nest of some *eekurit* ants. They dug down into the nest and found more of it. They decided to plant it in the ground, and it grew, and people began to cultivate it for food. And so finger-millet became the first crop of the Ngikuliak.[22]

This story is peculiar to the Ngikuliak. No Jie informant ever related it, and indeed the Paranilotic traditions are unanimous that sorghum was their original crop, with finger-millet gaining some importance only in the fairly recent past. It is probably of great significance, therefore, that Weatherby has had exactly the same tale recounted to him by Tepes informants, who also regard finger-millet as their original crop.

In relatively recent times tobacco is also recalled to have been an important crop, and the Ngikuliak claim to have known of it well before the Jie, although tobacco could only have been introduced in

[20] Lomare, J 129. This interview was conducted jointly with John Weatherby whose Tepes research assistant was also present. Despite several careful searches, the paintings at Maru were never found.
[21] Lomare, Looru, and Lomugur (Locan), J 78, and Lomare, J 129.
[22] Lomare, J 129.

post-Columban times. Nevertheless, as clay pipe-bowls found at some Ngikuliak sites appear to be associated with very early pre-iron cultures, and as Ngikuliak traditions indicate that pipe-smoking was of such importance as to form part of certain ritual observances, one must suspect that tobacco-smoking was preceded by the smoking of some other plant, such as hemp.[23]

Honey-gathering was also an important facet of Ngikuliak economic life, and honey is remembered as one of the items used for bride-wealth in traditional Ngikuliak society. The few remnant Ngikuliak families still appear to know more about the various types of bees than most Jie.

Of domestic animals, perhaps the most important to the Ngikuliak were dogs (presumably used in their hunting activities), and some Jie traditions spoke of the Ngikuliak formerly owning packs of up to one hundred.[24] In all probability they also owned sheep and goats, but not in very significant numbers. It is virtually certain that before the coming of the Paranilotes they owned no cattle, and even after their arrival many Ngikuliak families resisted owning them until very recently.

Although most Jie informants were in definite agreement that the Ngikuliak were originally without cattle (and Ngikuliak informants expressed the same traditions),[25] some Jie informants told two versions of a peculiar tradition which seemed at first to indicate that the Ngikuliak knew of cattle even before the Paranilotic-speakers:

> One day long ago an Ekuliakit called Lobeimoe went from Maru to Daidai and saw a cow and a bull there. Those were the first cattle that the Ngikuliak had seen. He went back to Maru and told the others about those strange animals. He returned to Daidai and this time saw six cattle. He told the Ngikuliak and also the Jie about them. The Jie and the Ngikuliak went together to trap those animals. They surrounded the whole area and killed all the wild animals, which tried to run away. But the cattle stood quietly and the people captured them. But it was the Jie, and not the Ngikuliak, who began to keep cattle, although Lobeimoe discovered them first.[26]

[23] I owe this observation to Roland Oliver. Ritual pipe-smoking amongst the Ngikuliak was performed during childbirth ceremonies.

[24] Apua, J 114.

[25] The very names 'Ngikuliak' (for the people) and 'Kulok' (for the group itself) are derived from *akilok*, Ajie for 'to trap'. By implication the name is applied to any 'poor people' without cattle. The remnant Ngikuliak now refer to themselves by that name and have forgotten any previous name by which their group may formerly have been known.

[26] Lotiang (Ekothowan) and Lengoyang, J 123.

A second tradition, although similar, is expressed in a rather different way:

> The Ngikuliak have always been at Maru. No one knows where they came from. They were the first people to learn about cattle. One day when they were out hunting they saw a cow grazing with wild animals at Daidai. They tried to capture it, but failed. They went back a second time and saw that the cow had a calf. They went a third time and saw three cattle. They went and told the Jie about those animals. The gazelles and the other wild animals ran away, but the cattle stood quietly and the Jie captured them. The Ngikuliak were foolish and ran off after the gazelles. The Jie saw the calf suckling its mother, and as they were clever, they tasted that milk and found it was good. And so it was the Jie who began keeping cattle although the Ngikuliak found them first.[27]

The Jie informants who related these traditions were from Lokatap and Kotiang territorial divisions respectively, the two divisions that have experienced the closest contacts with the Ngikuliak (and are usually the most scornful of them). The traditions clearly incorporate elements of an entirely separate Jie tradition, but are probably based mainly on a Ngikuliak tradition which explains how some of them joined with the Paranilotes after their arrival in Najie: .

> In the time of Ngikoria, the Ngikuliak used to go from Maru to Lokodokodwoi well at Dopeth for their water. Then one day they found hoof-prints there and followed them into the bush where they saw a bull and a cow. Those were the first cattle the Ngikuliak had seen. Lobeimoe was the man who actually found them, and he captured them and took them back to Maru. He gave the bull five calabashes of water and the cow four. They drank the water quickly and the other Ngikuliak were alarmed, saying, 'Those animals will drink all our water. Let us kill them'. But he [Lobeimoe] said, 'No, don't kill them. Let me take them back to the place where I found them, and I shall water them there'. So he took them to Dopeth and gave them water, and he went on to Lokwor in Kotiang and settled there with his cattle. Because he had those cattle he joined with the Jie and founded the Lokwor and Ngadakori clans.[28]

From this it can reasonably be suggested that the Jie versions are told not so much to suggest that the Ngikuliak were the original cattle owners (which all other evidence contradicts), but to under-score the 'foolishness' of the Ngikuliak in which so many Jie firmly believe.[29]

---

[27] Modo (and others), J 25.

[28] Lomare, J 129. For the separate Jie tradition, see Chapter IV.

[29] The Jie versions are extremely similar to a Bari tradition in which the *dupi* (suppressed) clans which occupied the Bari area before the arrival of the Bari

If a Jie tradition can be trusted, the Ngikuliak seem to have been fairly numerous people in the past, for they are recalled to have been 'so numerous as to surround completely the base of Maru when they danced the *elilia* [a circle dance]'.[30] It seems likely, however, that the Ngikuliak seldom assembled in any large numbers, but rather spent much of their time moving as fragmentary bands between the widely scattered hills and other localities which were their temporary homes. Undoubtedly, water was an especially difficult problem and dictated much of this movement, as is recalled in another Ngikuliak song:

Tepe nyakiru Maru, apena atowoto inaa.	There is rain at Maru, let us move there.
Eee, apena atowoto inaa.	Eee, let us move there.
Atepe nyakiru Lokiding, apena atowoto inaa	There is rain at Lokiding, let us move there.
Atepe nyakiru Kotiang, apena atowoto inaa.	There is rain at Kotiang, let us move there.[31]

Any more detailed reconstruction of their traditional socio-political organization is difficult to achieve from the oral traditions. Ngikuliak informants do not remember any names of constituent clans which their group may have once had, and the present subdivisions of the remnant Ngikuliak group can be best described as extended families, rather than clans or sub-clans. Jie traditions, although almost certainly exaggerated, indicate that the Ngikuliak social system was quite different from the Jie. 'The Ngikuliak had no clans as we do. They could marry whomever they pleased, even from their own family. Their wives were their own kinfolk. They didn't have to marry outside like other people.'[32]

[30] Apalodokoro (and others), J 23. If this can be taken literally, it would mean that the Ngikuliak numbered at least a couple of thousand. However, it should be noted that the concept of a people completely encircling the base of a mountain seems a popular one in Central Paranilotic tradition, and appears also in a Dodos tradition concerning the Poot group (D 3) and in a Nyakwai tradition concerning themselves (NY 2).

[31] Adome, J 62.

[32] Lowor (Elizeo) and Lobul, J 106.

lui (free) clans loose their cattle to the incoming *lui* because of their foolishness. See G. O. Whitehead, 'Suppressed Classes Among the Bari', *SNR* 34 (1953) 274. A parallel to the Jie versions can also be seen in the Pastoral Maasai myth concerning the origin of cattle in which the Dorobo are the original cattle-owners before losing them, again through their own foolishness. The myth is recorded in several sources including A. C. Hollis, *The Masai* (Oxford, 1905), pp. 226–9.

Political power seems to have been vested in individual leaders, of whom Awangaki (a diviner, who died at the beginning of this century) seems best remembered and also typical of his predecessors. Whether such leadership by individuals was confined to specific bands, or whether it extended over the entire group is really not clear. Nor is it clear in what manner these leaders were chosen, or to what extent they could exercise power.

Some recollection of the Ngikuliak religion is retained in the traditions. This religion appears to have been quite different from the Jie, and centred on a spirit cult. Although considerable mystery surrounds their ritual practices, some Jie informants expressed the belief that the Ngikuliak 'could talk with their dead people, to the spirits of their ancestors'. Although the Jie are in many ways scornful of the Ngikuliak, they are none the less universally believed to have close links with the supernatural.[33]

Weatherby's study of the Tepes has shown that their socio-religious system was based largely on an important spirit cult known as *aouyenit*. He argues convincingly that it was largely the *aouyenit* that has ensured the survival of the Tepes as an independent group, although completely surrounded by the dominant and expanding Karimojong. It seems likely that the Karimojong, standing in awe of Tepes mystical powers, as exercised in the *aouyenit* rituals, have always been reluctant to drive the Tepes from their mountain homes.[34] Karimojong informants largely supported Weatherby's picture, and clearly regarded the Tepes *aouyenit* with much the same respect as the Jie regard the mystical powers of the Ngikuliak. Furthermore, there are strong hints that the spirit cult of the Ngikuliak may have indeed borne a close resemblance to the Tepes *aouyenit*.[35]

The Ngikuliak appear to have experienced considerable cultural and linguistic influences from non-Fringe Cushitic-speaking sources by the time of the arrival of the main proto-Jie elements in Najie in the early eighteenth century. By that time, circumcision appears to have become one of their cultural features. Some Jie informants referred to them as 'the circumcised ones' in oral traditions, while

---

[33] Lokec (Lomorumoe) and others, J 49. It is commonly believed that trespassers into Ngikuliak places will be struck by lightning.

[34] Personal communication with Weatherby. See also his article, 'A Preliminary Note on the Sorat (Tepeth)', *UJ* 33 (1969).

[35] After a joint interview, the informant Lomare had a private conversation with Weatherby's Tepes assistant, Lokiru, in which he indicated that the Ngikuliak cult was a variation of the *aouyenit*.

the Ngikuliak themselves admitted to songs about circumcision which are still sung on ritual occasions:

| Isuwa ngisecec, isuwa ngibolony. | We the spoilt ones, we the circumcised. |
| Eee, Isuwa ngilenger, isuwa ngibolony. | Eee, we the circumcised, the circumcised.[36] |

Because circumcision does not appear to have been a cultural trait of either the Fringe Cushitic or Central Paranilotic-speaking groups, and because oral evidence and surviving place names (some very close to known areas of Ngikuliak occupation) indicate an early Kalenjin-speaking population, it is possible that the Ngikuliak may have borrowed circumcision from that source. The original Ngikuliak language seems to have been so entirely eclipsed by Paranilotic speech that it would be impossible now to detect any Kalenjin loan-words which might reinforce this theory. Still, the Tepes language does exhibit heavy Kalenjin borrowings, and so it is perhaps reasonable to conjecture that Kalenjin influence may have extended into the linguistic as well as the cultural realm of the Ngikuliak.

By the time of the eighteenth-century Jie genesis, the Ngikuliak had clearly experienced other contacts which were to alter their previous language to a Paranilotic dialect. Some traditions indicate that when Proto-Jie elements from Koten arrived in Najie and first made contact with the Ngikuliak, they were already speaking a language which was at least similar to Ajie.[37] At all events, it is clear that interactions between different peoples had gone on in what is now Najie long before the inception of any group called 'Jie'.

An examination of the Paranilotic-speaking peoples who were to provide the basic elements of an incipient Jie group is best begun by focusing attention on a concentration of peoples who once lived in

[36] Adome, J 62. The Jie are more scornful of the Ngikuliak practise of circumcision than any other aspect of their early culture. Very often Jie traditions describing the Ngikuliak practice link it with highly erotic and disgusting activities also supposedly performed by the Ngikuliak. For their part, the Ngikuliak informants were always most embarrassed by any question dealing with circumcision, and sometimes maintained that their ancestors were merely born without foreskins, and that no intentional circumcision operation was performed. Circumcision is certainly not practised now by the Ngikuliak.
[37] Some informants (for example Lowor (Elizeo) and Lobul, J 106) indicated that although the Ngikuliak language 'sounded like Ajie', it was largely unintelligible to the first Ajie-speaking pioneers who arrived from Koten.

the area of Koten and the Magos Hills and eastwards to the escarpment hills of east-central Karamoja (*see* Map 3). It was upon this concentration that both Gulliver and Nagashima based their historical reconstructions, and it is this concentration that has received the most attention in previously published sources. Elements of it were to become a major numerical segment of the proto-Jie community, and were profoundly to influence its linguistic, economic, and socio-political development.

Clans which can trace their ancestry back to this Koten–Magos group[38] are now found among the Jie, Karimojong, Turkana, and Dodos (and quite possibly among other Central Paranilotic-speaking peoples as well). In each tribal group, such clans share a common (if rather vague) tradition of having come to the Koten–Magos area from the north. The following Karimojong tradition is representative: 'In the beginning, all the people [of these clans] from among the Karimojong, Jie, Dodos, Toposa, and Turkana, came together from a place called 'Dongiro' which is far to the north, in the place called Sudan.'[39]

In other traditions the place in the north is variously termed 'Toposa', 'Nubi', or simply 'Sudan', and the aggregate of these traditions indicates the south-eastern corner of the present Republic of the Sudan as the previous home of the Koten–Magos group. In no instance was there any specific indication as to when this move from the north may have occurred: rather, it was 'long, long ago—perhaps at the very time when the world began'.[40]

There is general agreement that the people who came from the north were relatively poor, with only very limited numbers of livestock and rudimentary agriculture:

When the people came from the north, they had cattle, but only a few. They were really trappers. They would go into the bush to trap wild animals and to gather honey.[41]

[Before the dispersal of the Koten–Magos concentration] the people

---

[38] An alternative name for this group could be the 'Karamojong Cluster', as suggested by Gulliver. I have decided against using this term as I feel strongly that it implies an ethnocentric position of the present Karimojong peoples, unwarranted by the oral traditions. As much as I respect Webster's attempts to coin a name from Central Paranilotic terminology, I must also reject his term 'Ateker', for although it may be meaningful to the Iteso, it certainly does not convey the same picture of a 'family of related tribes' to the Jie and the other Paranilotic-speaking peoples of Karamoja.

[39] Loru (Enosi), BK 1.

[40] Ecak (Timothy), J 126.

[41] Lokimak, T 14.

THE BACKGROUND TO THE JIE GENESIS

cultivated, but they had only very small gardens. The only crop they knew how to grow was sorghum. There was too much sun in that area to grow very much.[42]

All indications are that hunting and gathering were probably the chief economic occupations of the group at the time of its migration from the north. The subsidiary occupations of animal husbandry and agriculture seem to have been of about equal importance. Jie traditions universally claim that 'God gave us cattle and sorghum on the same day'.

Another Jie tradition, if it can be accepted, provided additional information about the group before its arrival in the Koten–Magos area:

> The reason why the Jie and the other people came to Koten was because an old woman called Napeikisina [the one-breasted one] came from a long way off, crossing many rivers, to the land where they lived. She had a long knife with which she slew many people. The Jie and the others fled till they came to a large body of water which was too wide to cross. One of the women of the group begged God to make a path in the water, and the waters opened and the people crossed. Napeikisina followed them, but the waters closed and Napeikisina was swept away. The Jie and the others continued their journey. They had cattle, sheep, and goats with them, but they had no iron spears or knives. They used only sticks for fighting, and they had bows and blocked arrows to draw blood from their animals. At that time it was the custom for the women to walk naked, but on the way they grew ashamed, and the men slaughtered goats to provide skins for them. On their way the people also discovered gourds and learned to cultivate them.[43]

Those parts of this tradition concerned with 'Napeikisina', and especially the parting of the waters, are to be found in the mythology of many African peoples. Vansina, terming this type of story 'Wandersagen', listed the appearance of the 'parting of the waters' tale in no less than twenty-five societies, as widely separated as the Maasai and the Ashanti.[44] The Jie tale (which is also told to children in a slightly different form as a kind of folk-tale) seems to have been borrowed from the Turkana, who, in turn, had picked it up from peoples living even further east, possibly the Samburu. Indeed,

---

[42] Pelekec (and others), T 7.

[43] Looru (Sampson), J 9. There seems to be little mythology in the traditions of any Central Paranilotic people with which I am acquainted. In the existing mythology female characters often play a leading role, such as in this tradition.

[44] Op. cit., pp. 73–4.

Looru, the Jie informant who related the tale, differed from all other Jie informants in stating that the group came to Koten, not from the north, but from the east, in the direction of Turkana-land and Lake Rudolf.

While the possibility of one group arriving at Koten from the east cannot, of course, be ruled out, it would seem far more likely that the Napeikisina saga has merely been imposed on a more straightforward and factual (and much duller) account of the arrival of the Koten–Magos group from the north. If this were so, then the tradition, stripped of its embellishments, may indicate that the group left their previous homeland because of incursions of hostile peoples (represented in this version by the terrible female ogre), and that at the time of their migration they owned and bled livestock, were ignorant of iron, and permitted female nudity. Part of this picture would seem to be supported by other vague Jie recollections that 'long ago the Jie used only sharp stones for their tools and weapons',[45] and equally vague hints that Jie women were once unclothed.

Some Jie traditions recall more explicitly that when the group arrived in the Koten–Magos area they found others there before them: 'When the Jie and the others arrived in the Koten area, they found the Upe [Pokot] were already there. The Upe were the first people of that area. The [people who were to become] Bokora Karimojong quarrelled with them and fought them and drove them away to the south.'[46]

The Upe of these traditions were most probably a rearguard of the former Kalenjin-speaking population[47] which was responsible for place-names such as 'Toror', 'Sidok' (or 'Kicok'), and indeed 'Koten' itself, and, as suggested above, may have been the group

---

[45] Nakade (Peter), J 118. In no case was there ever any suggestion that the Koten–Magos Jie were their own iron-makers. Most informants agreed that iron was not commonly used until the development of their close economic association with the iron-making Labwor.

[46] Igira (Yaramoe) and others, J 17.

[47] In his book, *Southern Nilotic History* (Northwestern University Press, 1971), C. Ehret has concluded that roughly this same area was inhabited by a people he terms the 'Kenya–Kadam'. According to his hypothesis, this group did not speak a Kalenjin dialect, but rather a dialect of the considerably earlier 'Proto-Southern Nilotic', from which the 'Pre-Kalenjin' dialect was to evolve. If the 'Upe' of the Jie tradition can be equated with Ehret's 'Kenya–Kadam', then it would be strictly incorrect to regard those 'Upe' as 'Kalenjin-speakers'. Until Ehret's book has received wider attention, however, it is more expedient in any case to regard them as a Kalenjin-speaking group.

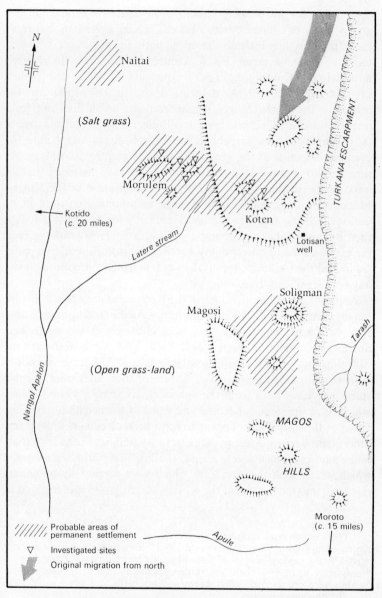

N

Naitai

(Salt grass)

Morulem

Kotido
(c. 20 miles)

Latere stream

Koten

TURKANA ESCARPMENT

Lotisan
well

Soligman

Magosi

Tarash

Nangol Apalon

(Open grass-land)

MAGOS

HILLS

Moroto
(c. 15 miles)

///// Probable areas of
       permanent settlement

▽   Investigated sites

    Original migration from north

Apule

**MAP 3. The area inhabited by the Koten–Magos Paranilotes
before c. 1720**

responsible for introducing circumcision to the Ngikuliak. If this group can be linked with Ehret's 'Kenya–Kadam peoples', then from his linguistically based hypothesis they would appear to have been overrun by a Central Paranilotic (in Ehret's terminology, 'Karimojong–Teso') expansion by about the middle of this millennium.[48] A date of approximately 1500 for the arrival of the Koten–Magos group from the north does not seem unreasonable and indeed, most traditions seem to indicate that a fairly lengthy time was spent in the Koten–Magos area before the eventual dispersal of the group in the early eighteenth century. As time passed animal husbandry appears to have assumed greater importance, so that by the end of its concentration in the Koten–Magos area the group was to emerge as primarily pastoral in its outlook.[49] If the area was similar climatically to the way it is today, then its fairly light rainfall and rolling grasslands would have been far better suited to an economy based on pastoralism and trapping (as indeed the traditions recall) than one in which agriculture played any very significant role.

Archaeological investigations in the Koten area presented a picture largely consistent with the oral traditions. As the traditions indicated they would be, habitation sites were clustered at the north and north-eastern base of Koten Hill itself, and north-westwards to Morulim and several smaller outlying hills in the same direction. Almost without exception a key feature of these sites were circular stone structures built from the spherical, conveniently sized stones which litter the slopes of Koten and some of the neighbouring hills. Some of these structures appear to have been dwellings, while a few others (some barely 3 feet in diameter) may well have been granaries. Some sites contained a few round, shallow-basin grinding stones,[50] which, taken with the structures which were supposedly granaries, reinforce the traditions that the Koten–Magos group was engaged in

[48] Ibid., pp. 69–70.

[49] There is universal agreement among Jie informants that the cattle of the Koten–Magos group were the same humped, short-horned zebu variety still herded by the modern peoples of Karamoja, and that humpless or long-horned breeds were unknown. There are further traditions that both bleeding and milking were practised and that horns of both cattle and small stock were shaped with stone hammers.

[50] The Koten grinding stones were found in far less profusion than the deep-basin grinding stones found at the sites further west. Furthermore, those at Koten were of an entirely different shape and were so much smaller than the massive deep-basin variety in the west as to appear almost miniature in comparison.

some cereal agriculture. Rather more of the stone structures (some 40 feet or more in diameter), however, appear to have been stock enclosures, and Jie traditions explicitly state that the Koten–Magos group constructed stone kraals for their cattle and small stock.

Unlike most archaeological sites in other parts of Karamoja, no surface potsherds of any kind were discovered at the Koten sites. Also, there was absolutely no evidence of any ironware, or iron slag, and the whole picture given was one of a relatively simple material culture, again generally in line with the impression given by the traditions.

Although Jie traditions indicate that the Koten–Morulim sites, relying on nearby Lotisan well for their water supply, were the most important settlements of the Koten–Magos group, mention is also made of other settlements both in the Magos Hills themselves to the south, and at Naitai to the north-west, neither of which was investigated. It seems likely that the group, its economy based so much on trapping and pastoralism, was not entirely tied to any one place, but ranged over a fairly wide area, of which the Koten–Morulim sites were but a focal point. Indeed, some traditions indicate that the group at times moved as far east as the headwaters of the Tarash River in search of seasonal grazing.

Some Jie traditions claim that the hills were used as observation posts from which to scout out fresh grazing lands:

> All those people at Koten—the Jie, Karimojong, Dodos—used to climb the hills to look out in various directions to see which areas looked best. That is how Koten got its name: from *kitek* [to gaze for a long time] or *Kiteo* [to look over there]. The [people who were to become] Jie looked out to the west to this very area in which we now live, and they saw it was good.[51]

It was from this westerly direction that there appeared, some time during the early part of the eighteenth century, a band of strangers called by the Koten–Magos peoples, *Ngikatapa* ('Bread-people', a

[51] Looru (Sampson), J 120. This is a good example of how many Central Paranilotic traditions attempt to explain the derivation of group or place names by drawing a false inference from a kernel of historical fact. That the Koten–Magos group did climb the hills to scout out likely grazing lands seems very probable, as the view from many of these hills is indeed panoramic and allows an observer to have at least a general idea of the surrounding country for thirty or more miles in any direction. The name 'Koten', however, seems certainly to have been of Kalenjin origin and to have pre-dated the arrival of the Koten–Magos group of Central Paranilotes. Such traditions which purport to explain how names were derived are often of the 'pleasing story' type mentioned above, and they provide great enjoyment to the Jie and other Central Paranilotes.

nickname which is still used by Central Paranilotic-speakers for their mainly Lwo-speaking, primarily agricultural, western neighbours). The arrival of these *Ngikatapa* strangers at Koten was to prove of great significance to the emerging Jie community, as will be seen in the following chapter.

The identity of these *Ngikatapa* who appeared in the Koten area from the west brings us to examine another major group which was to provide important elements to the Jie and the other emerging Central Paranilotic tribes. To do so, we must shift our attention away from the Koten–Magos group to look at areas further west, from central Karamoja to the frontiers of what is now Acholi District, and from there southwards to Teso District, and even to the area beyond Mt. Elgon.

Work by a number of historians, including Were, Webster, and Odada,[52] has shown that various Central Paranilotic-speaking peoples had established themselves in these areas to the west and south of Koten well before the Koten–Magos group began their first tentative expansions out of their area of concentration in the early eighteenth century. (See Chapter IV.) While some of these Paranilotes pushed well beyond the boundaries of what was to become Karamoja District, others were established within it. A good example is provided by a people called the Ngariama who inhabited the south-central portions of the area subsequently occupied by the Karimojong. A descendant of the group recalled:

> The original home of the Ngariama was at Lokales in Pian. The Ngariama were a tribe on their own. They were friendly with the Kumama [Iteso] and with their neighbours. The Ngariama and the Kumama spoke the same language as the Karimojong, but they had never been together with the Karimojong. . . . When the Ngariama lived at Lokales, the Karimojong lived beyond the Apule River in the north [e.g. in the direction of the Magos Hills].[53]

These various outlying Paranilotic-speaking peoples were to provide the basic elements for the Itesyo, Iteso, Kumam, and Langi,

---

[52] For the Itesyo, see G. Were, *A History of the Abaluyia of Western Kenya* (Nairobi, 1967), p. 57; for the Teso, see J. B. Webster, in *Tarikh*, 3, 2 (1970), and for Paranilotic groups along the present Acholi borderland see his chapter in the forthcoming *Uganda Before 1900*, Vol. i (East African Publishing House); for the Kumam see M. Odada, 'The Fusion of the Lwo and Ateker—the Kumam', unpublished seminar paper presented at Makerere University, 1971.

[53] Longorio, BK 9.

and they also provided important segments of all the emerging Central Paranilotic groups of Karamoja, north-western Kenya, and the south-eastern Sudan. Amongst the Jie they were to form the core of the Rengen major division, as well as provide a number of important clans to the other major division, Lokorwakol. It is therefore important to achieve some clear understanding of them and to draw some conclusions as to their probable origin.

These outlying Paranilotes had certain economic and cultural features in common which clearly differentiated them from the Koten–Magos concentration. While the Koten–Magos group, during its concentration in the drier eastern grasslands, steadily evolved a pastoral complex, these outlying groups appear to have retained an economy based largely on hunting and gathering, or else, in many cases, to have become increasingly more agricultural. The oral traditions of those groups pushing out from the southern and south-eastern frontiers of Karamoja, as well as those of groups within Karamoja itself, clearly reflect this. Of the Itesyo, Were has recorded that eleusine and millet grain were traditionally their chief food, with meat and milk of only secondary importance, while both Lawrance and Webster have collected Itseo traditions that indicate they were agriculturalists before beginning to own cattle, and Webster and Kagolo further indicate that their moves outwards from Karamoja were dictated by a need for better (agricultural) land and/or new hunting grounds.[54] A similar non-pastoral economy is pictured by the traditions of virtually all the outlying Paranilotic groups within Karamoja. Of most direct relevance to the emerging Jie community was a group called 'Loser' (the people called 'Ngiseera') which once occupied the Kotido area of what was to become Najie. Traditions of the descendants of these Ngiseera recall that 'originally the Loser didn't know about cattle. People lived by cultivating sorghum and by trapping wild animals. There were no cattle here [in Najie] at all'.[55]

Another of these outlying Paranilotic groups which was to play an important role in the development of the Jie community was a group called 'Poet' or 'Poot' which inhabited the western part of the borderland between what is now Najie and the country of the Dodos (*see* Map 4). While traditions of the descendants of this group

---

[54] G. Were, *Western Kenya Historical Texts* (Nairobi, 1967), p. 24; J. C. D. Lawrance, *The Iteso* (London, 1957), p. 7; Webster, in *Tarikh*, 3, 2 (1970); B. M. Kagolo, 'Tribal Names and Customs in Teso District', *UJ* 19 (1955), 42.

[55] Lonyala, J 81.

indicate that cattle were not entirely unknown, again they reveal that no great economic reliance was placed on them: 'At first, none of the Ngikaato [Poet] clans had any cattle, except the Korikituk, who had very few—one or two, like that. The people lived mainly by trapping wild animals.'[56]

The existence of such traditions in Karamoja where pastoralism has become so important an economic, sociological, and psychological factor is truly remarkable, and their validity, in light of this, seems certain. Furthermore, archaeological sites associated with some of these outlying Paranilotic groups exhibit features which strongly support a picture of a people with a non-pastoral economy.[57]

In addition to sharing a non-pastoral economic tradition, all available data suggest that these outlying Paranilotic groups shared a common range of clan observances (*ngitalia*) which again distinguished them from the Koten–Magos group. In Najie there is a remarkable correspondence in the ranges of *ngitalia* of those clans that were descended from various of these outlying Paranilotic groups. Although individual variations naturally occur,[58] most of these clans subscribe to a range of *ngitalia* which include the wearing of gazelle skins (or occasionally other wild-animal skins, sometimes in conjunction with goatskins) as some article of clothing by the women of the clan, an apron of small hollow sticks strung together (*ekalungur*) for newly married women, an avoidance of eating bushbuck (*akoloba*) and/or in some instances squirrel (*eceleku*), a finalization of marriage ceremony (*lomalol* or *lobunat*) in which an animal (usually a he-goat) is killed by ritual suffocation or, in a few instances, by disembowelling, and in many cases a prohibition against cutting or touching human hair in given circumstances, eating the intestines of animals, a song about gazelles or gazelle skins, and a mystical prohibition against outsiders attempting to take their livestock by force. Again, while there is no absolute correspondence, and individual variations occur, the clans which trace their descent from the Koten–Magos concentration in general dress their women

---

[56] Adupa (Sampson), D 12. Other outlying Paranilotic elements resident in Karamoja ultimately formed the core of the Nyakwai community which now lives in a chain of hills south-west of Najie (see Map 4). Again, traditions collected from descendants of these ancestors reveal that their ancestors were originally ignorant of cattle and relied mainly on trapping. Similar traditions were also collected by R. Herring during his work amongst the Nyakwai.

[57] See below, pp. 96 and 99–100.

[58] Jie informants were quite clear in their assertion that the range of *ngitalia* can and does change in exceptional circumstances, and it can be suggested that this correspondence in *ngitalia* was closer in the past than it is now.

FIG. 4. A comparison of the ranges of *ngitalia* of Jie clans representative of the Koten-Magos and Agricultural Paranilotic-speaking groups

I. KOTEN-MAGOS CLANS

CLAN	SKINS	APRONS	FOOD PROHIBITIONS	MARRIAGE CEREMONY	OTHER
Lodera	calf	*ekalungur*	none	*lokidori*	
Lodoca	calf	?	bushbuck	*lokidori*	
Lomejan	calf	*ngadalai*	none	*lokidori*	
Lopao	any	*ngadalai*	none	*lokidori*	
Ngikakere	calf or goat	? probably *ngadalai*	none (except one subdivision, bushbuck)	*lokidori*	
Toroi	calf, then goat			*lomatol* (ox)	

II. AGRICULTURAL PARANILOTIC CLANS

CLAN	SKINS	APRONS	FOOD PROHIBITIONS	MARRIAGE CEREMONY	OTHER
Jimos	goat, eland-trimmed	*ekalungur*	bushbuck	*lomalol*||*lobunat*	Gazelle song
Loser	gazelle	*ekalungur*	bushbuck	*lomalol*||*lobunat*	Gazelle song; prohibition about cutting children's hair; *Edeke* a god.
Poet	gazelle cloaks	*nyakaiya* or *ngidani*†	bushbuck and squirrel	*lobunat*	Prohibition against cutting children's hair; cannot touch their hair; their cattle cannot be taken by force; gazelle song.
Teso	gazelle cloaks	*ekalungur*	bushbuck	*lokidori*	Prohibition against cutting children's hair; *Edeke* a god.
Karewok	calf	*ekalungur*	none	*lobunat*	A disembowelling ritual.
Loposa	gazelle	? (probably *ekalungur*)	bushbuck	*lomalol*||*lobunat*	A disembowelling ritual.

† The *nyakaiya* or *ngidani* apron worn by brides of many Poet subdivisions is unique to them and consists of decorated leather thongs.

in calf-skins, often have their brides wear aprons decorated with iron beads (*ngadalai*), have no food prohibitions, and perform a finalization of marriage ceremony (generally called *lokidori* by the Jie) in which an ox is killed by spearing. The *ngitalia* of Jie clans representative of both groups are recorded in Figure 4.

Clans descended from various of these outlying Paranilotic groups were also incorporated into other Central Paranilotic societies, such as the Karimojong, Turkana, and Dodos. While the available evidence is not so abundant for these peoples, sufficient data have been collected to indicate that these clans subscribe to ranges of *ngitalia* that correspond largely to those of clans descended from outlying Paranilotes amongst the Jie.[59]

All available data, therefore, strongly suggest the existence of a number of Paranilotic-speaking groups who were primarily non-pastoral in economy and who subscribe generally to a very similar range of *ngitalia*, inhabiting much of central, southern, and western Karamoja, and spilling out into neighbouring areas, long before the group of Paranilotic-speakers concentrated in the Koten–Magos area began their own expansion. Because of their non-pastoral economic outlook, these outlying groups will henceforth be termed 'Agricultural Paranilotes'.[60] In the past, insufficient attention had been paid to the origins of these Agricultural Paranilotic groups, and several writers[61] assumed that they had once been part of the

[59] Specific examples from the Karimojong, Turkana, and Dodos can be found in my Ph.D. thesis, p. 170. From what sparse data that has been collected amongst the Iteso and Langi, a close parallel between the ranges of *ngitalia* of the clans of these peoples and the relevant Jie clans is again suggested. For the Iteso, see Lawrance (1957), op. cit., pp. 60–3, and F. L. Williams, 'Teso Clans', *UJ* 4 (1936). Additional information was provided by J. B. Webster and N. Nagashima in personal communication. For the Langi, see Driberg, op. cit., pp. 189–204.

Furthermore, the Iteso belief in a god called *Edeke* (meaning simply 'disease' in Ajie) is paralleled by only two Jie clans, Tesiyo and Loser, both clearly descended from outlying Paranilotic elements.

[60] It has been a great problem to find a satisfactory name to describe these various groups of non-Koten–Magos Paranilotes, as there was clearly no one name by which they all called themselves. In earlier writings, I used the blanket name 'Ngiseera' in an attempt to use some terminology of the groups themselves, but as the name applied to only one such group (and perhaps elements of certain others), I now feel that my use of this name was both incorrect and possibly misleading. I consequently find myself forced to adopt a term which at least describes their more or less common economic outlook which was to distinguish them clearly from the more pastorally oriented Koten–Magos group.

[61] Notably J. C. D. Lawrance, 'A History of the Teso to 1937', *UJ* 19 (1955), 12–14, also his 'The Karimojong Cluster—A Note', *Africa*, 23 (1953). Simi-

linguistically related community concentrated at Koten and Magos. This assumption was probably due at least in part to the ideas of Fr. A. Tarantino who noted that the four original clans of the Lango: Atek, Arak, Okarawok, and Otengoro also appeared universally among the 'Kumam, Abwor, Teso, Karimojong, and Jie'.[62] In fact Tarantino was mistaken, for although the four clans do appear among those groups made up largely of Agricultural Paranilotic elements now resident outside Karamoja (e.g. Kumam, Iteso, Lango), they certainly do not appear universally among those other Paranilotic groups, mainly resident in Karamoja or adjoining areas of Kenya and the Sudan, in which the Koten–Magos element is generally the stronger (e.g. Jie, Dodos, Karimojong, Toposa). With all of these latter groups there is evidence to indicate that wherever any of these 'universal' clans appear, they in fact represent groups of Agricultural Paranilotes absorbed by the expanding Koten–Magos elements during the eighteenth or early nineteenth centuries.[63] It seems clear, therefore, that Tarantino only succeeded in showing a probable link between various of the outlying Agricultural Paranilotic groups, and not a link between them and the Koten–Magos group, as he implies.

Nevertheless, Tarantino's conclusions undoubtedly did much to shape the ideas of subsequent writers. Only one observer, P. H. Gulliver, seriously questioned that the Iteso (and therefore, by extension, any other Agricultural Paranilotic group) were once part of the Koten–Magos concentration, or indeed (the linguistic evidence apart) whether any sort of link between them can be shown to have existed. Gulliver, while admitting that certain cultural similarities do exist, pointed out that there are also rather basic cultural

[62] See Tarantino, 'Lango Clans', *UJ* 13, 1 (1949), 109, and 'Notes on the Lango', *UJ* 13, 2 (1949), 145–6.

[63] Only one 'universal' clan ('Karewok' or 'Kathiwok') is found amongst the Jie and Toposa, while amongst the Dodos and Karimojong three of the clans appear. Only amongst the Turkana do all four clans appear, and here, significantly, all are found only within the Ngicuro division which was originally composed of Agricultural Paranilotic elements.

In the forthcoming *Uganda Before 1900*, vol. i, J. B. Webster makes the interesting suggestion that Arak (sometimes called 'Ararak') may have been an early vanguard of young men which pushed on ahead of the Koten–Magos group. However, I find any real support for such a notion entirely lacking from the oral traditions of the Koten–Magos group.

larly, Father C. I. Walshe ('Notes on the Kumam', *UJ* 11 (1947)) and A. C. A. Wright ('Notes on the Iteso Social Organization', *UJ* 9 (1942)) suggested a close link between that group and the Langi. Odada and Webster in some of their earlier writings also made similar suggestions.

differences (notably in their respective class systems based on time), as well as some important linguistic differences. As to the historical evidence of assuming any link between the Iteso (or any other Agricultural Paranilotic group) and the Koten–Magos group, Gulliver wrote: 'Neither Lawrance nor any other writer known to me has given any acceptable legend which definitely relates the origin of the Teso with the origin of any member of the Karamojong cluster'.[64]

In fact, a close examination of the various Agricultural Paranilotic oral traditions which had been collected at the time of Gulliver's writing merely indicates that those groups passed through some part of Karamoja during a migration from the north, or that they were 'neighbours' of the Koten–Magos group, or indeed that Agricultural Paranilotic and Koten–Magos elements existed as quite separate groups in Karamoja.[65]

Moreover, most oral traditions collected during 1969–71 either lacked any indications of links between the various Agricultural Paranilotic groups and the Koten–Magos concentration, or else repudiated such a link altogether. From the Agricultural Paranilotic point of view, the Ngariama tradition recorded above is a typical example. Many other Agricultural Paranilotic traditions similarly insisted that the Koten–Magos group 'were only our neighbours, and we did not even intermix with them'.

For their part, descendants of the Koten–Magos group related traditions which also repudiated any link between themselves and various Agricultural Paranilotic groups. When elements of the Koten–Magos concentration dispersed into their respective new homelands, in the eighteenth and nineteenth centuries, they encountered various Agricultural Paranilotic groups which they invariably saw as 'strangers' or 'different people' with whom they had certainly not been in the Koten–Magos area. Furthermore, Koten–Magos traditions very frequently emphasized the economic, cultural and even linguistic differences between themselves and the various groups of Agricultural Paranilotes.[66]

[64] Gulliver, op. cit. (1956) 214.

[65] Lawrance, loc. cit. (1955); Driberg, op. cit., p. 27; Tarantino, 'Notes on the Lango', pp. 147–8. While it is admittedly rather difficult to understand Lawrance's sources of information, his statement that the Iteso may have come from the Koten area where they split from the Jie appears to have been only his hypothesis, unsupported by Iteso oral evidence.

[66] A Karimojong tradition recorded by Dyson-Hudson (op. cit., pp. 262–3) and Lawrance (loc. cit. (1955), 12) has been interpreted by some observers as indicating a split between the (proto-) Karimojong and the (proto-) Iteso.

On the other hand, a very few oral traditions do suggest some definite links between the Koten–Magos concentration and some Agricultural Paranilotic groups. In most instances, however, these traditions are rather vague and strongly aetiological, and indicate that such links were very early, well before the eighteenth-century dispersal of the Koten–Magos group. Often, such traditions are basically *ex post facto* statements on the evolution of the different economies of the Koten–Magos pastoralists and the Agricultural Paranilotes. A good example is a Jie tradition concerning the Loser, an Agricultural Paranilotic group which once inhabited part of Najie and ultimately provided elements to the Langi and possibly other western groups:

> Long, long ago the Jie, Karimojong and the others who lived at Koten lived together with the Loser and other 'Ngikatapa' [a Jie nickname for their western neighbours] . . . They were all one people then. Then one day the people had to make a choice, and the Jie, Karimojong, and the other people of Koten chose cow-dung, while the Ngikatapa chose the residue of beer. So the Ngikatapa took sorghum with them and went off to the west to grow food, while the Koten people remained behind and raised cattle.[67]

The close correspondence between clan names and ranges of clan observances of the widely dispersed Agricultural Paranilotic groups, plus the oral evidence which repudiates any link between the

[67] Apalodokoro, Lomongin (Julio), and Inua (Lodweny), J 75 and J 128. Very similar (and also strongly aetiological) traditions can be found amongst many other East African peoples, including the Lango (Tarantino, 'Notes on the Lango', p. 146), the Maasai (A. C. Hollis, *The Masai*, pp. 272–3), and the Lacustrine Bantu (see, e.g. J. Roscoe, *The Bakitara or Banyoro* (Cambridge, 1923), for the story of Kamrasi).

Webster ('The Iteso During the Asonya', p. 5) has convincingly argued that amongst the Iteso, the name 'Iseera' (e.g. the people of the group 'Loser') appears to mean 'those who have gone on ahead' or 'pioneer'. The Jie, however, do not see the name as meaning 'pioneer' in any sense. Again, one is led to conclude that the term was originally employed by Agricultural Paranilotes to refer to advance elements of their own group.

During my own research, the tradition was related by only five Karimojong informants, all but one of whom were from clans of Agricultural Paranilotic origin. As Dyson-Hudson himself noted, this tradition 'exhibits some strange features'. My own interpretation is that it was originally an Agricultural Paranilotic tradition which simply states that while some of their people moved off to the west, others remained in their previous Karamoja homelands where they were assimilated by elements from the Koten–Magos concentration and thereby 'became Karimojong'. Again, Central Paranilotic traditions such as this one based on the supposed derivation of names are generally of the vague, 'pleasing tale' sort.

Agricultural Paranilotes and the Koten–Magos peoples, at least in the Koten–Magos area, suggests that the two groups may have undergone a very early separation, even pre-dating the arrival of either in Karamoja.

Exactly such a picture is suggested by many Agricultural Paranilotic traditions which indicate that when entry into Karamoja was made, it was done so by two distinct groups of Central Paranilotic-speaking peoples, each with its own constituent clans, ranges of clan observances, and linguistic differences. For example, a Labwor tradition tells of a migration of some of their ancestors into Karamoja from the north-west which clearly does not correspond to the migration of the Koten–Magos group from due north or north-east. According to the Labwor, this more westerly group followed a route which brought them southward through central and western parts of Karamoja, well to the west of Koten and Magos:

> They came from the Sudan via Mt. Orom and Kalomide, and on to Mt. Toror, where they halted. Some went westwards from there via Theno and Onogoropon looking for food. They pushed on to Koyo, Tartugo, Kodea, and Wialia, and then on towards the Moroto River. They occupied all those places until the great famine came and drove many of them to Lango and eastern Acholi.
>
> A second group also came from the same direction, but followed different routes to the south. The first of them went past Kalodwong and on into eastern Acholi, while those who came behind came from Orom to Kapeta, and then to Tikidani [in Ajie, 'Kotidani'] and settled near Kalanga mountain. Then some of them came on to Labwor, via Rwot mountain.[68]

Map 4 shows that such a route would have brought these people southwards through, or very close to, areas occupied, or once occupied, by the Eyan, Poet (or Poot), Loser, Nyakwai, and Labwor, all of whom either were descended mainly from, or at least incorporated considerable numbers of, Agricultural Paranilotic elements.

Other indications of a Paranilotic migration well to the west of

---

[68] Pidele (Otyang) and Okelo (Epui Woirono), L 9. The movement of one of these groups called 'Lango Tiro' by the eastern Acoli, toward Amyal on the present Karamoja–Acholi border has been tentatively dated by Webster as between 1598 and 1652. (Webster, 'The Peopling of Agago', p. 4. See also the forthcoming *A History of Uganda*, vol. i, section A).

In his researches amongst the Labwor and Nyakwai, Herring did not collect any tradition of a major dispersal at Toror. Nevertheless, his own reconstruction of this migration, the Toror dispersal apart, does not appear to differ greatly from mine.

the Koten–Magos area are provided by Lango traditions. Recent observers of the Langi, including Ogwal[69] and Tosh, have begun to pay closer attention to Lango clan histories, particularly with regard to traditions concerning their migrations before arriving at Mt. Otukei, the mountain on the Karamoja–Lango border from which so many Lango clans say they entered their present homeland. In virtually all cases where clans could recall an earlier homeland, they indicated places in that part of the southern Sudan more or less directly north of the natural pass at Mt. Orom. From that part of the Sudan (often named 'Sudan-Wila' in the Lango traditions), variously identified as 'Didinga', 'Lotuko', and 'Shilluk' (all given by Labwor traditions as well), the migration route to the south lay 'through east Acholi to Otuke', which, as Tosh suggests, seems reinforced by Driberg's impression that the 'Lango tribe as a whole originated near the Agoro hills which nowadays divide Acholi from Lotuko'.[70] As the same place-names along the route from the north, including Kodea (in the Labwor dialect; 'Adea Rock', in Lango) and Loyoroit (Labwor; 'Oyoriot', Lango), are mentioned in both Labwor and Lango traditions, there can hardly be any doubt that the traditions of the two peoples are describing the same migration. Finally, and very significantly, according to Ogwal's and Tosh's researches, branches of at least three of Tarantino's four 'universal' clans (Atek, Okarowok, and Otengoro) are among those Lango clans which trace their origin to the migration from 'Sudan-Wila'.[71]

There are additional indications that other Agricultural Paranilotic groups entered Karamoja from the same direction. The Eyan, for example, who now inhabit the eastern slopes of Mt. Orom itself, while unable to trace their origins further back than Orom, do indicate that their former homes were on the western slopes of the mountain, just above the Orom Pass.[72] The Poet (or Poot) group, also descended mainly from Agricultural Paranilotes, who once occupied the Kapeta River area at the southern end of the pass, have a tradition: 'We Poot came to this area [the Kopos area of Dodos] from the west. Our ancestors came from the direction of

---

[69] R. Ogwal, 'History of Lango Clans', unpublished manuscript, a copy of which is in the possession of the Makerere University Department of History.

[70] Tosh, op. cit., Chapter 1, p. 13; Driberg, op. cit., pp. 27–8.

[71] Ogwal, loc. cit., pp. 46 and 57–8; Tosh's data is included in the impressive card-file on Lango clans that he compiled during his research. I am very grateful to him for allowing me free access to this file.

[72] Lokidi (Antonio), Y 1. Eyan traditions also speak of some Labwor elements moving south from Orom.

Orom via Kamoce, and they were related to the Ngieyan who still live there. They came here as cultivators, without cattle.'[73]

Further south, the Miro, a group of Agricultural Paranilotes who occupied an area along the Omanimani River before the advent of Koten–Magos elements of the Karimojong, recall that:

> Our ancestors came here from the north-west, from the direction of the land that is now inhabited by the Lango Miro. We were originally the same people as those Lango Miro, and we left them behind in the north-west when we came here. The Karimojong were still living north of the Apule River at the time.[74]

There is also evidence that at least some of the Iteso clans may have entered their present homeland from roughly the same direction.[75] Moreover, a major (proto-) Iteso concentration existed in the Napak area on the eastern frontier of present-day Karamoja,[76] not far to the south of the headwaters of the Moroto River, that area into which Labwor traditions maintain that some Agricultural Paranilotic elements were pushing after the dispersal in the region of Mt. Toror.

There is an indication in Labwor traditions that while most of the Agricultural Paranilotes moved on to the west and the south, one group, having reached the vicinity of Mt. Toror with the main migration, veered off to the east and became the only Agricultural Paranilotic group to come into direct contact with the Koten–Magos group:

> At Mt. Toror, they stopped, and there was hunger there at Toror. Some of the people had a few cattle and others had none. Those who had a few cattle went away to the east to Koromoc, Looya, and the Tarash River, east of Koten. There were other Turkana, as well as Karimojong and Jie, living in that direction already, whose grazing land was Koten. The people who went east from Toror joined with the Turkana, and they themselves became Turkana. The other people at Toror moved west and became the Langi, as we have said.[77]

This tradition, with its mention of two 'Turkana' groups, was at first sight rather confusing. However, a widely known Turkana oral

[73] Atebe and Lokol, D 11.

[74] Muya (Nawot), MOK 1.

[75] See e.g., Webster, *Tarikh*, 3, 2 (1970), and Tarantino, 'Notes on the Lango', p. 146. Similar evidence was provided by traditions recorded in my own interviews: L 4, J 36, J 75, and J 114.

[76] Lawrance, op. cit. (1955), 12. The existence of this concentration was further supported by Karimojong traditions recorded in my interviews BK 7 and 9.

[77] Pidele (Otyang) and Okelo (Epui Woirono), L 9.

tradition which was recorded and published as early as the 1920s provides the key to understanding its true significance.[78] Several variations of it were collected in western and south-western Turkana from my own informants, the following being, in many ways, typical:

> Long ago, an old woman called Nayece came from the west from Najie gathering wild fruits. She came to the hill now called Moru Anayece near the Tarash River, where she settled. Then a bull (*engiro*) got lost in Najie and also came east, following the Tarash River, until he came to the place where Nayece was living. During the day the bull would go out to graze, and during the night he would sleep at Nayece's compound. Then eight young men, the children of Nayece, came from the west searching for her and for the bull which was lost. They tracked the bull and they found him together with Nayece, who was drying wild fruits she had collected. They remained there for some time and saw that there were many wild fruits and good grass. Then they returned to Najie and told the people there about the good area they had found. And so a large group of young men and girls took cattle and went to the east as though they were going to *ngauyoi* [dry-season cattle-camps]. They grazed their herds at Moru Anayece, and they decided to settle there. So at first the Turkana were people of the *ngauyoi*, and their real home had been Najie.[79]

The Jie clans which were originally part of the Koten–Magos concentration acknowledge a relationship with the Turkana, but have two seemingly contradictory traditions as to how the Turkana evolved. Many informants claimed that they 'never came west of Koten',[80] when the Koten–Magos dispersal took place in the early eighteenth century, but moved eastwards into the Tarash Valley before the Koten–Magos concentration began its break-up. Other informants, however, maintained that the Turkana were part of the dispersal, moving eastwards into Najie with the Jie elements of the Koten–Magos group, only to retrace their steps back to the east later on.

Very much in line with these Jie traditions, one observer, Nobuhiro Nagashima, in an unpublished paper written in 1968, suggested that the Turkana were made up of two distinct groups of Paranilotic-speaking peoples: one of which broke away from the embryonic Jie in Najie, and the other a group which pre-existed the arrival of the

[78] See among others: Lt. D. M. Hulley, 'Notes on the Turkana', E.A. 4325, Part I, 1920; J. Barton, 'Notes on the Turkana Tribe' (Part I), *JAS*, 20, 78 (Jan. 1921); and E. D. Emley, 'The Turkana of Kolosia District', *JRAI* 57 (1927).

[79] Eremon (and others), T3.

[80] Kere and Meron, J 64.

Jie break-aways in the Tarash River Valley area. Relying on the admittedly rather meagre oral evidence which had been collected at the time of his writing, Nagashima convincingly argued that the two major divisions now present in Turkana society represent the two groups that originally formed the tribe: the Ngicuro division representing an earlier Paranilotic group and the Ngimonia division representing the later arrivals from Najie.[81]

There are indications from more recent research in Turkana that the Turkana themselves regard Ngicuro as the older division. In the ceremony of *akiwodokin* or *angola*[82] in which groups pass through an improvised gate in an order prescribed by the order in which they settled in the land, Turkana informants were agreed that the Ngicuro groups invariably precede the Ngimonia when members of both divisions come together for a joint ceremony.

It is moreover interesting to consider the constituent clans of the Ngicuro division and their clan observances (*ngitalia*). To begin with, all four of Tarantino's 'universal' clans: Karewok, Katek, Tengor, and Rarak, appear in Turkana society exclusively among the Ngicuro division. Also included in that division were clans named 'Iteso' and 'Lokatap', whose original Agricultural Paranilotic affiliation is equally obvious.[83] The three Ngicuro clans amongst whom there was an opportunity to inquire concerning their clan observances all stated that those observances included the *lobunat* finalization of marriage ceremony and the wearing of gazelle skins, i.e. observances common to the range associated with the various Agricultural Paranilotic groups in Uganda. Not even a single instance of any of this range of observances was found among any clan of the other Turkana major division, Ngimonia.[84]

All this puts the Turkana tradition of origin in a new light. It can be suggested that this tradition is in fact a composite of two tradi-

[81] Nagashima, loc. cit.

[82] See above, p. 22.

[83] Gulliver, *A Preliminary Survey of the Turkana* (Cape Town, 1951), p. 68, further reports that A. C. A. Wright claimed that all of the same Turkana clan names which appear among the Ngibelai and Ngikamatak subdivisions of the Ngicuro are also found among the western Iteso.

[84] The three Ngicuro clans were Katek, Lobal, and Iteso; also the Lokatap clan performs a finalization of marriage ceremony involving disembowelling. Moreover, two Turkana clans with members in both major divisions, Loponga and Swalika, have the same *ngitalia*, which may indicate their original Ngicuro affiliation.

Although he was not specifically concerned with recording clan *ngitalia* during his research, Gulliver (ibid. p. 60) noted that the women of *every* Ngicuro clan are supposed to wear gazelle-skins.

tions: one relating to the origin of the earlier Ngicuro division, and the other to the later-arriving Ngimonia. In the first part of the tradition, the 'old woman' Nayece moves to the east in order to collect wild fruits, and it is not unreasonable to imagine the 'old woman' as representing a whole group of people, the Ngicuro, who (like many of the Agricultural Paranilotic groups in Uganda) placed a strong reliance on gathering for their subsistence. It is only later that the 'young men' come to the east to join 'Nayece' and introduce intensive pastoralism into the area. The tradition of young men searching for a lost bull is closely paralleled by a Jie tradition concerning the occupation of Najie by Koten–Magos elements, even the colour of the lost bull (*engiro*, 'light grey') being the same in both traditions.[85] Thus, the later-arriving 'young men' seem to have come from Jie elements of the Koten–Magos group who had already begun the occupation of Najie, as indeed some of the Jie traditions state. It is further suggested that these 'young men' represent the (more pastoral) founders of the Ngimonia major division.

There was sufficient agreement among many Turkana informants that the 'young men' settled in the Tarash River Valley during the generation-set Ngipalajam (*see* Figure 3), the same generation-set which Jie and Karimojong informants stated were alive when the Koten–Magos group dispersed in the early eighteenth century, and this is further supported by Turkana traditions recorded by McKean which mention 'Nyepalajam' as one of the generations which came from Najie to settle on the Tarash.[86] On the other hand, no informant was able to name the specific generation-set that was alive when Nayece settled in the east: only that it was 'long, long ago'. Moreover, in the Turkana tradition, not only does 'Nayece' precede the 'young men' in to the Tarash Valley but the young men go back and forth between Moru Anayece and their homes in the west a number of times (at least twice and, in one version, as many as four times) before finally settling in the east. Traditions of the Koten–Magos group, for their part, indicate that the people of that concentration were constantly on the move to find fresh pasturage and water for

[85] This is especially significant in that Dyson-Hudson states that there are no less than fifty-five hide designations in Akarimojong (op. cit., p. 97). For the Jie tradition, see Chapter IV.

[86] J. D. McKean, 'Northern Turkana History', in *Kenya Land Commission—Evidence and Memoranda*, vol. ii (London, 1934), p. 1758. The other generations mentioned by McKean are 'Emisse' and 'Edutan'. My Turkana informants identified 'Ngimis' or 'Ngimik' as the fathers of Ngipalajam, but none had heard of any generation-set similar to 'Edutan'.

their livestock, and that some of their transhumant movement took them to dry-season cattle-camps on the headwaters of the Tarash, hardly 20 miles east of Koten. It can be concluded, then, that while most of the Agricultural Paranilotes occupied areas to the west and south of Koten, one group of them, the ancestors of the Ngicuro Turkana, went to the east to the headwaters of the Tarash, and thus became the only Agricultural Paranilotic community to establish contacts with the concentration of pastoralists at Koten and Magos.[87]

There is evidence, then, that the Central Paranilotes entered Karamoja as two distinct groups, from two different directions, and, with the exception only of the proto-Ngicuro Turkana, that there was no further contact between the two groups until the early eighteenth century. As the oral traditions of the Iteso make it clear that they had arrived as far south as the eastern portions of their present country by the sixteenth century, the separation between the two Central Paranilotic-speaking groups must have taken place in the southern Sudan, well before even that early date. It is hardly surprising, therefore, that no specific memory of that separation has survived in Central Paranilotic oral tradition, although some of the vague traditions mentioning a separation between proto-Agricultural and proto-Koten–Magos Paranilotes in an unspecified area, might just reflect a very dim recollection of such an event somewhere in the southern Sudan.

Nor is it surprising that, when the Koten–Magos group began its eighteenth-century expansions south and west from its former concentration, most of the outlying Agricultural Paranilotic groups they encountered should have been regarded as 'different people' or 'strangers', after a period of separation and independent cultural, economic, and linguistic evolution which had lasted most probably for several centuries.[88] Many Agricultural groups experienced inter-

[87] It is also strongly suggested that the Kenya Itesyo whom K. R. Dundas ('The Wawanga and other Tribes of the Elgon District', *JRAI* 43 (1913), 62–3) and subsequent writers mention as having broken from 'the Turkana', in fact split off from the Ngicuro division, possibly before the arrival of the Ngimonia. According to Dundas's Itesyo clan list, nine Itesyo clan names also appear among the Turkana—all nine (again including the four 'universal' clans of Tarantino) only among the Turkana Ngicuro division. Not a single Ngimonia clan seems represented in Itesyo society.

[88] A strikingly close parallel to this suggested reconstruction of early Central Paranilotic history exists among the oral traditions of the Southern Paranilotic-speaking Pastoral Maasai. The Maasai traditions collected by Jacobs and recorded in his unpublished Oxford D.Phil. thesis, 'The Traditional Political Organization of the Pastoral Maasai', 1965, pp. 28–34, relate that during their migration from the north, the Maasai-speaking peoples divided into two major

actions with alien peoples during or before their southward migration, which would have made them seem even more unfamiliar to
the Koten–Magos group when contact was re-established in the
eighteenth century. The first of these interactions appears to have
been with Paranilotic-speaking groups of the southern Sudan,
peoples akin to the present-day Bari and Lotuko. While indications
of such contact are admittedly vague, they are sufficient in aggregate
to show that some early contact took place between the Agricultural
Central Paranilotes and Northern Paranilotes which was not
experienced by the Koten–Magos group.

From oral traditions of the eastern Acoli, Webster feels it possible
that elements of the Northern Paranilotic-speaking Lotuko pre-
existed the arrival of Lwo-speaking groups in the Agago area of
eastern Ahcoli, on or very close to the migration route of the Agricultural Paranilotic groups from the north, and a Labwor informant
of a clan which was probably of Agricultural Paranilotic affiliation
stated that his ancestors were 'once one people with the Lotuko and
spoke the Lotuko language'.[89] Moreover, at least five Bari clan
names appear to have existed among the Central Paranilotes, and
all of them seem to have originally been associated with the various
Agricultural Paranilotic groups, rather than with the Koten–Magos
group. The clans are: Karyak or Kariak ('Karewok', one of Tarantino's 'universal' clans), Sera ('Loser', the clan, and 'Ngiseera', the
people, among the Jie and Iteso, plus a Koten–Magos name for the
Langi as a whole), Rito ('Ngerepo' or 'Ngereto' among many Central
Paranilotic tribes), Gela ('Gelangole' among the Jie) and Lokaamiro
(quite possibly an early form of 'Miro' or 'Miiro', now applied to
the Lango and to an early Agricultural Paranilotic group in the
Karimojong area).[90] In addition, the Bari-speaking Kuku may well

[89] See Webster's chapter in *A History of Uganda*, vol. i. See also R. Herring's
chapter in the same work, and his 'Production and Exchange in Labwor,
Uganda', an unpublished paper presented at Dalhousie University, 1973.
Okidi (Simei), L 10.

[90] Bari clans are listed in A. C. Beaton, 'The Bari: Clan and Age-Class

groups, the *Il Maasai* following one route, and the *Iloikop* another. After their
separation the Il Maasai developed an economy based on intensive pastoralism
(much in the same way as the Koten–Magos group of Central Paranilotes),
while the Iloikop placed a stronger reliance on agriculture (much like various
groups of the Agricultural Central Paranilotes). When, in the nineteenth
century, elements of the two Maasai-speaking groups encountered one another
again in parts of Kenya and Tanzania, they did so virtually as strangers, the
Maasai nicknaming Iloikop groups *Ilmengenga* ('corpses', i.e. 'those who were
dead and suddenly come back to life'), *Ilmingana* ('the deaf mutes', from their
inability to speak 'proper' Maasai anymore), and *Ilumbwa* ('farmers').

be represented among the Labwor as the ritually important Jo-kakuku clan.

It is also recalled in many oral traditions that some of the Agricultural Paranilotes possessed the knowledge of iron-smelting when they came from the north, although it is extremely rare to find clans of Paranilotic origin acting as their own blacksmiths (and it has already been pointed out that the Koten–Magos group did not possess the art). There are indications that Paranilotic-speaking Eyan first taught the art to Lwo-speaking clans of the proto-Labwor (who were to become the pre-eminent blacksmiths of Karamoja). Herring has recorded Labwor traditions which state that it was two of their original clans, Kalanga and Apwor, both of Lotuko origin, who first learned of iron-making, far to the north.[91] The original source of this knowledge may well have been Madi groups absorbed as 'dupi ('serfs') by northern Paranilotes, and Fr. Crazzolara has suggested a connection between such clans as 'Eparadup' now found amongst some Agricultural Paranilotic communities and the absorbed 'dupi.[92]

There is, moreover, certain archaeological and ethnological evidence which appears to reinforce the idea of a Northern Paranilotic presence among the Central Agricultural Paranilotic groups. The circles of flat stones and the massive deep-basin grinding stones (so unlike the small round ones of the Koten sites) which are typical features of Agricultural Paranilotic settlement sites in western and central Karamoja bear a striking resemblance to those illustrated in photographs taken by C. G. Seligman in Bari villages, while a visit made to remote Eyan villages on the slopes of Mt. Orom revealed very similar stone circles still in use as shrines.[93] Ethnologically, the important Bari ritual functionary, the ngutu lo lori, 'the person of the

---

[91] Herring, 'Production and Exchange in Labwor', p. 4; also see his chapter in *A History of Uganda*, vol. i.

[92] Crazzolara, loc. cit. p. 207, and also his *The Lwoo* (Verona, 1954), Part III, p. 339.

[93] The photographs appear in C. F. and B. Z. Seligman, *Pagan Tribes of the Nilotic Sudan* (London, 1932).

Systems', *SNR* 19 (1936), 110–20. The Bari Panigilo or Panyari clan may be represented among the Eyan and Labwor as the 'Ki-panya', and 'Panyamenya' clans, respectively, and possibly among the Jie as the division called 'Panyan-gara'. Another Bari clan, Lodara, would seem to be represented among the Jie as 'Lodera', but available data seems to suggest that Lodera was originally affiliated with the Koten–Magos concentration. It is furthermore tempting to link the Lotuko place-name 'Kapoeta' (which can be translated as 'the place of the Poet') with the Poet group of Agricultural Central Paranilotes.

iron rod', who 'exorcises illness from the villages and whose symbol of office and tool is an iron rod', has an exact parallel in two Jie ritual functionaries, both of which come from clans of Agricultural Paranilotic origin, whose symbol of office and tool is the *anywil*, a bar of iron, used during times of widespread illness or famine.[94] Finally, there is evidence to conclude that the New Fire ritual which is of particular importance to the Jie and to the Ngikaato division of the Dodos may have been derived from a Northern Paranilotic (possibly Lotuko) source.[95]

While our knowledge of Northern Paranilotic history is still only sketchy, Bari traditions do indicate that, after a migration from the east, they had arrived on the east bank of the Nile by at least the mid-sixteenth century, when their Bekat Limat line of Rain Chiefs was established at Sindiru, some 40 miles south of Juba.[96] Such a migration would have taken them from or through at least part of the area claimed by many Agricultural Paranilotes as their previous homeland at some date before the mid-sixteenth century. Indeed, Mark Loro, a Makerere research student, in 1971 recorded a specific tradition of separation between the Northern Paranilotic Kakwa and the Iteso at Kapoeta towards the beginning of the sixteenth century.[97] It is hoped that additional research will do even

[94] Ibid., p. 254. The Jie clans are Lominit for the Ngikorwakol major division, and for the Rengen, some clans of the Lokatap division (probably Kalolet), virtually all of which were originally descended from Agricultural Paranilotes. It is tempting to see some connection between the Lominit and the Lotuko Lomini clan, but as the Jie clan was simply named from a kind of tree (*eminit*), this would seem questionable. Weatherby has collected Tepes traditions which recall that a people called 'Ngiminito' (the name of the people of a group called 'Lominit'), now disappeared, were early inhabitants of part of the country now inhabited by the Karimojong.

[95] See below, pp. 124–25. It is also worth noting that an important part of the preparation for the burial of a Bari rain-maker included the blocking of all the orifices of the body (ibid., p. 292). The *lobunat* or *lomalol* ceremony, performed only by those clans of Agricultural Paranilotic origin, in which an animal is ritually suffocated, includes the ceremonial blocking of all its orifices as it is put to death.

[96] A. C. Beaton, 'A Chapter in Bari History', *SNR* 17 (1934), 169.

[97] See Webster's chapter in *A History of Uganda*, vol. i. Both Webster and Herring in that same volume argue that there was probably a Northern Paranilotic population living in western Karamoja by the sixteenth century. My own evidence led me to conclude that Northern Paranilotic–Agricultural Central Paranilotic interactions took place in the southern Sudan, rather than in Karamoja, but I would concede that further investigations may well prove Webster and Herring correct. Both of these writers have also recently identified what they consider to be a Galla element here in the western parts of Karamoja, and especially in Lango. I can find nothing in my data which would support this view.

more to expand these tantalizing hints of Northern Paranilotic–Central Agricultural Paranilotic contact further.[98]

If Agricultural Central Paranilotic contact with Northern Paranilotic elements is thus only rather vaguely perceived, indications of
contacts between Agricultural Paranilotic groups and another alien
people, the Lwo, are, on the other hand, both abundant and clear.

Labwor traditions, for example, state that the Agricultural Paranilotic migration from the north was accompanied by a concurrent
Lwo migration from the same direction:

> The Langi [i.e. the Agricultural Paranilotes] and [Lwo-speaking clans
> of] the Labwor came together from north of Mt. Orom. They walked
> side by side but they were two different tribes, and they weren't really
> together. The Labwor spoke this present language [a Lwo dialect] and
> the Langi spoke Akarimojong. The Labwor walked slightly to the
> west and the Langi walked slightly to the east.[99]

Even among the Itesyo, the southernmost of the tribes descended
mainly from Agricultural Paranilotes, Were has recorded traditions
that Lwo-speaking peoples were their neighbours in the Sudan and
that the migrations of the two peoples southward were concurrent.[100]
Webster's eastern Acoli traditions likewise present a picture of
early eastern Acoli history in which the dominant theme is the
interaction between Lwo and Agricultural Paranilotic groups all
along the present Acholi–Karamoja frontier, down the length of
which, on either side, the migrations seem to have passed.[101]

Contacts between the two peoples were to bring about considerable linguistic, socio-political, and economic interactions, in which
the Lwo-speakers generally appear to have played the dominant role.
These effects, especially linguistic, are the most obvious in the case
of Kumam, Langi, and Labwor. In all of these societies the clans
that originally spoke a Paranilotic tongue were so influenced by Lwo
contacts that they entirely abandoned their previous language in
favour of Lwo dialects.[102] Such effects were not confined to those

---

[98] There is, as far as I know, no linguistic trace of any Northern Paranilotic
dialect among any of the peoples now living in Karamoja or in neighbouring
areas to the west or south. According to Fr. J. Flores of the Verona Mission,
Kaabong, the language of the Mening people, who live just north of the Nyangea near the Sudan border, is a Lotuko dialect. The Mening are, however, a
very recent immigrant group into Karamoja.

[99] Awok (Anjelo), L 6.

[100] Were, op. cit. (1967), p. 25.

[101] Webster and Herring, in *A History of Uganda*, vol. i.

[102] For the Kumam, see Odada, loc cit., and Walshe, loc. cit.; for the Langi,
see Tarantino, 'Notes on the Lango', and Tosh, op. cit., Chapter 1. The Lango

three societies, but extended to other Agricultural Paranilotic groups who by the eighteenth century had become bilingual. By that time, a kind of linguistic spectrum seems to have extended across central Karamoja. In the west, on the present Acholi–Karamoja frontier, and southward to the area of Otukei, people were predominantly, if not exclusively, Lwo-speaking, regardless of their original ethnic affiliation. Further east, in what was to become Najie and southern Dodos, they seem to have been increasingly more bilingual, so that descendants of the Poot or Poet group, roughly in the middle of the spectrum, are equally divided as to whether their ancestors' original language was Lwo or Paranilotic. Finally, in the extreme east, in the area of Koten and the Magos Hills, was that concentration of Paranilotes whose Lwo contacts had been no more than slight and who were predominantly or entirely Paranilotic-speaking. Labwor informants described it like this:

> Long ago, the Acoli, Labwor, and Langi were together and they all spoke a similar language. The Jie, Turkana, Dodos, and the Karimojong were together and they spoke a different language. But the Langi, who lived closer to the Jie than the others of our group, knew both languages equally well.[103]

The economic and socio-political influences of the Lwo upon many of the Agricultural Paranilotic groups will be discussed at greater length in the following chapters. For the time being it is sufficient to note that many oral traditions credit the Agricultural Paranilotes with the introduction of new crops and advanced agricultural techniques which were probably derived from a Lwo source, and at least one of their major habitation sites near the Kotidani River in west-central Karamoja exhibits terraced hillsides and irrigation channels, as well as the ubiquitous deep-basin grinding stones,

[103] Ongom (Justo) and Kiyonga (Matayo), L 3. Central Paranilotic dialects retained by Agricultural Paranilotic groups (such as the Iteso, whose contacts with Lwo-speakers must have been less intense) are still reasonably close to the Central Paranilotic dialects spoken by those peoples largely descended from the Koten–Magos group. In their *Non-Bantu Languages of North Eastern Africa* (London, 1956), pp. 109–11, A. N. Tucker and M. A. Bryan even describe Akarimojong, Ajie, and Adodos as belonging to what they term the 'Teso Language Group'. In recent personal communication, Professor Tucker described Ateso as a 'broken down form of Akarimojong', which has lost certain elements (such as the open/closed vowel sounds) only very recently.

---

adoption of a Lwo dialect has been so complete that Driberg, op. cit., argued that they were of Lwo origin. The Labwor evidence is mainly from my own researches, and here a number of important clans do, in fact, seem to have been originally Lwo-speaking.

all of which reflect an agricultural intensification and sophistication unrivalled by the Koten–Magos group. The agricultural intensity reflected by their sites throughout central Karamoja has led Nelson to describe them simply as 'a group of agriculturalists'.[104] Within the political sphere, some Agricultural Paranilotic groups appear to have been influenced by the Lwo concept of the *Rwot* (chief or king), and imparted it to several of the primordial Central Paranilotic societies of Karamoja.[105]

It is now possible to attempt a brief reconstruction of the situation in Karamoja before the beginning of the eighteenth century, on the eve of the Jie genesis. Throughout this reconstruction, reference to Map 4 is essential.

Bands of Fringe Cushitic-speaking peoples, who certainly represented one of the earliest populations of Karamoja and probably ranged over a wide area, were still found throughout the whole length of Karamoja. At the northern and southern extremities, the Teuso and Tepes inhabited the higher mountain regions, which served to isolate them from much outside influence. In the centre, however, the Ngikuliak (and probably to some extent the Nyangea, just to their north), inhabiting less imposing hills, were more open to contacts with outsiders, and seem to have experienced Kalenjin influences, probably before 1500. Those Kalenjin-speaking peoples, who apparently occupied considerable parts of Karamoja before the sixteenth century had disappeared by the eighteenth century, possibly assimilated or driven south by the southern advance of Central Paranilotic-speaking peoples from the southern Sudan. The Oropom, other early inhabitants of Karamoja, had also given up much of

---

[104] Nelson, loc. cit., p. 2. He classifies them as 'Group III', between a group of Late Stone Age peoples and the 'modern pastoral inhabitants'.

[105] See below, Chapter IV. Within the cultural sphere, the avoidance of bushbuck, which seems to have formed one of the range of *ngitalia* common to all the Agricultural Paranilotic groups, may have derived from a Lwo source. This process certainly occurred amongst Lwo groups themselves, and between them and Bantu-speaking kingdoms to their south-west, as described by F. K. Girling (*The Acholi of Uganda* (London, 1960), p. 77): 'There is a tendency, it seems, for common lineages to adopt taboos of the aristocratic lineages in their domain. The bushbuck is the most common of all totemic animals, and it is no coincidence that this is also the totem of the kings of Bunyoro-Kitara . . . as well as being that of the Rwot of Payera. A common lineage . . . which achieved sufficient numerical strength to establish itself independently . . . commonly adopted the totemic observances of the most important ruling lineages.' Webster (*A History of Uganda*, vol. i) further argues that the bushbuck may have been the totemic animal for most of the later Lwo royal clans, before their dispersal in Baar during their migration from the north, probably in the fifteenth century.

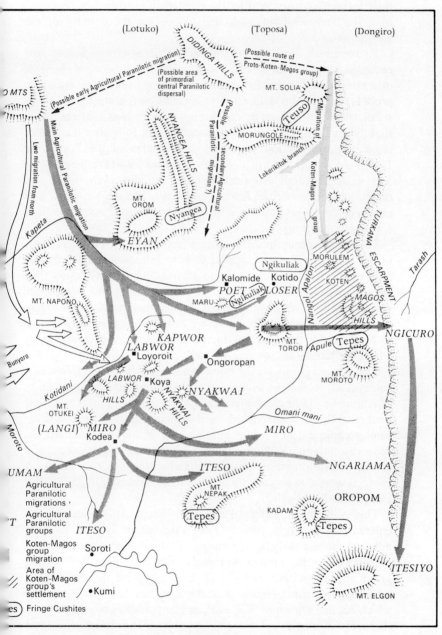

MAP 4. Groups in Karamoja before c. 1720

their former territory, and by the eighteenth century were confined to a small area within what was to become the country of the Karimojong.

To the north, possibly in that part of the southern Sudan now occupied by the Didinga or Lotuko, a separation between elements of a primordial Central Paranilotic group appears to have occurred, probably before the sixteenth century. It would seem that the two subdivisions drifted apart, one group moving west and the other slightly east. The eastern group turned south, following the line of rugged escarpment hills from the present area of the Toposa or Dongiro down to the Koten–Magos hill country where they halted. The western group also turned south, possibly even before the eastern group, entering Karamoja at the Mt. Orom pass, and experiencing close contacts with both Northern Paranilotic- and Lwo-speaking groups *en route.*

The eastern group, possibly after a brief clash with the rearguard of the retreating Kalenjin, appear to have found the grasslands and hills of the Koten–Magos area to their liking, and although they ranged considerably within that area, they remained a compact group within a somewhat limited area of concentration. Largely dependent on hunting and gathering activities at first, they appear to have steadily developed an increasing reliance on pastoralism, to which the Koten–Magos area was well suited.

The western group, on the other hand, appears to have followed a route which took them southward through the wetter, western parts of Karamoja. Their close interaction with Lwo-speaking peoples still further to the west introduced them to new food crops and agricultural techniques, and while hunting and gathering continued, in some cases, to play an important role in their economy, most of their groups became progressively more agriculturally oriented. These Lwo contacts were also profoundly to affect them linguistically, culturally, and politically.

This Agricultural Central Paranilotic group itself seems to have entered Karamoja in two streams. One group appears to have adhered more closely to the range of mountains capped by Mt. Napono along the present Karamoja–Acholi frontier. Part of this group appears to have pushed even further west into eastern Acholi, while the rest either remained at the Kotidani River as the group which became known as 'Kapwor', or else gradually moved on from that area westwards via Loyoroit into Labwor. The other Agricultural Paranilotic stream adhered to a more easterly route after emerging from the Orom pass, leaving splinter groups behind them as they came: the Eyan (probably the first to break off) remaining at Orom itself, the Poet or Poot remaining in the Kapeta River area between Orom and Kalomide, and the Loser and several smaller groups remaining in what was to become central Najie.[106] It was probably these Ngiseera or a related Agricultural Paranilotic group that exerted enough influence over Ngikuliak bands to cause them to adopt the Central Paranilotic dialect they were speaking by the eighteenth century.

Reaching Mt. Toror, the remainder of the group dispersed, possibly because of famine. While many of them (probably disenchanted by the steadily drier country into which they were moving) veered off to the west, others moved to the east, where, unlike any other Agricultural Paranilotic group, they established close contacts with the group concentrated at Koten and Magos, and formed the nucleus of the Ngicuro division of the Turkana, as well as providing considerable elements of the proto-Itesyo of Kenya.

Those who veered west from Toror either went up into the Nyakwai and Labwor highlands (from whence some appear to have returned again to the plains south of Toror), or else continued on through the highlands toward Otukei and the headwaters of the Moroto River. Here another dispersal must have occurred, for while some proto-Kuman and Iteso elements appear to have pushed on more or less directly into their present countries, other Agricultural Paranilotic elements including the Ngariama and part of the Miro and proto-Iteso swung away to the east again, occupying much of the country south of the Omanimani River which was subsequently to be occupied by the Karimojong.

Thus, the more pastoral Koten–Magos concentration was to be surrounded on three sides by groups of Agricultural Paranilotes who, although linguistically related to them and once part of the same primordial group in the southern Sudan, had by the beginning of the eighteenth century, after a separation of perhaps more than two centuries, evolved linguistic, economic, and socio-political differences which were to make them appear to be complete strangers. Many of these Agricultural Paranilotic groups were referred to as *Ngikatapa* ('bread people') as a somewhat disparaging comment on

---

[106] Some Labwor traditions vaguely indicate that yet another stream of Agricultural Paranilotes may have entered Karamoja to the *east* of Mt. Orom. Apparently Herring collected the same or similar traditions in his work amongst the Labwor, as well.

the economic outlook they had evolved. It was the appearance of some of these 'Ngikatapa' from the west early in the eighteenth century that was to be a very important factor in the dispersal of the Koten–Magos group, which led, in turn, to the formation of the distinct political entity called 'Ngijie', as well as many of the other political communities that now comprise the Central Paranilotes.

Previous observers have tended to concentrate their attention on only one or another of the major groups whose interactions were to bring about the formation of these political communities. Gulliver, and Ngashima following him, were most concerned with the Koten–Magos group. As the Jie family structure, closely tied up as it is with pastoral concerns, was most probably derived largely from the more pastorally oriented Koten–Magos group, it is hardly surprising that Gulliver, whose main concern was to achieve a detailed under-standing of that structure, should be more influenced by the traditions of Koten–Magos clans. Moreover, the traditions of those clans tend to be more dramatic and memorable, and are the most widely known throughout most of the Ngikorwakol major division.[107] It is very much to Gulliver's credit, therefore, that he should have so percept-ibly challenged the pre-existing notions that the Agricultural Parani-lotes were merely an advance guard which pushed out from the Koten–Magos concentration, and it is equally to Nagashima's credit that he did so much to point out the fundamental differences between the two major divisions of the Turkana and thus provide a valuable key with which to unlock the whole problem of the two Central Paranilotic-speaking groups.

On the other hand, Crazzolara, after years of historical research among Lwo- and Madi-speaking peoples, approached Central Paranilotic history, as it were, 'from the west'. It is not at all surpris-ing, therefore, that his main focus should have been on the more westerly Agricultural Paranilotic groups, rather at the expense of the Koten–Magos concentration.[108] Moreover, his identification of an

---

[107] During his stay in Najie, Gulliver lived with the Losogot clan of the Kotido division which was of Koten–Magos origin. Although Gulliver inter-viewed widely in Najie, my own experience clearly showed how difficult it is not to be influenced by the clan or territorial division with whom one is most closely associated.

[108] Although Crazzolara (loc. cit., 1960) does not specifically identify any of his informants in Karamoja, he does mention (p. 209) that he met them at Catholic Missions. As the Catholic Mission in Najie is located in the heart of Losilang territorial division where the Agricultural Paranilotic element is the stronger, it seems very likely that the traditions he was told were mainly, if not entirely, those of clans descended from various Agricultural Paranilotic groups.

'Eastern and Western Lango' may have been his interpretation of those traditions that do reflect the existence of the distinct Agricultural and Koten–Magos Paranilotic groups, and the general drift of his 'Lango' to the east may in fact have been a reflection of the very movements of various Agricultural Paranilotic people that brought them into contact with the Koten–Magos group.

CHAPTER IV

The Jie Genesis

BY the beginning of the eighteenth century, the increasingly strong pastoral outlook of the Koten–Magos group was causing serious ecological pressures within their area of concentration, and internecine feuds were engendered: 'Water was a problem at Koten. In the dry season everyone tried to water his cattle at once. This led to quarrels and fighting'.[1] Tempers became frayed and relatively minor incidents were blown out of proportion:

> At first there were no Bokora, no Jie—they were all one. But then there were quarrels. One day, boys were playing with bows and arrows as boys do, and one shot and killed another by mistake. There was a big quarrel. The parents of the boy who was killed and those who supported them became the Bokora. The parents of the other boy and their supporters became the Jie. Those who were to become the Bokora said, 'You have killed our child, and now we shall be enemies'.[2]

There are a number of versions of the manner in which the Koten–Magos group began to split up. For example, a Karimojong tradition, first recorded by Gulliver,[3] purports to explain the separation between themselves and the Jie with reference to the group-name of the latter. According to the Karimojong tale, the Jie were 'young men' who broke from their 'fathers', the Karimojong, by taking cattle to the dry-season cattle-camps (*ngauyoi*) and refusing to return with them. When ordered to return, the 'young men' resisted their elders with spears, whereupon the 'young men' formed their own tribe, *Ngijie*, 'the fighting people'.[4]

Traditions 'relating to general history' of this sort, which under-

---

[1] Igira (Yaramoi), Lokong, Muria (Longonyo), and Langlang, J 17.
[2] Nakade (Peter), J 57.
[3] Gulliver, op. cit, (1952), 5.
[4] This tradition was related by only one Jie and three Karimojong informants. The Karimojong informants were those of BK 1 and 2, whose clans, Katek and Lokatap, were probably not even part of the Koten–Magos concentration. The Jie was Ecak (Timothy), informant of J 5, J 48, and J 126, who, although an excellent informant, was one of the first Jie converts to Christianity, and lived for a number of years among the Karimojong at the Lotome B.C.M.S. Mission.

take to explain the derivation of a name, are often highly suspect. Previous observers, however, unaware of this, have frequently accepted this tradition literally, Nagashima even commenting that 'the Karimojong origin of the Jie is a case where neither traditions nor scholars have contradictory claims', and that such an origin can be accepted as 'historical fact'.[5]

The majority of traditions, however, indicate that the fragmentation of the Koten–Magos group was not directly caused by any single dramatic incident, but rather through a more gradual process of mounting ecological pressures and resulting intra-group frictions. It seems highly unlikely that at the time of their separation any of the constituent parts of the Koten–Magos group were known by their present tribal names, and those observers who have accepted the Karimojong tale as 'historical fact' have overlooked many Jie traditions which clearly state that they were not known by the name 'Ngijie' until fully a century after the dispersal of the Koten–Magos group.[6]

Thus some previous observers, including Gulliver and Nagashima, have been rather too concerned with determining the precise order in which various constituent groups of the Koten–Magos concentration are seen to have hived off from one another,[7] a concern of relatively minor importance. Moreover, the 'blame' for the break-up of the Koten–Magos concentration lay not with any one of its embryonic constituent parts, but with deep-seated problems of ecology and over-population.

By the early years of the eighteenth century, the Koten–Magos group had become separated into two major parts, each of which had drifted out to opposite peripheries of the area of concentration. In the southern part of the region, from the Magos Hills down to the Apule River, were elements which were to provide important segments of Karimojong, Dodos, and (some) Toposa society, while in the north-west, at Koten and Morulim hills, were

---

[5] Nagashima, loc. cit., p. 6.

[6] The concept of a new group being formed by the break-away of young men going to cattle-camps is a very popular one in Central Paranilotic oral tradition. Among the Jie alone, it is given as the reason for the splitting off of the (Ngimonia) Turkana, the (Ngikor) Toposa, the (Sudan) Jiye, and even the branches of several dispersed clans within Najie itself.

[7] As a result the Karimojong, who have been often regarded as the group from which all the other Central Paranilotes ultimately hived off, have attained an ethnocentric position among the Central Paranilotes totally unjustified by the oral traditions. For this reason terms such as the 'Karamojong Cluster' should be avoided.

other elements which were to form important segments of Jie, Turkana, Dongiro, (Sudan) Jiye, and (some) Toposa society (*see* Map 5).

In the words of Jie informants, 'the people who lived there in the east began to separate because of jealousy. The place became crowded and each group wanted to find enough land to live in. The Jie and their brothers the Turkana, Toposa, and Tobur lived together at Koten. The Karimojong and their brothers the Dodos were down at Magos'.[8] And from the Karimojong point of view, 'at first, all the people lived near Lotisan well near Koten. Then the Karimojong decided to leave that place because of hunger and because the Jie were quarrelling with them. So the Karimojong moved to the south and settled at Lokapel, Tutui, and the other areas near the Apule River'.[9]

To the majority of informants, the separation was simply 'long ago', while others, including some of the best Jie, Turkana, and Karimojong informants, agreed that the two major subdivisions were thus established on the peripheries of the Koten–Magos region at the time of the generation-set Ngipalajam. A comparison of Jie, Turkana, Karimojong, and Dodos generation-sets lends considerable support to the traditions of these informants. Figure 5 shows that Ngipalajam is the only remembered generation-set to which the Jie, Turkana, and Karimojong agree that they all concurrently belonged. Although no Dodos informant ever mentioned a generation-set called Ngipalajam, it was stated that a group called 'Ngimirio' was initiated at that time, and Jie informants claimed that an age-set or age-section of their Ngipalajam generation was called Ngimirio.[10] After Ngipalajam there is virtually no correspondence between the names of the generation-sets initiated concurrently by the four societies, which is exactly what one would expect if, as reliable informants have indicated, Ngipalajam was the last generation-set to be inaugurated before the irreparable fragmentation of the Koten–Magos group into its various parts.

On the other hand, the generation-sets before Ngipalajam might have been expected to be the same for all four societies, since all

---

[8] Dodoi (Lokwangiro) and Longoli (Apariong), J 88. The 'Tobur' in this tradition probably refers to those Labwor elements that did go west from Najie.

[9] Cero and Anyakun (Kilipa), BK 4.

[10] Despite interviews with some thirty Dodos informants, a clear understanding of their generation-set system was never achieved and so it is by no means certain that a Ngipalajam generation did not exist for them, as well.

would have been part of one Koten–Magos concentration. From Figure 5, however, it will be seen that the names of these generation-sets of the 'fathers' of Ngipalajam are different for each society. In no society did any reliable informant attempt to name any generation-set preceding the 'fathers' of the Ngipalajam, and some expressed the belief that the 'fathers' of Ngipalajam were 'the first people—those who lived when the world was created'. It is suggested that these names do not, in fact, refer to a generation-set as such but rather to the whole of the vaguely remembered (and partly mythological) epoch which preceeded the better-remembered and more factual historical epoch of Ngipalajam and the following generation-sets.[11] As Vansina has noted, 'in cases where a mythical period is contrasted with a historical one, the duration of the former is reduced to a single moment in time'.[12]

In his book on the Soga, D. H. Cohen makes the point that for them a number of cataclysmic events marked the division between the epochs of myth and of history to which a credible chronology could be assigned.[13] With the Koten–Magos group of Central Paranilotes, a very close parallel can be drawn, the immediate cataclysm being the disintegration of the group, which undoubtedly had its roots in the epoch preceding the inauguration of Ngipalajam. The Koten–Magos group had certainly been aware of mounting ecological pressures and resulting internecine feuds for some time before this. Nevertheless, in about 1720 when the new generation-set began its initiations, they were still enough of a corporate group to select the same generation-set name, Ngipalajam, for all their initiates. It was during the time spanned by the Ngipalajam initiations (c. 1720–60) that the group was to fragment irrevocably, and with that fragmentation the first embryonic stirrings of several new Central Paranilotic societies, including the Jie, became apparent. As those new

[11] I am very grateful to P. H. Gulliver, who in personal communication after my return from Uganda in 1971, first made this suggestion to me. As he pointed out at that time, the various names assigned to these 'fathers' of Ngipalajam are in themselves rather suspect. Whereas virtually all the generation-set names following them refer to an animal, or occasionally a plant or mineral, the names of these early 'generation-sets' seem rather to refer to people. With the Jie, for instance, *Ngisir* can be translated as 'the dandies' or the 'decorated people'. While the Turkana themselves do not seem to know the meaning of *Ngimis* or *Ngimiik*, there may well be some connection with the Southern Paranilotic *Il Mek*, the name applied to any non-Maasai peoples. The Karimojong *Ngikakwang* appears to mean 'the light-skinned people'.

[12] Vansina, op. cit., p. 101.

[13] D. H. Cohen, *The Historical Tradition of Busoga* (Oxford, 1972), pp. 68–9.

Fig. 5.

Comparison of Jie, Turkana, Karimojong, and Dodos Generation-Sets.†

	JIE	TURKANA (Ngimis or Ngimiik)	KARIMOJONG (Ngikakwang)	DODOS (Ngikorio)?
I	(Ngisir) (c. 1680?)			Ngimirio or Ngikaititi
II	Ngipalajam (c. 1720)	Ngipalajam	Ngipalajam	
	A. Ngimirio			
III	Ngikok (c. 1760)	Ngimute or Ngisuguru	Ngimirio	Ngiputiro
				A. Ngikok
IV	Ngisiroi (c. 1800)	Ngiputiro	Ngigetei I	Ngibaanga
V	Ngikokol (c. 1840)	Ngimoru I	Ngingatunyo	Ngikoria or Ngitiira
VI	Ngikosowa (c. 1880)	Ngirisai I	Ngitukoi	Ngitome
VII	Ngimugeto (c. 1920)	Ngimoru II	Ngimoru	Ngikamar (?)
VIII	Ngitome (1963)	Ngirisai II	Ngigetei II	(forming)

† There is less certainty regarding the reconstruction of the Dodos system than any of the others. My reconstruction of the Karimojong system corresponds exactly to that made by Mrs. D. Clark in 1950 ('Karimojong Age-groups and Clans', *UJ* 14 (1950), 215–17).

societies began to emerge, so too did the epoch of more chronologic-ally reliable and factual history.[14]

If the gradual disintegration of the Koten–Magos group was to signal this new epoch, there was another cataclysm, which, if it only somewhat indirectly affected the Koten–Magos peoples, was never-theless of key importance to the emergence of the new Central Paranilotic communities.

The traditions of the eastern Acoli and the Labwor recall a terrible famine, remembered by the Acoli as the 'Nyamdere', which brought great devastation to those primarily agricultural peoples, Lwo and Agricultural Paranilotic, who inhabited the borderland of present Karamoja and Acholi Districts. Some of Webster's Acoli informants still speak of the Nyamdere as 'the greatest of all famines',[15] and from a great deal of oral evidence, Webster has deduced that the famine took place sometime between the years 1706 and 1733. It is clear from both Acoli and Labwor oral evidence that a great deal of population movement all along the Acholi–Karamoja borderland resulted, as is indicated from the following Labwor tradition, which claims that a quarrel between Lwo and Agricultural Paranilotic groups 'caused' the famine:

> When the Morulem [division of the Labwor] arrived in their present area from Rwot [mountain], they found the Langi [Agricultural Paranilotes] still living in the Morulem area. There was a quarrel and Onyipo, the brother of Olemukan, the leader of the Morulem was killed. So the Labwor dug up an *ebele* plant and turned it to face those people who had done wrong, and the sun shone for seven years with no rain. This caused the great famine (*kec madit*), and all the people of the area were forced to disperse. Some went to Acholi and they are the present Payira. Others went to Lango and settled along the Ganotoro River. Others, including those who had a few cattle, went to the east to the Turkana [the Koten–Magos group] ... Even the Labwor who had caused that famine were affected by it, and most had to go up into the mountains to dig wild roots in order to stay alive.[16]

---

[14] The Gullivers (op. cit. (1953), p. 11) estimated that the break-up of the Koten–Magos group (or at least the Jie and Karimojong elements of the group) took place not long after 1700.

[15] J. B. Webster, 'Acholi Historical Texts', p. 23; see also his chapter in the forthcoming *A History of Uganda*, vol. i.

[16] Pidele (Otyang) and Okelo (Epui Woirono), L 9. The arrival of the Payira at this time is also recalled in Acoli tradition; see e.g. Webster, 'The Peopling of Agago', p. 9. There is no connection between the Labwor Morulem division and the hill called Morulim near Koten. Both names simply mean 'bare hill', a very common geographical feature in Karamoja.

As the tradition states, some of the famine refugees pushed east-wards across Karamoja towards the Koten–Magos concentration. While they appear to have come from many different areas along the Acholi–Karamoja borderland, the main group of refugees appears to have come from a place called Nasogolingokwo ('the place of dogs with long horns'),[17] not far from the present village of Kalongo in eastern Acholi District. Others came from the Adilang area further south, and others from the direction of Orom, to the north. These refugees seem to have been primarily Agricultural Paranilotic groups who had had considerable Lwo contacts, but there were clans of Lwo origin amongst them, too. In some instances they were bilingual in Lwo and Central Paranilotic dialects. Jie descendants of these refugees (who were given the nickname *Ngikatapa*, 'bread people', by the Koten–Magos group) described the homeland, way of life, and the dispersal of their ancestors:

> Our people, the Ngikatapa, came from Nasogolingokwo, or as the Acoli call it, 'Nasogolingwok', where they lived near a water hole in a river. The Ngikatapa dispersed there: one part went to the west to Acholi where they are now called Ngikalopio or Ngikatapa, and the other part came here to the east to Rengen [in Najie]. At Nasogolin-gokwo, our people spoke Ajie [Central Paranilotic], but those who went to the west also spoke *akibinibini* [the Jie term for any non-Central Paranilotic language, usually Lwo]. Our people cultivated sorghum and trapped animals, but they had no cattle ... At that time, the Nakapelimoru and the Panyangara [Jie elements of the Koten–Magos group] were there in the east [the informants pointed towards Koten, just visible on the horizon].[18]

The refugees' route took them eastwards across part of what was subsequently to become Najie. They seem to have marched rapidly past the Agricultural Paranilotic groups, such as the Loser and the Poet or Poot, which had originally been splinter groups, left behind in central Karamoja, as the main Agricultural Paranilotic migration

---

[17] According to Ogwal (loc. cit., p. 7), a branch of the Lango Atek clan also claims to have originated at this place (called Atunggwoktu in the Lwo dialect of the Langi). It may well have been an important Agricultural Paranilotic dispersal point. Herring thinks that the parts of this tradition dealing with the *ebele* plant and Olemukan refer to a famine of the nineteenth century. In my view, however, the dramatic *ebele* story probably *originally* referred to the 'Nyamdere', and was later grafted on to the tradition of the nineteenth century. Olemukan, however, may well have been a nineteenth-century figure, as Herring's data suggest.

[18] Lokwii, Wari, Locan (and others), J 95.

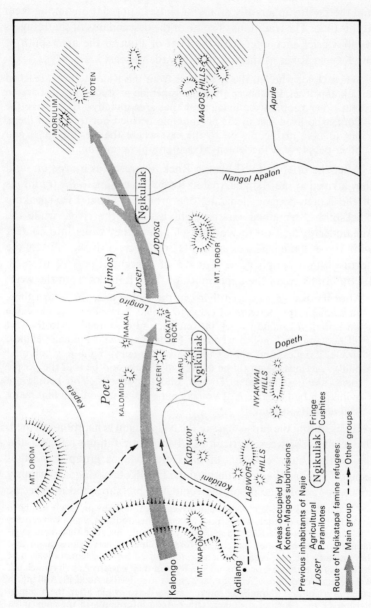

MAP 5. Central Karamoja *c.* 1710.

had moved down from the north. These groups were obviously not so badly affected by the 'Nyamdere' as those who lived further west, and there were apparently no major shifts in population among them at this time. The traditions of some of the descendants of the refugees recall a brief encounter with the Poet or Poot in the area south of the Kapeta River as they pushed towards the east:

> When Opio, who led the group east from the Kalongo area, reached Lokatap Rock in Rengen [Najie], his people paused. Opio discovered that other people were living near that area already—those were the Poot, who lived just to the north. Opio decided not to remain there, but to take his people on to the east where the Jie, Turkana, and other people [e.g. the Koten–Magos group] were living.[19]

After the brief halt at Lokatap Rock, the refugees moved on until they arrived at the Nangol Apalon River. According to the traditions of the Koten–Magos elements, one group of them, Lwo-speaking blacksmiths, remained on the right bank of the river, while the remainder pushed on to Koten itself where they came into contact with those Koten–Magos elements who were drifting out to the north-western periphery of the area of concentration (*see* Map 5). Jie traditions recall the appearance of these refugees from the west:

> After the people had been living in the Koten area for a long time, an *Ekatapit* [pl. *Ngikatapa*] came to Koten from the west. He came via Lobal to Lokatap Rock in Rengen, and continued on to the east till he came to Longiro where he found many wild animals: elands, giraffe, gazelles, and among them a bull [*engiro*, 'light-grey coloured bull') . . . He went on till he arrived at Koten, and he told the people there—the Jie, Turkana, Toposa, and the others, 'You people are living in a bad area here. If you come to the west, you will find many wild animals to hunt'.[20]

It was during the early stages of the Ngipalajam generation-set, then, that contact between Agricultural Paranilotic famine refugees and the north-western elements of the Koten–Magos group was established. The north-western subdivision of the Koten–Magos, obviously concerned about the mounting ecological pressures and internecine

[19] Okeo (Yonasan), L 11. Although now resident in Labwor, Okeo was born an Acoli, and his mother, from whom he heard this tradition, was a Rengen Jie.

[20] Nakade (Peter), J 57. Although many Jie traditions state that these 'Ngi-katapa' arrived at Koten as refugees from famine, other versions claim that they came to the east because of dissension caused by the unequal division of the liver of a hartebeest or kongoni at a feast in their eastern Acholi homeland. Webster has recorded a very similar version among the Acoli at Adilang in which Agricultural Paranilotes move eastwards to Najie after the unequal division of the heart of a duiker. Other Acoli informants in the same area maintained that the move was caused by a famine.

feuds which were besetting their group, seem to have welcomed the 'Ngikatapa' refugees' report of the good hunting grounds to the west, and the two peoples banded together for a large expedition into those western lands:

> So the people at Koten decided to go to the west with the *Ekatapit* to hunt those animals. They killed many of the wild animals, and then they captured the bull (*engiro*) which was also there, some grabbing its head and others its tail. The people saw that that place was good. They found hills of edible termites, and some men claimed them as their own. Other men claimed certain areas for their gardens, and others claimed good places on which to build houses, in case they should come there again. After that they tied the bull with a rope and returned to Koten . . . When they returned to Koten, they found that quarrels were still going on, and so they decided to move permanently to the good place which the *Ekatapit* had shown them in the west. It was thus that the Jie came to live in this place, Najie.[21]

The Koten–Magos and Agricultural Paranilotic settlers established themselves at the place called Daidai on the west bank of the Longiro River in what was to become Kotiang territorial division (*see* Map 6). According to their traditions, these place-names came about as a result of that first hunting expedition:

> There were many more wild animals here in Najie in those days than there are now, and so hunting was more important. The people settled at Daidai, which was so named because it was there that they beat out [*akidaidai*] the leather thongs used for snares. The whole area to the west was called Kotiang ['place of the wild animals'] because there were a great many wild animals there.[22]

> At first this river was not called Longiro—it had no name. It was named after the light-grey bull (*engiro*) which the people found grazing there with the wild animals.[23]

The advent of the Koten–Magos and Agricultural Paranilotic strangers from the east seems to have had a profound effect on the previous inhabitants of Najie. The first Ngikuliak bands were encountered as the newcomers pushed westwards through the eastern parts of Najie. According to some Jie traditions the Ngikuliak were terrified by the appearance of the strangers:

[21] Nakade (Peter), J 118, and (with others), J 16.
[22] Ecak (Timothy), J 5.
[23] Lobalong (Joseph) and Kere, J 12. The place-name derivations recorded in these traditions seem generally more reasonable than is often the case in 'traditions relating to general history', reinforcing the traditions that the new settlers first developed an interest in Najie as a fresh hunting ground.

They were afraid when they saw the cattle of the Jie for they had not seen cattle before. Some ran and hid in holes in the ground. If the Jie saw them hiding in a hole they would put the butts of their spears down the holes and lean on their spears, gazing off into the distance, as though they didn't know the Ngikuliak were there. The Ngikuliak, with spear butts pressing into their backs, would cry, 'Oh, Oh!' And the Jie would pretend to be surprised and say, 'Ah! So you are there? Come out!'[24]

Possibly because of such treatment, few of the Ngikuliak seem to have joined with the strangers at this time. Most fled to the relative fastness of their hills, especially Maru, and others appear to have abandoned Najie entirely, fleeing to the Acholi borderland to the west.[25] One of their songs laments:

Loceno! Eee, eee! Apena ion dang naboko.
(Loceno [a person's name]! Eee, eee. Let us now go to the turtles.)
Ament ngidwee Angilok ngakecelepon.
(The children of Angilok have brought the milking animals.)[26]

The largest of the Agricultural Paranilotic groups which were also previous inhabitants of Najie, the Loser and the closely related Loposa, reacted to the appearance of the strangers in much the same way as the Ngikuliak. Less affected by the 'Nyamdere' than the Agricultural Paranilotic and Lwo groups further west, they seem to have had little contact with the 'Ngikatapa' famine refugees who passed so rapidly through central Karamoja on their march towards Koten. However, with the return of those refugees in company with elements of the Koten–Magos group, seemingly bent on permanent settlement in Najie, most of the Loser and Loposa seem to have taken fright and moved off to the west:

The Ngiseera [Loser] used to live here in Kotido. They dug the water-holes at Nakere and Lomuth. They were mainly cultivators, although they may have had a few cattle as well. They spoke *akibinibini* [Lwo]. When they saw the Jie coming from the east, they were afraid and said, 'These people will fight us. Let us go to the west!'. The Jie didn't fight those people, but the Ngiseera went away to the west as the Jie

[24] Nakade (Peter), J 57.
[25] The appearance of Ngikuliak bands in eastern Acholi may be recalled in Acoli traditions which describe a people called 'Abunga' arriving in Potongo from Najie. Although they had some goats, it seems that they were primarily a hunting and gathering group. See Webster, 'Acholi Historical Texts', p. 16.
[26] Kere, Meron, and others. J 64. Turtles were eaten only in times of great hardship. 'Going to the turtles', therefore, would be roughly equivalent to the English 'going to the dogs', giving up hope entirely.

came from the east. Most of them went away, and only those who formed the Loser clan of Kotido remained behind.[27]

Most of the Loser and Loposa followed a route to the west which eventually brought them to Mt. Otukei and the eastern frontiers of Lango and Teso.[28] The descendants of those who remained behind in Najie still remember their emigrant kinsmen in a kind of pageant performed on ceremonial occasions. They place their chattels on their heads, load their donkeys, and form a line facing towards the west and Mt. Otukei, all as though they were preparing to migrate. They sing:

Apena atowoto, elwana Serer.	Let's move, Serer [Lango] is far away.
Apena atowoto, elwana Kumam.	Let's move, Kumam [Teso] is far away.
Elwana Serer, elwana Kumam.	Serer is far away, Kumam is far away.
Apena atowoto, elwana Serer e!	Let's move, Serer is far away, indeed![29]

The departure of the Loser and Loposa was closely followed by emigrations from Najie of considerable segments of the Koten–Magos group of new settlers. Hardly had the newcomers established themselves at Daidai when one segment of the Koten–Magos group, apparently disappointed in the new area, turned around and retraced their steps to the east:

> After the people came west from Koten, some found that conditions were not all they had hoped for . . . Some therefore took livestock and went back to the east saying, 'Lo! We have left the good grass behind us in the east. This place will kill our flocks'. And so they returned to the east and became Turkana.[30]

These emigrants, moving back through the old area of concentration and descending the escarpment to the headwaters of the Tarash, were to found the Ngimonia division of the Turkana.[31] Their own traditions clearly indicate their links with the group which moved from Koten to the Daidai area of Najie:

> After the people settled in Najie, two bulls strayed away to the east. The grandfather of my grandfather, Angirokol, whose generation-set was Ngipalajam, was the owner of one of those bulls, whose name was *engiro* [light grey]. My ancestors told me there is some connection between the name of that bull and the river called 'Longiro' in Najie.

[27] Mabuc (Loputuka), J 70 and J 85. A very similar tradition to this seems to have been collected by the Gullivers (op. cit. (1953), p. 10).
[28] See below, pp. 149 and 160.
[29] Adome, J 62.
[30] Lokala, Tede (Teko), Looru (Sampson) and others, J 9.
[31] See above, p. 93.

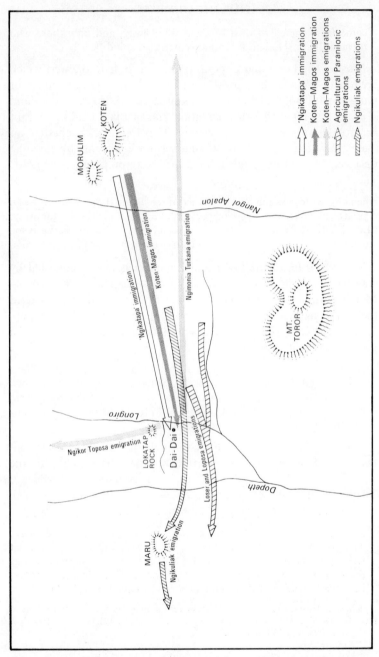

MAP 6. The Immigration from Koten to Central Najie and Subsequent Emigrations

People tracked those lost bulls to the east and found them living with
Nayece who was drying wild fruits at Moru Anayece near the Tarash.
. . . They saw that place was good, with fertile soil, good grass, and
many wild fruit. They carried the news back to Najie and many young
people decided to move to the east to the place of Nayece. All of this
happened in the time of the Ngipalajam.[32]

The Turkana tradition probably takes its inspiration from the Jie
tradition which records that first hunting expedition to the Longiro
River area of Najie and even the name of the Turkana leader
'Angirokol' sounds suspiciously like the name of the Jie leader,
'Orwakol'.[33] The most reliable Turkana informants were in agreement that the immigrants from Najie arrived on the Tarash while
the Ngipalajam were still initiating. This was further supported by
traditions collected by McKean in the 1930s, in which the immigrants
were remembered to have been of the 'Emisse, Edutan and Nyepalajam ages',[34] and a few of my own informants also mentioned that
members of the Ngimis or Ngimiik generation-set were among the
Najie immigrants. Although Ngimis or Ngimiik most probably represents the whole epoch that preceded Ngipalajam, in mentioning
'Ngimis' or 'Emisse', the Turkana traditions may have been recalling
that a considerable number of men initiated into the generation-set
(or sets) earlier than Ngipalajam were included in the emigration
from Najie. This would indicate that the Ngimonia migration from
Najie to Tarash took place well before the final stages of the
Ngipalajam initiations, and it would probably not be wrong to
estimate that it took place no later than about 1740.

Soon after the departure of the Ngimonia Turkana to the east,
other Koten–Magos elements departed to the north. Some of these
emigrants ultimately seem to have formed important segments of
the Dongiro and (Sudan) Jiye, but perhaps the majority of them
were part of the group which was to form the Ngikor division of
the Toposa. These emigrants appear to have gone north from
Daidai via the territory now inhabited by the Rengen major division
of the Jie (*see* Map 6), primarily in search of additional grazing
land:

[32] Lokimak, T 14. It is unusual to find any Central Paranilotic informant who
can recall the name of the grandfather of his grandfather. Lokimak's was
certainly a special case, however. He is well known throughout a surprisingly
large area of Turkana as the direct descendant of Angirokol, whom many
Turkana regard as the leader of the Najie emigrants.

[33] Both names are derived from *okol* which describes cattle with certain
black-and-white spotted markings.

[34] McKean, loc. cit., p. 1757.

The Ngikor went north from Najie to Loyoro [in Dodos] where they settled for some time before continuing on to their present homes-land in the Sudan. As recently as the Ngimugeto initiations [1920s], a large group of them came here to Najie to observe our initiations and to learn more about our customs. This shows that they were originally Jie.[35]

As this tradition recalls, most of the northern emigrants at first established themselves in the Loyoro area (which was ultimately to be occupied by the Dodos), a scant 25 miles north of Daidai in central Najie. Unlike any of the other emigrant groups, all of whom seem to have largely severed their contacts with Najie when they moved away, they remained in close contact with the Daidai settlers, and were probably rather more a northern vanguard of those settlers than a separate community.

Some traditions do make vague mention of a cattle disease and/or a famine at roughly the same time that the initial settlement at Daidai and the subsequent emigrations out of Najie were going on. The picture generally conveyed, however, is not one of any great disaster, but rather of shifts in population undertaken to avoid any excessive concentration of people in a confined area. For their part, the Agri-cultural Paranilotic Loser and Loposa were probably beginning to realize that the central Najie area was only marginally suited for their intensive agricultural specialization,[36] and the rather dramatic appearance of the strangers from the east was the catalytic event which set them in motion towards the more fertile lands they had reason to suspect existed to the west: 'Our ancestors, the Loposa, and their brothers, the Loser, were clever in the ways of cultivation. They had seen the rain passing to the west, even as it does now, and they realized there must be a fertile country there.'[37]

The Koten–Magos settlers, with the unfortunate internecine quarrels experienced in their previous area still fresh in their minds,

[35] Ecak (Timothy), J 48 and J 126. Ecak and several other informants men-tioned 'other Toposa' already living in the north before the Ngikor broke from the Jie. A number of non-Jie informants (including those of BK 2, BK 4, D 1, and L 10) stated that when the Koten–Magos group began its original journey southwards from the Sudan to the Koten–Magos area, some ele-ments of the group remained behind in the south-eastern Sudan. It is entirely possible that this did happen, but the matter is not really clear from Jie oral tradition.

[36] At the Loser and other Agricultural Paranilotic habitation sites in Najie, profusions of deep-basin grinding stones and the remains of stone granary supports attest to the intensive agriculture engaged in by these groups.

[37] Lonyangakan (and others), J 65.

must have been equally anxious to avoid any great demographic build-ups which might bring about the same severe ecological pressures that had beset them in the Koten–Magos area. Emigrations into surrounding areas were therefore inevitable. Several Jie traditions indicate that these emigrations dramatically reduced the population of Najie, which at the point of arrival of the new settlers from Koten, must for a short time have been very large indeed: 'I was told that at that time, the population of Najie was very much larger even than it is now. For a time every part of Najie was occupied and no place was empty. Then the Turkana, Toposa and all the other groups left the Jie and the population suddenly became much smaller.'[38]

The emigrations from Najie left behind two compact groups of settlers at Daidai: a remnant core of the Koten–Magos elements; and the 'Ngikatapa' famine refugees who had temporarily banded with them for the initial stages of the occupation of Central Najie. At the time of its settlement at Daidai, each of these groups had its own leader who owed his position of leadership to his hereditary office of *ekeworon* (pl. *ngikeworok*), 'ritual Fire-Maker'. The fire-maker of the Koten–Magos settlers at Daidai was called Orwakol, a man of the Toroi clan, while for the 'Ngikatapa' (or 'Rengen', as they soon became known), he was Oding (occasionally pronounced Odiny or Loding) of the Ratai clan.

The office of fire-maker and the ritual of New Fire generally have received very little attention from previous observers of Central Paranilotic societies.[39] Nevertheless, a New Fire ritual must have been a cultural feature of even the primordial Paranilotic-speaking community, for at least some vestige of such a ritual is still discernible among societies belonging to the Northern, Central, and Southern linguistic subdivisions which evolved from that primordial community. From the available data, the ritual seems strongest amongst the Central Paranilotic Toposa, Jie, and the Lokaato section of the Dodos, as well as amongst the Lotuko in the north,[40] and perhaps vaguest amongst the Southern Paranilotic Samburu and Pastoral Maasai, where only a faint recollection of the fire-makers

[38] Looru (Sampson), J 120.

[39] e.g. the Gullivers (op. cit. (1953), p. 50) devote only a few lines to the office, and Dyson-Hudson, op. cit., while making several rather vague mentions of a Karimojong New Fire ritual, virtually ignores the fire-makers themselves. Only slightly more attention was paid to the Toposa fire-makers by Beaton (in Nalder, op. cit., p. 69).

[40] See the Seligmans, op. cit., pp. 323–4.

and their New Fire rituals have been retained in the persons of the 'Fire-stick Elders', so important to age-set inaugurations.[41]

Among the Jie and the other societies in which the fire-makers and their New Fire ritual is so important, the ritual entails the extinguishing of all the old fires of the community and scattering the ashes to the wind. This is followed by the ceremonial rekindling of a New Fire by the fire-maker and his ritual assistants with sacred fire-sticks, and the relighting of all the fires of the land with brands from it. In general, the ritual is performed in times of great stress (famine, war, disease), and also in conjunction with the inauguration of a new generation-set.

It is very likely that the fire-makers of the Koten–Magos group at the time of its dispersal were primarily religious functionaries, accorded considerable respect, but commanding little or no obedience in even the vaguest political sense. Such a picture would certainly be consistent with the office as it now exists among the Karimojong and the Lomeris section of the Dodos: those societies in which the Koten–Magos elements experienced relatively little close interaction with Agricultural Paranilotic or Lwo communities.

Orwakol, therefore, was probably rather unusual for his time in being considered by the Koten–Magos elements of the proto-Jie settlers at Daidai as in any sense their 'leader'. The historical figure of Orwakol is now partly enshrouded by legend in Jie oral tradition, but he must have been a man of exceptional personal qualities, who would have been regarded as an 'outstanding individual' even without the benefit of his hereditary ritual office. Some informants went so far as to describe Orwakol as 'the first man', while others credited him with the invention of the generation-set system and, upon 'instruction from God', the New Fire ritual. More credibly, other informants claimed that Orwakol had been responsible for the establishment of several important ritual centres in the immediate vicinity of Daidai (still of great importance as foci for the politico-religious unity of one of the Jie divisions), the discovery of the pit of sacred clay (still used for smearing on important ritual occasions), and with the introduction of the *ekori* ceremony, a kind of annual harvest festival which seems peculiar to the Jie among the Central Paranilotes. As a symbol of office and probably as a focal point for some ritual activity, Orwakol and his Toroi kinsmen are remembered to have brought with them from Koten a wedge-shaped stone, about 3 feet in length, which they set up in the kraal of Orwakol's home-

[41] P. Spencer, *The Samburu* (London, 1965); Jacobs, loc. cit. (1965).

stead near Daidai.[42] Orwakol's homestead and the immediately
surrounding area was given the name *Lokorwakol*, 'Orwakol's place',
and the Koten–Magos settlers who regarded Orwakol as their leader
lived clustered around Lokorwakol, west of the Longiro River, in
Kotiang, considered by the Jie as their original territorial division.
It seems clear that Orwakol successfully made himself and his office
the focal point for the earliest feelings of their unique and independent identity by his group of followers. As a lasting tribute to him,
Kotiang is still said to 'give strength to the Jie because it was there
that Orwakol had his home,'[43] and the descendants of his Koten–
Magos followers, who were to form the core of one of the Jie major
divisions, still call themselves *Ngikorwakol*, 'Orwakol's people'.[44]

The fire-maker of the Agricultural Paranilotic famine refugees, the
'Ngikatapa' or Rengen, was a man called Oding, probably the son of
Opio, the man who had led the 'Ngikatapa' from the Acholi borderland to Koten. Rather less about Oding has been retained in the oral
traditions of the descendants of his band of followers, who were to
form the core of the Rengen division of the Jie. Like Orwakol, however, Oding appears to have been highly revered by his people, and is
still regarded by the Rengen as their 'great ancestor' (founder). Like
the descendants of Orwakol's Koten–Magos followers, the Rengen
still refer to themselves as *Ngikaloding* 'Oding's people'.

While any detailed description of the office of the Rengen fire-
maker as it existed at the time of Oding does not appear to have
survived in the traditions, it seems very likely that the functions of
the Agricultural Paranilotic fire-makers were rather different from
those of their Koten–Magos counterparts, and that many more
ritual trappings were associated with their office.[45] In function the
Agricultural Paranilotic fire-makers seem to have had very real
judicial powers and they had under their direct control the annual
agricultural cycle of the community. Ritual trappings associated with

[42] Lobilatum, J 51. Stones similar to this can be seen erected in the kraals of
almost all important Jie functionaries: fire-makers, assistant fire-makers,
asapanu leaders and so on. They closely resemble the flat stones of the circles,
which were presumably supports for granaries, at most Agricultural Paranilotic
habitation sites, but there is nothing in the oral traditions which suggests any
link. Similar stones also appear in the traditions of non-Jie societies, including
the Toposa (Nalder, op. cit., p. 66) and the Labwor (L 9).

[43] Akurameri (and others), J 7.

[44] By extension, the whole of the area now occupied by the Ngikorwakol is
now sometimes called *Lokorwakol*, 'Orwakol's place', although *Lokorwakol* is
usually reserved as the name for that part of Kotiang division in which Orwakol
had his homestead.

[45] See Chapter VI.

their office included elaborate burial ceremonies and symbols of office. Such functions and trappings do not appear to have been inherent in the office of the Toroi fire-makers, and were certainly not inherent in the office of the fire-makers of those other societies—Karimojong and Lomeris Dodos—in which the Koten–Magos element is the strongest. Among the Ngikorwakol, it was only after the office was usurped by a clan of Agricultural Paranilotic origin, the Jimos, that such functions and trappings appear to have become associated with the office. On the other hand, although the original fire-making clan of the Rengen, the Ratai, was later replaced by another, Kalolet, there is nothing to suggest that the functions and trappings of office as described above were introduced at the time of the replacement. Rather, it would appear that the new Rengen fire-makers inherited the office with all its functions and trappings intact from their predecessors.[46]

The case of the Dodos again strongly supports the supposition that inherent in the office of the Agricultural Paranilotic fire-makers were powers and functions not accorded to their Koten–Magos counterparts. One of the Dodos territorial sections, Lomeris, was descended mainly from elements of the Koten–Magos concentration, and the Lomeris fire-makers were apparently never regarded as more than respected ritual functionaries, without any real leadership role in their community. On the other hand, another section, Lokaato, was almost entirely composed of elements descended from the Poot (or Poet) and other closely related Agricultural Paranilotic groups; their fire-makers, quite unlike the Lomeris, possessed real judicial and economic powers and ritual trappings very similar to those of the Rengen fire-makers. In the course of Dodos history, the Lokaato fire-makers were to emerge as the most powerful of Dodos society:

> Although each Dodos section has its own fire-maker, it is the fire-maker of the Poot [clan of the Lokaato section] who leads all the others. The Poot fire-makers led the Dodos in everything. The Poot brought the office of fire-maker with them from the west, and they taught the other Dodos to be proper fire-makers.[47]

It seems very likely that the additional powers and trappings attached to the office of fire-maker by Agricultural Paranilotic groups such as the Rengen and Poot were a result of their unique contacts and interactions with Northern Paranilotic and/or Lwo-speaking

---

[46] See Chapter VI.
[47] Lokidap (and others), D 10.

groups during their migration southwards into western and central
Karamoja. Amongst the Northern Paranilotic Lotuko, the Seligmans
noted that the fire-makers were also the rain-makers (*kobu*), functionaries accorded real political, as well as ritual, powers,[48] and so part
of the inspiration for the development of more powerful Agricultural
Paranilotic fire-makers may have been provided by that, or possibly
another, Northern Paranilotic source. Clearly, additional inspiration
was provided by the Lwo. Contact with the Lwo caused many
Agricultural Paranilotic groups either to abandon their original
language entirely in favour of Lwo dialects, or to become bilingual.[49]
Many seem to have been affected by the Lwo concept of the *Rwot*
(pl. *Rwodi*), which has been translated as 'hereditary chief' or 'king'.
Such Agricultural Paranilotic groups as the Rengen Jie and the
Lokaato Dodos seem to have been so much influenced by the Lwo
concept that some of the functions and rituals accorded to the *Rwodi*
were borrowed by the Agricultural Paranilotes and invested in the
persons of their fire-makers.

The *Gwelo* and *Yeko Kodi* ceremonies performed by Lwo kings,
in which tribute in the form of agricultural produce is brought to
them, and by which their control over the annual agricultural cycle
is expressed, were borrowed in their entirety by some Agricultural
Paranilotic groups and bestowed on their fire-makers. In the same
way, the Jimos, the Agricultural Paranilotic clan which eventually
usurped the office of fire-maker of the Ngikorwakol Jie from the
Toroi clan, also seems to have borrowed from the Lwo the *Goyo Bal
Gang Pa Rwot*, a rain-making ceremony performed by their kings.[50]
The judicial powers accorded by the Agricultural Paranilotes to their
fire-makers were also probably inspired by similar powers accorded
to their kings by the Lwo, although, as Webster has shown, in the
case of many eastern Acholi kingdoms, these powers were increasingly shared between the kings and their *Lukwena* and later their
Twon Lok advisory councils.[51] Most of the ritual trappings associated

[48] For a description of the ritual see the Seligmans, op. cit., pp. 323–4. See
also C. G. and B. Z. Seligman, 'The Social Organization of the Lotuko', *SNR*
8 (1926), 3, for a description of the *kobu*.
[49] See above, pp. 98–9.
[50] The Lwo ceremonies were described by Webster in personal communication, and in his 'Acholi Historical Texts', pp. 83–4. Similar ceremonies in which
tribute is accorded the kings are also described by Girling, op. cit., pp. 96–7.
The Seligmans (op. cit. (1932), p. 248) also mention a similar sort of tribute in
agricultural produce being given by the Bari to their rain-makers.
[51] Webster, 'State Formation and the Development of Political Institutions
in Eastern Acholi', pp. 4–5.

with the Agricultural Paranilotic fire-makers also seem to have been derived from Lwo sources. The symbol of office of the Rengen Jie fire-makers, for example, is a sacred spear (called simply *akwara*, 'the spear') made entirely of iron, without the wooden shaft of other Jie spears. A number of eastern Acholi kingdoms have exactly such a spear among the royal regalia of their kings, the spear of the Ajali kingdom which 'has no name, nor handle'[52] being a prime example. Finally, the burial ritual for deceased Lwo kings, which entails dressing the corpse with certain ornaments and the killing of a black bull,[53] seems to have an almost exact parallel in the internment rituals performed for the Rengen and Jimos fire-makers.[54]

While there does not seem to be any specific recollection in Jie oral tradition that the fire-makers of the Agricultural Paranilotic groups were thus influenced by their interactions with Northern Paranilotic- and/or Lwo-speaking peoples, informants frequently expressed the belief that the Agricultural Paranilotes were influenced in a general way by others during their residence in the west:

> In the west, the Ngikatapa borrowed the customs of other people, and came with those customs to Najie. It happened like this. Suppose a man comes to Najie from the west with seeds he has borrowed there. Suppose he digs his garden and plants those seeds while the person in the neighbouring garden plants his usual seeds, those of Najie. And lo! The person who has borrowed the new seeds finds that his garden has yielded well. Is he not well pleased? Will he not say, 'These seeds have suited me well!'? Will he not continue to use the seeds he has borrowed? It was thus with the Ngikatapa.[55]

Other traditions specially name the Lwo-speaking Acoli as the people who so influenced the 'Ngikatapa' in the west: 'Oding and his people, the Rengen, came here from the Acoli. The Rengen are

---

[52] Webster, 'Acholi Historical Texts', p. 148. Girling (op. cit., p. 116) also mentions a similar spear 'all in one piece with an iron shaft' as being part of the royal regalia of the kings of Patiko.

[53] Webster, 'Acholi Historical Texts', p. 115.

[54] It is fair to admit that no observer of two other groups descended largely from Agricultural Paranilotes, the Iteso and the Langi, ever mentioned any New Fire ritual or hereditary fire-makers in those societies. It is inconceivable that the ritual and the office did not at one time exist in those societies, and one is forced to conclude that because the various observers were not aware of the importance of the ritual to many other Paranilotic societies, they simply did not attempt to collect any data regarding the ritual and its functionaries. Certainly the ritual did exist in two other societies descended largely from Agricultural Paranilotes, the Labwor and the Nyakwai, as my own and Herring's data attest.

[55] Amuk (Akitibuin), J 89.

different than the other Jie. Their customs are different—they are the customs of the Acoli.'[56] It would therefore seem reasonable to suppose that by the time of the initial occupation of central Najie, the Rengen contacts with Lwo-speaking (and perhaps to a lesser extent, with Northern Paranilotic-speaking) peoples, experienced during their migration from the north and during their period of settlement in the Acholi–Karamoja borderland, had already added new dimensions to the pre-existing office of fire-maker. It can be suggested that a position of leadership similar to (if not greater than) the one that Orwakol must have won largely through his own outstanding personal qualities, may have been accorded to Oding simply as his hereditary right.

It is clear that both Orwakol and Oding were strong and much revered leaders, and that their groups of followers, each with its own distinctly different economic and cultural background, soon realized that any very close political union (which would have implied at least some degree of assimilation of one group by the other) was unworkable.[57] Not long after their arrival at Daidai, the two groups therefore drew apart to form their own largely autonomous communities, in a manner which, significantly, is described in the oral traditions in terms of the fire-makers. The following tradition (although somewhat biased towards the Ngikorwakol point of view) typically describes the separation:

At Daidai both Orwakol and Oding set about to make New Fire. Orwakol's fire was kindled first, and so Oding came to him and said, 'It is foolish for us both to try to make New Fire here in the same place'. And so Orwakol gave him a brand of his fire, and Oding took his people and went to Lokatap Rock in Rengen, and settled there. And so there came to be two 'homesteads' of the Jie: Orwakol's, which was here in Lokorwakol; and Oding's which was there in Rengen.[58]

[56] Anunu and Cope, J 28. One area into which Lwo influence apparently did not extend was that of religion, as none of the Agricultural Paranilotic peoples who became part of the Jie appears to have possessed any notion of the *Jok*.

[57] The general impression given by the oral traditions is that the two groups were of roughly the same numerical size when they established themselves at Daidai. The present numerical superiority of the Ngikorwakol could be easily accounted for by the facts that the Ngikorwakol were to assimilate greater numbers of aliens than the Rengen, that an entire Rengen division was to be destroyed in a war, and that a major segment of the Rengen population (the Kadokini) emigrated to a Ngikorwakol territorial division.

[58] Mabuc (Loputuka), J 70. The Jie tradition quoted here is in some ways strikingly similar to one recorded by Crazzolara, *The Lwoo*, pp. 376–7, in which a New Fire ritual and sacred fire-sticks play an important part in the

Other Ngikorwakol and Rengen traditions state that the separation was caused because the two fire-makers 'grew jealous of each other',[59] but there was universal agreement that it was Oding and his people who moved away from the Ngikorwakol, still clustered near Daidai. Most of the Rengen settlements were established in what became Kadwoman territorial division, but, as the above tradition indicates, Lokatap Rock (the same place recalled in the traditions as a stopping place for the 'Ngikatapa' famine refugees on their migration to the east) became the focal point of the area pioneered by the Rengen separatists, very much as Daidai was to remain the focal point for the Ngikorwakol (see Map 7). According to some Rengen traditions, the rock itself (a large granite outcropping which rises up dramatically out of the surrounding flat plain) was consecrated as a ritual centre in a most unusual way:

> When the Rengen first arrived at Lokatap Rock, they found no wild creatures living there. But then a diviner (emuron) had a dream, and he instructed the people to go and trap rock hyraxes and bring them to the rock. The people trapped hyraxes and released them at the rock. The emuron told the people not to kill the hyraxes for as long as they should live at Lokatap Rock, so long would the Rengen endure. There is also at Lokatap Rock a very large black snake that has a white feather growing from its head. That snake is really a great person who lived long ago, and some of the elders say it is Oding himself. It visits the new-born babies during the night after their birth and licks them with its tongue to bless them.[60]

The traditions of both Jie major divisions agree that the separation between the Ngikorwakol and the Rengen was not, however, absolute:

> After the people came from the east, they divided Najie into two parts: Lokorwakol, under the great ancestor Orwakol; and Rengen, under

[59] Jie interviews including J 4, 20, 31, and 88. Some informants related a tradition which claimed that Orwakol and Oding were twin brothers. These traditions contradict the great mass of evidence provided by other traditions, both Ngikorwakol and Rengen, in which the arrival of Oding's group of 'Ngikatapa' refugees from the west is related in great detail. The suggestion that Orwakol and Oding were the closest relatives most probably came about as a reflection of the close co-operation which grew up between the two Jie major divisions during the late nineteenth century.

[60] Aringole, J 107. A very large number of hyraxes still inhabit the rock, and although the Rengen do kill hyraxes other than those at Lokatap, the ones at the rock are never harmed in any way and are, as a result, quite tame. The Ngikorwakol have no sacred animals.

extension of the rule of the Reeli group of the Padzulu Madi over the neighbouring Kagiri.

its leader, Oding. The people of both areas took part in the settlement of Najie, but in each area the people had their own customs. It
was discovered that New Fire couldn't be made if they sat together,
and so they moved apart so that they could make New Fire separately.
But you must not suppose that because they moved apart, one group
was the Jie and the other group was not. No! We are all—Ngikorwakol and Rengen—thoroughly Jie.[61]

It is difficult to be certain of precisely in what ways the two groups
remained linked. It is clear that each group's ritual activity was
conducted independently, and it would seem that each was responsible for the dry-season movement of its own livestock. However,
both groups appear to have been known to outsiders by a common
name, *Ngiro* (probably best translated as 'the people of the Longiro
River'), and to have shared as their common emblem the honey
badger or ratel (*ekor*).[62] Both groups also used the sacred clay from
the pit near Daidai for ritual smearing during the most important
ceremonies.

Through mutual influence between the groups, the Koten–Magos
settlers who were the core of the Ngikorwakol major division seem
to have rapidly learned new skills from the Agricultural Paranilotic
Rengen:

> The people who went to the west [from Koten] grew only small gar-
> dens of sorghum before they moved. But when they arrived there
> [in Najie] they learned to be good cultivators and they grew large
> fields of sorghum. They soon learned about other crops, as well.[63]

> When the people went west to Najie they had houses like ours
> [the rough shelters of the Turkana], but when they arrived there in
> Najie they learned to build the good houses which they now live
> in.[64]

The Rengen appear to have been rapidly influenced by the more
pastoral outlook of the Koten–Magos Ngikorwakol. Although even
their own traditions indicate that they were without cattle when they

[61] Lobalong (Joseph) and Kere, J 12.
[62] The emblems of various Karimojong sections are described in detail by
Dyson-Hudson, op. cit., pp. 127–30. The emblematic association of the Jie
with the honey badger is clearly more of a totemic association than is the case
with any of the Karimojong sections. There is a strong Jie prohibition against
killing their emblematic animal, and a major ritual, the *Ekor* ceremony, is
prescribed should a honey badger inadvertently be slain.
[63] Pelekec, Akwawi, Eregai, and Etele, T 7.
[64] Lokuu, Meri, Lomanat, and Lomoru, T 8. These informants indicated that
the Ngikorwakol Jie learned pottery-making after their settlement in Najie.

arrived from the Acholi borderland, by the time of their separation from the Ngikorwakol at Daidai they had clearly acquired livestock, as the traditions of both major divisions make reference to the movement of Rengen herds and to the problems of grazing and watering. The Rengen also appear to have adopted the Ngikorwakol generation set system, and although their initiations were conducted separately, they were invariably to copy the names of the Ngikorwakol generation-sets, and even most age-sets.[65]

While some kind of theoretical co-operation must have existed between the two emerging major divisions at the time of their separation at Daidai, and while each group clearly exerted certain influences over the other, soon after their separation each group embarked on a period of territorial expansion during which they occupied areas roughly equivalent to their present areas of permanent settlement:

> When the people [Ngikorwakol] came from Koten, Orwakol was their leader, and the leader of *ngitalia* [customs], and his people were like the people of one homestead. But then the single seed (*ekinyo mit*) which came from the east was spread all over Najie as the people began to spread from Lokorwakol to all parts of Najie.[66]

While the emigrations of such groups as the Ngiseera, Ngimonia Turkana, and Ngikor Toposa had greatly reduced the population of central Najie, the remaining core of Ngikorwakol clustered near Daidai were obviously concerned about the possibility of overtaxing the resources of that region, and therefore decided that expansion was necessary: 'The Jie remembered the troubles at Koten caused by the lack of water. They saw that there was only a limited amount of water at Longiro and so people decided it was best to settle other areas.'[67] As this tradition indicates, water was the most important of the expansions:

> The Jie territorial divisions were established so that all the people could live near sufficient water. Other considerations were not so important. If they wanted fresh hunting grounds, for instance, they

[65] It seems practically impossible to achieve any understanding of what sort of age-class system the Agricultural Paranilotes may have initially had. Those groups that experienced close contacts with the Koten–Magos elements universally appear to have adopted their generation-set systems. For those groups that were less influenced by the Koten–Magos peoples, such as the Iteso and Langi, it is difficult to deduce anything very meaningful from the descriptions of twentieth-century observers such as Lawrance, Wright or Driberg, all of whom observed those societies at a point when their class systems had already been abandoned.

[66] Loceny (Natwanga), J 83.

[67] Lothike (Elawa), J 131.

could always go out from Najie into the bush to hunt animals, but they needed to have water close to their homes.[68]

While most of the Ngikorwakol settlers pushed out from Kotiang into the southern and eastern parts of Najie, the Rengen settled areas generally to the north-west, in the direction of Lokatap Rock (*see* Map 7). Whatever co-operation existed between the two groups during the initial occupation of central Najie must have decreased to some extent, as their respective settlers drew further apart from each other and from the Daidai area.

Those informants who mentioned the generation-set of the settlers who pushed out from Daidai were almost universally agreed that it was Ngipalajam, the generation-set inaugurated at Koten about 1720, just before the arrival of the 'Ngikatapa' famine refugees. There are indications that by the time of expansions from Daidai these Ngipalajam had become relatively senior men. Many traditions, for example, indicate that this pioneering and settlement of Najie was carried out mainly by groups of kinsmen: small compact clans or lineages, and so references to 'Ngipalajam settlers' may well be to the *leaders* of these groups of agnatically related bands of settlers. In that case, these Ngipalajam leaders would have been relatively senior men, and it would therefore seem likely that the next generation-set, Ngikok, whose initiations began about 1760, was inaugurated just before the settlers began their migrations out from Daidai. Some informants specifically indicated that the Ngikok were initiating at least by the time that some of the more outlying Lokorwakol areas were being settled. Other informants spoke of the 'sons of Orwakol' as the settlers who moved out from Daidai to form the various territorial divisions.[69] Orwakol, who was a senior man even at the time of the migration from Koten to Daidai must have belonged to the generation-set which preceded Ngipalajam,[70] for it is recalled that Loyale (sometimes pronounced 'Loyala' or 'Aoyaleng'), his son and successor, was a Ngipalajam initiate. Although there are no traditions specifically describing Orwakol's death, it

[68] Lobalang (Joseph), Logwela (Gonye), and Lodon (Kapelinyong), J 40.

[69] In most cases, informants used the term 'sons of Orwakol' to mean the whole generation-set which followed that of Orwakol. Two informants, Lodon (Kapelinyong) and Logwela (Gonye), J 3, used the term in a more literal way, stating that 'Orwakol's seven sons founded the seven divisions of Lokorwakol'.

[70] Hardly any informants ventured any opinion on the generation-set to which Orwakol himself belonged. A very few rather tentatively suggested 'Ngisir', but as noted above 'Ngisir' probably refers to a whole epoch, rather than to a specific generation-set.

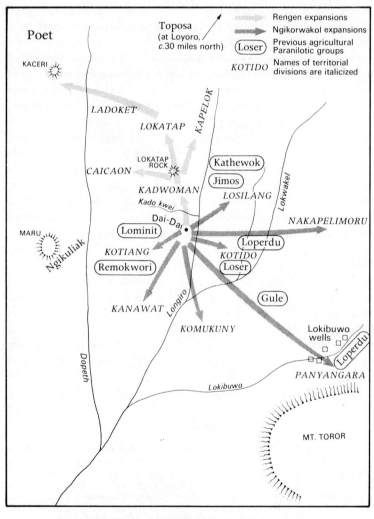

Poet

KACERI

LADOKET

LOKATAP

KAPELOK

Toposa
(at Loyoro,
c.30 miles north)

Rengen expansions
Ngikorwakol expansions
(Loser) Previous agricultural
         Paranilotic groups
KOTIDO   Names of territorial
         divisions are italicized

LOKATAP
ROCK

CAICAON

KADWOMAN

Kado kwei

Dai-Dai

(Lominit)

MARU

Ngikuliak

KOTIANG

(Remokwori)

Kathewok

(Jimos)

LOSILANG

Lokwakel

NAKAPELIMORU

(Loperdu)

KOTIDO

(Loser)

(Gule)

KANAWAT

Longiro

KOMUKUNY

Dopeth

Lokibuwo
wells

(Loperdu)

PANYANGARA

Lokibuwo

MT. TOROR

MAP 7. The settlement of Najie and the establishment
of the territorial divisions.

seems very likely that he died just as the settlers began pushing out
from Daidai to the other parts of Najie some time around 1760.
Loyale appears to have been invested as the new fire-maker before
the Ngikorwakol expansion was properly under way. In order to
prove his succession to his father's office, Loyale submitted himself
to a ritual test:

> After the Ngikatapa [Rengen] had gone to their rock, but when the
> other people [Ngikorwakol] were still at Daidai, the people met
> together at Daidai to decide on their new fire-maker, as Orwakol was
> dead. Loyala, who was my own ancestor, knew that he should be the
> successor of Orwakol, but there were others who wanted to be the
> fire-maker, as well. Each of these people blew air into the vagina of a
> cow in turn, and when Loyala's turn came, he blew and the cow
> immediately fell dead. And the people said, 'Truly, he is the one to
> be our fire-maker'.[71]

According to the traditions and to their 'rank' in the *angola*
ceremony, the territorial divisions of Lokorwakol were established
in the following order: Kotiang (the area of original settlement west
of Daidai), Losilang, Kanawat, Komukuny, Kotido, Panyangara,
and finally Nakapelimoru. All the divisions appear to have been
established within a span of relatively few years, all having been
settled by clan leaders of the Ngipalajam generation-set. This seems
to have been true even for those which were the last to be established,
as a Panyangara tradition indicates: 'My father told me that the
Ngimirio and Ngingatunyo [stated by many informants to have been
age-sets or age-sections of Ngipalajam] were initiated when the Jie
came to Longiro from Koten. When the Panyangara went away from
Longiro to Lokibuwo, they were led by those same Ngingatunyo.'[72]

In all cases, the Lokorwakol territorial divisons appear to have been
settled peacefully, although in the establishment of some divisions,
considerable numbers of pre-existing aliens were encountered and
assimilated by the Daidai pioneers. The largest alien populations
were found in Kotido and Losilang territorial divisions. In Kotido
these were mainly remnants of the Ngiseera group of Agricultural
Paranilotes, most of whom had fled to the west with the arrival of
the Koten strangers. They were absorbed into Kotido division as the
large and important Loser clan. Another alien people of Kotido
were the Ngipeerwo, assimilated as the smaller Loperdu clan, who
were probably another Agricultural Paranilotic group, but without

---

[71] Koroc (Lokepon), J 103.
[72] Lothike (Elawa), J 131.

any tradition of immigration: 'Our ancestors said that we Ngipeerwo were the first clan to dwell here in Kotido. Even the Ngiseera, who came here from the direction of Obote's place [i.e. Lango], found us here when they came. Our fathers said there is no story of the Peerwo coming from any other area.'[73]

Perhaps an even larger alien population existed in Losilang. One of the two Losilang subdivisions, Lojoo, seems to have been entirely descended from this population, dominated by the large and ritually important Jimos clan,[74] with a smaller clan, Kathewok. Like the Ngipeerwo of Kotido, these clans often claim that they have no traditions of immigration, but have 'always lived in Najie'. However, both clans were probably of Agricultural Paranilotic origin,[75] and arrived in Najie from the west, as is indeed indicated by the traditions of other informants of these clans:

> Our people came here from Tobur [Labwor]. We were related to the people there in Tobur, and when our ancestors arrived here in Najie they spoke the language still spoken by the Tobur [a Lwo dialect]. Our people arrived here searching for food before the other Jie came here. When they arrived here from Magos and other places, our ancestors began to mix with them and learned their language.[76]

The Acoli of Adilang (just to the west of the Labwor Hills) also have traditions which refer to this Lojoo group of the Losilang: 'Losilang [in Jie] are known as "Otilang". They lived here first and then moved to Jie-land. It was a man who left Adilang and went to Jie-land to found that clan . . . he spoke Lwo. He went without quarrelling here. The Otilang and Adilang continued to visit each other up until the present.'[77]

Still, as there are no references to specific generation-sets or

[73] Namuya (Ngorok) and Kwenye, J 105.
[74] See below, Chapter VI.
[75] Kathewok is a variation of 'Karewok', one of Tarantino's 'universal clans'. While there is also evidence for a Lwo origin of the Jimos (see Crazzolara, loc. cit. (1960), p. 209), the evidence seems rather stronger that they were Paranilotes who had undergone tremendous Lwo influences (see Webster, 'Acholi Historical Texts', p. 190). Herring has suggested an interconnection between the Nyakwai clans, Kajimo and Ikaruwok, which seems especially significant when we consider that Jimos and Kathewok were so closely associated in Lojoo.
[76] Ngorok (Ekone–Alokol), J 77.
[77] From J. B. Webster's 'Acholi Historical Text No. 63', recorded in 'Acholi Historical Texts', pp. 28–9. However there seems to be some confusion among the Adilang Acoli regarding their connection with the Losilang Jie, and some of Webster's informants claimed that it was a group from Losilang that moved west from Najie to establish the Adilang kingdom.

famines, it is impossible to be certain from either Jie or Acoli traditions exactly when this Lojoo group of Losilang arrived in Najie.
While they may well have been earlier inhabitants of Najie, who
(like the Ngiseera) arrived there during the original migration of the
Agricultural Paranilotes into Karamoja from the north-west, it is
possible that they may have been refugees from the western 'Nyamdere' famine, who entered Najie more or less simultaneously with,
but separately from, the Rengen. Archaeological evidence tends to
support the first hypothesis, for the Jimos homesteads are located
on a great mound which was clearly built up over a long period of
previous settlement and contains great numbers of half-buried deep-
basin grinding stones. The only other mound of a comparable size
in Najie is that upon which the Loser homesteads are built, and so it
seems quite probable that both the Loser and the Jimos represent
groups who have been living at their present locations considerably
longer than other Jie clans. Moreover, some Jie traditions speak of
the Jimos having 'already established their ritual grove at *Moru
Eker*'[78] while the Lokorwakol were still clustered near Daidai, which
again may indicate that the Lojoo group were earlier inhabitants of
Najie.

The other Ngikorwakol territorial divisions appear to have assimilated far fewer aliens during the pioneering of their own areas. The
pioneers of Kotiang territorial division, establishing their homesteads
westwards from the original settlements around Daidai to the Dopeth
River, came into closest contact with the Ngikuliak bands at Maru,
just beyond the Dopeth. Few, if any, Ngikuliak appear to have been
assimilated at this time, however, and the only aliens who appear to
have been absorbed were two small groups of Agricultural Paranilotes: the Remokwori, and part of the clan now called Lominit.[79]
Similarly, during the settlement of Panyangara territorial division,
only another small branch of the same Ngipeerwo who were encountered by the settlers of Kotido, and possibly a tiny group known as
'Gule', were encountered and absorbed. During the initial settlement
of Komukuny, Kanawat, and Nakapelimoru divisions, apparently
no alien groups were encountered, and so the first inhabitants of
these areas seem to have been exclusively Koten–Magos peoples.

Virtually from the moment of its establishment, therefore, almost

[78] Koroc (Lokepon), J 103.
[79] According to Tosh's clan-file, Remokwori is clearly represented in Lango
society as 'Oremakori'. One such Oremakori group is part of the Arak clan,
another of Tarantino's 'universal' clans.

every Lokorwakol territorial division began to emerge as a unit unique and distinct from any other. It would seem highly likely that feelings of loyalty and interdependence grew up very rapidly between the men who pushed out together from Daidai to share the common hardships and adventure of settling a given territorial division. As the settlement of each division was undertaken by a few small compact clans, those feelings of loyalty were to some extent underlined by ties of kinship. Moreover, the divisions had widely different experiences of encountering and assimilating alien populations, ranging from the case of the Losilang pioneers who settled in an area where they encountered a strongly Lwo-influenced population of Agricultural Paranilotes, probably about as numerous as themselves, to the case of the Kanawat who settled an apparently uninhabited area.

In most cases, however, Lokorwakol oral tradition contains disappointingly little information concerning the actual establishment of the various territorial divisions. In no case does there seem to have been any kind of conflict between the Koten–Magos pioneers from Daidai and any alien groups with which they may have come into contact, and in no case is there any indications that any such alien group was removed from its area of habitation by the newcomers. As is borne out by even present-day settlement patterns, the clans of the first Koten–Magos pioneers to move into a new division from Daidai chose for themselves the best of the available settlement sites (usually on a ridge) and the most fertile of the available agricultural land (usually along river or stream beds), but again there is nothing to indicate any infringement on the land traditionally cultivated by pre-existing populations.

In most instances, the absorbed alien populations formed their own separate clans of the new territorial divisions, but in a few cases they appear to have formed a close association with one or another of the Koten–Magos clans of the new settlers. The case of the Loperdu of Kotido provides a good example:

> We Ngipeerwo are sometimes referred to as 'Lokocil', and some people even think that we and the Lokocil clan have one *etal* [are one clan]. However, we have different *ngitalia* and we are not really related at all. Our close association with them came about because when they arrived here they became our neighbours and good friends. We marry each others' daughters. When one of us slaughters an ox, the other comes and shares it.[80]

[80] Namuya (Ngorok) and Kwenye, J 105. The Lokocil were not, in fact, one of the original clans of Koten–Magos origin to settle in Kotido, but were

Convenient natural boundaries between the divisions (usually rivers or streams) seem to have been easily agreed upon, and no instance of conflict caused by any boundary dispute is mentioned in any tradition. The settlement of the new territorial divisions was by all indications so peacefully and smoothly carried out that there was probably little of note to be passed on by the oral traditions to following generations.

The one exception seems to have been the Panyangara territorial division, concerning whose establishment a great deal more appears to have been retained in their traditions than is the case with the other divisions. This is undoubtedly due to a major engineering feat performed by the Panyangara settlers, unparalleled by any of the others. Initially, the Panyangara established themselves some miles south of their present location, at the northern foot of Mt. Toror near the Lokibuwo River. The discovery of the area by the first Panyangara pioneers is said to have taken place in this way:

> When the Jie were all still together [at Daidai], some came south to Lokibuwo and Toror to hunt. There they met some Ngipeerwo living near the big *epeerwo* tree from which they derived their name. The Ngipeerwo showed them it was a good area and so some of the people decided to go and settle there permanently with the Ngipeerwo.[81]

The pre-existing Ngipeerwo had made a discovery which was to be of great importance to the Panyangara settlers from Daidai: 'When the first Panyangara came to Lokibuwo they found that . . . the Ngipeerwo had discovered that there was a great deal of water there, and so those people of Panyangara decided to dig the Lokibuwo wells.'[82] The wells have not been used intensively for over a century and have consequently fallen into considerable disrepair. Nevertheless, a system of water-holes, all heavily silted in, but still up to 12 or 15 feet deep, interconnected by a complex system of channels and canals, is still clearly discernible. Panyangara traditions speak of 'ladders' of six or eight men being formed to hand up hide buckets of water from the wells to waiting herds. The system is all the more remarkable in that Panyangara traditions agree that the excavations were accomplished mainly with wooden digging sticks

[81] Looru (Sampson), J 120.
[82] Lothike (Elawa), J 131.

---

probably Koten–Magos peoples who went first to Dodos before coming to Kotido not very long after its establishment.

and hide buckets.[83] It is hardly surprising, then, that the Panyangara should have retained considerable information concerning the digging of the wells and the concurrent establishment of their territorial division, even the work-song of the Panyangara settlers who dug the wells still being remembered by their descendants:

Ji, o-oh! Lokibuwo tolakar yong!	Oh! Lokibuwo, you will be happy!
Apotu atapapakan.	Your fathers have come.
Apotu ngikonidwe.	Your children have come.[84]

While the Ngikorwakol were thus expanding to the south and east, establishing their territorial divisions, and assimilating alien peoples, the Rengen pioneers were pushing mainly towards the north-west from their ritual centre at Lokatap Rock. The Rengen settlers who remained south of Lokatap Rock, nearest to Daidai, formed Kadwoman territorial division, bordered on the south by the Kadokwei River, which was recognized as the boundary between the Rengen and the Ngikorwakol. Included in that division were the homesteads of Ratai, the Rengen fire-making clan, which were located near the site of the present Cilapus homesteads. The settlements at Lokatap Rock itself, and on to the north, formed Lokatap territorial division. Other Rengen settlers pushed back towards the east, forming Kapelok territorial division, whose eastern boundary was the Longiro River, while other settlers pushed west, forming Caicaon territorial division which was bounded on the west by the Dopeth River. The fifth division, Ladoket, was established north-west of Caicaon, its settlers crossing the Dopeth and pushing steadily northwards in the direction of the Kapeta River (see Map 7).

Unlike many of the Lokorwakol divisions, the Rengen do not appear to have encountered any substantial numbers of pre-existing aliens as they settled their new areas.[85] Some Rengen traditions, however, claim that one of the leaders of the 'Ngikatapa' (some specifically mention Oding), returned to Acholi as the Rengen expansion began in order to recruit additional settlers from his people who had remained in the west despite the Nyamdere famine:

[83] To the best of my knowledge, these are the only deep wells in Karamoja. In comparison to the deep wells of Tanzania Maasai-land, these at Lokibuwo seem like very deep water-holes, though the system of interconnecting channels seems unique.

[84] Lokiru, Acau, and Aupe, J 10. All the Panyangara were adamant that there was no trace of the deep wells before their arrival in the area.

[85] Some traditions (e.g. J 102) speak of some Ngipeerwo inhabiting part of the Kapelok area, but it seems more likely that these Ngipeerwo were immigrants from Kotido who arrived well after the Rengen divisions were established.

'The leader of our people returned to Acholi and collected the rest of our people who had remained there. He brought them back to Lokatap in Rengen where he told them to settle.'[86]

The Rengen soon realized that the areas around Kaceri and Makal to the north-west were by far the best watered and most fertile areas of northern Najie, and large numbers of pioneers, led by the Ladoket, but joined by individuals and families from all the other Rengen territorial divisions, spilled across the Dopeth and pushed on into these areas. As the Rengen vanguard began the settlement of the Kaceri area, they realized that others had been living in that area not long before:

> When the Rengen arrived at Kaceri, they saw grind-stones and circles of flat stones which had been the supports for granaries here at the base of this mountain. The mountain itself was called 'Poet', for the people who had lived here were those same Poet who occupied the whole area from Makal up to the Kapeta River.[87]

These Poet, a splinter group left behind in the wake of the main Agricultural Paranilotic migration into Karamoja from the north-west, were the same people with whom Opio and his 'Ngikatapa' famine refugees had had brief contact on their journey to Koten from the Acholi borderland. They seem to have been a fairly numerous and powerful people, and from the beginning they must have presented a considerable barrier to further Rengen expansions towards the north-west and the Kapeta River.

There are some indications, however, that the Rengen probably did not envisage any immediate threat from their Poet neighbours. Some traditions claim that they were not alone as they expanded to the north, but that 'the Rengen and the Toposa went north together'.[88] Other traditions suggest that the Toposa in fact emigrated to the north some years before the start of the Rengen expansion, but fairly strong bonds between the Ngikor Toposa at Loyoro in Dodos and the Jie appear to have been retained.[89] It seems probable that the Toposa had their closest contacts with the Rengen settlers who were pushing across the Dopeth to the north (*see* Map 7). With the friendly Toposa on their right flank, the Rengen pioneers were probably not much concerned by the presence of the Poet between themselves and the Kapeta River.

[86] Lokayan, J 124.
[87] Lokayan, J 124.
[88] Angura and Koroc (Lopirya), J 101.
[89] See above, p. 120.

By about 1770, as the Ngipalajam initiations were brought to a close and more and more members of the succeeding generation-set Ngikok, were initiated, the emerging Jie (or more properly 'Ngiro') community had already evolved its two major divisions and constituent territorial divisions, and had undergone a period of expansion and settlement in which an area roughly equivalent to present Najie was occupied.

While the expansions of both major divisions were carried out rapidly and peacefully, each expansion was markedly dissimilar from the other. While the Lokorwakol expansion led to the formation of seven divisions, scattered over a fairly large area from the east bank of the Dopeth River in the north-west to the foot of Mt. Toror in the south-west, the Rengen expansion was focused towards one direction only, the north-west, which resulted in the formation of five more compactly grouped divisions. While the Koten–Magos elements who formed the core of the Lokorwakol assimilated considerable numbers of pre-existing aliens, thereby underlining feelings of their own unique and separate identities among many of their territorial divisions, the Agricultural Paranilotic 'Ngikatapa', who were the Rengen, assimilated few, if any, outsiders. Possibly because of this, and very probably because of the stronger unifying factor provided by their more powerful fire-makers, feelings of corporate identity among the Rengen were more strongly focused on the group as a whole, rather than on the constituent territorial divisions.

CHAPTER V

The Jie and their Northern and Western Neighbours in the Late Eighteenth and Early Nineteenth Centuries

THE bickerings of the Koten–Magos peoples, described in Chapter IV, had created two major subdivisions which drifted out to opposite peripheries of their area of concentration. While elements of the northern subdivisions made contact with 'Ngikatapa' famine refugees, and with them moved westwards to Najie to form the core of the Jie community, the southern subdivisions remained clustered in the area from the Magos Hills down to the Apule River (*see* Map 5). Apart from those two major subdivisions, there was also a third group in Karamoja which was composed of basically the same Central Paranilotic-speaking elements. This third group, which ultimately provided the basic elements of the Lokorikituk section of the Dodos, appears to have broken away from the original migration of the Koten–Magos group from the southern Sudan before it actually arrived in its area of concentration at Koten and the Magos Hills. According to many of the Koten–Magos traditions, these Lokorikituk remained in the area from the Napore Hills (north-west of present-day Kaabong township) south-westwards toward the Nyangea Hills (*see* Map 8), where they existed as a community largely independent of the Koten–Magos concentration: 'When the Jie, Turkana, Karimojong, and the others were living at Magos, the [Lokorikituk] Dodos were not with them. They lived in the north and associated with the Napore and Ngikuliak [Teuso]. They obtained their water from the wells at Samuke.'[1]

As the Lokorwakol and Rengen major divisions of the embryonic Jie community began to expand outwards from Daidai, the territorial entity of Najie gradually began to take shape. Except to the north-west, however, where Rengen pioneers pushing across the Dopeth River began to impinge on the fringes of the area occupied by the Agricultural Paranilotic Poet, Najie as yet had nothing even

[1] Ecak (Timothy), J 5.

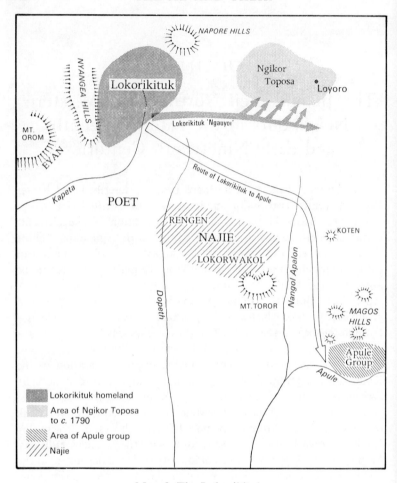

MAP 8. The Lokorikituk.

approaching discernible frontiers. Elsewhere to the north, Jie settlement areas and grazing lands simply gave way to uninhabited bush
country, beyond which, further north, lay the settlements and grazing
areas of the emigrant Ngikor Toposa. Even further north, a series
of events in which the Lokorikituk group played a key role, was to
culminate in the definition of the northern frontier of Najie.

After the departure of the northern subdivision of the Koten–
Magos group to Najie, part of the Lokorikituk are remembered to
have left their homeland and to have travelled south, probably

some time after 1760, eventually joining with the southern sub-division concentrated on the northern banks of the Apule River: 'When the Ngiputiro generation-set was initiating, some of our people left Nyangea and went south to the Apule River. They found the Karimojong living right on the banks of the river and our people joined them.'[2]

The newcomers spent only a very short time along the Apule, and finding conditions not to their liking, they retraced their steps to the north, but now in the company of some of the Apule peoples who were eventually to form the Lomeris section of the Dodos and some divisions of the Toposa:

> Our people went south to the place known as 'Karimojong Rock' near Apule where they settled with the Karimojong. Our people settled there only for a while because they saw that the population at Apule was very large. They decided to return to their homes in the north, and with them came some of those Apule people who were the Toposa.[3]

While part of the Lokorikituk were thus making their sojourn to Apule, the rest of the group remained settled in the old area near Nyangea. Again, the people who were ultimately to form the Ngikor division of the Toposa, having broken away from the Jie settlers at Daidai, established themselves in the Loyoro area of southern Dodos and seem to have been in fairly close contact with the Rengen Jie settlers who were pioneering areas northward from Lokatap Rock.[4] The Lokorikituk at Nyangea began to cast a covetous eye south-eastwards towards the area occupied by these Ngikor Toposa, how-ever, and finally devised a clever stratagem to gain control of that area. An articulate Dodos informant explained how it was accomplished:

> The Dodos were originally settled near Karikalet in western Nyangea. To the south-east of them were the Toposa. The Dodos began sending

---

[2] Lodio (Matayo), Dapala (Musa), and Lobong (Juma), D 6. Karimojong traditions (e.g. BK 2) also recall the arrival of the Lokorikituk from the north.
It seems likely that the migration of the Lokorikituk to the Apule was caused by a famine. In personal communication, J. Weatherby informed me of a Nyangea tradition that they once lived with the 'Dodos' (presumably the Lokorikituk) at Morungole until a famine drove them south-westwards toward the Nyangea Hills from whence it is recalled that the Dodos went on towards the south-east. W. Deshler ('Factors Influencing the Present Population Distri-bution in Dodoso County of Karamoja District', an unpublished paper pre-pared for the East African Institute of Social Research in 1954, p. 4) also mentions a migration of the Nyangea and Napore in the same area.
[3] Longatunymoe (Kasimoto) and Meri (Adunia), D 7.
[4] See Map 8.

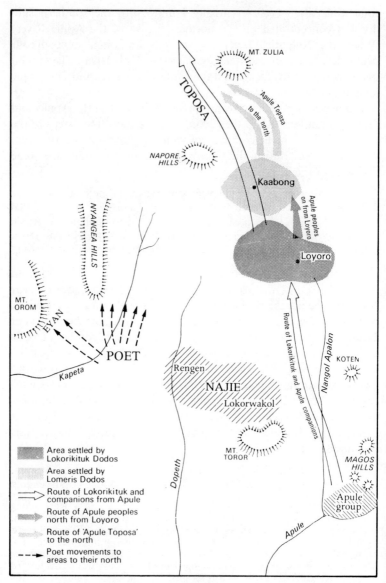

MAP 9. The expulsion of the Toposa and the occupation of Dodos.

their cattle-camps in that direction, and they saw that the cattle which went to these eastern areas became very fat—not like the poor 'Katap' cattle which grazed at Nyangea. When the young men of the cattle-camps returned to Nyangea, they said to the elders, 'The grass is good in the east. Let us, the young men, go back there and test the strength of the Toposa. The Toposa and the Jie are brothers. Let us try to separate them so that we can fight the Toposa by themselves, without having to fight their brothers, the Jie, as well'. And so the young men went back to the east with their cattle, but this time with shields on their arms, and all the women and children were left behind at Nyangea. The young men established cattle-camps at Karwa, Nangoleseme, Longomo, Nagoroete, Narengecoto, Nakuuma, and Lopemu [all located between Nyangea and Lyoro]. Several hundred young men remained in each place. And so, without any war being declared, the Dodos gradually moved in between the Jie and the Toposa. When they were successfully between them, the young men suddenly attacked the Toposa. They captured the Toposa wells at Loyoro, Komokatai, and Loalam. Fighting went on for nearly three years, and then the Toposa began to go away to the north.[5]

The rout of the Toposa appears to have been made complete with the timely arrival from the south of the other Lokorikituk, returning from their southern sojourn, together with their Apule companions. No sooner than this group arrived in the Loyoro area, however, when the Lokorikituk and some of the Apule elements began to quarrel, and some of the latter joined the exodus of the defeated Ngikor Toposa who were streaming northwards past Morungole into the southern Sudan:

After they arrived at Loyoro, those [people who were to become] Toposa who had accompanied our people on the return from Apule began to quarrel. Men became jealous of other men's herds; men became angry if the cattle of others trampled their gardens. And so our people and those Toposa began to fight each other with sticks, and finally they decided to go away to the north.[6]

The Lokorikituk group established themselves in the former Ngikor Toposa homeland around Loyoro, while those Apule peoples who had not quarrelled with them and gone away with the Toposa group moved some miles to the north and established themselves in the area around the present township of Kaabong (*see* Map 9). The two groups, which became the Lokorikituk and Lomeris sections

[5] Lokoel (Musa), D 9.
[6] Longatunymoe (Kasimoto) and Meri (Adunia), D 7.

respectively, thus brought about the first emergence of a Dodos political community and probably just before 1800,[7] had begun the occupation and settlement of much of the present Dodos homeland.

While the genesis of the Dodos and the expulsion of the Toposa was thus going on to their north, the Jie were continuing their occupation and settlement of Najie. The events in the north probably had little effect on most of the Ngikorwakol, whose territories were mainly in the southern and eastern parts of Najie. For the Rengen, however, the replacement of the Toposa by the emerging Dodos community was of greater concern. After the occupation of the Kaceri–Kalomide area, the advance of the Rengen pioneers across the Dopeth River ground to a halt. The traditions recall that beyond Kalomide lay increasingly large numbers of the Agricultural Paranilotic Poet and their Lwo allies, and it seems very likely that the Rengen, now without their Toposa 'brothers' on their right flank were hesitant to continue any determined push north-westwards into the Poet territory towards the Kapeta River.

This is not to imply that there was any overt conflict between the Rengen pioneers and either the Poet or the emerging Dodos at this time. Many traditions indicate that the Rengen (sometimes even accompanied by members of the northern Lokorwakol territorial divisions) did in fact penetrate the Poet territory, not as permanent settlements, but as temporary cattle-camps, to which the basically agricultural Poet allowed access to the important Kapeta watering points:

> After the other people, such as the Turkana and the Ngiseera, went away from Najie, the Jie began looking for places to send their cattle-camps. The Rengen, with some of the Kotiang, began going up to Kapeta to the cattle-camps. Their camps were at Lokapel, Makal, Lolelia, Lomatere, Loberis [all in the direction of the Kapeta River] and such places . . . In those days there was no trouble with the Dodos [Poet] who lived in that area.[8]

It is likely that at this time, both the Poet and the emerging Dodos had temporarily transferred their attentions away from the south and from the Rengen pioneers. The emigration of the Ngikorikituk Dodos from the Nyangea area to Loyoro had created a temporary

---

[7] The difficulty of achieving precise dating for these events is discussed in my London Ph.D. thesis, pp. 274–5.

[8] Adia (Lokongukuyo) and Kojo, J 93. A large percentage of the Poet were eventually to form the third Dodos section, Lokaato, and so, many Jie informants have a tendency to refer to the Poet as 'Dodos'. See Chapter VI.

territorial vacuum to the north-east which the Poet rapidly filled.[9] Similarly, the emerging Lokorikituk and Lomeris sections of the Dodos seem to have been primarily concerned with the settlement of territories largely to the north at this time, and so there was little, if any, pressure along the northern frontier of the Rengen (*see* Map 9). Still, from the very early stages of their northern expansion, the Rengen must have been rather uneasy about the proximity of their two powerful northern neighbours, the Poet and the Dodos.

During their occupation and settlement of eastern and southern Najie, the Lokorwakol territorial divisions came into contact with no numerically powerful or potentially hostile alien groups such as the Poet or Dodos. The alien populations encountered by the Ngikorwakol pioneers were relatively small ones which were rapidly and smoothly assimilated during their expansions. Apparently the only non-assimilated aliens directly contacted by the Ngikorwakol pioneers were some Nyakwai elements encountered by Panyangara cattle-camps which pushed south-westwards from the settlements near the Lokibuwo deep wells: 'The Panyangara cattle-camps used to go from Lokibuwo up to Kopua and Kailong in Nyakwai for grass and water. At first, the Jie and the Nyakwai lived peacefully, without quarrels between them.'[10]

As this tradition states, the Ngikorwakol relations with the Nyakwai appear to have been (at least initially) friendly, and there is absolutely no indication that the Ngikorwakol regarded their numerically weak south-western neighbours as any threat.

Indeed, the only alien group whom the Ngikorwakol regarded as a potential menace were the people known as 'Kapwor', whose settlements, near Katipus mountain west of the headwaters of the Kotidani (or Tikidani) River, were a good 30 miles west of any Lokorwakol territorial division (*see* Map 10). Despite the distance between them, the Ngikorwakol were, from the very early days of the occupation and settlement of Najie, nevertheless keenly aware of the existence of the Kapwor: 'While the Jie were settling this area [Najie], the Kapwor were there in the west at Kotidani. Those Kapwor would

[9] It was probably at this time that some Poet also joined with the Ngieyan Agricultural Paranilotes at Mt. Orom, where they formed the Poot clan. An Eyan informant (Antonio Lokidi, Y 1) mentioned that their arrival was at least partially dictated by a famine and a plague of locusts.

[10] Longoli (Apanyemuge), J 104. Herring ('Origin and Development . . .', p. 9) recorded a Nyakwai tradition which seems to refer to the appearance of these same Jie cattle-camps.

sometimes hold big ceremonies and the dust kicked up by their dances would be seen by the Jie far to the east in Najie. And the Jie would look to the west and say, "There are the Kapwor".'[11]

The Kotidani River area, which was the home of the Kapwor, is one of the best-watered and most fertile areas in central Karamoja. As it lay directly across the main migration route from the Orom pass southwards into Karamoja (see Map 4), it appears to have been a convenient stopping-place for many of the Agricultural Paranilotic- and some of the Lwo-speaking groups which followed that route southwards into Karamoja. Consequently, it is sometimes difficult to describe accurately the composition of the Kapwor group at a given point in time. At some fairly remote date the area may have contained a considerable Ngikuliak population. Some Jie traditions mentioned Ngikuliak settlements in the area, and Ngikuliak informants agreed that some of their ancestors lived at Kiruu cave, a few miles north of Katipus mountain.[12] A great many sherds of 'deep-grooved' pottery found at one Katipus site (which seems clearly separate from other sites in that area) afford some support to these traditions.

Nevertheless, it seems certain that, by the time of the eighteenth-century occupation of Najie by the Ngikorwakol and the Rengen, the Ngikuliak inhabitants of the Kotidani area had been largely, if not entirely, replaced by Agricultural Paranilotic groups from the north. Many Labwor clans were descended from these northern immigrants, and their traditions describe in some detail the arrival of their ancestors from the north:

> The Kapwor came from far to the north, in the Sudan. We were once one people with the Lotuko, and our original language was like theirs. Our present language [a Lwo dialect] was learned from people like the Acoli as we came from the north ... After leaving the Sudan, the Kapwor settled at Tulelo at Didinga, west of Kidepo. There were no people in that area at that time. The Didinga were not yet there. From Tulelo, the Kapwor moved south to Apore, but the Napore people were not there at that time. From Apore, the Kapwor came south to Tikidani [Kotidani] and settled there ... The people who settled at Tikidani were composed of many clans. The Kapwor were the largest clan, however, and so the whole group was known as 'Kapwor'. The Kalanga and other clans were also there.[13]

Some traditions indicate that the Agricultural Paranilotic Kapwor may have been soon joined at Kotidani by some clans which were

[11] Logwela and Kere, J 125.
[12] Lomare, Looru, and Lomugur (Locan), J 78.
[13] Okidi (Simei), L 10.

originally Lwo-speaking. Other traditions state that at least part of
the Loser and (possibly) the Loposa groups of Agricultural Paranilotes, the earlier inhabitants of Najie who fled to the west with the
advent of the Koten immigrants, also joined with the Kapwor at
Katipus mountain during the first half of the eighteenth century:
'Most of our people went west from Nakere water-hole in Kotido
and never returned . . . They went first to Kotidani where they
became one people with the Kapwor before they moved on to *Serer*
[Lango].'[14] Labwor traditions also mention these Ngiseera who
oined the Kapwor from the east: 'The people who came from the
north settled at Tikidani, which is sometimes called "Apwor", and
at Nyanga mountain, which is near by. The people called "Iseera"
also came to that place from the place called "Loser", which is in
Kotido near the [present] prison.'[15]

The traditions agree that the people at Kotidani were basically
agricultural, with sorghum as their main crop, but that they also
owned fairly large numbers of cattle, unlike many other Agricultural
Paranilotic groups. There is also agreement that some of the Kapwor
were skilled blacksmiths and smelters, and that during the occupation
and settlement of Najie by the Ngikorwakol and Rengen, the Kapwor
population at Kotidani was a very large one indeed: 'The Kapwor
were very numerous. They occupied the entire area from Camkok to
Longori, north-west of Katipus mountain, and southwards as far as
Kamorumoru, and westwards as far as Longaro. We cannot be sure
if they were more numerous than the Jie or not, but our ancestors
said that they were truly very many.'[16]

Archaeological investigations in the Kotidani area lent considerable support to the traditions. Visits to the area described in the
preceding tradition confirmed that it was once inhabited by a very
large population (*see* Map 10). Habitation sites appear to be scattered
throughout the entire area, with probably the greatest concentrations
between Katipus mountain and the Kotidani River. In some places
it is impossible to take a step without grinding potsherds underfoot.
Early in 1971 a rapid survey of the southern and eastern slopes of
Katipus was undertaken, and in that area alone (which probably
represents only one corner of the entire site) there were 173 of the
massive deep-basin grinding stones, a large number of circles
of upright flat stones, about thirty cairns (possibly burials), and

[14] Lokwii (Nakeapan) and Lonyala, J 42.
[15] Okeo (Yonasan), L 11.
[16] Logwela and Kere, J 125.

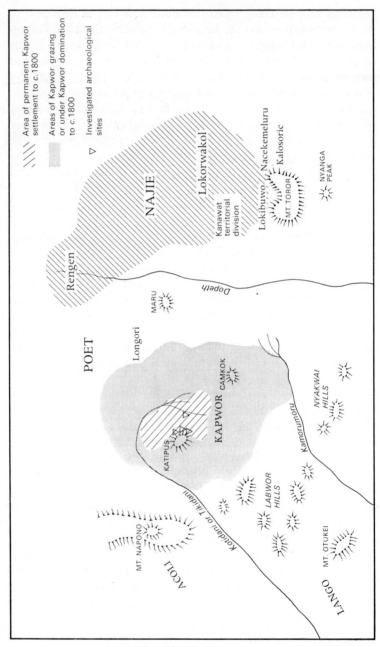

MAP 10. The Kapwor.

three smelting furnaces with accompanying slag-heaps, two of them inside stone circles. Evidence of agricultural terracing and probably man-made channels was also still discernible on the mountain slopes. It would probably be reasonable to estimate that the Kotidani population once numbered several thousand, and a detailed survey of the whole site might indicate an even larger number.

Although the expansion of the Ngikorwakol Jie did not bring them into any prolonged contact or immediate territorial rivalry with these numerically powerful westerners,[17] there were undoubtedly some fears that the Kapwor herds might soon be encroaching on grazing and watering resources claimed by some of the Ngikorwakol territorial divisions. While the permanent settlements of the Kapwor were some distance from Lokorwakol, the grazing lands of the Kapwor cattle lay to the east of the permanent settlements, in the direction of Najie (*see* Map 10).

By about 1770 the second age-set of the Ngikok generation-set was being initiated throughout Najie. The traditions recall that the young men who composed this age-set were a troublesome lot and that the elders had to take steps to castigate them: '[Members of] the second age-set of Ngikok were rude. They insulted the elders and the elders ordered that they should be beaten.'[18]

In obedience to the elders' orders, the senior age-set of the Ngikok fell upon their juniors and administered *ameto* (group punishment) to them in the form of a severe beating with switches. It is important to note, however, that only the Ngikorwakol Ngikok appear to have been involved, and that the Ngikok initiates of the Rengen, still in the process of settling the Kaceri–Kalomide area to the north-west of the Dopeth River, do not seem to have been included. In an attempt to escape further beatings and to recover some of their lost dignity, the junior Ngikok of the various Ngikorwakol territorial divisions fled as a group into the bush. Some traditions recall that the initiates of Kanawat territorial division (the one that lay closest to the Kapwor) led the flight, and certainly the route taken by the fugitives led them westwards from Kanawat. As they wandered in the bush, the temporary outcasts came to the hill which was subsequently named *Camkok*:

---

[17] Some informants claimed that some Kapwor iron was traded to the Jie. While this seems entirely reasonable, there is still nothing to indicate any close or prolonged contact between the two groups.

[18] Mabuc (Loputuke), J 112.

The young men of the Ngikok came to a hill where there was water
and they halted there to drink and to rest. One of them climbed that
hill and looked out to the west. Then he returned to his companions
and said, 'Brothers, come with me for I have seen animals grazing
just to the west. They seem to be elands, but I am not certain, so come
and see for yourselves'. And so all of those Ngikok climbed the hill
and looked to the west. They saw that those animals were not elands,
but the cattle of the Kapwor, who used that area for their pastures.[19]

Although they had not expected to become engaged in any military
conflict and had gone to the bush unarmed, the Ngikok initiates,
noting that the Kapwor herds were only lightly guarded, are recalled
to have immediately siezed the opportunity and raided them:

And so the Ngikok attacked the Kapwor who guarded those herds and
they captured all the cattle. They took the cattle back to Najie re-
joicing, and when the people saw them coming, they were surprised,
and they praised their sons. The Ngikok were well pleased and said,
'Truly, God has been very good to us. Here are all of the cattle of the
Kapwor which we have taken without a real fight'. And so that hill
from which they raided the Kapwor was given the name *Camkok*
[roughly, 'the place which brings good fortune to the Ngikok'] to
honour them.[20]

Although an initial raid may have been made on the Kapwor in
the manner described in the widely known 'Camkok tradition', the
tradition may in fact be a rather truncated recollection of a whole
period of raiding against the Kapwor. Still, Jie traditions do record
only this one raid, and make no mention of any retaliatory raids by
the Kapwor. The Jie therefore, seem to have been the more successful
in whatever conflict went on between the two peoples, and undoubtedly any Jie fears concerning the potential threat posed by the
Kapwor must have diminished after the success (or successes) of the
Ngikok.

The 'Camkok traditions' give considerable insight into an important
aspect of the Jie historical experience: that is, the authority of the
elders, as expressed within the context of the generation-set system.
The nineteenth century was to see the rise of hereditary functionaries
(the fire-makers and war-leaders) whose offices were largely external

[19] Apalodokoro, Lomongin (Julio), and Inua, J 23. These informants differed
from others in claiming that the Ngikok went to the bush, not to escape further
punishment, but because they were commanded to by the elders in order to
search for honey as an added chastisement after their beatings.
[20] Kulomoi (Apaesiyaai), Lowosia (Apaecorod), and Apalopetaa, J 13.

to the generation-set system.[21] Before this time, the generation-set system must have had an extremely important integrative effect on the loose Jie socio-political system, as indeed it still does to some extent even today. While the statements of contemporary Jie elders may tend to idealize the importance of gerontocratic aspects of the Jie political structure in the past, the oral traditions do make it clear that while the authority of the elders was primarily ritual, in some instances that authority decidedly verged on the political.

To the Jie, seniority can be achieved only within the context of the generation-set system. Biological age in itself is not sufficient.[22] As the men of a given age-set advance in seniority, they are thought to 'grow closer to God', and the authority which they steadily accrue is thought to be directly derived from this supernatural source. The surviving members of the most senior sets in existence at any point in time therefore command the greatest respect and obedience, in direct proportion to their closest proximity to God:

> The age-sets of the oldest men have the most power. That is because they have grown close to God (*Akuj*) over many years. They can truly bless the people. Even if they become foolish and speak like children, still they are wise, because they are the oldest age-sets. Until they die, they are the most powerful.[23]

The Jie system, then, is a truer gerontocracy than is the case with the class systems based on time of many other East African societies. Other societies, including even the southern neighbours of the Jie, the Karimojong, whose generation-set system seems in many other ways very close to the Jie, make it mandatory that elders 'retire' once they achieve a given seniority within the framework of their system.[24] With the Jie, however, there is no such notion of 'retirement' of elders, and they are highly critical of those societies, such as the Karimojong, who practise such 'retirement':

> When Karimojong elders become very old men they just stay at home and sleep. We don't do things that way. With us the oldest men—those of the most senior age-sets—continue to lead the prayers and make decisions until they die. For the oldest men to be excluded would spoil everything. If elders are made to stay at home they become very sad and sleep all the time, and soon they die.[25]

[21] See below, Chapters VI and VII.
[22] See Gulliver, *Art Organization of lhe Jie*, pp. 148 and 165; also Dyson-Hudson, op. cit., p. 181.
[23] Mabuc (Loputuke), J 112.
[24] Dyson-Hudson, op. cit., pp. 193–4.
[25] Kere and Meron, J 64. My Jie research assistant was quite appalled on

Even after their 'sons'', generation is elevated to elderhood, the survivors of the senior Jie generation-set continue to wield authority and are still considered the 'true elders'. In 1963, for example, when the Ngimugeto generation-set was raised to elderhood by the surviving Ngikosowa elders in a 'promotion' ceremony, those Ngikosowa by no means relinquished any of their authority:

> The ceremony to promote [*akitopolor*, to raise up] the Ngimugeto was held at about the same time that our grandsons, the Ngitome, began their initiations. The Ngikosowa and Ngimugeto went to Nayan [ritual grove] where many oxen were sacrificed. The Ngikosowa were on one side and the Ngimugeto on the other. Then the Ngikosowa blessed their sons [the Ngimugeto] and raised them up and told them, 'Come! Sit here on this side with us. Be elders.' But those Ngimugeto were not really able to do anything after this ceremony that they could not do before. The Ngikosowa still have the power [*apedor*], and we shall have it until we are all dead. The Ngimugeto must still ask our permission before they can do things.[26]

From the moment of their initiation, when they are given a ritual beating by members of the age-set immediately senior, men are constantly and acutely aware of the authority and powers of those senior to themselves in the generation-set system. Until an age-set junior to themselves is formed, the most recent initiates perform the more menial tasks on ritual occasions, collecting firewood and sorghum stalks, and roasting the sacrificial animal on an open fire. This last job is made even more difficult by the incessant badgering and orders hurled at them by all the senior age-sets. On such occasions their obedience is constantly tested by senior men who give the junior age-set minute shreds of meat to roast, the loss of which can cause punishment to be meted out to the entire age-set. On the other hand, patient obedience is rewarded by gifts of choice pieces of meat handed back to the junior men by their seniors. As the most

---

[26] Dodoi (Lokwangiro), Longoli (Apariong), and others, J 88.

Ngimugeto informants always readily acknowledged that although they themselves were elders (*ngikaskou*), they were also 'those in the middle', and that their 'fathers', Ngikosowa, were still the 'big people of the land'.

Nevertheless, seniority with its coincident authority is often relative to a given situation. As Gulliver, op. cit. (1953), p. 157 has noted, it is sometimes possible for a man to be very senior within his own kinship group or neighbourhood, and still relatively junior within the framework of the generation-set system as a whole.

---

several occasions during our interviews among the Karimojong at the lack of respect shown by even fairly young men to some of the aged 'retired' elders who served as informants.

junior men are thus playing their menial role during rituals, the most senior men demonstrate their supernaturally derived powers and their proximity to God, by leading the prayers and in general supervising the ceremonies upon which the Jie community relies for its well-being.

While the seniority and authority of the elders is thus demonstrated most clearly on ritual occasions, it is often impossible to draw any clear distinction between the authority of Jie elders which is expressed only within a ritual context, and that which finds practical expression in some other, non-ritual, sphere.[27] For example, the annual *akiwodokin* ceremony performed by each territorial division to 'free the cattle' for their departure to the dry-season cattle-camps, the senior elders demonstrate their ritual authority by acting as supervisors and by lightly beating and spattering with clay the representatives of each clan as they pass through an improvised gate. While their authority is thus symbolically expressed within a ritual context, it clearly can be seen to extend into the economic sphere, viz. by effectively controlling the movement of livestock. In the words of the Jie:

> Before the young men go to the cattle camps, an *akiwodokin* . . . ceremony is held. It is conducted by the oldest men [senior elders] who beat them and throw clay at them. This is to show that the oldest men have the power. They do this so that the young men will know they must return when the elders call them . . . Thus, it is the oldest men who decide how cattle should move, even though they remain at the homesteads and do not themselves go to the cattle-camps.[28]

In other ways the expression of the elders' authority is constant, especially in the regulation of privileges extended to junior age-sets. Many of these privileges concern the wearing of certain head-dresses and ornaments:

> When the sons of a generation-set are initiated, that generation-set is usually given permission by their own fathers to grow their hair and to fashion the mudded head-dress (*emedot*) . . . [Before that time, they] cannot wear the mudded head-dress, but only the red hair-bag (*atokot*) . . . The young men must obey the elders and wear only what they are told.[29]

[27] Cf. A. R. Radcliffe-Brown (in Fortes and Evans-Pritchard, eds. *African Political Systems* (London, 1940), p. xxi), 'In Africa it is often hardly possible to separate, even in thought, political office from ritual office'.

[28] Lobalong (Joseph), Logwela (Gonye), and Lodon (Kapelingyong), J 40.

[29] Loporon (Cila) and Munyes, J 94.

Each generation-set wears only certain ornaments and feathers. For example, we Ngimugeto wore red feathers at first, but then our fathers, Ngikosowa, ordered us to stop wearing them and we obeyed. We asked them for their permission to wear black feathers, and finally they agreed. They also ordered us to stop wearing 'red iron' [copper] ornaments and told us to wear 'yellow iron' [brass]. We were also forbidden to wear ivory bracelets.[30]

There are indications that before the rise of the hereditary functionaries in the nineteenth century the powers of elders, as derived from their senior status in the generation-set system, were of considerable importance with the more purely judicial and political spheres. Some informants recalled, for instance, that the elders were once able to order the cessation of internecine quarrels:

> Long ago, the elders could stop a fight merely by drawing a line in the sand and telling the young men who were fighting to sit down quietly on their own side of the line. In those days people obeyed the elders because they were greatly respected. They were much more respected and feared than is the Government nowadays. After the young men stopped fighting and sat down, the elders would take the case to the fire-maker, and long ago, the elders could even judge the case themselves.[31]

Other informants stated that, before the rise of Loriang, the great Jie war-leader, in the late nineteenth century, military affairs were largely under the control of the elders:

> In the time before Loriang, the war-leaders used to go to the elders to ask their permission to attack such and such a place. They would bring the elders gifts of tobacco, milk, or *emuna* [a mixture of honey and meat], so that the elders might bless them, saying, 'Go! Let the enemy sleep. They will not see you until your army is already upon them'. Diviners did not play any important part in the preparations for war. It was the elders who were important. They were like gods. They decided which places to attack. They were the ones who smeared the warriors with light-yellow clay.[32]

With the death of a fire-maker, it was the elders who chose his successor, a right which they continued to exercise even during the

---

[30] Mabuc (Loputuke), J 112. For the wearing of brass and copper ornaments by alternate generation-sets among the Karimojong, see Dyson-Hudson, op. cit., p. 157; and for the Pokot, see J. G. Peristiany, 'The Age-set System of the Pastoral Pokot', *Africa*, 21, 3 (1951), 290. It is unclear whether exactly the same custom was adhered to by the Jie.

[31] Dodoi (Lokwangiro) and Longoli (Apariong), J 88.

[32] Lobalong (Joseph), Logwela (Gonye), and Lodon (Kapelinyong), J 40.

early and mid-nineteenth century when the importance and authority of the fire-makers was at its height:

> The old men—the elders—choose the new fire-maker. They come from every territorial division to Looi [ritual grove] where they have a big meeting. When they have decided, the old men return to their own territorial divisions where they have their own ceremonies to announce to the people who has been chosen. And the people say, 'Truly, our fathers have chosen wisely'.[33]

It is clear that the authority and powers of the elders, although largely expressed in a ritual situation, were not confined exclusively to ritual matter, but were of economic, judicial, and political relevance, as well. As to the manner in which they command the obedience and respect of their juniors, Gulliver has stressed that the elders, having grown close to God, rely upon supernatural sanctions to uphold their authority. In Gulliver's words, disobedience to the elders is 'a sacrilege, with punishment from the High God',[34] and Jie informants agree that supernatural sanctions, in the form of curses (or, nearly as severe, the withholding of blessings) were indeed an important means by which the elders traditionally have wielded their authority: 'If the young men disobey the elders in any way, or if they refuse to return with the cattle from the cattle-camps, the elders can curse them. If the young men are very disobedient, the elders can say to them, "Let all of you die! Let all of the cattle with you die".'[35]

The informants were equally in agreement, however, that the elders also traditionally relied on other, more secular, sanctions to uphold their authority:

> These days, it is the Government that forces the young men to return from the cattle-camps. But in the past, it was the elders who ensured that they would return. It was the elders who ordered the young men to do all things. If the young men disobeyed their 'fathers', they could be cursed and forced to slaughter an ox in payment. Then they would be forgiven. If they disobeyed a second time, the elders could say to the age-mates of those disobedient ones, 'Your brothers have disobeyed us!'. The disobedient ones would then be beaten by their fellows and brought to the elders where they would kill another ox. And they would be forgiven. If even a third time they disobeyed, again they were beaten and killed yet another ox. But if they

[33] Logwee, J 56.

[34] Gulliver, op. cit. (1953), p. 161. Gulliver still maintains that the authority of the elders was strictly within the ritual sphere and did not extend into other areas. This remains as a point of disagreement between us.

[35] Lobalong (Joseph), Logwela (Gonye), and Lodon (Kapelinyong), J 40.

disobeyed again, the elders would let them go their own way, without blessings.[36]

On some occasions, beatings and fines would be administered to only a single offender, but at other times an entire age-set was punished, in retribution for an offence committed by some or all of its members. Such group punishment was called *ameto*, and was usually meted out by a senior age-set of the same generation as the offenders, upon orders from the elders:

> In the past, if young men disobeyed the elders, or if they were rude, or if they sat on their elders' stools or 'stole' [wore] their ornaments, the elders would order them to be beaten and driven from the villages into the bush where they would remain until they got oxen to slaughter for the elders. This was *ameto*. The elders would usually order the next older age-set to beat the age-set of those who had done wrong. When I was young, my own age-set, Ngimoru [of Ngikosowa], was beaten by Ngidewa [also of Ngikosowa]. We feared them.[37]

The authority of the elders, then, as demonstrated with recourse to the physical sanctions of *ameto*, was clearly the underlying factor that brought about the largely accidental raid by the chastized Ngikok on the Kapwor herds. Their authority may well have been expressed in a military context following this raid, by the elders' giving organization and direction to a whole series of raids, now incapsulated by the one 'Camkok tradition'. In any case, such organization and direction was clearly provided by the elders in other military conflicts in the years following the Camkok raid.

The Camkok raid also demonstrates the important integrative function provided by the generation-set system. Membership of a generation-set clearly cut across and transcended membership of the segmentary clans and territorial divisions, and on an occasion such as the Camkok raid, allowed a degree of socio-political cohesion sufficient for corporate participation by members of the seven Lokorwakol territorial divisions in the achievement of a common goal.[38] The exclusion of the Rengen Ngikok initiates, on the other hand, underlines the independent operation of each major division's

---

[36] Alinga, Lowot, Lothigiria, and Narecom, J 41.

[37] Lobalong (Joseph), J 130. A fairly close parallel to the Jie *ameto* may have existed in the whip fights between Iteso age-sets, as described by Lawrance (op. cit. (1957), p. 75) and Wright ('Notes on the Iteso Social Organization', p. 71).

[38] See Gulliver, op. cit. (1953), pp. 166–8, for his discussion of the importance of the generation-set system in the social integration of the Jie.

generation-set system, and strongly suggests that such cohesion was practically expressed only on the level of the major division, and not on the level of the 'Ngiro' community as a whole. Furthermore, although the Rengen generation-set system seems to have been, like the Lokorwakol system, an integrative factor, the cohesion which existed between the five Rengen divisions may have derived more strongly from their more compact territorial organization and, perhaps even more important, from their more powerful fire-makers. The traditions recall that shortly after the successful raiding of the Kapwor cattle, western Karamoja was beset by another terrible famine, caused by a prolonged drought similar in proportion and effect to the Nyamdere perhaps eighty years before.[39] Like the Nyamdere, this famine, remembered in Acoli tradition as the 'Laparanat', most seriously affected the more agricultural peoples along the Karamoja–Acoli borderland, and again like the Nyamdere, caused considerable population movement in that area.[40] One of the most badly affected of these western groups was the Kapwor who, with their cattle already lost to the Ngikok, now were faced with a total crop failure, and were forced to abandon their vast Kotidani sites:

> The people at Tikidani had no root crops. Their food was grain, mainly sorghum. When the drought came all the sorghum died and the people were left with no food at all. The only thing they could do was to disperse and search for wild fruits. The Iseera who were there left first and went west towards Otukei. There they had another famine and they went on to Lango. Other people went to Paicam in Acholi. The Paibwor [clan] settled at Pajule near Kitgum [in Acholi], the Pajima settled at Labongo at Kitgum, and the Jo-langa settled at Gulu [in Acholi].[41]

[39] Jie traditions recall that the famine occurred after the Camkok raid, but still during the time of the Ngikok initiations, and therefore some time between about 1770 and 1800. From genealogies collected during his work in eastern Acholi, Webster, in personal communication, estimated that the famine occurred some time during the last two decades of the eighteenth century, and in the tables at the end of his 'Acholi Historical Texts', estimated that the effects of the famine were being felt in eastern Acholi between 1787 and 1814. From genealogical reckonings made during his work with the Tepes, Weatherby, in personal communication, estimated that the famine occurred in the 1780s.

[40] While the matter is far from clear, some groups may also have emigrated from Najie at this time. For a discussion of these groups, see p. 305 of my London Ph.D. thesis.

[41] Okeo (Yonasan), L 11. The arrival in eastern Acholi of these Kapwor refugees from the Laparanat seems to be generally recalled in Acoli tradition; see for example Webster, 'Acholi Historical Texts', p. 46.

The Ngiseera refugees from Kotidani, pushing westward through the Labwor Hills, are remembered to have joined with 'other Ngiseera' (probably those who followed a different route from Najie to Otukei) and 'Miiro' (probably a group that branched off from the original Agricultural Paranilotic migration from the southern Sudan) peoples whom they found living in the Mt. Otukei area already and, after a second famine (or perhaps really a continuation of the Laparanat), pushed further west into eastern Lango. Observers of the Lango, such as Driberg, Crazzolara, and more recently Tosh,[42] are in agreement that by about 1800 large numbers of proto-Lango immigrants were streaming westwards from Otukei into the eastern parts of the area they now occupy, and it can be reasonably suggested that the catalyst which directly triggered off this immigration was the Laparanat and the consequent arrival at Otukei of considerable numbers of refugee Ngiseera and Kapwor from the populous Kotidani sites.

By the time of their emigration westwards, the Agricultural Paranilotes had already experienced close Lwo contacts over a long period. Many of their groups were bilingual in both Lwo and Paranilotic dialects and almost all had developed an intensive agricultural specialization. This picture is further supported by the traditions related by Tosh's Lango informants, which recalled that when their ancestors were in the Otukei area, they were already Lwo-speaking (although bilingualism was to continue to some extent after the movement westwards from Otukei) and that they knew of a variety of crops, many of which were unknown to the Jie and other peoples further east.[43] For more than a quarter of a century, scholars including Driberg, Tarantino, and Ogot,[44] have sought to find a solution to the complex problems concerning the ethnic make-up of the Lango, and how, where, and when the Langi evolved their Lwo dialect and agricultural specialization. The key to such problems must lie in first understanding the historical experience of the Lwo-influenced Agricultural Paranilotic groups who, streaming westwards out of Karamoja to escape the effects of the Laparanat, provided major elements of the emerging Lango. The solution to the Lango problems lies, not in Lango, as most of the previous observers have thought, but rather east of Mt. Otukei, in western Karamoja.

---

[42] Driberg, op. cit., p. 31; Crazzolara, loc. cit. (1960), 200; Tosh, op. cit., p. 19.

[43] Tosh, op. cit., p. 15.

[44] Driberg, op. cit., pp. 23–32; Tarantino, 'Notes on the Lango'; Ogot, op. cit., pp. 48–62.

Not all of the refugees from Kotidani emigrated west, however, and a few, desperate in the face of famine, fled to the east towards Najie. As with the Nyamdere two generations before, Najie does not seem to have been as badly affected by the drought as the Acholi borderland. The balanced economy steadily evolved by the 'Ngiro' community during its period of pioneering and settlement protected its people from the worst effects of the famine, allowing them to rely on their livestock until sufficient rain returned for a sorghum crop to be planted. Still, the Laparanat undoubtedly caused considerable hardships for the people of Najie, and the reception given to the first of the Kapwor refugees was a hostile one indeed:

> The famine was so great that some of the Kapwor were even forced to go to Najie where the sorghum was growing again. There the Jie killed them and stuffed their mouths with the green sorghum, saying, 'You see! Those people are thieves who came here to steal our grain; so let them eat it!'.[45]

Some of those Kapwor refugees who went westwards from Kotidani may have included a large group under a leader called Odanga who stayed briefly among the eastern Acholi kingdoms before turning south and entering the Labwor Hills, although this is by no means certain.[46] Others, including part of the Ngiseera and Loposa groups of Agricultural Paranilotes who had abandoned central Najie to the Koten strangers nearly a century before, retraced their steps eastwards from Otukei, back towards Najie. While the Ngiseera made for the Kotidani sites, most of the Loposa seem to have passed to the south and entered the settled areas of Najie itself. By this time the drought which had caused the Laparanat was over and the worst effects of the famine had passed. The Ngiseera who attempted to re-establish themselves at Kotidani, however, found that the area had been occupied by others during their sojourn at Otukei: 'At Otukei, the Ngiseera split up. Most went west to Serer [Lango], but others, together with some of the Loposa, turned again towards Najie. When they came again to Kotidani they found that Acoli people had settled there while they [the Ngiseera] were at Otukei.'[47]

---

[45] Okec (Ruben), Angole, and Lojok, L 1.

[46] From rather sparse genealogical data from Labwor, I initially assumed that Odanga's group was most probably one of those displaced by the Laparanat. Herring, however, is of the opinion that the traditions I collected describe earlier dispersals brought about by the Nyamdere famine in 1720. As Herring has far more corroborative data from both Labwor and Acholi sources, his interpretation is probably more correct.

[47] Lokong (Israel), J 97.

As this tradition indicates, these newcomers were western people, basically Lwo in ethnic as well as linguistic affiliation, from the kingdoms of eastern Acholi, who had fled to the east after an internecine quarrel in their eastern Acholi homeland and had arrived in the Kotidani area, recently vacated by the Kapwor:

> My ancestors belonged to the Acoli clan Pajimu. There was a dance at which one of my ancestors killed a member of the Komongo group [of the Acoli], and the Komongo took revenge by killing two of our people. Our people retaliated, killing ten Komongo. Then they ran away to the east to Kotidani, and when they saw the Ngiseera or Miro coming from the west, they joined with them ... We have now become the Ngikaloding sub-clan of Sinotoi, but we were originally Acoli people. Even now our clan observances include a song to remind us of our Acoli ancestors:
>
> | Eur, eur, Katapa | Smelling, smelling [of] Katapa |
> | Ngokosi kinei, eur Katapa | Our goats, smelling [of] Katapa |
> | Ngakosi tuk, eur Katapa | Our cattle, smelling [of] Katapa |
>
> When we sing of 'Katapa', it refers to Acoli. We still use sim-sim to entice our new-born babies to suckle, as did our Acoli ancestors.[48]

The Ngiseera and the Acoli newcomers were almost immediately joined by another Lwo group which arrived at Kotidani from the west. These people, having suffered considerably during the Laparanat in their eastern Acholi homelands, appear to have been searching for a new land in which to settle:

> My clan is now called 'Kapor' because it was once settled at Tikidani. Originally my ancestors came from Paicam in Acholi. They were driven by hunger from Acholi to Tikidani where they found the Ngiseera, who had arrived there from the west, and people called 'Kapor' [the Acoli group described in the preceding tradition], who had come from Acholi. The older Ngiseera could speak a language like Ajie, which was their original language, but their young people were all speaking Acoli. Our people joined those at Tikidani, and we became known as 'Kapor', too. The people lived all over the Tikidani area, but the Ngiseera stayed on one side and the people who had come from Acholi stayed on the other. Both groups got their water from the Tikidani wells.[49]

Although the traditions are rather vague as to the reason, this new population did not remain long at Kotidani, but began moving again towards the east and Najie.[50] Most Jie informants agreed that this

---

[48] Lokec (Lomorumoe) and others, J 49 and 96.

[49] Akejan, J 71.

[50] Most traditions list 'hunger' or a 'lack of water' for the move, and it is possible that the last effects of the Laparanat may have still been felt in the west.

move was undertaken after the Ngisiroi generation-set, or even more specifically the Ngimadanga age-section of Ngisiroi, had begun their initiations. Figure 3 shows that the second age-section of Ngisiroi would have been initiating from about 1810, and so the worst effects of the Laparanat were by this time probably at least a decade in the past, and normal conditions once again prevailed in Najie. The migrants soon encountered Jie cattle-camps which had moved west to occupy the former grazing lands of the dispersed Kapwor. Unlike the reception given to the Kapwor starvelings who had arrived in Najie some years earlier when the effects of the Laparanat were still very much in evidence, these Ngiseera and Acoli immigrants were well received, first by the cattle-camps and finally by even the settled population of Najie. The Ngiseera were welcomed by their cousins who had remained behind in Najie and had become the Loser clan of Kotido, while the Loposa returned to their previous homes in what had become Komukuny territorial division, where they joined with the numerically small Lodera, a clan of Koten–Magos origin. Even the arrival of Acoli 'Kapwor', who had no previous ties with Najie, was at least tolerated by the Jie. Most of them went to the northern foot of Mt. Toror, where they settled at Nacekemeleru, Kalosoric, and Locarangikapor on the periphery of the Panyangara settlements clustered near the Lokibuwo deep wells. From their Toror homes, the newcomers gradually strived to forge a closer relationship with the Panyangara. In one instance, a whole group of these Acoli Kapwor soon joined with their Panyangara neighbours: 'After the Kapwor came from Kotidani to Nacekemeleru, some came to Lokibuwo where they joined with the Loperdu, the same people who had first discovered the water at Lokibuwo.'[51]

In other instances, individual Kapwor made an independent effort for closer integration with the Jie: 'A Kapwor might become friends with a Jie and perhaps go with his friend to raid the cattle of some enemy. Those cattle would be used to build up his [the Kapwor's] herd, and with them he could marry Jie wives. That is how the Kapwor came to be Jie.'[52]

[51] Lothike (Elawa), J 131.
[52] Dodoi (Lokwangiro), J 89.

Other traditions claim that the move was caused by Acoli attacks, but it is very likely that these traditions were confusing these 'Kapwor' with the Jie famine refugees of nearly a hundred years later, who most certainly did experience conflicts with the Acoli.

The Acoli Kapwor and the Lwo-influenced Ngiseera clearly injected yet another western 'Katapa' element into the emerging Jie community. Unlike the earlier 'Ngikatapa', the Rengen, who had formed their own largely separate and independent division, these immigrants diffused themselves amongst several of the Lokorwakol territorial divisions which had previously been mainly composed of Koten–Magos clans. The Kotidani immigrants brought with them a variety of western animals and crops, previously unknown, or at least little used, in Najie:

> When those 'Miro' [Ngiseera and Loposa] returned here from the west with those Kapor, they spoke both Ajie and *akibinibini* [Lwo]. They brought with them the first hens and a new type of sheep with long tails. They also knew of many new crops: sim-sim, groundnuts, sweet potatoes and cow-peas, which they began planting in Najie. Before this time, the Jie had only sorghum, *ngadekele* [a kind of pumpkin], and cucumbers.[53]

In addition, both the Ngiseera and the Acoli immigrants were skilled in an art not practised by any of the Jie, but which was quickly abandoned once they settled amongst the 'Ngiro':

> When they were at Tikidani, both the Ngiseera and the Kapor of Acholi knew how to make iron. Have you not seen their smelting furnaces there? The Ngiseera could make iron when they came to Tikidani from the west [from Otukei]—the Kapor did not teach them. When the people left Tikidani to come to live in Najie, they stopped making iron. When they were at Tikidani they had no cattle, but when they came to Najie, they acquired cattle and therefore stopped making iron.[54]

The case of the Kotidani immigrants was paralleled by that of some of the pre-existing Agricultural Paranilotic groups of Najie, absorbed during the Jie genesis during the earlier part of the eighteenth century. Like the Kotidani peoples, some of the earlier Agricultural Paranilotic inhabitants of Najie are recalled to have originally possessed the art of iron-smelting, but to have abandoned it when they were assimilated into 'Ngiro' society with its emerging balanced economy, in which transhumant pastoralism played so important a role. It was soon discovered that the management of transhumant herds and a permanent forge was exceedingly difficult: 'At first some of the people of Najie could make their own iron, but

53 Lokec (Lomorumoe) and Arini, J 96.
54 Akejan, J 71.

then they stopped. They found that a man cannot work bellows if he is herding cattle.'[55]

The Koten–Magos peoples were never iron-makers. It is difficult to be certain of exactly when they were first introduced to iron implements, but the first recollections of iron in their oral traditions is that obtained while they were still concentrated in the Koten–Magos area from the Agricultural Paranilotic Ngieyan of Mt. Orom.[56] According to their own traditions, the Ngieyan claim that they were the original iron-smelters in northern and central Karamoja, and that they were responsible for teaching other Agricultural Paranilotic groups the art.[57]

Be this as it may, just before their early eighteenth-century dispersal at Koten, the proto-Jie elements of the Koten–Magos group were obtaining iron from other Agricultural Paranilotic groups which had arrived on the Nangol Apalon River from the west as part of the 'Ngikatapa' exodus from the Nyamdere. Other Jie traditions claim that the Koten–Magos peoples were obtaining iron from the west even well before their dispersal: 'When the people were at Koten, the Ngiseera or Ngimiro lived here in Najie. They were iron-making people and so the people of Koten used to obtain spears and other things from them.'[58]

During the evolution of the 'Ngiro' community and its occupation and settlement of Najie during the latter part of the eighteenth century, by far the most iron was coming in from the west, and although some Rengen groups continued to obtain iron from the Ngieyan, that northern source declined considerably in importance. The chief western supplier of iron was the emerging Labwor community, a heterogenous collection of Agricultural Paranilotic clans, influenced to various degrees by their contacts with the Lwo, with a leavening of elements which were Lwo in ethnic as well as linguistic affiliation. Many of those who settled in the Labwor Hills were skilled smelters and smiths, and because the Labwor economy, unlike that of the Jie, was based almost exclusively on sedentary cultivation, the emerging Labwor found it quite convenient to maintain permanent forges, which could be readily supplied with the charcoal obtainable from the forests which covered many of the hills. Except for the Camkok raid against the Kapwor and the hostile

[55] Longok (Erisa), J 1.
[56] Interviews including J 109 and 124, T 14, B K 5, 7, and 8.
[57] Lokidi (Antonio), Y 1.
[58] Mabuc (Loputuke), J 85.

reception given to the first of the Laparanat refugees, Jie relations
with all the various western elements from which the Labwor community derives were basically good. After Laparanat, relations
between the Jie and Labwor steadily improved until a close interdependence and co-operation grew up between the two peoples.

The basis of this close relationship was the iron trade. Although
a few small deposits of rather inferior iron ore existed in the Labwor
Hills, the largest deposits of good quality ore in Central Karamoja
were located at Mt. Toror. From an early date the Labwor seem to
have made use of the Mt. Toror ore, although the mountain and its
mines came firmly under the control of the Jie during their occupation and settlement of Najie during the latter part of the eighteenth
century. The Panyangara territorial division of the Ngikorwakol
established itself at the Lokibuwo deep wells and the northern foot
of Toror, just below the mouth of the great central valley of the
mountain in which the largest iron deposits were located. Moreover,
the cattle-camps of the Panyangara and some of the other Ngikorwakol divisions ranged the plains between the Labwor Hills and
Toror. Their control over the raw material ensured that the Jie
would be the favoured customers of Labwor smiths, a fact which
was to be of critical importance during the Jie fight for survival
during the second half of the nineteenth century. The Jie never had
the inclination (nor perhaps the ability) to mine the ore themselves,
and it was always the Labwor who regularly sent mining parties up
into the mountain. In accord with the friendly relations growing up
between the two peoples, the Jie who occupied the Labwor route to
the mountain made the miners' journey as easy as possible: 'The Jie
never charged us any tolls to pass through their country or to dig at
the mountain. The Labwor would always have many friends among
the Jie and they would often spend the night with their Jie friends
on their way to and from the mountain.'[59]

Toror itself was uninhabited, except for a band of Fringe Cushitic-
speaking Tepes who occasionally came from their settlements at
Nyanga peak south of Toror to camp in the caves high up on the
mountain. The Labwor, realizing that the mountain had very little
permanent water, never made any serious attempt to form a colony
there, and although from time to time individual smiths constructed
smelting furnaces near the iron mines, most of the ore was loaded
into leather sacks and carried by the miners back to their own
country, where they were met on the frontiers by Labwor women

[59] Okidi (Simei), L 10.

who would carry the sacks the remaining distance.[60] Although every Labwor clan seems to have included both smelters and smiths, some individuals were more intensively engaged in the manufacture of iron goods than others, and by the late eighteenth century at least some kept a ready stock of ironware on hand for their Jie customers: 'There were some men who were especially expert in making spears and other iron goods. These lived almost entirely by their skill. They always kept a number of spears or hoes or axes on hand in their homes where the Jie could come and choose the things they wanted.'[61]

Other Labwor blacksmiths would make itinerant journeys to Najie, hawking their wares from settlement to settlement. Such journeys, however, were apparently undertaken only intermittently, especially when the smiths felt *ekicwan* (literally, 'a need for meat'), for livestock was the chief commodity exchanged by the Jie for the ironware. The standard price of a spear was a he-goat, while a large bull or ox would fetch an axe, a cow-bell, and four spears, or as many as ten of the long chains that the Jie used as ornaments or to make the pubic aprons worn by unmarried girls.[62] As the rates of exchange indicate, young or female animals were seldom traded, and it was more usual for male or barren female animals, extraneous to the generative functions of the Jie herds, but sufficient to satisfy the Labwor *ekicwan*, to be exchanged.[63]

The commerce was extremely important to both parties and the interrelationship that resulted from it was so close that by the early twentieth century many early European visitors believed that the two peoples were historically one tribal group, despite the disparity in their languages and economies. In the words of Labwor informants, however, 'some people have said that the Jie and Labwor are brothers. In fact, both groups have always been separate tribes, but the Jie have always come to us for their iron. Because of iron, the two tribes became friends, until finally they agreed to become even like brothers.'[64] And in the words of the Jie:

The Tobur [Labwor] have always been there in their hills. They were not with us. But over the years, the Jie have always gone to the Tobur

[60] Okec (Ruben) and others, L 1.
[61] Ongom (Justo) and Kiyonga (Matayo), L 3.
[62] Interviews including L 2 and 3, J 33 and 34.
[63] For a fuller discussion of this iron trade, see R. Herring, 'Production and Exchange in Labwor, Uganda'.
[64] Ogira (Jebedayo) and Oceng, L 4.

to trade oxen for spears and cow-bells, and the Tobur have come to that 'mountain of iron' [Toror] with leather sacks to gather the iron rocks. And so we became friends. In war-time, the Jie never kill the Tobur. In the dry season we graze our herds in the country of the Tobur. As the livestock have mixed, so have the people. And now it is as though we have become related.[65]

With such a close interrelationship ensuring that Jie demands for ironware would be satisfied, it can be readily understood why the Jie were apparently little concerned by the fact that those western peoples who possessed the knowledge of iron-making invariably abandoned their forges when assimilated into the 'Ngiro' community.

[65] Lowot, Loworo, Lobwal (and others), J 8.

CHAPTER VI

Developments of the Early Nineteenth Century

1. THE JIMOS AND THE RISE OF THE FIRE-MAKERS

DURING the first part of the nineteenth century, the hereditary fire-makers (*ngikeworok*, s. *ekeworon*) of the Lokorwakol major division achieved a new importance. This was accomplished through the replacement of the old fire-making clan, Toroi, by a new clan of hereditary fire-makers, Jimos of Losilang. With the succession of the Jimos, the office of fire-maker became an important focus for the closer integration of the still largely independent territorial divisions of the Lokorwakol major division. To examine the rise of the Ngikorwakol fire-makers, we must first direct our attention back to Loyale, the Toroi fire-maker who had succeeded his illustrious father, Orwakol, just after the middle of the eighteenth century. Loyale probably died just before the expulsion of the Toposa by the Dodos and the subsequent Laparanat famine.[1] Very little concerning Loyale has been passed down by the Jie oral traditions, and it may be concluded that he lacked the charisma which had so distinguished his father. In fairness, however, it must be remembered that while Orwakol was the fire-maker of a territorially compact group settled near Daidai, Loyale was fire-maker to a community of pioneers whose energies were being directed towards the occupation and settlement of areas further and further afield from Daidai and Kotiang, 'the home of Orwakol'. Although not entirely certain, the name of Loyale's son and successor was probably Lowatamoe.[2] Like Loyale, Lowatamoe submitted himself to a ritual test in order to prove his succession over a number of rival Toroi claimants:

[1] See Chapter V.
[2] The blame for this uncertainty lies less with Jie oral tradition than with my own inadvertant confusion of two different fire-makers, Cukamoe and Lowatamoe, during my field research. This mistake was not detected until after my return to London. As a result Lowatamoe was almost totally ignored in my questioning. Fortunately, several good Jie informants spontaneously provided a number of traditions regarding this important figure.

Lowatamoe was selected as fire-maker in this way: several men of Toroi all claimed to be the new fire-maker and so each had to smear his sandals with fat and leave them outside his homestead at night. During the night, hyenas came and ate all the sandals except those of Lowatamoe ... The next morning the people came and said, 'Truly, we have found our new fire-maker'.[3]

Soon after his succession, however, the son of Loyale with his branch of the Toroi clan left Kotiang and, travelling some miles south, established himself in Kanawat territorial division. The move from Kotiang to Kanawat is almost universally remembered by the Ngikorwakol, but not a single tradition suggested any reason for it. To have abandoned 'the home of Orwakol' and to have established residence in a new territorial division was a very serious step, and one can only conclude that an intra-clan quarrel had developed amongst the Toroi, possibly arising from some ill-feeling over the succession. This view is supported by the fact that the office of hereditary generation-set leader was retained by the Toroi branch which remained in Kotiang, although before this the offices of fire-maker and generation-set leader were always held by the same man.

There is nothing in the traditions that suggests that the Lokor-wakol office of fire-maker underwent any major changes after the move from Kotiang to Kanawat. Lowatamoe, like all of his Koten–Magos predecessors (with the notable exception of Orwakol) appears to have been solely a respected ritual functionary whose duties and powers did not extend beyond his performance of the ceremonies in which he was the acknowledged specialist. It is very likely that Lowatamoe would have been called upon to perform the New Fire ritual at least once during the Laparanat, but no specific recollection of such an event appears to have been retained in the traditions. The traditions do specifically recall that whenever the Kanawat fire-makers performed the New Fire ritual, it was at Moru Eker ritual grove in the south-western corner of Losilang territorial division, not far from Daidai, which lay just to the west across the Longiro River. While the fire-makers of Kotiang may have also used this same grove, they also seem to have used other groves established by Orwakol himself in Kotiang. It is notable that Moru Eker was

---

[3] Looru (Sampson), Nangiro, and Lothike (Elawa), J 52. It is well worth noting the interchange that elicited this information. To my question, 'Can you tell me any traditions regarding Cukamoe, the son of Loyale?', the informants replied, 'Cukamoe? No, you mean Lowatamoe. Haven't the Kanawat told you of Lowatamoe?'. This was one of the occasions where I wrongly assumed that 'Lowatamoe' was merely another name for Cukamoe.

traditionally the ritual centre of the Jimos, an Agricultural Paranilotic group assimilated during the occupation of Najie, who had
emerged as the ritual specialists of Losilang.

The connection between the Toroi of Kanawat and the Jimos of
Losilang was not only that of Moru Eker ritual grove. The traditions
state that the daughter of the Toroi fire-maker was married by a man
of the Jimos who belonged to the Ngikok generation-set. The girl,
Lowatamoe's eldest child, was married some time before the birth of
Cukamoe, Lowatamoe's only surviving son. Soon after the birth of
Cukamoe, the Toroi fire-maker, by now an elderly man, died. His
death was to be of major consequence to the whole institution of the
Lokorwakol fire-maker: 'When the old fire-maker died, Cukamoe
was only a young boy. The eldest sister of Cukamoe had been
married by a man of the Jimos of Losilang and she took the New
Fire ritual away from Kanawat to those people of Losilang.'[4]

The daughter of Lowatamoe and her Jimos husband (neither of
whose names have survived in the traditions) had a son of their own,
Lomanio, who was somewhat older than his maternal uncle, Cukamoe (see Figure 6). Arguing that Cukamoe was too young to perform
the duties of fire-maker and that no other suitable candidates existed
amongst the Kanawat branch of the Toroi, the Jimos claimed that
the succession should be accorded to Lomanio through his mother,
Lowatamoe's eldest child. Although the Jimos argument was a
flimsy one, the Lokorwakol had probably never faced any similar
situation in the past, and the Jimos secured enough support from the
senior elders for Lomanio to be formally installed as the new fire-
maker. The Toroi, apparently still divided amongst themselves, were
unable to present any unified opposition to the Jimos claims.
Although the Kanawat division duly selected Cukamoe as the new
fire-maker and installed him in a ceremony of their own, the office
had irrevocably passed to the Jimos, and although his father seems
to have served as a kind of regent for some years, Lomanio was
regarded by virtually all of the Lokorwakol as their new fire-maker.[5]

With the succession of the Jimos line of fire-makers, the office and

---

[4] Inua (Lodweny), Apalodokoro, and Lomongin (Julio), J 128. Other
Kanawat informants (including Apua and Lonying, J 114) indicated that
Lowatamoe had had several sons before Cukamoe, but that all had died, pre-
sumably in infancy. Be this as it may, informants were in agreement that
Cukamoe was the eldest surviving son and clearly first in line for succession
to the office of fire-maker.

[5] The name Lomanio means 'he who pretends' and it is of course tempting to
see an equivalent to the English 'Pretender' or 'Usurper'. However, the Jie
do not seem to have assigned specifically that meaning to the name.

the New Fire ritual underwent some important changes. Like their
Rengen counterparts, the Jimos fire-makers began to perform an
important ritual role in the annual agricultural cycle by which they
in fact demonstrated their regulation of it: 'When planting time
came, the people of all the Lokorwakol territorial divisions would
gather at Lomukura to ask the fire-maker's permission to begin
sowing. If he decided the time was right, he would bless them by
smearing them with clay.'[6] Having given his blessing to the people,
the fire-maker would bless the seeds, which implied his permission
for planting to begin: 'The fire-maker would bless the sorghum seeds
and then distribute them to the territorial divisions, saying, "Go
now, and plant your gardens".'[7]

At harvest time the first of the new grain and the first brew of beer
was brought to the fire-maker to taste: 'When the new sorghum was
ripe, people from each territorial division would bring the fire-maker
baskets of grain and he would be the first man to taste a handful of
each division's grain. In the same way, the first of the new beer
would be brought, and he would take the first sips.'[8]

The Jimos fire-makers furthermore adhered to a number of strict
food prohibitions, apparently not observed by their Toroi predecessors:

> The fire-makers of the Jimos could not eat the meat of cattle that had
> died of natural causes—only those that were slaughtered for rituals.
> They could eat only the grain that was grown in Najie, and none
> from the outside.[9]

> The fire-makers from Losilang could eat only food that came from
> Najie. They could not eat any wild fruits, such as *emongot*. They
> could eat only the meat from the shoulder or the ribs of slaughtered
> oxen.[10]

In place of the heavy and unwieldy wedge-shaped stones set up in
the kraals of the Toroi fire-makers, the Jimos chose as their symbol
of office an iron axe (which they had probably used in the performance of their Losilang ritual duties before their accession to the

[6] Lowot (Lomugereng), J 99.
[7] Kenye (Apeamaler), J 63.
[8] Lowot (Lomugereng), J 99. The Kanawat informants of J 114 claimed that
gifts of grain and other things were frequently brought to the Kanawat fire-
makers, but these were the only informants who indicated that any such tribute
was accorded to the Toroi fire-makers. Moreover, their statements may well
have been referring specifically to the Kanawat fire-maker, Cukamoe, who
held the office in Kanawat only after the Jimos succession.
[9] Longok (Erisa), J 86.
[10] Looru (Sampson) and others, J 52.

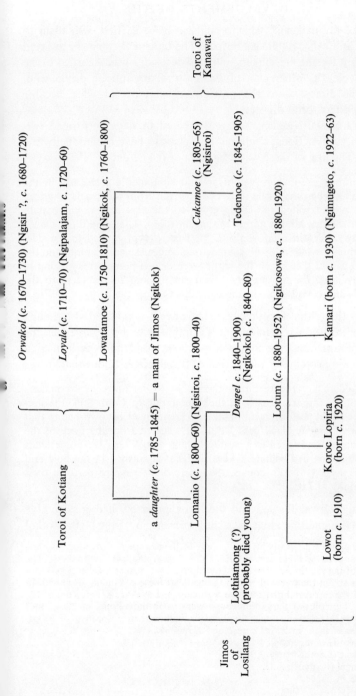

Orwakol (c. 1670–1730) (Ngisir ?, c. 1680–1720)

Loyale (c. 1710–70) (Ngipalajam, c. 1720–60)

Lowatamoe (c. 1750–1810) (Ngikok, c. 1760–1800)

Toroi of Kotiang

Toroi of Kanawat

a *daughter* (c. 1785–1845) = a man of Jimos (Ngikok)

Lomanio (c. 1800–60) (Ngisiroi, c. 1800–40)

Cukamoe (c. 1805–65) (Ngisiroi)

Tedemoe (c. 1845–1905)

Dengel c. 1840–1900) (Ngikokol, c. 1840–80)

Lotum (c. 1880–1952) (Ngikosowa, c. 1880–1920)

Kamari (born c. 1930) (Ngimugeto, c. 1922–63)

Lothiamong (?) (probably died young)

Koroc Lopiria (born c. 1920)

Lowot (born c. 1910)

Jimos of Losilang

Note: The dates of the various fire-makers in this diagram are, of course, only approximate. Lacking concrete data, a life-span of 60 years is assigned to each fire-maker and a 30- to 35-year span is estimated between each man and his father. While this is arbitrary, the system invariably places a fire-maker within the span of the initiations of the generation-set to which the traditions state he belonged. Therefore, the margin of error is probably not too great.

office of fire-maker),[11] which could easily be carried with them to rituals and other public gatherings. The task of keeping the axe and bearing it for the fire-makers on ritual occasions was accorded to the Kathewok, the other clan of Agricultural Paranilotic origin who, with the Jimos, were the previous inhabitants of what became Losilang territorial division.[12]

The Jimos fire-makers are remembered to have performed two other ritual functions; again neither seems to have been done by the Toroi. The first of these was a blessing of the herds:

> The Jimos fire-makers would go and sit under a tree early in the morning when the cattle were being driven from the kraals to graze. They would watch the cattle going to the east and would remain under the tree all day gazing in that direction. They would not glance in any other direction—only to the east. If they looked to the side, bad things would happen: there would be disease and famine; and the cattle would die. When the cattle were driven home after grazing in the evening, the fire-makers would get up and follow them to the kraals and bless them. He did all of this to bless the herds of the Jie.[13]

The other ritual function was that of rain-making; and although the congregation of senior elders continued to be regarded as the chief rain-makers, the Jimos fire-makers sometimes performed a rain-making ceremony before that of the elders at Looi ritual grove:

> The elders are the real rain-makers in Najie, and the fire-makers played no important part in their ceremony at Looi. Still, the fire-maker could perform a rain-making ceremony of his own before that of the elders. A black goat would be selected from the flock of the fire-maker, and taken to a certain hole in a rock near the homesteads of the Jimos in Losilang. There the goat is washed in the hole and then released. If rain comes, the elders don't have to perform their ceremony at Looi.[14]

Loyale, Orwakol's son and successor, probably had considerable difficulty in exerting any very strong influence over the Ngikorwakol

---

[11] The Jimos were probably the 'people of the axe' (*ngika–aep*) for Losilang *angola* and *akiwodokin* ceremonies before becoming the fire-makers. The 'people of the axe' in each territorial division are the men of a given clan whose duty it is to cut the tree with which the 'gate' at these ceremonies is closed. In many of the territorial divisions the 'people of the axe' are drawn from a clan (usually Agricultural Paranilotic) who were early inhabitants of Najie, and they enjoy a relatively high ritual status within their respective divisions, regardless of their 'order' at *angola* and *akiwodokin*.

[12] Lowot (Lomugereng), J 132.

[13] Lowot (Lomugereng), J 99.

[14] Dengel (Kamari), J 53.

pioneers who were pushing further and further east and south-east from the original settlements around Daidai.[15] As the seven divisions of Lokorwakol were settled, the homesteads of the Kotiang Toroi were left in the north-western corner of the area, in close proximity to the more important ritual groves established by Orwakol, but some distance from the homesteads of the more recently established eastern and south-eastern territorial divisions (*see* Maps 2 and 7). With the removal of the Toroi fire-maker to Kanawat, the distance between the fire-maker and many of the eastern areas was even further increased. While the homesteads of the Jimos in south-western Losilang were rather more towards the geographical centre of the Lokorwakol settled area, the new fire-makers were clearly concerned that sufficient contact between themselves and the various territorial divisions was not being made. To remedy the situation, the Jimos fire-makers would undertake a progress through Lokor-wakol before the performance of major rituals, visiting each territorial division in turn, and softening a black goatskin in their hands to proclaim their identity:

> The fire-maker of Losilang would always take a goatskin and soften it in his hands before an important ceremony. He would come with the skin to Daidai where he would give it to the fire-maker of my family [Toroi of Kotiang], and together both men would move on to the homesteads of the people of Loreumoe. From there, they would go on to Kanawat, to be joined by another fire-maker, and from there to Komukunyo and then Panyangara, where a man from Ngikalo-riang [the clan of the war-leader] joined them. From there they would go on to Nakapelimoru, and finally they all return to Kotido. If New Fire is to be made, the fire-sticks would be prepared while the fire-maker is making his journey.[16]

As this tradition indicates, the Jimos fire-makers appointed a hereditary 'assistant' from each of the Lokorwakol divisions. In a gesture of calculated diplomacy, the chief of these assistants was chosen from the branch of the Toroi that had remained in Kotiang at the 'home of Orwakol' and still provided the hereditary generation-set leaders. Nevertheless, ritual occasions provided an opportunity

---

[15] See Chapter IV.

[16] Koroc (Lokepon) and Lodio (Apaedongol), J 73. Several reliable Jie informants (including those of J 58) described similar progresses being undertaken by Loyale and other Toroi fire-makers, and so the Jimos probably cannot be credited with having devised the progress. Other informants (including those of J 96) indicated that the Jimos fire-makers used their progress in order to spread any important news (not necessarily concerned with ritual performances) throughout Lokorwakol.

for the Jimos clearly to demonstrate that ritual supremacy had
passed from Orwakol's people to themselves: 'The Jimos are the
most important of the fire-makers and the Toroi of Kotiang are only
second in importance. When an ox is slaughtered at an important
ritual, the people of Losilang [the Jimos] get the right shoulder and
the Kotiang [the Toroi] get the left shoulder.[17]

Two of the other 'assistants', those of Komukuny and Nakapelimoru, were selected from branches of the Jimos that had emigrated
from Losilang to settle in those areas, while in the other divisions,
the assistants were chosen from clans that already enjoyed high
ritual prestige in their own areas.[18] Besides accompanying the fire-
maker on his progress, the 'assistant' fire-makers also participated
directly in the New Fire ceremony:

> When 'the land is heavy' [i.e. when there is trouble] and New Fire
> is to be made, all the fire-makers gather at Moru Eker [ritual grove].
> The Jimos fire-maker begins to twirl the fire-stick and then the fire-
> maker of the Toroi takes over from him. The fire-makers of the other
> divisions assist by holding the piece into which the fire-stick is drilled,
> and they can take over the twirling should the Jimos or the Toroi
> fire-maker require them.[19]

New Fire continued to be kindled by the Jimos during times of
great crisis and in conjunction with generation-set inaugurations: the
same occasions on which it had been kindled by the Toroi. The fire-
sticks themselves were changed, however. Whereas the Toroi had
used sticks of *ekaliye* wood, the Jimos used only sticks of *ethegethege*,
a tree which grows in profusion in their ritual grove, Moru Eker,[20]
although the sticks were still referred to as *epit ka Orwakol*,
'Orwakol's fire-sticks'. Adding considerably to the difficulty of their
task, but demonstrating their proficiency, the Jimos fire-makers
moreover insisted on using only green *ethegethege* sticks, newly cut
from a living branch.

[17] Lokeler, J 102. The Toroi of Kanawat were eventually accorded the second-
ranked assistant, but apparently only after the death of Cukamoe, who continued to function as an independent fire-maker in his own territorial division
while the rest of Najie acknowledged Lomanio.

[18] According to some informants, however, only the Jimos fire-maker and
his Kotiang assistant were of real importance: 'The Jimos of Losilang and the
family of Koroc [the Toroi] of Kotiang are the most important of the fire-
makers. The fire-makers of the other divisions are only helpers. They are just
vultures who come running when an ox is to be slaughtered.' (Teko Ekalam,
J 76.)

[19] Koroc (Lokepon), J 73.

[20] John Wilson kindly identified 'ekaliye' as *Grewia trichocarpa* and
'ethegethege' as *Cordia ovalis.*

The powers and authority of the Jimos fire-makers were also extended into legal and judicial spheres. The fire-makers could order the cessation of internecine feuds, decide cases, and moreover enforce their decisions, if necessary:

> The fire-makers of the Jimos could judge cases. Should a Jie kill another Jie, their two groups would fight, but if the fire-maker ordered them not to, they would stop. He was the only man [individual] in Najie who could do that. People would hear his words. People had to obey him. If they didn't stop fighting immediately, the fire-maker would go to them and say, 'Why do you fight when I have told you not to?'. He could even order young men to be sent to prevent them from fighting. The fire-maker would then judge who was wrong and would make them pay a fine [akibut, to pay cattle in compensation] to those they had wronged.[21]

The homestead of the fire-makers was also considered a sanctuary for fugitives, who might flee there to escape immediate retribution for some crime, and to lay their case before the judgement of the fire-maker: 'If a man had wronged another, he could run to the home of the fire-maker in Losilang and be safe. No one could follow him there. No one could beat him there.[22]

Finally, the Jimos adopted a new form of burial ritual for their fire-makers which, if not so elaborate as the burial rituals of the Rengen fire-makers, was nevertheless more elaborate than the burial rituals accorded to the Toroi:

> After the old fire-maker has died and has been buried, his bones are dug up and special ceremonies are performed, usually at about the same time that his successor is chosen. But the fire-makers of the Jimos are not buried with any of their possessions. It is only the Rengen who do that.[23]

> When the fire-maker has been dead for some time, his bones are dug up and ceremonies are held. A black ox is slaughtered and beer is brewed. Then the bones are reburied.[24]

With the accession of the Jimos fire-makers, then, the Lokorwakol office of fire-maker was elevated from that of a relatively powerless ritual functionary to an office which more closely resembled that of

[21] Lopeirinyet (Angura), J 87. The senior elders could, as a group, also order the cessation of fighting, but after the accession of the Jimos fire-makers, they deferred all judgement to them.
[22] Looru (Sampson), and others, J 52.
[23] Lowot (Lomugereng), J 99.
[24] Iluputh (and others), J 100.

the Rengen. While of obvious significance to the Lokorwakol major division of the developing Jie community, the rise of the Jimos fire-makers is also of wider significance in that it sheds considerable light on the whole question of the diffusion of the concept of the *rwot* (king). The case of the Jimos is a clear example of the transference of the concept from primarily agricultural Lwo peoples to a group of Agricultural Paranilotes, who, in their turn, introduced the concept to primarily pastoral elements of Koten–Magos origin, grafting various aspects of Lwo kingship to the pre-existing Paranilotic office of hereditary fire-maker. Therefore, the case of the Jimos may provide fresh evidence to the long debate between 'diffusionists' and 'anti-diffusionists', and do something towards finally resolving that debate once and for all.[25]

Although well over a century had gone by since the Agricultural Paranilotic Jimos had entered Najie from the west, it seems reasonable to deduce that the Jimos, like the Rengen 'Ngikatapa', had been profoundly influenced by contacts with western peoples, especially those who were linguistically and culturally Lwo. Like the Rengen, the Jimos appear to have been deeply impressed with the Lwo concept of the *rwot*, and certainly many of the same powers, ceremonies, and ritual trappings accorded by the Lwo to their kings were assumed by the Jimos *ngikeworok* after their accession. It would, moreover, seem likely that a recollection of kingship was retained within the context of Losilang ritual activity, led by the Jimos and performed at their ritual centre at Moru Eker. It can furthermore be suggested that the Jimos, desirous of extending their powers and ritual authority from Losilang to the rest of Lokorwakol, may have consciously planned a strategem by which to secure the office of hereditary fire-maker. They seem to have taken the fullest

[25] A very clear picture of a similar diffusion of the concept of the *rwot* in western Acholi is provided by R. Atkinson in his 'State Formation and Development in Western Acholi', an unpublished seminar paper presented at Makerere University in August 1971. Atkinson argues, however, that in western Acholi a rather 'refined version' of the *rwot*-ship was introduced from Bunyoro by Palwo immigrants only after about 1680. Important features of the *rwot*-ship brought in from Bunyoro included the ownership of royal drums and the payment of certain kinds of tribute (different both in kind and in concept than the tribute accorded to the Jimos fire-makers). There would hardly have been time for either the Jimos or the Rengen to have been influenced by the version of the *rwot*-ship introduced into western Acholi by the Palwo. Rather, the Lwo-speakers who influenced the Jimos and Rengen must have been one of the groups which (as all recent observers of the Acholi agree) pre-existed the arrival of the Palwo in eastern Acholi and along the western Karamoja borderland, at least from the mid-seventeenth century.

possible advantage of the Toroi schism by establishing affinal ties with the Kanawat branch and by inducing the Kanawat fire-maker to use Moru Eker as the ritual grove for making New Fire. Again, their claim to the succession appears to have been perfectly timed, and having just secured that succession, their appointment of the Kotiang Toroi as their most important assistants betrays an element of studied calculation.

The increased power of the Jimos fire-makers undoubtedly cut into that traditionally wielded by the Ngikorwakol senior elders, perhaps most clearly in the judicial sphere. In many other ways, however, the traditional duties and authority accorded to the elders continued unchanged after the accession of the Jimos. In military matters, for example, the Jimos fire-makers began to take a more active role in ritual preparation for war, such as smearing the warriors with clay before battle,[26] but the actual direction of armies and raiding parties, and the overall planning of strategy remained strictly the province of the senior elders and the hereditary war leaders. The senior elders also continued to exercise their right to select the successor of a deceased fire-maker, although their choice was at least theoretically limited to only one of the sons of the old fire-maker.[27] Indeed, the traditions make it clear that the Jimos owed their succession to the office of fire-maker largely to the support given to their claim by the elders, and that, however well planned their own strategem to secure the office may have been, they could never have attained the office without the vital backing of the elders. In many ways, the relationship between the elders and the fire-maker seems to have been remarkably similar to the one that existed between the elders of the eastern Acholi kingdoms and their kings, of which Webster has written: 'The king (*rwot*) reigned, but hardly ruled without the almost unanimous consent of the elders'.[28]

With the attainment of the office of fire-maker, the relationship between the Jimos fire-makers and the senior elders found expression in their close co-operation, especially on important ritual occasions.

[26] Lokec (Lomorumoe) and Arini, J 96.

[27] The personal qualities looked for in a prospective candidate were basically gentleness and humility. Primogeniture was of little importance, and the traditions state that in choosing a new fire-maker more flamboyant elder sons were frequently passed over in favour of a quieter junior one.

[28] Webster, 'State Formation and Fragmentation in Agago', p. 4. Like the Jie, the Acoli elders chose a new king from among the old king's sons (Webster, 'Acholi Historical Texts', p. 13) and in personal communication Webster stated that the qualities looked for by the Acoli elders in their new king exactly paralleled those sought by Jie elders in their fire-makers.

The presence of the senior elders was deemed desirable on those occasions (especially the kindling of New Fire) led by the fire-makers, and in the same way, the presence of the fire-maker was expected on those occasions on which the ritual leadership was provided by the elders:

> The elders are the ones who conduct the rain-making ceremony at Looi, and the fire-maker has no special role. But he was expected to attend, and is given the meat from the right shoulder of the sacrificial ox . . . The fire-maker also has no special role at the *angola* ceremony at Nayan or Daidai, but he must be present together with the 'big' elders.[29]

The co-operation between the elders and the fire-makers was further reflected in their sharing of authority on the level of the major division. While the elders could 'approach the fire-maker and tell him it was time to make New Fire',[30] they would also 'discuss important matters and then take their decisions to the *ekeworon* to hear his opinion',[31] and even in the important duty of selecting a new fire-maker, 'the elders would meet under a tree with the men of the Jimos to decide together who should be chosen'.[32] The Ngikor-wakol fire-makers, traditionally only religious functionaries, thus achieved a new status with the accession of the Jimos, by which they received an authority which transcended the ritual sphere. As with the Rengen, the office of Ngikorwakol fire-maker after the Jimos accession undoubtedly became a focus for more intensive feelings of the corporate unity of the major division and, with the institution of the generation-set system, helped to cut across the segmentary loyal-ties focused on clan or territorial division. Something of the corporate identity the Ngikorwakol had experienced nearly a century before, when they were clustered near Daidai under Orwakol, was recaptured through the integrative force provided by the Jimos fire-makers. The authority and importance of the fire-makers at the height of their power after the Jimos accession is clearly retained in Jie tra-ditions:

> The Jimos were the most important people in Najie. The people of Koroc [the Toroi of Kotiang] were important because they led the generation-sets, and the people of Loriang [the Lodaca of Panyangara] were important because they led in wars. But the Jimos were more

[29] Dengel (Kamari), J 53.
[30] Dengel (Kamari), J 53.
[31] Looru (Sampson) and others, J 52.
[32] Dodoi (Lokuangiro), Longoi (Apariong), and Lodon, J 88.

important than either, because they had all the power concerning New Fire and all the customs of the Jie.[33]

The Jie never had chiefs. Only the Acoli and the other 'Ngikatapa' had them. But the fire-makers of the Jimos were like big chiefs (*ekapalon*) of the Jie. They were as big [important] as the A.D.C. is now. They led the Jie in all things. They judged cases. They 'opened the gate' for war [i.e. by smearing the warriors], although the actual leading of the armies was, of course, not their job.[34]

Jie tradition concerning the importance of the fire-makers also made an impression on at least one early European observer of Karamoja, E. J. Wayland, who noted: 'In the "old days" there were two chiefs [of the Jie] . . . under each chief was grouped certain sections of the tribe, so that it was virtually divided into two. They were *not* wizards, but chiefs.'[35]

2. THE DEFEAT OF THE POET

While the accession of the Jimos fire-makers undoubtedly did much to strengthen the political integration of the Ngikorwakol, other processes were also in operation which were to modify further the strongly independent natures of the territorial divisions. These processes entailed the internal movement of clan and sub-clan groups within the settled area of Najie. Such internal movement was of course typical of the historical experiences of many other African peoples, and very often had the effect of transforming a segmentary collection of clans and/or other units into something which more closely resembled a nation. A prime example is Buganda, where the clan territories of the pre-Kintu period progressively disappeared in the face of the inter-territorial movement by various clan sections. With the Jie these processes began with the return of the Agricultural Paranilotic Ngiseera and Loposa, together with their Lwo companions,

[33] Mabuc (Loputuke), J 85.

[34] Lokepon (Koroc) and Lodio (Apaedongol), J 73. The reference to 'A.D.C.' is to the Assistant District Commissioner of Jie and Labwor Counties, the highest ranking government official with whom the average Jie comes into any kind of contact.

[35] E. J. Wayland, 'Preliminary Studies of the Tribes of Karamoja', *JRAI* 61 (1931) 224. Wayland's reference to 'wizards' is to diviners. While the Jie had a variety of diviners, mainly benevolent, extremely few seem to have ever played any very important role in Jie society. In all cases, their powers were strictly ancillary to those of the senior elders, the fire-makers, and the war-leaders. (This view was also held by the Gullivers, op. cit. (1953), p. 49.) Except for a few Jie diviners, such as the female diviner, Lodul, and Loingolem of Panyangara, both of whom achieved a society-wide reputation, the most highly respected diviners consulted by the Jie came from neighbouring societies, including the Acoli, Dodoso, and Ngikuliak. A full discussion of Jie diviners is included in my London Ph.D. thesis.

whose arrival injected a considerable western influence into not
one, but several Lokorwakol territorial divisions, thereby blurr-
ing to some extent the uniqueness of those divisions. By the early
years of the nineteenth century, a certain amount of population
movement between the various parts of Najie was also discernible.
By that time many of the small compact clans which had participated
in the initial occupation and settlement of the territorial divisions had
grown tremendously, and several of the larger clans had begun to
splinter and branch out to other areas. The fire-maker Lowatamoe,
who took his branch of the Toroi from Kotiang to Kanawat, and the
two sub-clans of the Jimos which moved from Losilang to Komukuny and Nakapelimoru[36] are good examples of the process. Another
example is provided by the descendants of the patriarch Kere of the
Lokore clan of Kanawat. By 1800 (i.e. the end of Ngikok initiations)
the ridge on which the Lokore had settled in Kanawat had become
overcrowded, and some of Kere's sons and grandsons (often called
Ngikakere, 'Kere's people') began to move away from the Kanawat
homesteads to set themselves up as Lokore sub-clans in several
parts of Panyangara and Nakapelimoru territorial divisions. The
reasons for their movements were varied: family quarrels, shortages
of food (presumably agricultural produce), supernaturally caused
misfortunes, or simply a desire to live in a new area. In the words of
a descendant of one of the separatists:

> Clans often break up if they become too large. They find that there is
> not enough food, or they see another area which seems like a good
> place to live. Our clan originated in Kanawat, but then some ·men
> moved here to Thiokol and Kadoca [both in Nakapelimoru] while
> others went first to Lokibuwo and then to Kapuyon [in Panyangara].
> We now belong to these places, but we still remember that Kanawat
> was the home of our ancestors. Was not Kere the 'father' of us all?
> Do we not all share one *etal*?[37]

In some cases, such emigrant branches of dispersed clans settled
close to affinal or maternal kinsmen in their adopted territorial
divisions. As the tradition indicates, dispersed sub-clans, although
almost invariably granted full membership in their new divisions,
never forgot their origins and would often continue to regard their

[36] See above.

[37] Nakwo, J 115. The leader of the Lokore branch at Kapuyon left Kanawat
because he felt he was being asked to provide too many sacrificial oxen for
Kanawat rituals. The Lokore branches do *not*, in fact, still share one range
of clan observances (*ngitalia*, s. *etal*). Nakwo used the term 'one *etal*' loosely,
to mean 'descended from a common source'.

old divisions as the 'home of our fathers'. In a sense, therefore, many such migrant sub-clans regarded themselves, and were regarded by others, as belonging to two territorial divisions, and the independent and unique identity of many divisions was thereby further blurred.

The internal population movement of Najie even transcended major-division boundaries, and sometime during the early years of the nineteenth century (during the early stages of Ngisiroi initiations) a large contingent of Rengen immigrants arrived in Lokorwakol and established themselves as the Kadokini subdivision of Panyangara. These Rengen, representing several clans, mainly of Lokatap territorial division, continued to perform their rituals separately from the other Panyangara, but were regarded as at least territorially part of Lokorwakol, and began to take an active part in the everyday economic and domestic life of the Ngikorwakol.

The arrival of the Kadokini was in fact symptomatic of increasing turmoil all along the north-western Rengen frontier. The expulsion of the Toposa at the end of the eighteenth century had created a territorial vacuum which caused both the Agricultural Paranilotic Poet and the emerging Dodos community temporarily to shift their attention northwards, away from the Rengen vanguard which was pioneering the Kaceri and Kalomide areas, north-west of the Dopeth River.[38] Within a very few years, however, the Poet were feeling the effects of a famine (quite possibly the Laparanat), brought on by a drought and a plague of locusts, and many of them were forced to take temporary refuge with the Ngieyan on Mt. Orom, or even further west along part of the Acholi borderland not so badly affected by the famine:

> When the famine came, the Poot [Poet] and the clans who were with them: the Titi, Kathengor, and Kalobur, went away to the west. Some went to Orom and others went to eastern Acholi where the hunger was not so great. The Poot group had no cattle, but after a time, they looked again to the east and saw that the people there [Rengen Jie and Lokorikituk Dodos] were rich [in cattle]. So they said, 'Let us return to the east'. Most of them returned, but a few remained behind in the west and became Acoli and continued to be farmers. Those who remained are known by various names including Kadwera, Karyangabu, and Gule.[39]

[38] See Chapter V.
[39] Adupa (Sampson), D 12. Other informants, including those of D10, agreed that the Poot group went to the Paimol area of north-eastern Acholi. The arrival of the Poot in Paimol is still recalled in Acoli traditions collected by Webster ('Acholi Historical Texts', pp. 80–94) in which they are referred to by the same names given in Adupa's testimony above.

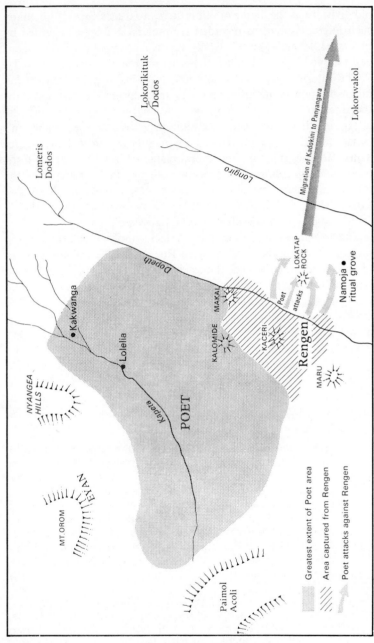

MAP 11. The Poet.

When those Poet who had gone to the west returned to their former area south-east of the Kapeta River, they found that the Toposa, who had been driven north by the Dodos, were concentrated north of Mt. Morungole near the present border with the Sudan. From there, the Toposa were launching raids against the Dodos who were still settling their former country:

> When the Poot arrived here from Acholi, the Toposa around Morungole were raiding the Dodos to the south. Some of the Poot helped the Dodos in their fights and the Toposa were finally defeated and driven even further north. The Poot [re-]settled the areas around Komoce, Loruu, and Makal to the north of Najie, and some began to associate closely with the Dodos because of *ekicwan* [lit. 'a need for meat'].[40]

Although some of the Poet thus lent support to the Dodos, others appear to have formed a closer association with the Rengen Jie: 'The Poet lived between the Jie and the Dodos, but they were neither one nor the other. They sometimes acted as spies for Jie raiding parties who wanted to steal Dodos cattle, and of course this made the Dodos very angry.[41]

Sandwiched between the Rengen Jie to the south and the Lokorikituk Dodos to the east (see Map 11), the Poet found it increasingly difficult to establish any firm policy which would ally them to one side or the other, and therefore succeeded in incurring the animosity of both. Open hostility first broke out with the Jie. Although Jie cattle-camps had been permitted to use the important Kapeta watering points before the famine, with their return from the west, the Poet became resentful of the Jie intrusions, and forbade further use of the Kapeta by the Jie. The population growth, both human and bovine, which had necessitated the population shifts in Najie, however, were undoubtedly beginning to put considerable pressures on available resources, and the Rengen and the northern Ngikorwakol divisions who relied on the Kapeta area for dry-season water and grazing clearly considered it of vital importance. The Jie cattle-camps, ignoring the Poet dictum, continued to push through Poet territory towards the Kapeta. The Poet reaction was swift and decisive:

> Trouble began to grow between the Jie and the Poet. Whenever the Jie cattle-camps tried to go up to Kapeta, the Poet would refuse to let them pass and would take their cattle. Finally, the Jie had enough and began to resist the Poet with spears. But this led to

[40] Lokidap (and others), D 10.
[41] Cope, J 28.

big Poet attacks, not only against the cattle-camps, but against Niaje, as well.[42]

Initially, the Poet attacks were extremely successful. The Jie cattle-camps were expelled and the Poet warriors over-ran the vanguard of the Rengen settlers who had occupied the Kaceri and Kalimode area, hurling them back across the Dopeth River and taking the area for themselves (see Map 11). In the process, Ladoket, the northernmost of the Rengen territorial divisions was swallowed up and ceased to exist: 'Before it was attacked and overrun, Ladoket was the fifth Rengen territorial division. After the attacks, however, it was no more. Only a few of the Ladoket people survived. They were forced to join with the Kapelok division where they still exist as a small clan called "Ladoket".'[43]

The Poet, flushed with their successes, even launched attacks across the Dopeth into the heart of the Rengen settled area which caused the emigration of the Kadokini to the safety of Panyangara.[44] The Rengen fell back on Namoja ritual grove, just south of Lokatap Rock (they were probably somewhat encouraged to see that the hyraxes were still there), and decided to undertake a drastic change in their ritual leadership. There appears to have been a strong feeling among the Rengen that their defeats were at least partially attributable to the ineffectiveness of their Ratai fire-maker, a descendant of Oding, and the people gathered at Namoja clamoured for his removal. It seems likely that considerable ill-feeling was engendered against the Ratai, whose homesteads south of Lokatap Rock had escaped the Poet onslaughts, by those Rengen who had borne the brunt of the attacks and had lost their homes and properties. In any case, the Kalolet, the clan chosen to replace the Ratai as the Rengen fire-makers, was clearly one of those driven from their home area by the Poet. The original name of the clan was Lodoi, but when they were forced to abandon their homesteads and flee to an area in Lokatap near a salt lick (*elet*), they took the name 'Kalolet' as a bitter reminder of their expulsion. The first Kalolet fire-maker chosen by the Rengen elders to replace the Ratai was a man called Loimanyang of the Ngisiroi generation-set. Unfortunately, the tradition related by his great-grandson, Acap, the present Rengen fire-maker, fails to reflect the drama which the replacement must have occasioned:

[42] Lobeerei and Lokwange, J 98.
[43] Lokayan, J 124.
[44] A Kadokini tradition of their emigration is recorded above in Chapter II.

My clan was not the original fire-making clan of the Rengen. The Ratai of Kadwoman were the fire-makers before us. They are also known as Ngikaloding, because they were the children [descendants] of Oding himself. But then the Ratai became very bad fire-makers. They were spoiling the ritual. Terrible things were happening in Rengen. So it was decided that my clan should take over.[45]

The transfer of the office of fire-maker from the Ratai to the Kalo-let does not seem to have entailed any major changes in either the office or the New Fire ritual, as had been the case with the transfer of the Lokorwakol office from the Toroi to the Jimos. The Kalolet seem to have inherited from the Ratai an office which was strikingly similar to that developed by the Jimos on their accession, and there is a clear parallel between most of the powers and the functions accorded the fire-makers of both major divisions. One difference between the two major divisions was the occasions on which New Fire was made. As with the Ngikorwakol, the Rengen fire-makers were expected to make New Fire in times of great stress, but in contrast, New Fire was not kindled in conjunction with the inaugura-tion of a new Rengen generation-set, although the fire-maker was called upon to smear the first initiates with ritual clay.[46] Another major difference was that at the burials of deceased Rengen fire-makers a more elaborate ritual was used than at the burials of either the Toroi or even the Jimos:

When the fire-maker of the Rengen dies, he is buried with his clothing, ornaments, and other possessions, even his sleeping hides. Gourds of milk are also buried with him. The fire-maker is the only man of the Rengen who is buried like that. The other Jie [the Ngikorwakol] do not bury anyone like that. The fire-maker is buried with his head point-ed to the east, lying on his left side. People bring milk and pour it on his grave. They also bring food, some of which they eat themselves, and some of which is left on the grave. After some years, the bones of the fire-maker are dug up and a special ceremony is held. A goat is killed and the bones of the fire-maker are put in the skin and taken to the place where New Fire is made [Moru Anamit]. There they are buried under a pile of stones. All of the fire-makers are there at Moru Anamit.[47]

The only other differences appear to have been very minor ones: having a spear, rather than an axe or wedge-shaped stone as their symbol of office; referring to the fire-sticks (which were of *ethegethege*

[45] Acap (Lodioki), J 108.
[46] Interviews including J 60, 91, 93, 95, and 108.
[47] Acap (Lodioki), J 108.

wood, like the Jimos) as *epit kaloding*, 'Oding's fire-sticks'; and
possibly not following the same sort of ritual progress as the fire-
makers of the more dispersed Ngikorwakol.

Having thus chosen a new line of fire-makers, the Rengen felt
themselves ready to begin a counter-offensive against the victorious
Poet. They first enlisted the help of the rest of the Jie community, the
Ngikorwakol, whose northern divisions undoubtedly felt the loss of
the Kapeta water rights almost as severely as the Rengen. In the
same way that the internal population movement within Najie had
helped to effect the closer integration of the Jie community, so now
did the opportunity to combine in unified warfare against a common
enemy serve to develop further the awareness of their 'Jie-ness' by
both major divisions. Considerable numbers of Ngikorwakol warriors responded to the Rengen call. These warriors were men of the
Ngisiroi generation-set, the sons of the Ngikok who as young men
had successfully raided the Kapwor. Some Jie informants indicated
that some of the more junior age-sets of the Ngisiroi, including
the Ngimadanga, Ngiwapeto, and Ngiyarameri (see Figure 3),
had already been initiated and took part in the offensive against
the Poet,[48] and there was almost universal agreement that the
Ngiseera and Loposa, together with their Acoli companions, had
already returned from the west. A date towards the end of the time
spanned by Ngisiroi initiations, e.g. between about 1830 and 1840,
seems indicated for this campaign. Perhaps the exploits of the Ngikorwakol Ngikok against the Kapwor had established a military tradition which the Ngisiroi felt they had to emulate; perhaps the
replacement of the Ratai fire-makers with the Kalolet had boosted the
flagging spirits of the Rengen. Whatever the reason, the campaign
of the combined Jie forces almost immediately reversed the losses
suffered by the Rengen. The first thrust of the Ngisiroi swept the
Poet from their newly acquired areas of Kaceri and Kalomide, and
soon the Jie attacks were pushing northwards to the banks of
the Kapeta, capturing their wells at Kalomide, Lolelia, and at the
Kapeta itself. Finally, the Lwo allies of the Poet who had been
settled with them for some generations abandoned their friends
in the face of the increasingly severe incursions and fled to the
west: 'The Poet were really composed of two groups: the Poet
themselves, and the Ngimuto, who were people like Acoli. The Jie
attacks split them up. . . . The Ngimuto went directly to the west

---

[48] Interviews including J 24, 59, and 100.

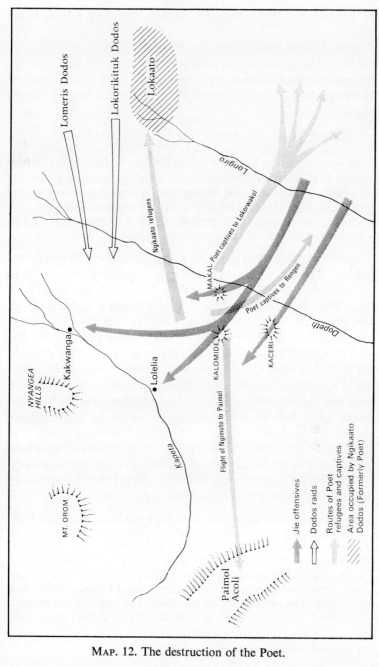

MAP. 12. The destruction of the Poet.

to Paimol in Acholi where they settled. They can still be found there.[49]

With the Poet reeling from the Jie assaults, the Dodos took advantage of the situation and fell upon the eastern flank of the Poet. Large numbers of the Poet were taken captive, and according to one Dodos tradition, an entire band of them was taken in a curious manner:

> When the people were fighting the Poet, the Dodos found a whole group of them gathered at Kamoce [a hill north of Kalomide]. They were dancing to the sound of a *nyethui* bird . . . When the bird cried, those Poet would dance to its sound. They had left their spears and other weapons to one side, and the Dodos surrounded them, cutting them off from their weapons. The Dodos captured them all: men, women, children, all! . . . The Dodos decided to bring them to their homes and make them become Dodos, as well.[50]

With their Muto allies gone, Jie attacks hammering them from the south, and Dodos raids carrying off large numbers of their people to the east, the Poet resistance crumbled. Jie cattle-camps could once again have free access to the Kapeta resources, and the northwestern frontier of the Rengen was secured. Like the Dodos, the victorious Jie took large numbers of Poet captives and brought them back to Najie. Poet groups were thus scattered quite literally throughout Najie (see Map 12). A considerable number were assimilated by the Lokatap territorial division of the Rengen where they formed a large and important clan. Other Poet groups were absorbed by four of the seven Lokorwakol territorial divisions: Losilang, Kotido, Panyangara, and Nakapelimoru. Although they were brought to Najie as defeated enemies, the Poet universally seem to have been well treated by their captors, and almost immediately steps were taken to ensure their full integration into Jie society. A tradition of the Kotido Poet clan is typical of their experience:

> When our ancestors were dispersed from the Kalomide area which had been their homes, many came here to Najie. My own people came here to Kotido, and when they arrived the Losogot [clan] were kind to them. They married the daughters of our people and gave them cattle for bride-wealth so that they could become rich. In time, our people also married the daughters of the Losogot. Before our ancestors came here, they were cultivators and had only few cattle. It was the Losogot who first gave us many cattle. Even now, many

[49] Naluk, J 79.
[50] Ngole (Paulo) and others, D 3.

people refer to our clan as 'Losogot' as well as 'Poet'. But we are not really Losogot, of course. We are simply their good friends, and we marry each others' daughters.[51]

Those Poet who were taken by the Losilang territorial division were also treated well, but were given special tasks to perform for the Jimos fire-makers as a reminder of their conquest:

My people, the Poet, once lived at Makal together with the Muto Acoli, and also at Longor and the wells at Kapeta. When the Jie attacked my people, the Muto ran back to their mountain in Acholi, and my people were defeated. The father of my grandfather was one of those brought here to live in Najie. The Poet could speak Ajie at that time, but they spoke the Acoli language better. The father of my grandfather and his group of the Poet were brought here to Losilang. They were given the task of helping the fire-makers. It was God's will, and so it became our work to build the entire granary [of the fire-maker]—even to the poles and the roof; and then we filled it with grain to the very top.[52]

At the same time, however, the Jimos entrusted the Poet with important ritual duties, making them the 'people of the axe' (ngika–aep) for the Losilang angola ceremonies, and even allowing them to assist the Kathewok as the 'people of the axe' for the angola ceremonies performed by the Ngikorwakol major division as a whole.[53]

Those Poet who were taken by the Dodos were joined by others who arrived in the Kopos area voluntarily, fleeing the victorious Jie. So large was the Poet population in Dodos that they were able to form their own largely autonomous Dodos section, Ngikaato ('those of the west'), centred on Kopos, to the west of the Lokorikutik section and south of the Lomeris (see Map 12). The newcomers quickly gained considerable ritual importance in their new community and henceforth provided the most important Dodos fire-makers, similar in function to those of the Jimos and Kalolet among the Jie. With the addition of this third section, the Dodos community was now entering the final stages of its evolution. Although composed of many of the same Koten–Magos and Agricultural Paranilotic elements as the Jie, the Dodos evolutionary experience had been rather different and entirely separate from that of the Jie community. At the time of the final destruction of the Poet in about 1840, there can be no doubt that the Dodos regarded the Jie as an alien community

[51] Lokeler, J 102.
[52] Lopeirinyet (Angura), J 87.
[53] Longok (Erisa), J 86; Lowot (Lomugereng), J 132.

whose newly won control over the Kapeta grazing and watering resources was viewed with both envy and resentment.

3. THE EASTERN AND SOUTHERN NEIGHBOURS OF THE JIE

An important factor in the complete victory of the Jie over the Poet was the steady supply of iron weapons from the friendly Labwor. By the time of the Poet war, the Jie had secured yet another source of ironware. The originally Fringe Cushitic-speaking Ngikuliak hunters and gatherers, who had retreated to the fastness of Maru Hill with the advent of the immigrants from Koten, had for more than a century existed quite separately from the Jie community to the east. Gradually, however, an important symbiotic relationship had grown up between the two peoples, with the Ngikuliak exchanging game-meat, honey, ostrich-eggshell beads, wild-animal skins, and shields, sandals, and other articles made from hides, in exchange for barren livestock and milk.[54] As a result of a famine (most probably the Laparanat), some impoverished Labwor blacksmiths arrived at Maru from the west and were taken in by the Ngikuliak. In gratitude, the Labwor taught Lolemutum, a leader of the Ngikuliak, the art of iron-making before departing to their own country with the return of better times.[55] Lolemutum and his band of Ngikuliak set up foundries at Maru and began to fashion various kinds of ironware to trade with the Jie. Some Ngikuliak even copied the Labwor and began to make itinerant journeys around Najie, hawking their wares from settlement to settlement.[56] Because of their inherent belief in the 'inferiority' of the Ngikuliak,[57] Jie traditions which describe the poor quality and workmanship of their ironware should be treated with caution. Still, it seems clear that the Ngikuliak were not as skilled as the Labwor, and that the Ngikuliak did concentrate on making ornaments and smaller pieces of ironware: 'The Ngikuliak learned to make iron, but not very well. They could make iron beads and chains and such things, but they couldn't make useful things like spears or axes.'[58]

At any rate, it seems very likely that the Ngikuliak smiths were able to meet much of the Jie demand for iron ornaments and chains

[54] Interviews including J 4, 65, and 78.
[55] Interviews including J 28, 129, and L 6.
[56] Apangolen, J 67.
[57] See Chapter III.
[58] Loper (and others), J 38. Archaeological investigations at Maru revealed the remains of both spears and axes, however, and Ngikuliak informants claimed that limited numbers of these articles were made by their ancestors.

for pubic aprons by the time of the Poet war. Undoubtedly this permitted the more skilful Labwor to focus their energies on the manufacture of iron weapons which played so decisive a role in the crushing of the Poet.

By the early years of the nineteenth century, then, it is clear that the Jie demand for ironware was easily being met by the Labwor, and to a lesser extent by the Ngikuliak. By a date which must have corresponded closely to the commencement of the Poet war (about 1810–20), the smiths were obviously capable of producing a surfeit of ironware, for the Jie were beginning to play an increasingly important middle-man role in the traffic of Labwor iron goods eastwards to the Turkana. Ironware was not the only commodity being traded to the Turkana. A fairly constant flow of a variety of trade stems appears to have gone on between the two peoples throughout the latter part of the eighteenth and the entire nineteenth centuries. Amongst the Jie, the women of Nakapelimoru territorial division became relatively skilled potters, and their cooking and water pots were held in great esteem by the Turkana, none of whom could make pottery of their own. Although it happened no more often than once in several years, Najie was sometimes blessed with an exceedingly good rainy season, and at such times there would be a great surplus of sorghum and other agricultural produce. During such 'good years', it was not uncommon for a considerable amount of grain and other produce to be traded to the Turkana: 'When times were good in Najie, the Turkana used to drive cattle to Najie, to trade them for sorghum. Often the Turkana took donkeys with them to carry the food back to their homes.'[59]

As this tradition indicates, it was mainly livestock (especially cattle) that the Turkana exchanged for the Jie (or Labwor) goods, although a special blue clay, used for mudding their elaborate head-dresses, and found only in Turkana-land, was in great demand by the Jie. Perhaps somewhat curiously, the Jie seem to have been little concerned with making any substantial profit from their commercial activity, and certainly nothing resembling a class of 'professional' traders ever arose among the Jie (with the exception of those who appeared temporarily after the great disasters of the late nineteenth century).[60] As there was considerable intermarriage between the Jie and Turkana throughout their entire historical experience, much of the commercial activity was conducted between affinal kinsmen.

[59] Pelekec, Akwawi, and others, T 7.
[60] See Chapter VII.

Indeed, a number of traditions recall that goods were sometimes 'given freely' by one group to the other, although a reciprocal gift was clearly expected when the original donors should fall upon harder times.[61]

As we saw in Chapter IV, the emigration of the dissatisfied Ngimonia Turkana had taken them eastwards from Najie, back across the Koten–Magos area, and on down the escarpment to the headwaters of the Tarash River where they joined with the pre-existing Ngicuro. The Turkana community which thus evolved along the headwaters of the Tarash soon became aware of the existence of other peoples just to their east. At night the Turkana could see fires flickering on Pelekec and other hills, and young men were sent out to investigate:

> As the Turkana began to push out from Moru Anayece [on the upper Tarash], they encountered 'red people' (*arengak angowat*). We say they were 'red people' because they had very light skins. They also coloured their hair and bodies red with clay. They were different from the Turkana or the people who were in Najie, all of whom were black people. Those 'red people' were the Ngikor [Samburu]. The Turkana fought them and drove them away from the places near Tarash.[62]

It seems likely that these first conflicts with the Samburu took place during the time spanned by the initiations of the Nginute (or Ngisuguru) generation-set, which probably initiated between about 1760 and 1800 (see Figure 5.). Having taken the Pelekec area, the Turkana appear to have been satisfied for a time with its occupation and settlement and with raiding those Samburu who lived beyond Pelekec for livestock (whereby they acquired their first camels). During the initiations of the next generation-set, Ngiputiro (*c*. 1800–40), however, the Turkana embarked on a period of territorial expansion quite unparalleled by any other Central Paranilotic-speaking people. The first of the Turkana wars of expansion was directed against those Samburu between Pelekec and the western shore of Lake Rudolf. The Samburu, together with the Rendille and Boran peoples with whom they were allied, were handed a series of massive defeats. Large numbers of them were captured and assimilated into Turkana society, and the survivors were beaten back, first to

---

[61] This is very much in line with the notion of 'bond friendship', a relationship entered into by non-kinsmen to establish reciprocal stock rights. See Gulliver, *Family Herds*, pp. 209–12.

[62] Eregai, Eri, and Mana, T 18.

the shores of the lake, and finally right around its southern tip into the country still occupied by the Samburu south-east of the lake. According to traditions collected by Spencer amongst the Samburu, the vanguard of the expanding Turkana was pushing south-eastwards from Lake Rudolf towards Lake Baringo during the initiations of the Kipayang age-set of the Samburu, which was initiating between about 1823 and 1837,[63] and Dundas, writing in 1910, estimated that the expansion had successfully penetrated to Baringo by about 1840.[64]

While the centre of the Turkana expansion thus drove the Samburu and their allies east, and then south-east around the lake, a northern and a southern wing of the expanding Turkana swung out from the centre. The northern wing smashed pockets of Dongiro at Loriono-tom, Mogila, and Songot in what was to become north-western Turkana-land, and drove them north into the Sudan. Dodos settlers who had begun to descend the escarpment into the Oropoi and the Ngimoruitai areas were also attacked and beaten back up the escarpment into Karamoja. The southern wing of the Turkana encountered a community of Kalenjin-speaking Pokot ('Upe' to the Turkana) near Losogom in what was to become southern Turkana-land, and split it in two: one group fleeing southwards to the safety of the Pokot Hills; and the other trekking northwards across central Turkana-land to the northern tip of Lake Rudolf where they formed the core of the Merille people ('Malire' to the Turkana). The Turkana southern wing also encountered an extremely heterogeneous group, remembered in the traditions as 'Ngisigari', who lived all around the massif known as Moru Apalon ('the great mountain') or Moru Asigar ('the mountain of the Ngisigari)', just below the escarpment, in what became south-western Turkana-land. Those Ngisigari, who appear to have been a loose confederation of Kalenjin-, Southern Paranilotic-, and Central Paranilotic-speaking elements, were utterly routed by the Turkana attacks, and like the Pokot–Merille group, widely dispersed. A large proportion of them, reeling under the Turkana onslaught and smitten almost simultaneously with a famine

[63] P. Spencer, *Nomads in Alliance* (London, 1973), pp. 150-53. Gulliver also described the expansion of the Turkana in his *Preliminary Survey of the Turkana*.

[64] K. R. Dundas, 'Notes on the Tribes Inhabiting the Baringo District', *JRAI* 40 (1910), 50–1. From observations he made in the 1880s, von Hohnel concluded that the Samburu had been driven from the western side of Lake Rudolf 'a few decades ago' (*The Discovery of Lakes Rudolf and Stefanie*, ii, 185). On p. 236 he again estimates that the event took place about fifty years before, i.e. about 1835.

caused by a drought, abandoned Moru Apalon and fled to the north-
west towards Lake Rudolf. Many of them only reached the area near
Moru Eris west of the lake before the group halted, and large numbers died of starvation and exhaustion. A place called *Kabosan*
('rotten') still marks the area in which their corpses littered the
ground. Some of the survivors eventually reached the lake, while
others moved southwards to the Turkwell River, but both groups
were soon absorbed into Turkana society where they still exist as the
Ngisigari division. Many of the other Ngisigari, including most of
the Central Paranilotic-speaking elements, also abandoned Moru
Apalon, and retreated to the west, climbing the escarpment to enter
Karamoja in the Apule River area. In the span of a single generation-
set, then, the Turkana swept aside all opposition and occupied a
vast territorial area almost equivalent in size to the area they presently
inhabit. Their population was greatly increased by the absorption of
vast numbers of defeated aliens.

The Turkana, who included no smelters or blacksmiths in their
numbers, were forced to rely almost entirely on the friendly Jie for a
supply of Labwor-made iron weapons. Turkana traditions still recall the important supporting role in the expansion played by the Jie:
'The Ngikor, Upe, Malire, and Karimojong were all defeated and
driven from this land by our ancestors. All those people were defeated
with spears made by the Labwor and brought to us by our Jie
friends.'[65]

The expansion of the Turkana was to be of great, if somewhat in-
direct, consequence to the Jie community. The Ngisigari con-
federation at Moru Apalon was made up of such diverse elements
that it is difficult to be completely certain of its exact composition.
Nevertheless, it does seem certain that it was partly made up of
Central Paranilotic-speaking elements from that group of Koten–
Magos peoples who had occupied the Apule River area south of the
Magos Hills some time in the early part of the eighteenth century.
When the southern subdivision of the Koten–Magos group occupied
the Apule area, some of them, including the majority of those who
were eventually to form the Matheniko section of the Karimojong,
spilled eastwards down the escarpment where they occupied areas
along the western foot of Moru Apalon and became part of the
Ngisigari confederation (see Map 13). Both Karimojong and Turkana
traditions clearly recall their presence at Moru Apalon and their subsequent expulsion during the Turkana wars of expansion:

[65] Lokimak, T 14.

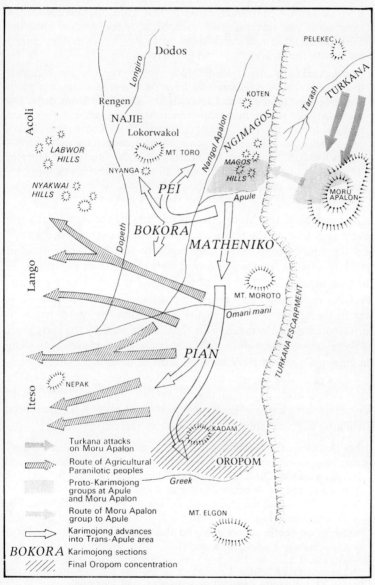

MAP. 13 The expansion of the Karimojong.

When the Bokora [section of the Karimojong] were living at Nakwa-kipi near Apule, our Matheniko ancestors were down there at Moru Apalon, at the well called Lokepoto. The Turkana lived to the east at that time and they referred to our people as 'Ngisigari'. There is still a big clan of the Matheniko called by that name. Our people herded their cattle and planted their gardens at Moru Apalon until the Turkana attacked and drove them up to Apule, where they joined again with the Bokora.[66]

Moru Apalon is often called 'Moru Asigar' because the Ngisigari lived there. Those Ngisigari who lived on this side of the mountain were Ngikor [Samburu] and I myself am descended from them. On the other side of the mountain were other Ngisigari, but they were really Karimojong. They were at Akwapua, Sogo, Lokoromeri, Loke-poto, and other places. Only some of the Karimojong were there—others lived up there above the escarpment in the direction of Moroto. Then the Turkana came and chased all the Ngisigari away. My own ancestors were captured and became Turkana, while those Karimo-jong ran back to their brothers up there [in Karamoja].[67]

The arrival of the Moru Apalon refugees in the Apule area put severe pressures on the resources of the already overcrowded area,[68] and the Apule group desperately began to search for new areas in which to expand. To the north-west were the Jie, well established in the area beyond Mt. Toror, and to the east and north-east were the Turkana occupying every area along the foot of the escarpment. It was to the south, then, across the Apule, that the group began to turn its attention. Fortunately for them, there were by the early years of the nineteenth century considerable population movements going on amongst many of those peoples, most of them Agricultural Para-eniloties (see Map 4), who had been the previous inhabitants of the trans-Apule area. Much of this movement was westwards out of Karamoja into eastern Teso, and it is remembered to have been caused by a 'great famine', most probably the Laparanat:

My ancestors, the Ngariama, lived at Lokales [in the southern part of what was to become the Karimojong area], and their neighbours and friends were the Kumama [Iteso] . . . Then came the great famine. The Ngariama and the Kumama had had a few cattle, but they all died. No rain fell and all the crops died. All the people had to disperse. The Kumama went away to the west, while the Ngariama also dispersed, some going north, others going to the mountains to join the Tepes

[66] Emanikor and Lodum, MTK 1.
[67] Nawoto, T 19.
[68] The emigration of the Lokorikituk in the late eighteenth century (see Chapter V) apparently provided only marginal and temporary relief to the overcrowded conditions on the Apule.

or the Ngiyale [Sebei]. The group called 'Miro' who lived near Napak
were also forced to go to the west where they became known as
'Ngiseera'. The Oropom were also affected by the famine, but they
were different people who were mainly cattle-herders, and so it was
not so bad for them . . . Not long after the famine the Karimojong,
who had been living north of the Apule, began coming south into
this land and took it for their own.[69]

Given such an opportunity, the Apule people, who were soon to
form the core of the Karimojong community, poured across the
river and took up residence in the areas recently vacated by the Agricultural Paranilotic emigrants, assimilating those pockets of them
who had remained behind. For the most part, the occupation of the
trans-Apule area was a peaceful one, and it was only when the immigrants began to encounter the sizeable Oropom population in the
Kaceliba area well to the south of the Apule that they met with any
resistance (see Map 13). The Oropom, who were by this time an
extremely heterogenous group composed of many different linguistic
elements, were, as the preceding tradition states, a largely pastoral
people, and they had remained virtually intact during the famine.
Nevertheless, their resistance melted in the face of Karimojong
attacks, and soon they found themselves in a very desperate situation:

The Karimojong kept beating the Oropom and drove them further
and further south. Finally the Oropom became tired of running. They
began killing their cattle to make leather ropes out of their skins.
They tied themselves together with those ropes so that none could
run away. They said, 'We are tired of running—it is better that we
should all die here together'.[70]

Writing in 1916, Captain Turpin reported that the destruction of
the Oropom took place during the time of the grandfathers of his
informants, and Lawrance and, more recently Wilson, have agreed
that the Oropom were dispersed by about 1830.[71] From Sebei oral
tradition, Weatherby has similarly estimated that the first Karimojong raids directed against the Mt. Elgon area were pushing southwards across the headwaters of the Greek River sometimes during the
1830s.[72] These dates for the southern expansion of the Karimojong

[69] Longorio, BK 9.
[70] Loyep (John) and Lobanyang (Esero), BK 2.
[71] C. A. Turpin, 'The Occupation of the Turkwel River Area by the Karama-
jong Tribe', *UJ* 12 (1948), and E.A. 2364, Part III; Lawrance, op. cit. (1957),
p. 10; Wilson, loc. cit. (1970), 126.
[72] J. M. Weatherby, 'Inter-Tribal Warfare on Mt. Elgon in the Nineteenth
and Twentieth Centuries', *UJ* 26 (1962), 200, 204, and map on p. 210. From

and the destruction of the Oropom tie in well with Karimojong traditions which state that the occupation of the trans-Apule area went
on during the time of the initiations of the Ngigete generation-set
and was complete by the time that the following generation-set,
Ngingatunyo, was inaugurated. Figure 5 shows that dates thus
indicated would be between about 1800 and 1840.

Except for the resistance offered by the Oropom, the occupation
of most of the territory beyond the Apule was carried out both peacefully and rapidly. By about 1840 the people who had crossed the
Apule, together with those pockets of previous inhabitants whom
they had assimilated, had evolved the Karimojong community,
composed of three major, and several minor, territorial sections. The
Matheniko, one of the major sections, which comprised many of the
former 'Ngisigari' elements of Moru Apalon, inhabited the area
southwards from the Apule and around the eastern foot of Mt.
Moroto, while the Pian, another of the major sections, composed
mainly of Matheniko break-aways, lived further south, in the areas
once inhabited by the Ngariama and Oropom. The third major
section, the Bokora, occupied the more western parts of the newly
acquired area, with territory extending almost as far north as the
southern foot of Mt. Toror, beyond which lay Najie. Two of the
minor sections, the Ngipei, just to the south-east of Toror, and
the Ngimagos, living in part of the area once inhabited by the Koten–
Magos concentration, also occupied territories which lay adjacent
to Najie (see Map 13). Unwittingly, then, the supplying of iron
weapons by the Jie community to their friends, the Turkana, had
helped to set off a rapid chain of events which culminated in the
appearance of a numerically powerful community along much of the
southern and south-eastern frontier of Najie.

By some date just before the mid-nineteenth century, the Jie were
becoming aware of the Karimojong presence to the south and south-
east, while to the north they were even more keenly aware of the
presence of the longer-established Dodos. By the middle of the
nineteenth century, therefore, virtually all of the independent Agricultural Paranilotic communities were gone, having retreated westwards out of Karamoja, or having been assimilated by the new, more
heterogeneous Central Paranilotic-speaking societies which replaced

---

Tepes oral traditions and genealogies, Weatherby, in personal communication,
estimated that the first Karimojong settlers coming south from the Apule
had established themselves in the Moroto area perhaps a decade before these
raids on Elgon.

them. The Jie community found itself in the rather unenviable position of being sandwiched between its more numerically powerful northern and southern neighbours, each of whom, like the Jie, based a large part of its economy on transhumant pastoralism. Although all three communities contained a core of clans descended from elements of the Koten–Magos concentration, together with assimilated Agricultural Paranilotic and other elements, each had undergone its own peculiar evolution, unparalleled by the other two. It is hardly surprising that by mid-century each group regarded itself as completely different and totally independent from the others. Nor is it surprising that, as each community strove to assert its control over important resources of water, grazing, and salt-licks on the peripheries of its settled area, friction between them should develop. Because of its unfortunate geographical position and its numerical inferiority, the Jie community was to be at the centre of this friction which, from the middle of the nineteenth century, ushered in an era of conflict unlike any that had gone before, an era which was to be of critical importance to the development of the Jie community.

CHAPTER VII

The Era of Warfare, Disasters, and Strangers.

BEFORE the second half of the nineteenth century, the Jie community had experienced little in the way of major military conflict. The one great exception to an otherwise basically peaceful history was the Poet war in which the armies of the Ngisiroi generation-set had crushed the last major Agricultural Paranilotic community in north-central Karamoja.[1] While one suspects that the 'Camkok tradition' may be a truncated recollection of a rather longer conflict with the western Kapwor, there is nothing to suggest that whatever fighting may have occurred was any more than a series of intensive cattle raids. Jie traditions do indicate that a certain amount of desultory raiding against other neighbouring peoples went on before the mid-nineteenth century, but such activity was clearly more in the nature of petty thievery than outright warfare. In the words of Jie informants, 'before the time of Eluii [a battle-leader who was active from about the middle of the century] there were raids and people fought with whips. But there were not the same big wars as there were afterwards.'[2]

Even in the years following the inauguration in about 1840 of the Ngikokol generation-set, the sons of the victorious Ngisiroi, conflict with neighbouring peoples does not appear to have been very serious, as the following traditions describing a raid on the Acoli demonstrate:

> After their inauguration, the young men of the Ngikokol stayed at the cattle-camps in the west for several years without coming home, and they began to think of themselves as very strong and brave. Their fathers, the Ngimadanga [age-set of Ngisiroi], became very angry with them for not coming home and they gave them the nickname *Ngiki-wan* [little children]. The Ngikokol therefore organized a big raid against the Acoli at Logili without telling their fathers, but they were badly defeated by the Acoli . . .[3]

[1] See Chapter VI.
[2] Nakade (Peter), Loceng (Natwanga), and others, J 16.
[3] Teko (Apalokoero), Acukwa (Urule), Lokoryang (Edoon), and Lokori (Atiangolem), J 21.

After they were beaten by the Acoli, they ran back to the Kanamuget River which they found swollen with rain. Some of them managed to escape, but many were swept away and drowned. Those who escaped came back to Najie with only one [captured] cow.[4]

However, the evolution of the Dodos and Karimojong communities to the north and south of Najie, respectively, steadily built up pressures in the peripheral grazing areas of Najie, as the cattle-camps of all three communities strove to assert their control over vital dry-season resources.[5] By the middle of the nineteenth century such rivalries were most acute along the borderland near Mt. Toror, which separated the southern territorial divisions of the Ngikorwakol from the northern settlements of the Bokora Karimojong. The Pan-yangara, who were the southernmost of the Ngikorwakol divisions, clustered near their deep wells at Lokibuwo, experienced the closest contacts with the newly arriving Bokora:

The Karimojong found that they lacked grass and sorghum in their old area [i.e. the Apule River area], and their cattle were dying. Some therefore came to the north-west towards Toror. Those were the Bokora. When they first arrived, they found the Panyangara settled near Toror and at first there was peace. The Bokora made an agreement with the Panyangara and all was well. But then they grew jealous for they saw that the Jie had many cattle and much sorghum and that their place was good. It was mostly the young men of the Bokora who lived near Toror, and they began to raid the Jie cattle, as young men do.[6]

The friction engendered in the Toror area had its first effects, not on either of the main participants, but on two of the smaller groups who unfortunately inhabited neighbouring areas. The first to be affected were a group of Fringe-Cushitic-speaking Tepes, who were mainly engaged in trapping and gathering on Toror itself and on Nyanga, an isolated peak just to the south. Seeking to turn the rivalry to their advantage, the Tepes tried to join in the cattle-raiding themselves, but only incurred the swift retribution of the Karimojong and the Jie, and were forced to abandon their homes and flee south to another Tepes community on Mt. Moroto.[7] Like the Tepes, the Nyakwai who lived in the hills south-west of Toror, also tried their hand at raiding, and succeeded in making off with a number of Jie

[4] Lokelo (Anjelo), and others, J 43.
[5] See Chapter VI.
[6] Looru (Sampson), Tede (Teko), and others, J 9.
[7] Lonyangakan (and others), J 65. Other informants, including those of J 30 and 131, stated that a chronic shortage of water contributed to their departure.

cattle before several of the southern divisions of Lokorwakol banded together and launched so severe an attack on them that the Nyakwai were even forced to flee from their hills for a time.[8] This open conflict with the Tepes and Nyakwai may have done much temporarily to relieve the friction which was building up between the Jie and Bokora. At any rate, the first major hostilities along the new frontiers were not in the Toror area, but further east in the Koten and Magos Hills area which had been the former homeland of the Koten–Magos group.

By the middle of the nineteenth century, the area was occupied by a people who took their name, 'Ngimagos', from the Magos Hills, and who were closely associated with Karimojong sections to their west and south by that date.[9] The Jie and the Turkana had maintained a fairly close relationship largely based on the trade in Labwor ironware, and by some date not long after 1850, both the Turkana and the Jie clearly regarded the Ngimagos, inhabiting the area between Najie and the Turkana escarpment, as a hindrance to free passage between the two areas: 'After the Turkana went away from Najie to Tarash, the Ngimagos, who lived at Koten and Magos, began to cause trouble. If Turkana tried to come to Najie for any reason, the Ngimagos would ambush them near Koten. This angered the Turkana and the Jie, and the Turkana began to fight them.[10]

The Ngimagos further provoked the Jie by raiding their cattle-camps near Kocolut on the eastern periphery of Najie, and the young men of the Ngikokol generation-set (mainly, if not exclusively, those of the Ngikorwakol territorial divisions) began to attack the Ngimagos from the west, while the Turkana continued their attacks from the east. The joint attacks had the effect of pushing the Ngimagos into a more confined area centred on the Magos Hills, and most probably did much to further strengthen the ties between the Ngimagos and the neighbouring Karimojong sections.[11]

While the conflict with the Ngimagos thus provided some relief to the tensions along the Mt. Toror frontier, that relief was only short-

[8] Adiaka and Adiako (Cesere), NY 2; also Herring, 'Origins and Development', pp. 9–10. Herring estimates that the Nyakwai returned to their hills between about 1840 and 1850 after their dispersal by the Jie.

[9] The origin of the Magos remains somewhat of a mystery. There are some strong hints that the group contained a strong Agricultural Paranilotic element, partly composed of Ngieyan emigrants from Mt. Orom. See my London Ph.D. thesis, p. 375, for a fuller discussion.

[10] Longeria and Nakwo, J 115.

[11] Lobilatum and Lopacura, J 46.

lived, and very soon the situation in the Toror area deteriorated into open hostility between the Bokora and the Panyangara territorial division. The trouble began when a large number of Bokora young men crossed the grazing lands separating the settlements of the rival communities and drove their herds into the settled area of the Panyangara. There was a brief clash at Nakoret Amoni, not far west of the Panyangara settlements clustered near the Lokibuwo deep wells, and then the Bokora pushed on towards the Lokibuwo area itself:

> When the Ngikoria [or Ngikokol] generation-set were young men, the Bokora arrived at the Panyangara settlements near Toror with their cattle just at harvest time. The Bokora herds were guarded by a great number of warriors, and they saw that they were more numerous than the Panyangara warriors. The Bokora began to feel pride, and they said, 'We have brought our cattle to feed on your sorghum. Do not refuse, or it will mean great trouble for you'. But the Jie were clever, and tricked them, saying, 'You speak truly. We can see you are many and we are few. Give us four days so that we can gather all our sorghum for your cattle and then we shall give it to you'. So the Bokora moved back a bit and built kraals just at the foot of the mountain, and they waited. On the fourth day the Bokora drove their cattle back towards the Jie settlements. But in those four days, the Panyangara had prepared themselves for battle, and had asked the other Jie to come to their assistance.[12]

There followed what was probably to be the greatest single military engagement that the Jie had yet experienced:

> When the Bokora came to feed their cattle on the sorghum of the Panyangara, the other Jie, including even the Rengen, came to help the Panyangara. A very great battle was fought. The fighting was very confused, with everyone fighting together. It was difficult to be sure who was a friend and who was an enemy. The fighting was so confused that the place where the battle was fought is still called *Nangodiai* [from *akingodia*, 'to mix up people together in one place'].[13]

The battle lasted for almost an entire day, but by evening the Bokora had been badly defeated and were in full retreat. Large numbers of the Bokora cattle were taken by the victors, some being captured even by the Panyangara women who followed close behind the advance of the warriors. Small groups of Bokora fled up the slopes of Mt. Toror seeking refuge on the heights, but many were tracked

[12] Nakade (Peter), Loceng (Natwanga), and others, J 16.
[13] Alinga (and others), J 41.

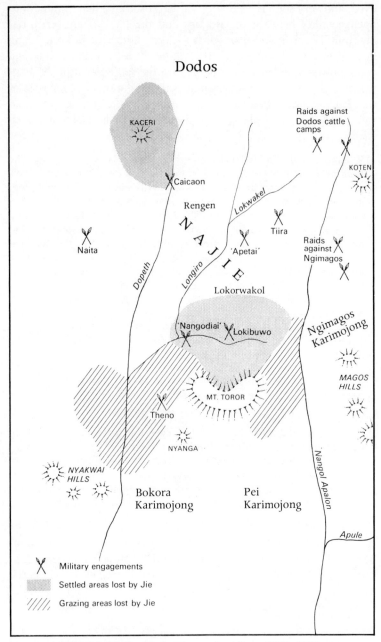

MAP 14. Major Jie battles and raids. *c.* 1860–1902.

down and killed. Informants indicated that the Ngimuria age-section of the Ngikokol formed the basis of the Jie army and that some Ngisiroi (presumably of the junior age-sets) were also active enough to participate in the fighting. It was further stated that most of the Bokora warriors belonged to the Ngikadokoi age-set of their Ngingatunyo generation-set (*see* Figure 3 and Figure 5). From all indications, therefore, the battle of Nangodiai must have taken place about 1860; and from that date nearly continuous warfare was to rage in central Karamoja until the second decade of the twentieth century.

The confused mêlée of the battle of Nangodiai provides an opportunity to examine briefly the Jie military system as it existed at that time. Until the end of the nineteenth century, Jie military organization and tactics were little more than rudimentary, and informants indicated that before the Ngikokol generation-set, anything that could even vaguely be termed a battle formation was totally lacking: 'Before the Ngikoria [or Ngikokol] began their initiations, there were no special arrangements of Jie armies. Everyone would go together in one big group.'[14]

It seems, therefore, that the armies that raided the Kapwor and defeated the Poet were hardly more than armed mobs. Personal bravery was geatly admired and encouraged, and men who killed an enemy in battle were honoured with a 'battle name', and were allowed to scar their breasts and shoulders and to cut the ears of their oxen in a special way. Men of outstanding courage and physical prowess became 'battle-leaders' to whom a band of twenty or so warriors might attach themselves as a kind of 'private company'. Most Jie military activity until after the middle of the nineteenth century took the form of intermittent raiding rather than large-scale campaigns, and a great many of these raids were carried out by a handful of men of a 'private company' under the leadership of their chosen battle-leader. Typical of such battle-leaders was Eluii, a man of Komukuny territorial division and a member of the Ngimuria age-set of the Ngikokol generation-set, who was active during the mid-nineteenth century. Although commanding only a small band of warriors from his own immediate neighbourhood, his bravery and success in raiding is still widely remembered in Jie oral tradition: 'Eluii was a brave warrior and a great cattle raider (*ekeerwon*). He would take five or ten men, or even go alone, and capture large numbers of enemy cattle. He was very fierce ... He used to go

---

[14] Atoong, Lokapel, Looru, and Modo, J 25.

against the enemies like a madman and crush any who dared to fight him.'[15]

While the fame of the battle-leaders depended largely on their success in raids, they also acted as rallying points and often provided the only effective leadership for their 'private companies' in larger-scale military actions: 'Long ago, Jie armies had no special leaders except for the brave men who would encourage others by their example.[16]

The chief weapons of the Jie were willowy, eight-foot spears made for them by the Labwor smiths, and heavy rectangular shields made by the Jie themselves or by Ngikuliak trappers from the hides of buffalo, rhino, elephant, and especially giraffe. Fighting-sticks, wrist- and finger-knives were used to a much lesser extent in hand to hand fighting. Most warriors carried two spears which they had been trained to use from early childhood by throwing sticks through a rolling *ekorobe* hoop, and the average warrior could invariably hit a moving target at 25 yards or more. Formal military training did not exist, but the rigours (and indeed the dangers) of their life at the cattle-camps in itself served to toughen the young men both physically and psychologically. At dances and rituals, boys had a frequent opportunity to observe mock battles and to watch the stylized dodging and bobbing used by the warriors as a means of defence against enemy spears in a battle situation. From adolescence, young men developed rivalries over girls which often culminated in whip or stick fights in which severe scarring and broken bones were frequent, and their initiation into the generation-set system ensured that young men learned discipline and respect for authority.[17]

With the beginning of Ngikokol initiations in about 1840, when the Karimojong and Dodos pressures along the frontiers of Najie were beginning to become apparent, a military organization or offensive actions was devised, based on the *nganyameta* (age-sets) of the men who composed the army: 'Armies would be arranged by age-sets. The senior age-set would be placed in the centre, with the others formed up to the right and left. The army would then advance toward the enemy like the fingers of a hand, with each "finger" being one age-set.'[18]

The constituent age-sets would be distinguished by the wearing of particular feathers and other decorations proper to their status in the

---

[15] Apei (Adolungiro), Lokomolo, and Lotyang, J 22; also J 18 and 34.
[16] Lobilatum, J 11.
[17] Interviews including J 18, 44 and 125.
[18] Lowot, Loworo, Lobwal and others, J 8. See Fig. 7.

generation-set system, with more senior age-sets tending to wear elaborate ostrich feather head-dresses and baboon-skin capes, and the juniors wearing only a single plume.[19] Tactics, however, continued to be conceived of in terms of raiding, and the capture of livestock was often considered more important than decisively defeating the enemy:

> In a big fight the various age-sets of the army had their own jobs to do. I mean, the older age-sets would try to capture the cattle of the enemy, and the younger age-sets, who had little experience in fighting, would be told to drive the cattle back towards Najie while the older age-sets protected them.[20]

Although the armies were thus (at least theoretically) organized by age-sets, each 'finger' of the battle formation continued to be composed largely of the 'private companies' owing allegiance mainly, if not entirely, to their own chosen battle-leader. Thus, a Jie army before the latter part of the nineteenth century was more of a patchwork of independent squadrons than a cohesive army. With this organization and these tactics, it is hardly surprising that the battle against the Karimojong at Toror should have been called *Nangodiai*: 'confusion'.

Such tactics and organization appear to have been typical of all the Central Paranilotic societies of that time. The Jie did have one at least potentially important refinement, however: the hereditary war-leader (*ekapalon ka-ajore*). Each Jie major division had its own clan from which the leaders were chosen; for the Ngikorwakol it was the Lodoca of Panyangara division, and for the Rengen it was a branch of the Kalolet of Logatap division, the same clan that provided the Rengen fire-makers after about 1830. The earliest of the Lodoca war leaders specifically recalled in the traditions is Meron, a member of the Ngikok generation-set who was succeeded before the middle of the nineteenth century by his son, Acuka, who belonged to the Ngisiroi generation-set. Acuka's Rengen contemporary was a man called Natebele, who was a member of the Ngiyarameri age-set of the Ngisiroi.[21]

Although in theory the hereditary war-leader was regarded as the commander of all the military forces of his major-division, in practise his authority was minimal. The actual planning of large-scale raids and other military activities was entrusted to the congregation of

---

[19] Lokec (Lomoramoe), Lomoni (Belukamoe), and Apeyo (Coban), J 49.
[20] Angura (and others), J 19.
[21] Lobwal, J-34; Kojo (Looya) and Lolwanamoe, J 60.

senior elders, while ritual preparations were carried out by the fire-makers, and to a much lesser extent, by the diviners. As we have seen, the actual leadership on the battle-field was mainly provided by the individual battle-leaders over their largely autonomous 'private companies', and by far the majority of military activity took the form of small-scale raids, again under the leadership of individual battle-leaders. Eluii, the Komukuny battle-leader and raider, is far better remembered in Jie oral tradition than the hereditary war-leader, Acuka, who was theoretically his commander. The role of the hereditary war-leader, therefore, appears to have been little more than that of a figure-head who might at best hope to have some say in deciding matters of strategy (such as they were) and perhaps provide a certain cohesive element to bring about some integration of the highly segmentary armies. His control over an army was marginal, and after a successful operation he would go entirely un-heeded as his warriors brawled among themselves to lay claim to captured cattle or other booty.[22]

The Jie therefore largely ignored the potential importance of their hereditary war-leaders and relied instead on a military system in which personal courage and independent action were the main in-gredients. While such a system was apparently adequate enough during the long era which preceded the mid-nineteenth century, it was to prove totally inadequate in the martial era which followed.

At approximately the same time that the tensions in the Toror area erupted into serious conflict at Nangodiai, there was also in-creasing friction along the north-western frontier of Najie. The cause of this friction was the by now familiar problem of the Kapeta watering points and grazing lands. The Jie victory over the Agricul-tural Paranilotic Poet had ensured free access to the Kapeta for the cattle-camps of the Rengen and the northern territorial divisions of the Lokorwakol, but had added considerably to the strength of the Dodos community as large numbers of Poet refugees fled east to form the Lokaato section. The Dodos, by now a fully evolved and expanding community, eyed the Kapeta resources with envy, and the Lokaato section, nearest to Najie, was still smouldering with resent-ment towards those who had driven their ancestors from their home-land. Jie traditions recall a number of relatively minor skirmishes with the Dodos in the area west of the Dopeth River, and although no battle of the magnitude of Nangodiai was fought, the Rengen settlers who had reoccupied the Kaceri area began to fall back and

[22] Lowor (Elizeo) and others, J 58.

gradually abandoned the whole of the trans-Dopeth area once again. Although they had felt secure enough to send a contingent to the aid of the Panyangara, within a very short time thereafter, the Rengen found themselves fully occupied in maintaining their control over their north-western resources in the face of ever-increasing Dodos incursions. The Lokorwakol divisions, themselves concerned with Karimojong pressures to the south and south-east, could offer little support to the Rengen, who were forced to deal with the Dodos virtually alone: 'When the Rengen began fighting the Dodos across the Dopeth, the Ngikorwakol were busy with their fights with the Bokora. Only a few men would go from here [Lokorwakol] to help them fight the Dodos. Most of the Ngikorwakol warriors had to remain in Lokorwakol.[23]

By a date soon after the middle of the nineteenth century, then, the Jie were experiencing increasing pressures along much of their southern and northern frontiers. To the Dodos and Karimojong, the Jie, or more correctly, the 'Ngiro' community (as it was still called at that time) represented a barrier to the expansions of their own frontiers and an impediment to their asserting control over vital resources in the peripheral areas. In reflection of the annoyance they felt towards their troublesome neighbours and the increased frictions which were growing up between them, both the Dodos and the Karimojong began to refer to the 'Ngiro' by a new nickname:

At first our people were called 'Ngiro' because we lived here in the land near the Longiro River ... Then the wars came. At first there were only fights with whips and then with clubs. Finally there were fights with spears. Our ancestors began to fight the Dodos and Karimojong more and more over the use of water-holes. We resisted the attacks of all those enemies. Our grandfathers began to be called *Ngijie* ['the fighting people'] by those enemies because they fought well, even though those enemies were many more than we were.[24]

Thus, instead of resenting the new nickname which was meant to be a scornful statement on their truculence, as seen through the eyes of their northern and southern rivals, both the Ngikorwakol and the Rengen accepted the name with pride and would henceforth refer to themselves as *Ngijie*.

The victory of the Jie at Nangodiai was to be short-lived. There soon were renewed and increasingly intense Karimojong pressures in the Toror area. While the main Jie settlements in the Toror area

---

[23] Lothike (Elawa), Longok (Apacelem), and Ekongor, J 29.
[24] Apei (Adolungiro), Lokomolo, and Lotyang, J 22; also J 7, 99, and 104.

were those of the Panyangara, focused on the Lokibuwo deep wells, the neighbours of the Panyangara, the Komukuny, had also established settlements in the southern part of their own division, not far to the west of Lokibuwo. Up to the time of the battle of Nangodiai, the Komukuny contributed much to the defence of the Toror area, and the Panyangara appear to have regarded them as their firmest allies. As Karimojong pressures once again increased after Nangodiai, however, the Kokumuny appear to have tired of the constant friction in the area, and decided to pull their settlements back to the northern parts of their division in central Najie. As they watched their erstwhile allies moving away to the north, the young men of the Panyangara became furious and perpetrated an action unparalleled in Jie historical experience:

> When the Panyangara were settled at Lokibuwo, Nacailap, and Kaicodo, the Komukuny lived nearby at Lakanyam and in the Nangodiai area. When the enemies [Karimojong] began to attack that area more and more frequently, the Komukuny decided to leave that area. They decided to go north and leave the Panyangara to fight the enemies alone. The Panyangara became very angry and they cried: 'Let us go and castrate their bulls!' They attacked the Komukuny with whips and clubs and there was a big fight. Finally the Panyangara were beaten, and they went back to Lokibuwo alone while the Komukuny went on to the north. This was the only time that Jie ever fought with other Jie in that way. Even in this fight, however, the young men used only sticks and no spears.[25]

Never before had a Jie territorial division fought with another in this way, and apparently the senior elders and even the Jimos firemakers were powerless to prevent it. With the retreat of the Komukuny, Bokora and neighbouring Pei Karimojong attacks on the Panyangara took on an added intensity. Some of the immigrant Kapwor who had not settled with the Panyangara at Lokibuwo had established themselves on the south-eastern side of Toror, and their settlements were soon wiped out by Karimojong onslaughts, as were outlying Panyangara settlements in the Theno area to the south-west.[26] The Karimojong armies followed up these successes by attacking the settlements clustered at Lokibuwo itself, with disastrous results for the Panyangara:

[25] Looru (Sampson) and others, J 52. The phrase 'let us go and castrate their bulls' (*apena atouto ngikec maaniko*) is used by the Jie only when they are very angry, and its meaning is 'to fight and completely subdue someone'.
[26] Interviews including J 7 and 63.

After the settlements at Theno and elsewhere on the western side of Toror were defeated, all of the Panyangara gathered north of the mountain. The Karimojong attacked again and the Panyangara were finally driven from their homes. They fled north across the Lokwakel and Lopurokoca Rivers, retreating back into Najie. Then the Panyangara made peace with the Bokora and they were allowed to move back into some parts of the area.[27]

Informants were agreed that the Panyangara were driven from Lokibuwo when the Ngimuria age-section of Ngikokol was still initiating and that the following age-section, Ngieleki, were still uninitiated boys. It would seem, then, that only a very short time had passed since the battle of Nangodiai, and it is very likely that the Panyangara were expelled sometime during the early 1860s. While it is recalled that the Panyangara recovered some of their lost territory with the peace that quickly followed their expulsion, they do not appear to have returned to the Lokibuwo deep wells, and the grazing lands beyond Toror were firmly retained by the victorious Bokora and Pei Karimojong (see Map 14).

It was not only territory and resources that were lost in the Panyangara expulsion. During the final battle at Lokibuwo, Acuka, the hereditary war-leader of the Ngikorwakol was slain, trying vainly to rally the remnants of his division's warriors. Teko, his eldest son, was duly selected as his successor by the Ngikorwakol elders. No one paid much attention to a younger son, Loriang, who fled northwards from the devastation and defeat at Lokibuwo as an uninitiated boy.

The peace that followed the expulsion of the Panyangara was again short-lived. Conflict appears to have started again when a strong Karimojong raiding party attacked a concentration of Jie cattle-camps at Naita, west of the settled area of Najie. The young men of the cattle-camps rapidly raised the alarm and managed to hold off the Karimojong until reinforcements from other cattle-camps and from the homesteads in Najie arrived and drove the raiders off. The action is still recalled in a Jie war song:

Oh, oh, i-yo, Naita!	Oh! Naita!
Lili! Torutu nyabore.	Lili [the sound of the alarm]. Help the cattle-camps.
Aremo ngimoe nyabore.	Enemies are attacking the cattle-camps.
Ngijie torutu nyabore Naita!	Jie, help the cattle-camps at Naita!

[27] Akuremeri (and others), J 7. See my London Ph. D. thesis, p. 388, for information on Jie peace-making ceremonies.

Apotu ngimoe lore, Naita.   The enemies have come to [our] home,
                              Naita.
Lili! Ngimoe Naita!   Lili! Enemies [at] Naita.[28]

The largely unsuccessful raid on Naita was quickly followed by a major Karimojong offensive campaign. Many Jie traditions claim that the objective of the campaign was to 'wipe out the Jie completely, and the Karimojong sent all of their warriors for this purpose,'[29] while others additionally claim that the Karimojong offensive was co-ordinated with a simultaneous one by the Dodos:

> In those days the Jie were too few to be an aggressive people. Najie was only a small place, like the testicles of a donkey. The Jie could only sit and wait for their powerful enemies to attack them. After the Panyangara were driven from Lokibuwo, the Karimojong went to visit the Dodos and they said, 'Why should we leave these Jie here? They are very few and their place is small. You, Dodos, attack them from the north, and we Karimojong will attack them from the south. They cannot fight us both'. The Karimojong sent a very large army to attack the Jie. Their warriors were drawn up in a line from Toror all the way up to Nakapelimoru [a distance of several miles]. They moved north like a fishing net, burning homesteads and killing many people. At the same time, the Dodos made their own attacks from the north. But the Jie fought very bravely and truly they won their name, *Ngijie* ['the fighting people'].[30]

The campaign, which was given the name *Apetai* ('everywhere'), came very close to being a complete success. In a single day all of the territorial divisions of Lokorwakol were overrun, and the Ngikorwakol retreated north-westwards across the Longiro River into Rengen. Here the unified major divisions put up a fierce last-ditch resistance, and after a very uneasy night, during which the Karimoong warriors slept in the Ngikorwakol homesteads, the young men from the western cattle-camps arrived in Rengen. With the young men of the cattle-camps swelling their numbers, the Jie offered even stiffer resistance to the Karimojong attacks the following day, and during the confused fighting a large Karimojong contingent was trapped at the Agar-Etuko ford in the Lokwakel River and wiped out

---

[28] Nyaramoe, Lokong (Israel), and a group of women, J 37.
[29] Kojo (Looya) and Lolwanamoe, J 60.
[30] Akuremeri (and others), J 7. The Dodos informants of D 3 strongly denied that there was any planned co-ordination between themselves and the Karimojong in these attacks. Whether the co-ordination was consciously planned or not, it still had the same effect of making the Jie fight on two fronts at once.

almost to a man. With this defeat, the Karimojong lost heart and fell
back to the south, abandoning the Lokorwakol settlement area, but
carrying off a great many cattle and other booty, and leaving utter
devastation behind them. The Dodos (who had certainly not pressed
home their offensive with the same determination as the Karimojong) also withdrew, and for the moment, at any rate, the Jie community had survived.[31]

The defeats that they suffered throughout the 1860s undoubtedly
did much to make the Jie community keenly aware of its numerical
inferiority. Jie traditions indicate that both the Karimojong and
the Dodos outnumbered them considerably during the latter half of
the nineteenth century, but they do not make any statement regarding the actual numbers of the respective populations. The earliest
estimate of the population of Najie was that made by H. M. Tufnell,
in 1911, and he concluded that the total adult male population was
'not more than 1500'. In the same year, he estimated that the total
adult male population of the Karimojong was about 'five or six
thousand'.[32] In 1919 Captain Chidlaw-Roberts estimated the Karimojong and Jie adult male populations at 5,298 and 1,869, respectively, and in that same year the *total* population of the Dodos was
estimated at 20,000, which would mean an adult male population of
about 4,000.[33] As all three of the Dodos major sections appear to
have actively waged war on the Jie, it is clear that the Dodos alone
outnumbered the Jie by about two to one, at least by 1919. Not all
of the Karimojong sections took a very active role in the fighting
with the Jie, but even subtracting the adult male populations of the
Pian section (who apparently played virtually no part in the wars
with the Jie) and the Tome section (who lent only occasional support
to the other sections), the adult male population of the other Karimojong sections still stood at about 4,000 in 1919, again outnumber-
ing the Jie by about two to one.[34] In 1919, therefore, the Jie were

[31] Interviews including J 48, 60, 64, and 85.
[32] Tufnell's Reports: 11 Oct. and 11 Sept. 1911, E.A. 2119.
[33] The 1919 estimates are recorded by Barber, op. cit. (1968), pp. 80 and 89.
The estimates were made in reports kept in the Moroto Archives, all of which
were unfortunately destroyed just before Uganda independence. In the following year Chidlaw-Roberts again made estimates of the *total* populations and
his figures were: 'Karamoja Proper' (i.e. Karimojong), 33,000; Jie, 11,000;
Dodos, 20,000; Nyangea and Napore, 3,000 (Capt. J. R. Chidlaw-Roberts,
Report on the Karamoja District of the Uganda Protectorate (Government
Printer, Entebbe, 1920), p. 2).
[34] A breakdown of the populations of the individual Karimojong sections in
1919, based on the destroyed Moroto records, is given by Dyson-Hudson,
op. cit., p. 135.

probably collectively outnumbered four to one by their northern and southern enemies. Although the populations of the three communities probably changed between the 1860s and the 1910s,[35] it would seem reasonable to assume that the ratio between those populations remained fairly constant during that period and to conclude that at the commencement of the long era of conflict the Jie were on some occasions fighting enemy forces as much as four times greater than themselves.

In an attempt to redress the balance, the Jie appear to have actively encouraged the immigration of alien refugees to Najie where they were incorporated into the Jie community. While great famines such as the Nyamdere and the Laparanat resulted in major population movements, it should not be supposed that shifts in population were confined solely to such times. Throughout much of the eighteenth and nineteenth centuries, there appears to have been an almost constant ebbing and flowing of small groups of people, and even of individuals, across much of Karamoja. Like the internal population movement discernible within Najie itself, this constant movement of small groups was attributable to a variety of reasons including feuds, legal troubles, and the myriad minor famines and 'hungry times' which incessantly beset various parts of Karamoja.

Following the early emigrations of the Ngimonia Turkana, Ngikor Toposa, and various Agricultural Paranilotic groups from Najie, a growing Jie population had pioneered new areas and tapped new resources to meet their expanding needs, and had then undertaken internal shifts of population to achieve a more perfect adjustment. When times were good, considerable alien populations, such as the returning Ngiseera and Loposa, together with their Lwo allies, and later the Poet war captives, were absorbed with relative ease. When times were less favourable, alien populations, such as the first of the unfortunate Kapwor starvelings, would be denied entry. With the rise of the powerful Dodos and Karimojong societies to their north and south, the Jie began to find increasing difficulty in maintaining their control over the vital resources of the peripheral areas, and ultimately control over even the more vital settled area of central Najie seemed to be dangerously close to slipping from their grasp. By the 1860s, therefore, the Jie were very anxious to build up their numbers

---

[35] It is quite possible that the populations of the three communities were greater in the 1860s than in the 1910s. The long period of wars, as well as the great disasters of the late nineteenth century, most probably reduced them all.

quickly, and the recruiting of immigrant aliens must have seemed a convenient means of doing it.

Sometime after about 1840 (i.e. during the Ngikokol initiations) a number of the Ngikuliak hunter-gatherers who had lived a largely independent existence at Maru and on other hills came down and joined with the Kotiang division of the Ngikorwakol, forming a major part of two clans, Ngadakori and Lokwor.[36] Then, during the middle years of the nineteenth century, immigrants from the neighbouring Nyakwai, Labwor and Acoli, as well as the more distant Iteso, were incorporated into several territorial divisions of the Jie community. Even immigrants from the enemies of the Jie, the Dodos and Karimojong, began to arrive in Najie, and were also welcomed. In most cases, the immigrants arrived as impoverished refugees, and while many initially provided services for the Jie, they were kindly treated, as traditions of both the immigrants and their hosts recall:

> Strangers came here to Losilang from other tribes. They came as poor people and they served as herdsmen for the original clans here and helped them to dig their wells and do all kinds of work. They would be welcomed with food, for there were few people in Najie at that time, and those strangers helped to increase the numbers of the Jie.[37]

After a time, the immigrants would be asked to help the Jie armies, either by serving as warriors, or by acting as spies against their former people. If the newcomers agreed and proved themselves loyal to their adopted community, they would be completely absorbed into Jie society and considered as 'thoroughly Jie' as the members of even the oldest clans:

> Strangers would come here from the Acoli, Dodos, Nyakwai, and other places. Often they would work as herdsmen for us when they came. If they decided to remain permanently, they were asked to help us fight our wars. If they went on raids and fought in battles, they were given food and captured cattle, so that they could marry wives, and they became Jie.[38]

> My clan is now known as Ngikalopetum. My grandfather, Longamelem, originally came here from Dodos. When he came here, he found that the Jie had few cattle and needed more. The Jie allowed him to settle with them, and asked for his help. He took some of the

[36] See the tradition describing the manner in which these Ngikuliak 'became Jie', in Chapter III.
[37] Loyang (and others), J 19.
[38] Igira (Yaramoe), Lokong, Muria (Longonyo), and Langlang, J 17.

Jie warriors and led them back to Dodos and showed them the homestead of Lokolong, where he knew there were many cattle. The Jie
raided those cattle and brought them back to Najie. It was thus that
Longamalem became a Jie.[39]

While the incorporation of aliens helped to swell the ranks of the
Jie at a critical moment in their history, and the services provided
by immigrant spies were helpful to Jie raiding activity, it is obvious
that not enough immigrants were absorbed to alter significantly the
serious disparity in numbers which existed between the Jie and their
enemies. Clearly, a solution to the military problems which beset the
Jie after the middle of the nineteenth century could not be achieved
only by increasing their numbers. Nevertheless most of the traditions
of these assimilated alien groups stress that they were absorbed as
Jie, rather than as members of a specific territorial division or even
a major division. The increasing pressures of their northern and
southern enemies had done much to blur even further the distinct
autonomy and uniqueness which had formerly been so strong a
feature of the constituent territorial divisions, and to foster an increasing awareness of the integration and unity of a Jie community.

If the Apetai campaign brought devastation to much of Najie, it
also appears to have at least temporarily exhausted the offensive
capabilities of the Karimojong armies. Although the campaign had
failed to destroy the Jie, the Karimojong must have been well satisfied with its results. With the Panyangara and Komukuny Jie driven
away, their own northern frontier was reasonably secure and large
tracts of grazing land as well as important watering resources in the
Toror area had come under their control (*see* Map 14). Neither Karimojong nor Jie oral tradition indicates that any major battles or
campaigns were fought in the years immediately following Apetai,
and it would seem that the old pattern of intermittent raids returned
while each side built up its strength for the inevitable renewal of
more serious conflict.

The encroachment of the Karimojong to the south forced the Jie
to readjust both settlement and grazing patterns. Many of the Panyangara settled near the immigrant Kadokini in the northern part of
their division at Kapuyon, an admirable defensive position near the
confluence of the Lokwakel and Loputh Rivers. The Komakuny
established most of their settlements just to the west of Kapuyon,
again in the northern part of their division and close to the geo-

[39] Acukwa (Urule), J 91.

graphical centre of Najie. In place of the individual homesteads (*ngireria*) or 'clan hamlets', many of the territorial divisions banded their settlements together into a single giant complex, completely surrounded by one stout defensive barricade, and all of the territorial divisions pulled in their outlying homesteads towards the geographical centre of the settled area: 'During the worst of the wars the Jie settlements were all clustered together like those of Nakapelimoru are now. For example, all of the homesteads of Kotido were between Looi and the place where the prison now stands. I myself do not remember seeing the settlements like that, but my grandfather said it was like that in his time.'[40]

With the loss of the grazing lands and water-points near Toror, the Jie cattle-camps had to intensify their activity in other areas. While some of the Panyangara continued to use areas near the Nyakwai Hills, many more cattle-camps began to use the western grazing lands bordering the Labwor and Acoli, with whom relations were basically good. Although pressures from the Dodos were mounting, they had yet to effect the same intensive mobilization as the Karimojong, and the cattle-camps of the Rengen, joined now by increasing numbers of Ngikorwakol, continued to push northwards to the vital grazing and water at Kapeta.[41]

By the mid-1870s, both the Karimojong and the Jie had probably recovered from the effects of the Apetai campaign and were ready for a renewal of serious fighting. In about 1876,[42] however, war preparations were disrupted by a cattle disease which raged through much of Karamoja, decimating the herds of Karimojong and Jie alike. According to Jie informants, the disease, called *Loongoripoko* ('the dark soup', from the foul broth made from the carcasses of cattle which were killed by the disease), appeared near the end of Ngikokol initiations, and its effects are remembered to have been very serious: '*Loongoripoko* came some years before *Lopid*. It killed a great many cattle. Even the cattle which were very healthy and fat grew thinner and thinner until finally they died.'[43]

[40] Akuremeri, J 47. The reference to Nakapelimoru is to the settlements of the Wotokau subdivision which have remained clustered together, surrounded by a barricade, quite unlike other Jie settlements.

[41] Interviews including J 93, 94, and 104.

[42] The date was estimated by Captain Turpin in 1916. Although he terms the disease "Logipi", there can be little doubt that it corresponded to the Jie "Loogoripoko". In an appendix to Turpin (loc. cit. (1948) 165), J. M. Watson, the Agricultural Officer in Karamoja, described "Logipi" as a disease of "watery swelling" and tentatively identified it as black-quarter.

[43] Lobowal J 34.

While Jie oral tradition makes a few vague mentions of cattle diseases which had preceded *Loongoripoko*, informants were agreed that this was the first time that a disease had reached such epidemic proportions. In the past, famines had usually been caused by prolonged droughts which resulted in serious crop failures, and the semi-pastoral peoples of central and eastern Karamoja had invariably fared much better than the primarily agricultural peoples along the western borderlands. With *Loongoripoko*, the situation was reversed, and the Jie and the other peoples of Karamoja found themselves having to rely on their sorghum and other agricultural produce while they began the long process of rebuilding their herds. While the disease did cause considerable hardship and suffering, it also provided a further respite to the resumption of major military conflict between the Bokora and the Jie. Spasmodic raiding continued, but as the herds of each side were equally destroyed, both peoples appear to have turned their attentions to other, more profitable, areas for most of their raiding activity.

Soon after the disease (and still within the span of the Ngikokol initiations), the Jie again began to raid the Ngimagos to the east, against whom they had fought so successfully perhaps a quarter of a century before. In the years that had elapsed, some of the Ngimagos had come north from the Magos Hills and resettled the area around Lotisan well near Koten. From there, the Ngimagos began to interfere with the movements of Jie cattle-camps, and the Jie finally launched a major attack on them:

> The Ngimagos were divided into several groups. One group was called 'Ngikorio', another lived down in the Magos Hills, and the third, under a leader called Lokothowa, settled near Lotisan. The young men of the Ngikokol went to Koculut in the east and there assembled an army. They attacked the Ngimagos at Lotisan and those in the Magos Hills and drove them away. The Ngimagos fled to Lokales in Pian [in the southern part of the Karimojong area] where they joined with the Pian. Their descendants can still be found there today.[44]

The attacks on the Ngimagos were the first successes won by Jie armies in many years and must have done much to revive their flagging spirits. The expulsion of the Ngimagos also resulted in a number of captured cattle to help the restocking of Jie herds, and it ensured that at least the eastern grazing lands were for the time being secure. However, the Jie had not seen the last of Lokothowa, the

[44] Lobilatum and Lopacure, J 11.

young leader of the Lotisan band of the Ngimagos. Although thirty years were to pass before the Jie saw him again, his eventual re-appearance would usher in a whole new era.

Soon after the expulsion of the Ngimagos and the inauguration of the next Jie generation-set, Ngikosowa—in about 1880—brown-skinned strangers appeared in Karamoja. The first of these strangers, who were known to the Jie as *Habaci*, arrived in Najie from the north. They had come from the area to the north of Lake Rudolf which was, by the end of the decade, to be incorporated within Menelik's expanding Ethiopian empire, and in their baggy cloth garments, mounted on strange four-footed creatures, and carrying for weapons sticks which made a fearful noise and gave off a terrible odour, they presented an exceedingly weird spectacle to the astonished Jie. Jie traditions maintain that at first there was little intercourse with these *Habaci*. Each group appears to have been rather distrustful of the other, and while the strangers invariably came with an inter-preter, most could not speak a single word of Ajie and there were clearly considerable problems of communication: 'When the first *Habaci* began coming here, the Jie thought they were very strange people indeed. We had not seen 'red' people like them before. We didn't understand why they had come here and at first the people were afraid they had come to kill us.'[45]

The mutual distrust quickly led to friction which was expressed in an armed clash between the Jie and one of the first of the bands of strangers:

> The only time the Jie had any real trouble with those people was at the beginning, when the first came. Some of them killed two Jie brothers and stole their cattle. The Jie were very angry. Our young men surrounded their camp at Nalingakan, and there was a battle in which people on both sides were killed. Night came, and while the Jie were waiting for dawn, the traders slipped out of their camp and went away.[46]

After this initial unpleasantness, relations with the *Habaci* stran-gers steadily improved, and later in the decade other strangers, Swahili from the East African coast, known to the Jie as *Acumpa*, who were reaching the final frontier of their long-distance caravan routes, began to visit Najie from the south. The primary purpose of the visits of both these groups of strangers was to hunt the large

[45] Loburkan, J 122.
[46] Lotiang (Ekothowan) and Lengoyang, J 123.

herds of elephants which roamed the peripheral areas of Najie, and occasionally even appeared in the settled areas where they wrecked havoc in the sorghum fields. Many Jie traditions refer to the strangers as 'those who carried the tusks of elephants' and make it clear that they did not attempt to establish themselves even semi-permanently in Najie, but merely made very brief visits:

> Those people never stayed in Najie. They would only come with their horses and donkeys to shoot elephants with their guns. Often they would arrive in Najie in the morning and hunt all day and then go away at night to wherever they had come from. Sometimes they would camp for a night or two in Najie, but no more.[47]

By the early 1890s, the visits of both groups of hunters to Najie were becoming more frequent. The earlier troubles with the *Habaci* were now a thing of the past, and both groups (especially the *Acumpa*) made a very real effort to establish cordial relations with the Jie: 'When the *Acumpa* came here, they used to give presents of rice to women and children. Our people would accept it, but then throw it away into the bush after the *Acumpa* had gone on because they were not used to such strange food.'[48]

Many of the strangers learnt Ajie and some even assumed Jie-style 'ox-names' (a kind of nickname) and composed their own ox 'praise songs', much to the delight of their Jie hosts. Although the strangers were primarily hunters, they also engaged in some trading activities with the Jie, mainly in order to supplement their rations whilst on hunting expeditions. In exchange for grain, milk, meat, and even fire-wood, the hunters gave beads, copper, and brass wire, and some ironware, and sometimes they would make presents to the Jie of the game they shot. Both the *Habaci* and *Acumpa* tried to induce Jie men to serve as guides and porters, and occasionally even to give them active help in their elephant hunting, but met with little success.[49] After the initial misunderstandings and friction with the *Habaci*, the Jie realized that they had nothing to fear from the strangers, and, being already under considerable pressure from their Karimojong and Dodos rivals, they were undoubtedly anxious to avoid any unnecessary conflict. The newcomers, for their part, wanted good relations with the Jie so that their hunting could be carried on in peace, and welcome additions to their sparse rations easily obtained. The impression strongly conveyed in most of the Jie traditions is that

---

[47] Lothike (Elawa), Longok (Apacelem), and Ekongor, J 29; also J 65.
[48] Looru (Sampson), J 120.
[49] Interviews including J 17, 33, 36, 38, 45, 66, 89, 127, and 128.

the hunters were regarded as peaceful, rather eccentric, and indeed almost comical characters:

> The *Acumpa* came here from the south-east when the Ngikosowa were initiating. They only wanted to shoot elephants, and they brought beads, wire, and other things to trade ... they had many donkeys to carry their things and herds of goats which they ate. They wore loose dark cloth on their bodies. They loved to eat meat and ate great quantities of it. They used to wipe their hands and even the oil off their mouths onto their clothes after eating.[50]

> The *Acumpa* and the *Habaci* came here riding on horses. They wore clothes and they were very hairy people with long beards and long noses which caused the Jie girls to laugh.[51]

> Those who came here to shoot elephants and trade things never caused trouble, except once, when there was that fight at Nalingakan. Other than that, they were peaceful. They never killed any of the Jie or took away any of our women or children.[52]

As the *Habaci* and *Acumpa* hunters began to make more frequent visits to Najie, the Jie continued the long process of building up their herds after the depredations of *Loongoripoko*. By the end of the 1880s, both the Jie and their Karimojong rivals had recovered nearly sufficient strength to renew active warfare, but in about 1887 another cattle disease, called *Loukoi* by the Jie, broke out in Karamoja, and again the herds of both peoples were decimated. Once more the Jie and the other semi-pastoral peoples of Karamoja set about to rebuild their herds, but this time the process was hardly under way before yet another disease, called *Lopid* by the Jie, completely devastated the remnants of the herds, probably in 1894.[53] '*Loukoi* came and killed many of the cattle. Then, when I was a small boy, *Lopid* came and killed almost all that were left.'[54]

Completing the grim irony of the disastrous situation, *Lopid* was almost immediately followed by a further outbreak of *Loukoi* (some

---

[50] Aringole, Lomulen (Puten), Loibok (Daudi), and others, J 26.

[51] Lobwal, J 34.

[52] Lodon (Kapelinyong) and Meron, J 127. It is interesting to compare statements made by Webster's Acoli informants regarding some of these same traders, viz: 'The Cumpa first came here during the reign of [Rwot] Lakiti. He did not worry about them because they were only harmless traders' (Webster, 'Acholi Historical Texts', p. 90).

[53] The dates for *Loukoi* and *Lopid* were estimated by Captain Turpin, loc. cit. (1948), 163. In his appendix to the article (p. 165), Watson at least tentatively identified *Loukoi* as pleuro-pneumonia and *Lopid* as a disease of the East Coast fever variety. Turpin, however, was of the opinion that 'Lopit' was in fact rinderpest.

[54] Iteba. J 39.

informants refer to it as *Lopetun* or *Loiloo*), a very poor harvest caused by a drought and a plague of locusts, and finally an epidemic of smallpox (*emeri* to the Jie) which took a heavy toll amongst the human population. The series of disasters wreaked incomprehensible suffering on the Jie, and the grim recollections of Jie elders can only partially echo the terrible consequences:

> Most Jie were left with no food at all. Nothing. They went up towards Kapeta and gathered wild fruits. My own grandfather lived like a monkey collecting wild things in the bush. He was left with only a donkey, a cow, and a few goats . . . How could he feed his family on these?[55]
>
> When the smallpox came I was about twenty years old . . . I caught the disease and was too weak even to stand up . . . My father and my grandfather both caught it. Many people in my [extended] family died of it.[56]
>
> Nearly all the cattle in Najie died. Only one bull, belonging to Loka-long of Panyangara, was left in all of Najie. People used to bring their cows to his bull to be serviced, and they would even come to him to buy cow-dung with which to smear the walls and floors of theis houses. I remember that my father had only two cows left out of hir entire herd. Many people went to the bush and hunted wild animals.[57]

A few fortunate Jie had sufficiently large flocks of sheep and goats (which were unaffected by the diseases and managed to live by browsing during the drought) to provide food for their families until the crisis had passed, but a great many either turned to hunting and gathering, or else fled from Najie, to take refuge with the primarily agricultural western peoples who had escaped the worst effects of the disasters. A few of those who turned to hunting and gathering were taken in by the Ngikuliak bands, while others formed bands of their own, and wandered in the bush in the peripheral areas of Najie. Of those who fled to the west, some ventured as far as the eastern frontiers of the Langi and Iteso,[58] although most

[55] Amuk (Akitibuin), J 89.
[56] Akuremeri, J 47.
[57] Longoli (Apanyemuge), J 104.
[58] Some of those who fled to eastern Lango included members of the Loser clan of Kotido, descendants of the same large Agricultural Paranilotic group which also provided a considerable segment of the Lango population. With the discovery that some of the Jie refugees were Ngiseera, the Langi are remembered to have immediately begun calling them 'brothers' and providing them with gifts of milk and meat. As fully a century had passed since any of the Jie and Lango Ngiseera had existed as one community, the Jie were astonished, but none the less delighted at their treatment. (Teko, Ekalam, J 76.) Other Jie refugees were not given such favoured treatment by the Langi, however.

sought refuge with the Labwor and several of the kingdoms of eastern Acholi.[59]

The Jie who died or who fled from Najie (at least temporarily) must have represented a very considerable proportion of the entire population. Both the Karimojong and the Dodos appear to have been about as badly affected as the Jie. In 1916 Turpin estimated that fully half of the Bokora section of the Karimojong had fled westwards to the Iteso, where many died of hunger or were killed by those with whom they hoped to find refuge.[60] Many other Karimojong fled to the bush to exist by hunting and gathering, and H. H. Austin of Major Macdonald's Nile expedition found members of them in a very impoverished state beyond the headwaters of the Turkwel River in 1897.[61] Many of the Dodos (who were perhaps slightly less devastated by the disasters than either the Jie or Karimojong), fled to Orom or the Nyangea Hills with what cattle remained, while many others were forced to turn to hunting and gathering.[62]

The first relief to the shattered communities of Karamoja was provided by the elephant-hunting strangers (especially the *Acumpa*, it would seem) who enterprisingly bought up large herds of cattle in areas unaffected by the diseases, and drove them to Karamoja, in order to trade them to the impoverished Karimojong, Jie and Dodos:

> After *Lopid* killed almost all the cattle, a few people managed to live off their sheep and goats, while others hunted in the bush. Others went to Acholi and other places to beg food from their friends and kinsmen. But then the *Acumpa* came with herds of cattle to trade to the Jie for elephant tusks and donkeys.[63]

The Jie, who had been merely indifferent to the hunting activities of the *Acumpa* and *Habaci* before the great disasters, now began to

[59] Interviews including J 15, 36, 38, 57, 80, 111, 113, 114, 118, 121, L 9, 10, and 11. Some Jie refugees went to the Kotidani area where they were referred to as 'Kapwor', as had been the Agricultural Paranilotic and Lwo Kapwor who had lived there fully a century before. This Kotidani group was also referred to as *Ngioapakiru*, 'those who follow the rain'.

While the matter is not clear, some Jie refugees appear to have fled Najie some years before the great disasters. These groups, including the 'Adilang' who went from Losilang to Acholi, and the Rikitai, who went from Panyangara to Bokora, are discussed in my London Ph.D. thesis.

[60] Turpin, loc. cit. (1948), 163.

[61] H. H. Austin, *With Macdonald in Uganda* (London, 1903), pp. 70–1; also MTK 3.

[62] Akurun and Alinga, D 13; also Turpin, loc. cit.

[63] Lopor (and others), J 38.

take a very active role in the elphant hunting. A few Jie were trusted enough to be lent rifles with which to shoot elephants themselves; others accompanied the traders as guides and porters, while many more, who had temporarily turned to hunting smaller game, began to hunt elephants with spears or traps. In exchange for their ivory or services, the Jie received considerable numbers of healthy livestock which served as a good basis from which to restock their herds. It is to their credit that the strangers did not take advantage of the situation to exploit the impoverished Jie, whose oral traditions recall that extremely good prices were paid for the ivory, a pair of large tusks fetching as many as thirty cattle.[64]

While the most immediate relief was thus provided by the *Acumpa* and, to a lesser extent the *Habaci*, the Jie themselves took steps to aid their recovery through their own commercial enterprise. The Jie had traditionally played a rather passive middle-man role in the transfer of Labwor ironware to the Turkana, but the volume of that commerce rose with the increase in demand, such as the Turkana wars of expansion earlier in the nineteenth century had provided. After the devastation caused by the great disasters, many Jie began to take full advantage of their convenient geographical situation and became (at least for the moment) full-time traders. To the west, the Labwor (whose livestock consisted mainly of goats rather than cattle) were relatively unaffected by *Loukoi* and *Lopid*, and during the following crop failure, they had escaped the worst effects of the famine by trading ironware to the Langi and other western peoples for grain.[65] To the east, the arid plains of Turkana-land had escaped the cattle diseases altogether, and as few Turkana were engaged in any cultivation, the locusts and the crop failure had no real effect on them.[66] The impoverished Jie middle-men were now much concerned with making as substantial a profit as possible, and exploited their more fortunate neighbours to the fullest possible extent:

After *Lopid*, many Jie got cattle again from the Turkana. They would take a he-goat to the Labwor and buy a spear. They would take that spear to Turkana and exchange it for a small milch-cow. They would take the cow back to the Labwor and trade it for several spears, and then go back to Turkana again with those spears and buy several cattle. They would continue like that until soon they had a herd again.[67]

[64] Interviews including J 127 and L 3.
[65] Okidi (Simei), L 10.
[66] Gulliver, *A Preliminary Survey of the Turkana*, p. 151.
[67] Lobwal, J 34.

Through the help provided by the *Acumpa* and *Habaci*, as well as through their own commercial ingenuity, the Jie began a fairly rapid recovery from the decimation of the great disasters. While some of the refugees who had fled from Najie, either just before, or as a result of the great disasters, would never return, increasingly large numbers did begin to return from their hunting and gathering life in the bush, or from their temporary refuge with neighbouring peoples, to their old settlement areas in Najie. While their own rates of recovery were perhaps somewhat slower than that of the Jie, the Karimojong and Dodos also took advantage of their contacts with the *Acumpa* and *Habaci* and were soon engaged in restocking their herds, as well. As their recovery progressed, the old and as yet unanswered questions concerning the disputed resources along their frontiers with the Jie began to be re-examined. While the inexorable train of disasters had precluded any renewal of the major battles of the 1860s, each community fully realized that such a renewal was ultimately inevitable.

At some date just before the great disasters, Teko, the Lokorwakol war-leader who had succeeded his father, Acuka, killed by the Karimojong at Lokibuwo, himself died. Teko was apparently without issue, and the succession devolved upon his younger half-brother, Loriang. Loriang, who had fled as a young uninitiated boy from the defeat at Lokibuwo, had now grown into young manhood, and had been initiated into the Ngitukoi age-set of Ngikokol. Although it was not immediately apparent, the Karimojong spear which had killed Acuka and eventually led to Loriang's succession was, in an ironic sense, to be the most decisive ever thrown in the cause of the Jie community.

At the time of his succession, however, Loriang hardly presented a very imposing figure. He was still a fairly young man, both biologically and socially. Although the Ngikosowa generation-set was inaugurated just before his succession, his own age-set was but the penultimate of the preceding generation-set, and he was still considered the 'son' of the aged survivors of Ngisiroi, who were still the senior elders. Physically, he was very short for a Jie (only about 5′ 6″), light complexioned, with a marked habit of bending forward and hunching his shoulders when he walked. He had a passion for ornaments, wearing a great many strings of yellow beads and iron wire around his neck, ivory bracelets, and several sets of ear-rings. Despite his age and his size, he had gone on a number of raids and fought bravely, and warrior's scars on both shoulders proclaimed that he had killed enemies.[68]

The terrible years of the great disasters provided no opportunity for Loriang to exert even the minimal leadership which was accorded by the Jie to their hereditary war-leaders, and Loriang (and certainly Teko before him) was initially somewhat overshadowed by the older and more experienced Rengen war-leader, Natebele, a contemporary of his father, Acuka.[69] Not long after the last of the series of great disasters took place, however, fighting broke out again, and Loriang was afforded his first opportunity to participate in a major battle. The Dodos, who had been perhaps somewhat less seriously affected by the disasters than the other peoples of Karamoja, managed to assemble a large army, and launched an attack on the settlements of Nakapelimoru, the north-eastern territorial division of Lokorwakol. A Jie informant who witnessed the battle as a young boy described the early stages of the attack:

> Before the Dodos attacked the place called Tiira in Nakapelimoru, my own grandmother, Awapawothit, an *amuron* [diviner], had already predicted they would come. Early on the morning of that battle my father had sent me to scare birds from the sorghum fields, and I heard someone calling his ox-name, 'Nyeturot!', Nyeturot!, away in the distance. I looked to the north, and although it was still rather dark, I could see the white feathers of warriors' head-dresses. I ran back to my father's kraal, and he told me to drive the cattle away towards Panyangara [to the south]. Everyone was crying out and shouting the alarm.[70]

The warriors of Nakapelimoru, heavily outnumbered, fell back on the Kadakimot River where they were reinforced from neighbouring Panyangara by a small contingent which included Loriang. The defenders offered fierce resistance, and the Dodos wasted considerable time in methodically searching the Jie kraals which were still rather empty of cattle after the great disasters.[71] By a stroke of good fortune, a strong Jie raiding party, composed mainly of Rengen warriors, the arch-enemies of the Dodos, had set off the night before for a raid of their own on some Dodos cattle-camps which had recently been established in the east near Koten. Another elderly Jie informant who

---

[68] This description was built up mainly from the testimony of Lobwel (J 34), one of Loriang's two surviving sons, and Apalodokoro (J 23), his grandson.

[69] Kojo (Looya) and Lolwanamoe, J 60.

[70] Nakade (Peter), J 57.

[71] Lobilatum, J 51.

was himself a young warrior in the raiding party described what happened: 'We were on our way to attack the Dodos when we came across a trail which had recently been made by a great many men. We realized that the Dodos must have sent an army to attack the Nakapelimoru and so we hurried back to Tiira where we saw those Dodos attacking.'[72]

The Jie raiding party fell on the Dodos from the rear, while those defending the line along the Kadakimot River, being further reinforced by small bands of warriors which had trickled in from other parts of Najie, launched a frontal counter-attack. Caught between the two attacks, the Dodos broke and fled back to their own country, but while they suffered some casualties, most of their army escaped. The traditions agree that the Jie warriors were drawn mainly from the Ngieleki age-section of Ngikokol and from the Ngikwei age-set of Ngikosowa, and that the Dodos army was composed largely of men of the Ngimothingo age-set.[73] From these and other indications, it would appear that the battle of Tiira was fought sometime during the final few years of the nineteenth century.

To Loriang, the battle (in which he seems to have played no very great part) was a valuable lesson in practical military tactics. It served as a clear indication of the critical importance of a rapid mobilization of forces in a defensive action such as Tiira. It was plain that the Dodos had come dangerously close to winning a great victory. Had it not been for the fortuitous arrival of the strong Rengen raiding party at the rear of the Dodos, the men of the thin defensive line on the Kadakimot River, to which the fragmentary bands of reinforcements from other parts of Najie had rallied so slowly, could not have hoped to stall the Dodos advance, however bravely they had fought. Jie military organization, based on the age-sets and the small 'private companies' of the myriad individual battle-leaders had again proved dangerously inadequate to meet the demands of large-scale defensive actions: 'In the days before Loriang when the Jie were attacked by their enemies, the Karimojong and Dodos, there was not time to arrange the army in any special way. There was no time for preparations. There was no time to say, "That man is brave. Let him go first [i.e. let him lead us]".'[74]

After the battle of Tiira, therefore, Loriang for the first time began to display the mastery of military science and tactics which was to

[72] Lopeirinyet (Angura), J 87.
[73] Interviews including J 33, 98, 109, and 118.
[74] Akuremeri and Nakothia, J 7.

win for him a place in Jie history, rivalled only by the quasi-mytho-
logical founders of the divisions, Orwakol and Oding. While one
must suspect that Loriang had been formulating his plans for many
years, the battle of Tiira seems to have codified them, and soon after
the battle he announced sweeping changes in the whole military
organization. Fully understanding the crucial importance of interior

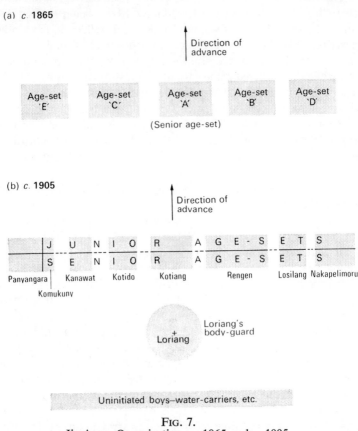

FIG. 7.
Jie Army Organization, *c.* 1865 and *c.* 1905.

lines in defensive actions, Loriang substituted an organization based
on the Lokorwakol territorial divisions (which, since the defeats of
the 1860s had been crowded together into a compact geographical
area) in place of the more unwieldy traditional organization based
on generation- and age-sets. It was hoped that such an organization
would permit a much more rapid and efficient mobilization of large

forces in case of attack, and henceforth men would be fighting in the company of their kinsmen and neighbours. The same organization could also be employed in offensive operations, and Loriang devised offensive tactics which called for the forming up of each territorial division as its own 'battalion' of a battle-line, in which each 'battalion' was to have its own assigned and recognized place. Panyangara and Nakapelimoru divisions (the ones that had experienced the heaviest of the raiding and fighting with the Karimojong and Dodos) were assigned the élite flank positions of this proposed offensive organization, with the battalions of the other territorial divisions formed up between them. The formation, from right to left, was to be Nakapelimoru, Losilang, Kotiang, Kotido, Kanawat, and Panyangara (with whom the Komukuny formed up as a small separate battalion of their own).[75] The old organization based on the generation-set system was not entirely abandoned, however, and Loriang's plans called for each battalion to be internally arranged by age-sets, at least in offensive actions. This organization, as it subsequently functioned in combat situations, was described by elders who in their youth were part of it:

> The Jie army was really arranged by territorial divisions. Each division was arranged as its own small army within the big army. But age-sets were also important. That is, the younger men were in the front of each battalion because they could move well and run quickly. The older men who could not run so quickly, but who had fought many times, came behind. Sometimes the plan would be for the young men to attack the enemy and then suddenly break off and rush away, as though they were beaten. The enemy would chase them. Then the older men, who had concealed themselves to the rear, would jump up from their hiding places and ambush the enemy, who would be surrounded and defeated.[76]

As well as reorganizing the formation of the army, Loriang actively began to take steps to reduce the independent action and the inordinate authority of the individual battle-leaders who led the 'private companies'. Realizing that little could be gained by small-scale and unco-ordinated raiding activity, and that an army composed largely of a patchwork of small, largely autonomous bands

[75] Interviews including J 33, 59 and 90. The informants of J 18 indicated that when the offensive organization was subsequently put into practice, the Panyangara and Nakapelimoru usually occupied the flank positions, but would occasionally form up together to oppose the strongest part of an enemy's battle-line, wherever that point might be.
[76] Nakade (Peter), Lowal (Logorengok), and others, J 16.

could hardly hope to gain major victories, Loriang was anxious to bring the battle-leaders firmly under his own control:

> Loriang forbade small groups of warriors to go on raids of their own, as they had done in the past. He made all the warriors of every territorial division come together to one place to form one army which he himself led. Before his time, armies had been small and were never united, and they were always defeated.[77]

> Loriang made sure that warriors were prevented from raiding without his permission. Warriors were forbidden to fight unless Loriang himself gathered them together or unless they were actually attacked by the enemy. He would always plan the wars, and sometimes small groups of warriors would go out on a raid, but only when Loriang sent them.[78]

The hereditary war-leaders had been accorded respect, but hardly any great authority by the Jie community, and it should not be supposed that Loriang's plans were accepted immediately upon his suggestion. On the contrary, there is ample evidence that in order to effect his reorganization Loriang first actively sought the support and backing of the senior elders:

> After he became the war-leader, Loriang would give presents of beer or even oxen to the very old men—those who walked with sticks. He did this to get their permission to do the things he wanted to do. No war-leader before Loriang ever did these things, and no war-leader before him ever led all the Jie in one army, as Loriang did.[79]

> Loriang used to bring all the oldest men to his home to seek their blessing. He made sure that all came, and he saw to it that the very old men would be carried there if they could not walk. They would stay with him for as long as a week and each day he would present them with gifts of food and tobacco. The elders were pleased with Loriang and they sharpened his spear and stuck it into a tree, saying, 'Kill our enemies like this!'. Then they gave him a stick of *ekaliye* wood which they spat on and blessed. They performed for him a kind of *angola* ceremony in which they swept his way clear and made a gate of grass, *abukut* [wild sisal], *ekathuruga* [small ant-hills] and *alakas* [a type of plant]. Loriang went through the gate and all the biggest elders blessed him. They collected small stones together and pretended they were cattle, in the way that small boys do, and they made sounds like cattle, 'Bauu! Bauu!', saying, 'These are the cattle which Loriang brings to the Jie from the enemies.'[80]

[77] Lothike (Elawa) and Looru (Sampson), J 52.
[78] Lobalong (Joseph) and Kere, J 12.
[79] Lobalong (Joseph) and Kere, J 12.
[80] Lowor (Elizeo) and others, J 58.

With the blessings of the senior elders, therefore, Loriang's planned reorganization was begun, and his prohibition against independent activity by the battle-leaders and their private companies was reinforced by the ritual sanctions of the elders. Loriang's innovations were sceptically received by many of the older warriors who were the veterans of Acuka's and Teko's time; and the individual battle-leaders certainly relinquished their authority only grudgingly. While Loriang's subsequent successes must have erased most of the ill-feeling that his plans engendered, there is still perhaps an echo of resentment in some Jie oral tradition: 'With Loriang, the Jie armies were always arranged in a special way. But our enemies, the Dodos and Karimojong, did not fight in this way. They continued to fight us bravely, like men, without big leaders or special formations.[81]

Somewhat ironically, Loriang's innovations were to be given their first test, not against either of the principal enemies, the Karimojong or Dodos, but against the primarily agricultural western neighbours of the Jie, the kingdoms of eastern Acoli. Traditionally, Jie relations with western peoples had been basically good. Except for the Ngikok raids against the Kapwor herds, the subsequent hostile reception given to the first of the Kapwor famine refugees, the expulsion of the Lwo allies of the Poet, and a few isolated raids, such as the disastrous one undertaken by the Ngikokol, contacts between the Jie and the 'Ngikatapa' had been mainly peaceful. Indeed, after the defeats of the 1860s, Jie cattle-camps had become very dependent on grazing and watering resources along their western frontiers, and during the terrible hardships of the great disasters, many Jie refugees had turned to the Acoli and other western groups for refuge and help. Furthermore, a considerable proportion of the Jie community was originally descended from the same ethno-linguistic elements which also comprised important segments of the western populations, and close contacts were maintained between the two groups by affinal ties.

The deterioration of good relations between the Jie and Acoli began during the great disasters. While many bands of Jie refugees had been amicably received, others had been given a poor reception by the Acoli from whom they sought help:

> During the troubles, many Jie went to the Acoli for help. Sometimes, if a man and his wife went there to get food, the Acoli would kill the man and take his wife.[82]

---

[81] Lowot, Loworo, Lobwal, Anyik, and Aporu, J 8.
[82] Lokong (Israel) and Loweei, J 36.

During the famine which followed *Lopid*, many Jie women used to go to Acholi to get food, but often the Acoli refused to let them return to Najie and kept them.[83]

A number of informants stated that Jie children were also taken by the Acoli and that some of these were sold as slaves in exchange for substantial numbers of muzzle-loading muskets to traders who had begun making frequent visits to eastern Acholi.[84] While bad feeling was thus engendered over the treatment of some Jie refugees it was the Labwor who were the direct cause of armed conflict between the Jie and Acoli. Having become embroiled in a feud of their own with the Acoli, the Labwor turned to the Jie for support, and because of their close interdependence based on the iron trade, the Jie felt obliged to side with their iron-making friends. Jie cattle-camps watering and grazing near Loyoroit in north-eastern Labwor were caught between the feuding Labwor and Acoli, and stock was lost: 'Acoli attacked our cattle-camps at Loyoroit and stole goats at the same time that they were fighting the Labwor . . . All the cattle-camps were withdrawn to the east, but the Acoli followed them and attacked again.'[85]

The Jie realized that relations with the Acoli were deteriorating, but they were apparently busy on two other fronts simultaneously, driving Dodos cattle-camps out of the Koten area to the east after a sharp engagement at Logum, and then launching a successful raid against a Dodos leader called Amodule to the north. Spies sent out by the Acoli, erroneously interpreting black excrement of Jie who had been drinking blood and milk to mean that the Jie were suffering from dysentery, returned with reports that the Jie were in a weakened condition and not expecting an attack. This intelligence led to the mobilization of what Webster has described as 'the largest military

---

[83] Lotiang (Ekothowan) and Lengoyang, J 123.

[84] The identity of the traders who supplied the Acoli with muskets seems rather uncertain from the oral traditions. Several Jie and a Labwor informant spoke of these traders as 'Nubians' (*Nginubi, Wa-Nubi*, or *Jo-Nubi*, depending on the language in which the testimony was given), but it appears quite certain that Baker's Nubians on the Nile, although they did join with the Acoli for raids on the Dodos, never allowed any fire-arms to pass into Acoli hands. Rather, the suppliers of the guns were almost certainly the traders whom the Acoli called 'Cumpa'. Although the Jie referred to the Swahili as 'Acumpa', there can be little doubt that the Acoli 'Cumpa' were not Swahili, but rather Ethiopian traders, and that they were the ones who supplied the muskets. See B. Webster (with J. E. Lamphear,)'The Jie–Acholi War: Oral Evidence from Two Sides of the Battle Front', *UJ* 35 (1971), 32.

[85] Lowot, Koki, Locero, and Riamakol, J 45.

force ever mustered by the Acholi kingdoms of Agago',[86] accompanied by no less than six kings and all their outstanding military leaders, and composed of at least 2,000 warriors. This massive force, armed mainly with muskets, and supported by spearmen, launched a multi-pronged dawn attack which according to all Jie tradition took them completely by surprise. The focus of the attack was Caicaon territorial division in Rengen, although settlements in Kotiang division of Lokorwakol were also overrun by one Acoli wing.[87]

The Acoli army, partly impeded because of a rain-storm which had drenched much of their powder the night before, was held back for more than an hour by a pitifully small band of Jie warriors from the immediate neighbourhood under the command of their local battle-leaders. However, despite wet powder, enough of the Acoli firearms were functioning to inflict terrible casualties on the Jie defenders, who managed to hold a thin defensive line only through sheer courage and bravado. This delaying action was just sufficient for Loriang's new organization of territorial division-based battalions to go into operation, and one after another, the unified battalions arrived on the battle-field with almost incredible speed and efficiency to shore up the defensive line in front of Caicaon. Finally, even the 'élite' battalions of Panyangara and Nakapelimoru, the most distant from the battle-field, arrived under the personal direction of Loriang, and the Acoli army, which was already beginning to withdraw, lost all semblance of order and ran. At this point, Loriang demonstrated his great military skill by drawing in all the battalions of his army, as well as all the Rengen warriors, into a unified force and launched a methodical and well-organized pursuit of the Acoli, which turned a successful defence into a resounding victory.

The battle was, in a sense, reflective of all Jie military history: the Jie endured through sheer courage and personal bravery until a more efficient and better-organized system finally allowed them to take the offensive. The success of Loriang's new organization can be gauged by the fact that a Jie force, outnumbered by at least four to one and armed with entirely traditional weapons, had decisively defeated the largest force ever faced by a Jie army, and one heavily armed with fire-arms besides. The Acoli sustained staggering casualties, and large numbers of their muskets fell into Jie hands. While the numbers of Acoli slain can never be known, among the dead were some

[86] Webster, loc. cit., p. 34.
[87] A detailed description of this battle, from both the Jie and Acoli points of view, can be found in Lamphear and Webster, ibid.

of the most important leaders of the eastern Acoli, including Rye-marot, king of Lira Palwo and leader of the Council of eastern Acoli kings; Lojun, king of Paiper; Cana Gola, war-leader of Pader; and Lakut, war leader of Paimol.[88]

Soon after the battle of Caicaon, which was fought in about 1902,[89] Loriang demonstrated that he also possessed considerable diplomatic skill. He was instrumental in forging a working military alliance with the same Acoli kingdoms which his battalions had defeated at Caicaon, and he also played an important role in concluding a peace with the Nyakwai with whom trouble had broken out through an unfortunate misunderstanding:

> The Jie went to attack some Karimojong cattle-camps which were near Lolung, below the Nyakwai Hills. At the same time, some Nyakwai happened to come down from their hills and were passing near Lolung. The Jie saw them and attacked them, thinking they were Karimojong. It was only after they had been fighting for some time that the Jie realized their mistake.[90]

Although his battalions could have smashed the numerically weak Nyakwai in a concerted thrust, Loriang wisely chose to make peace with them, thereby conserving his forces and ensuring that the Nyakwai would remain neutral in the resumption of full-scale warfare with the Karimojong, which he knew to be imminent. Loriang's diplomacy was to be justified, for almost immediately the Bokora Karimojong began a series of determined forays against those Jie cattle-camps that were still located on the open plains between Mt. Toror and the Nyakwai Hills. First at Nagum and then at Naorot just outside the settled area of Najie, the Bokora, probably under the command of a courageous battle-leader called Apaomielem, launched successful raids which resulted in the capture of considerable Jie livestock.[91]

After these setbacks, all the cattle-camps from the area were recalled to Najie, and Loriang set about to inaugurate the second phase of his planned military innovations. Although his new battalions had

---

[88] Personal communication with Webster; also Okeo (Yonasan), L 11. A Jie song, recorded in Lamphear and Webster, also lists the Acoli leaders who fell.

[89] Approximately this date was indicated by the elephant hunter, 'Karamoja' Bell (*Wanderings of an Elephant Hunter*) who was told of the battle during a visit to Najie in 1905.

[90] Lothike (Elawa), J 131. Herring recorded a similar Nyakwai tradition which states that Loriang himself concluded the subsequent peace.

[91] Nakong (and others), BK 8; also MTK 3.

performed superbly in the defence of Najie at Caicaon, Loriang realized that the outlying cattle-camps, guarded only by small bands of herdsmen, would continue to be vulnerable to attacks, no matter how efficient his strategy for the defence of the settled area of Najie might be. To Loriang the answer to the problem was obvious: his battalions would take the offensive, and carry the war for the first time to the settled areas of his enemies. Loriang decided that attacks should be concentrated on the Bokora, Pei, and other allied Karimojong sections, which he correctly assessed as the most imminently threatening.

After the victory at Caicaon, much of the scepticism concerning Loriang and his innovations had died away, and with the commencement of his campaigns against the Karimojong, Loriang carried his changes even further. He recruited a number of especially skilled observers who could impersonate the dialects and imitate the dress of the enemies, and used them as a spy network which would remain for long periods in or near enemy country before bringing back intelligence reports. He also employed a number of runners who stayed near his homestead and served as messengers who could be sent out quickly to the various territorial divisions with orders to muster their battalions for a campaign. He also selected a personal bodyguard from amongst the bravest and most skilful warriors of every territorial division and age-set. Jie warriors considered it a great honour to be selected for this bodyguard, and by choosing many of the same battle-leaders whose independent authority he had reduced, Loriang considerably assuaged any ill feeling they still harboured. Armed only with the sacred stick given him by the senior elders, Loriang would march ahead of his battalions before the commencement of action, waving the stick towards the enemy to ensure Jie success. Just as the fighting began, Loriang would retire to the rear of his battle-line, from where he could direct the course of the battle, to be surrounded by his bodyguard which would be employed only as a kind of élite reserve in a desperate situation, or to form a rearguard after the army began its march back to Najie after the fighting.[92] After a successful attack, Loriang himself would supervise the division of captured cattle and other booty, giving each battalion a certain number based both on its size and on its performance in the battle, and thus ending the confused internecine mêlées which had been a typical feature of the division of booty in the past:

[92] Interviews including J 8, 12, 18 and 34.

Loriang controlled his army very well. After a battle he would himself divide the captured cattle among his men, saying, 'I do not want you to struggle over these cattle. I shall divide them fairly amongst you'. Of course Loriang, because he was a great man, could take as many as he wanted for himself. It was the way in which he organized the army which made him great, and we warriors knew that.[93]

In many ways Loriang's greatest achievement, however, was his inclusion of other elements into his Ngikorwakol army, the most important of whom were the relatively independent warriors of the Rengen division. The battle of Caicaon had been fought mainly on Rengen soil and although the traditional battle leaders of the Rengen and their 'private companies' had fought bravely, they were clearly impressed with the efficiency and the success of Loriang's newly organized Ngikorwakol battalions. Soon after Caicaon, but before the commencement of his campaigns against the Karimojong, Loriang sent his messengers to Rengen to recruit a contingent of Rengen warriors. At this early stage, Loriang did not attempt to undercut the authority of the individual Rengen battle leaders, and the first recruits were selected from among those Rengen warriors who did not owe their primary loyalty to any 'private company': 'Loriang's messengers came here to Rengen to select men for his army. Loriang had told those messengers not to select the very fierce warriors who were known for their great bravery, but rather those who had good characters (*ejokak ngipitesie*) and could be trusted to obey him.[94]

After the initial successes of Loriang's offensive campaigns, however, the entire Rengen army, 'private companies' and all, came firmly under his command and was included as its own battalion in the Jie line of battle between the battalions of Kotiang and Losilang (their closest Ngikorwakol neighbours).[95] Apart from the Rengen, other, totally alien, elements were incorporated into Loriang's army. A contingent of Labwor warriors, some armed with fire-arms, under their own war-leader, Logo, joined their traditional friends for the wars against the Karimojong. Later, after his campaigns were well under way, a force from the same Acoli kingdoms which had attacked Caicaon, and led by many of the same leaders who had fought there arrived in Najie with presents for Loriang as an inducement to let

[93] Nakade (Peter), and others, J 16; also J 12, 52, and 58.
[94] Ekudi and Morunyang, J 15.
[95] Interviews including J 59, 91 and 95.

them join his army and share in the spoils. Loriang accepted both their gifts and their aid, and by the end of his campaigns, a large number of Acoli, mostly musketeers, were distributed throughout his battalions.[96]

While one cannot be completely certain, all available indications suggest that the army which Loriang fielded in his offensive campaigns included approximately 500 Jie fighting men. In addition to the warriors, informants stated that an almost equal number of boys in their early teens would often accompany an army to carry shields and water, to drive off captured cattle, and to gain valuable experience in battle (much in the same way as the *uDibi* of a Zulu army). Other men were employed as guards of the cattle-camps, and a rather smaller additional force, composed mainly of men from younger age-sets, was detailed by Loriang to remain in the settled area of Najie as a kind of 'home guard'. Informants were agreed that Loriang's Acoli and Labwor allies were less numerous than the Jie warriors, but that they did constitute a considerable segment of the army. It is probably reasonably correct to estimate that the allies were about half as numerous as the Jie warriors, and so it is likely that, by the end of his campaigns, Loriang was commanding a force of approximately 750 fighting men, plus several hundred boys.

Finally, Loriang instituted a rather complex chain of command system by which his orders could be smoothly executed. His immediate lieutenants were the individual commanders of the territorial-division-based battalions. Each of these men was appointed by Loriang to command all the warriors from his own territorial division and was responsible for their rapid mobilization upon receiving his orders. The chief of these lieutenants was Aleper, the commander of the Kotido battalion, who acted as second-in-command to Loriang and was often entrusted with the task of actually mustering the army.[97] Unlike Loriang, the battalion commanders went into battle fully armed and were expected to take an active part in the fighting. Directly subordinate to the orders of each battalion commander were a number of lesser officers, apparently selected by

---

[96] Interviews including J 15, 19, 34, 109; L 1, 4, 9; BK 5 and 7.

[97] Information about Aleper and the other battalion commanders was supplied by informants including those of J 76, 92 and 98. Among those informants were Lokong (Israel) and Teko (Ekalam), two of Aleper's sons. Lokong also described some of his father's exploits in his booklet *Lokong Tells His Story* written in conjunction with the Revd. H. Paget-Wilkes, published by the B.C.M.S. (London, 1930).

their respective commanders. Jie informants who were at least somewhat familiar with British military terminology described them like
this:

> Loriang was of course the most important leader of the army, but
> under him there were others who were also chosen to be leaders. Some
> of the bigger leaders were from the Ngieleki [age-section of Ngikokol]
> and they were like 'sergeants' (*ngisergenti*). Others were from the
> Ngikosowa [generation-set] and they were less important, like 'cor-
> porals' (*ngikorporali*).[98]

Loriang's Karimojong campaigns began with an attack against the
Pei, the weakest of the Karimojong sections which opposed the Jie,
and who inhabited the territory to the south-east of Mt. Toror.
Typically, Loriang first sent a party to spy out the Pei, but the party
was discovered and wiped out except for one man, Longabon, who
hid in a pumpkin garden and made his way back to Loriang with a
detailed report of the Pei strength and the locations of their cattle.
Loriang gathered his battalions and attacked the Pei, handing them
a massive defeat and captured large numbers of their livestock. This
initial success was followed in rapid succession by other victories at
Nakaterot, Lokitela-angimoru, Juuru, and Namugit, during which
the Pei and Bokora Karimojong, who had for so many years controlled the resources of peripheral areas which the Jie considered to
be theirs, began to fall back on the heartland of their own countries,
abandoning disputed grazing areas and watering points to the victorious Jie. Entire herds of captured Karimojong livestock began to
flow back into Najie, and very soon the Jie realized that they were
already in possession of more cattle than they had been even in the
days before the great disasters. Taking advantage of the momentum
of his victorious army, Loriang even launched far-flung attacks
against the Dodos at Loyoro and at Kamuria (near the present
township of Kaabong) to the north, and against the Matheniko
Karimojong at Moru Akero (near present-day Moroto township) to
the south, from which the successful Jie warriors returned with booty
which included even a herd of camels.[99] These successes proved that
Loriang's victorious army could raid almost with impunity up and
down much of the whole length of Karamoja, and it was at this

[98] Lopacure and Lobilatum, J 46.
[99] The Jie claim that these were the only camels they ever owned and even
that ownership was to be short-lived. According to Jie tradition most of the
camels soon died after feeding on the *egorogoethe* plant (identified by Mr.
Wilson as *courbonia sp.*) which grows in profusion in Najie; the survivors ran
away and made their way back to the Matheniko.

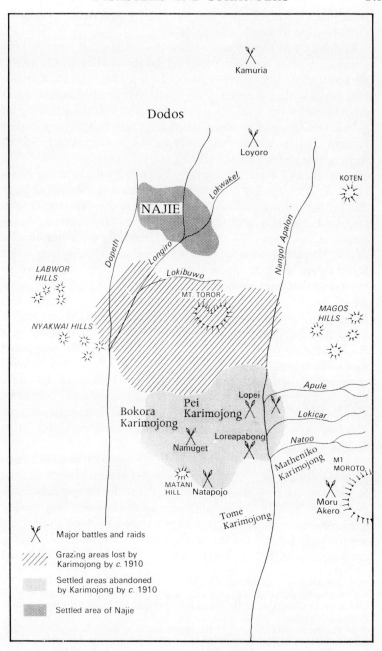

MAP 15. Loriang's Offensive Campaigns, *c.* 1902–1910.

point that the Rengen army and the Labwor and Acoli contingents came flocking to him.

Loriang's next victory was against the combined Pei and Bokora settlements which had withdrawn behind the Lokicar River, well to the south of Mt. Toror. While part of his force captured the Karimojong herds as they were led down to the river to drink, another laid an ambush for the Karimojong warriors who had been holding an *ekimonwor* dance at Ateleng nearby. As the Karimojong rushed towards the river to save their herds, Loriang's men jumped up from their hiding places and slaughtered large numbers of them.[100] The engagement at Lokicar was quickly followed by the battle of Nata-pojo, in which the Jie army, for the first time incorporating large numbers of Labwor and Acoli, made a thrust deep into the Bokora heartland, attacking settlements near Matani Hill, inflicting heavy casualties, and capturing cattle which (according to the testimonies of many Jie who witnessed it) formed a line 'several miles long' when being driven back to Najie. Others recalled that cattle were so numerous that even women and uninitiated boys were given some during the division of booty after the battle. Even so, Natapojo was rather less of a success than most of Loriang's other battles and raids, for even as the victorious Jie were starting home with their booty, a Karimojong force, determined to recoup some of the staggering losses which were being inflicted upon their people, took a different route and arrived in Najie before Loriang and his army. In a very rapid raid, the Karimojong, sweeping away the resistance offered by the novices of the Jie 'home guard', fell upon Jie homesteads near Kalomuny Rock in Kotido and captured a number of Jie cattle, making off with them just before the return of the Jie army.[101]

Natapojo was followed by the last major battle of Loriang's campaigns, Loreapabong, which was fought in October 1910.[102] At least in terms of the casualties inflicted, it was to be the greatest battle ever fought by a Jie army, with the possible exception only of Caicaon. Accounts are agreed that large numbers of Acoli musketeers were present for this battle. As the Jie army advanced on a heavy concentration of Bokora settlements, the Acoli kept up a concerted

[100] The ambush was described by Lobilatum, J 51, who took part in it.

[101] Jie informants of J 51, 111, and 125, and Karimojong informants of BK 8 and 9, gave accounts of this battle which corresponded in even the most minute details.

[102] The battle was a subject of the report made by Capt. T. Grant, the Political Officer of the Turkwel Mission on 13 Feb. 1911. In his report Grant states that the battle took place five months before. E.A. 1049, Part II.

fire to cover the advance, retiring behind the protection of Jie shields to reload before presenting another volley.[103] The rolling volleys of musketry did much to confuse the Karimojong, and Jie veterans of the battle recall that except for a few brave individuals, comparatively little resistance was offered. When the Jie spearmen got in amongst the Karimojong homesteads, the affair turned into a massacre. The recollections of Karimojong survivors recall something of the grim efficiency of the Jie and allied forces:

> I was a young man when Loriang came to Loreapabong. We ran into our houses to hide. The Jie beat on the houses and when the people came out, they were all speared. I was speared here in my hip—you can still see the scar. The Jie killed everyone in my family, and left me for dead.[104]
> When Loriang attacked us at Loreapabong, many Acoli and Tobur [Labwor] came with him. A great many of our people were killed. Many were shot by the guns of the Acoli. Don't ask me what sort of guns they were—I don't know. Do you think there was time to look carefully at those guns? No! They kept firing the guns—'puu! puu!' If anyone even stopped long enough to make the sign of his ox's horns with his hands, he was shot down.[105]

Loreapabong was to mark the pinnacle of Jie military success under Loriang. The engagement secured a vast number of additional livestock to swell even further the Jie herds, and the victorious Jie armies had also brought back large numbers of captured young women and children to be incorporated into the Jie community.[106] In 1909 'Karamoja' Bell could describe the Jie as 'a small but very compact, rich, and independent tribe' who were 'so rich in cattle and sheep as to be indifferent to other sources of meat supply'.[107] Two years later Tufnell, the Karamoja Touring Officer, could similarly describe them as 'extremely rich in flocks and herds'.[108] Loriang's army had firmly secured all the frontiers of Najie. The important

[103] The musketry tactics were described by Kere, J 125.
[104] Anyakun (Kilipa), BK 4.
[105] Nakong, BK 8. In the same way that men frequently called their 'ox names' as a battle-cry, the shape of a favourite ox's horns would also be imitated with the hands to encourage a warrior in battle. Grant, loc. cit., reported that the 'Karamojans had little or no chance of defending themselves' and that the Jie army 'massacred hundreds of them'.
[106] Jie informants stated that Loriang's army captured far greater numbers of cattle from the Karimojong than were being captured from them in the intensive Turkana raids of 1968–71. According to the records at Kotido Police Post, 5,288 Jie cattle were reported stolen by the Turkana between April 1969 and October 1970.
[107] W. D. M. Bell, *Karamojo Safari* (London, 1949), pp. 135 and 142.
[108] Report of H. M. Tufnell, 4 Oct. 1911, E.A. 2119.

244 THE ERA OF WARFARE

disputed resources in the Toror area were again under Jie control, and all of the lost territory of the Panyangara and Komukuny was regained. Indeed, the Pei and Bokora Karimojong had had to abandon much of their northern areas and had been pushed far to the south: 'Before Loriang began attacking us, our people lived at Lokicar and Natoo and as far north as the place where the Apule and Nangol Apalon Rivers meet. When Loriang came, the people were forced to move away to the south'.[109]

In 1911, a year after the battle of Loreapabong, the Karamoja Touring Officer reported that the Jie 'have driven all the people from the northern portion of the Bokora country, captured all their stock and carried off many of their women and children. I pointed out to them (the Karimojong) that they had probably only themselves to blame as being the more numerous tribe they had no doubt freely raided the Jiwe in the past . . .'. In September of that year, the same officer was in command of a patrol which passed through areas near Mt. Toror, and observed that the country of the Pei section, 'which was formerly the limit of the Bokora', was now 'all uninhabited country', except for large herds of game which ranged freely in the former settled areas of the Pei and Bokora.[110]

Similarly, the reports of another British officer stated that by about 1904 the Dodos of the Loyoro area (the Lokorikituk) had fled northwards, away from Najie, because of Jie and Turkana attacks. He further noted that the southern Dodos who had not fled to the north (presumably the Ngikaato of the Kopos area) were constantly harassed by Jie attacks, with little or no support being given them by the northern Dodos sections [111] (see Map 15).

To both his enemies and to his own people, Loriang had succeeded in becoming an almost legendary figure during his own lifetime. At Jie dances and on ceremonial occasions the most popular song being sung was one listing his victories, to which new verses were being added in rapid succession:

Ah oo Karenga yee, Kirem Karenga.	Ah, oh, Karenga, yee; we have attacked Karenga.
Kirem Natoo, ah oo!	We have attacked Natoo, ah, oh!
Kirem Lopei, ah oo!	We have attacked Lopei, ah, oh!
Kirem Natapojo, ah oo!	We have attacked Natapojo, ah, oh!
Loreapabong, ah oo!	Loreapabong, ah, oh![112]

[109] Lotiang (Kilipa) and Dengel, BK 5; also BK 3, 6, and 8.
[110] H. M. Tufnell's Report, 11 Sept. 1911. E.A. 2119.
[111] Report of C. A. Turpin, Northern Karamoja Garrison, 29 Feb. 1906, E.A. 4325, Part I.
[112] A large group of Kanawat elders, J 43.

To his own warriors, he was a hero without parallel, and surviving veterans of his army are still lavish in their praise of him sixty years after his campaigns: 'I fought in Loriang's army in all of the battles against the Bokora. We captured cattle because of Loriang. We killed enemies because of Loriang. We won great victories because of Loriang. He was a great man. He was a great leader. He was a great Jie.'[113] Indeed, to many informants it was only through the efforts of Loriang that the Jie endured as an independent community: 'Before we were warriors, the Karimojong and the Dodos always came to attack us in Najie. Then the people went to Loriang and they cried, "Loriang! The Jie are dying!". And when Loriang began to make war on the Bokora and the Dodos, the Jie began to win great victories and Najie was in danger no longer.'[114]

While Loriang clearly achieved his dramatic rise largely through his own unquestionable abilities, it must be noted that the Jie community, hard pressed by stronger enemies and decimated by the great disasters, was desperately ripe for the rise of some outstanding leader of Loriang's calibre. The office of hereditary war-leader provided the framework within which Loriang's rise was made possible, but again Loriang himself must be credited with consolidating heretofore unknown powers in the office.

The fire-makers who had consolidated considerable authority in their own offices during the earlier part of the nineteenth century, and had done much to encourage the closer integration of each Jie division, are hardly mentioned in Jie traditions pertaining to the great epoch of warfare which spanned the last half of the nineteenth and the first decade of the twentieth centuries. Both the Ngikorwakol fire-makers, Dengel and his son Lotum, and the Rengen fire-makers, Acap and his son Lodioki, who held the offices during this period seem to have been entirely satisfactory and to have performed their duties adequately.[115] Many informants stated that New Fire was kindled a number of times during the critical stages of the wars and even more often during the terrible years of the great disasters. The fire-maker of Lokorwakol is further remembered to have kindled New Fire with the inauguration of the Ngikosowa generation-set in

[113] Naluk, J 79.

[114] Lowot, Loworo, Lobwal (and others), J 8.

[115] A single discordant note was struck by the informants of J 58 who laid at least part of the blame for the Jie defeats before the rise of Loriang on the Jimos fire-maker. It is significant that two of these three informants were from Toroi, the clan from whom the Jimos had taken over the office.

about 1880. Clearly the fire-makers, who were indeed chosen because they were 'gentle and kind' and because they 'did not fight or quarrel',[116] were incapable of providing the kind of leadership necessary in the long era of warfare. As they were not expected to take any part in warfare, except for the ritual smearing of warriors before a campaign, their own role in this military epoch was eclipsed first by the individual battle-leaders, and then, and to an even greater extent, by Loriang. While they continued to provide valuable foci for the ritual unity and the political homogeneity of their respective major divisions, their practical role became ancillary to that of Loriang, whose leadership transcended the major divisions to embrace the Jie community as a whole.

Loriang's authority also impinged on that traditionally accorded to the congregation of senior elders. While he was extremely tactful in his dealings with them, and throughout his career took definite steps to curry their favour and support, nevertheless by the end of his Karimojong campaigns he had assumed much of the responsibility for determining strategic policies which had formerly been the concern of the elders. The traditions make it very clear that Loriang himself decided upon the targets his army would attack. He was sometimes advised by the elders, but more often he seems to have made his decisions alone, or in private council with his trusted battalion commanders, after which his messengers would be sent to inform the senior elders gathered at Looi ritual grove of his plans.[117] Although the elders often performed the necessary augury of reading animal intestines before a campaign, Loriang is also remembered to have been especially skilled at reading intestines and often performed the task himself.[118]

The great victories won by the Jie army in their offensive campaigns were directly due to Loriang's superior military organization and tactics. By integrating the Ngikorwakol and Rengen warriors into a unified and highly efficient army, representative of the entire Jie community, Loriang had defeated piecemeal the fragmentary armies of his enemies, based largely on individual sections of their communities:

[116] Lowakori (Ansilmo), J 90; Angura and Koroc (Lopirya), J 101.
[117] Interviews including J 76 and 97.
[118] Interviews including J 18, 33 and 51. Despite the assertions by some Karimojong informants that Loriang was 'a great diviner' or 'a great magician', the Jie are quite definite that he was not a diviner as such. Some informants did mention a diviner in whom Loriang put considerable trust and consulted frequently.

It was mainly the Bokora [section of the Karimojong] who fought
Loriang. The Matheniko [section] did not fight the Jie very often—
we had our own wars with the Turkana and the Upe [Pokot].[119]

The Tome [section of the Karimojong] would sometimes join with
the Bokora and the Pei to fight Loriang, but most of the fighting was
done by the armies of those sections. Loriang never came here to
attack the Tome, and so there was not much reason for us to fight
him.[120]

Each section of the Dodos had its own army and they usually fought
their wars separately . . . They hardly ever came together to form one
big army.[121]

It is furthermore clear that the enemy armies lacked the sophisticated organization and the internal cohesion of Loriang's force:

Karimojong armies were arranged by age-sets . . . but the various sets
had no special place in the army or any fixed duties. They all just
went and fought fiercely and tried to capture cattle. The various sets
would say to one another, 'If you leave this fight or get into trouble
because you are not brave, do not expect us to help you. We must all
remain together.[122]

Finally, both the Karimojong and Dodos entirely lacked the concept of a hereditary war-leader who was even nominally in charge of
the whole army of any section, and during Loriang's campaigns
neither group produced any leader who could emulate his military
ability or qualities of leadership. Amongst the Dodos, the war-
leader Lokoto, who was a leader of the Lomeris section, possessed
considerable bravery and skill, as did Lokuta, a leader of the Lokaato
section, but Dodos traditions make it clear that they were only two
amongst many: 'During the wars with Loriang, the Dodos had no
one war leader for all the Dodos armies. Each section had its own
leader. Lomeris was led by Lokoto and Lopwa. The people of
Loyoro [the Ngikorikituk] were led by Loitareng and Pokoyto. Other
leaders at that time were Dorino, Napaja, Ilangokan, and Lokuta.[123]

Similarly, the Karimojong were led by a number of 'fierce men' who
seem to have corresponded closely to the Jie battle-leaders before

[119] Lotipu, Lomonyang, and Ocom, MTK 3.
[120] Loram (Ecai) and Balo (Arengimoe), TK 1.
[121] Ngole (Paulo) and Loyarakori (Apalowak), D 3. In 1916 C. A. Turpin
of the Northern Garrison similarly noted that after about 1904 there was little
co-operation between the various Dodos sections in fighting the Jie. Turpin's
Report, 29 Feb. 1916, E.A. 4325, Part I.
[122] Nakong and Angela, BK 8.
[123] Akurun and Alinga, D 13; also D 1, 3, 5, and 8.

the rise of Loriang. Typical of these was Nakinei of the Bokora who owned a musket and commanded a small band of warriors who chose to 'follow his gun'.[124] Opposing Loriang, then, was an array of petty Karimojong leaders which equalled that of the Dodos: 'Many Karimojong war-leaders fought Loriang. They included Nakiapan, Lokurio, Lowokorwok, Edareng, and Wacom. But the Karimojong had no one like Loriang who led all our armies. Our leaders were just brave men who enjoyed fighting.'[125]

By the time of the battle of Loreapabong, other strangers had been making an appearance in some parts of Karamoja for more than a decade. Unlike the brown-skinned *Habaci* and *Acumpa*, these strangers were pale-skinned, and Loingolem, a skilled Panyangara diviner who had lived earlier in the nineteenth century had predicted that such people would someday appear in Najie.[126] Until after the battle of Loreapabong, however, few of these European strangers had visited Najie, and those who had were, like the *Habaci* and *Acumpa*, primarily concerned with shooting elephants and doing a bit of trading. Of these European hunters, probably the best remembered in Jie tradition is W. D. M. ('Karamoja') Bell, referred to by the Jie simply as 'Bwana Bell'. Another is recalled to have been a tall man with a bushy black beard who constantly laughed in a booming voice. Some elders remember him as a German (in fact, he may well have been an Italian), and claim that he got on poorly with the *Acumpa* hunters and traders who were also active in Najie at that time.[127]

While it was Bell or one of the other hunters who thus became the first European to visit Najie during the first few years of the twentieth century, Europeans had been at least vaguely aware of the Jie by the early 1880s. The first written mention of the Jie appears to have been made by Emin Pasha in May 1881 at his Acholi base, Pajule. Emin wrote: 'Lirem, or Lorem, adjoins Lobbor [Labwor] on the north and is called Aje, after its inhabitants; it is very populous . . . The district of Koliang lies next to that of Lirem. Behind it, towards the east-north-east is the district of Bognia . . .'[128] Although Emin

---

[124] Loyep (John) and Lobanyang (Esero), BK 2.

[125] Lotimong (Kilipa), Dengel (and others), BK 5; also BK 3 and 4.

[126] Anunu and Cope, J 28.

[127] Interviews including J 36 and 120.

[128] G. Schweinfurth, *et. al.* (eds.), *Emin Pasha in Central Africa* (London 1888), p. 252. Before leaving Acholi in 1872, Samuel Baker was informed of a country called 'Lobbohr' which is clearly Labwor, although an expedition

gave these notes 'with great reserve' because his information was 'gained from Negroes' (ibid.), and, given that place- and group-names as recorded by early European observers often bear little resemblance to their correct pronunciations, it nevertheless seems reasonably clear that 'Lirem, or Lorem' refers to *Lorengen* (the area of the Rengen division), that 'Koliang' is Kotiang territorial division (which does indeed border Rengen), and that 'Bognia' probably refers to the (Ngi)Bongia, an important clan of the Lokorikituk Dodos, who did live to the north of Najie.[129]

In 1897, the Government of the British Protectorate of Uganda made plans for its first appearance in Karamoja, an area previously ignored. In that year Major J. R. L. Macdonald was invited by Lord Salisbury to command an expeditionary force, initially called 'The Juba Expedition', whose task it would be to march rapidly north-wards concluding treaties with all indigenous tribes, thereby asserting British claims over the peripheries of their sphere of influence as delimited in agreements of 1890 and 1891. In this way it was hoped that access to the Upper Nile by both the French and the Belgians would be denied without any direct clash, and that any Ethiopian expansionist movements to the south and south-west would be effectively checked. After a false start in 1897, Macdonald's force finally arrived in Karamoja the next year. Macdonald detached two patrols from his column, sending one under Kirkpatrick to explore Lake Kyoga and then to make contact with the Nyakwai, while the other, under Austin, descended the Turkana escarpment to explore Lake Rudolf. Macdonald himself led the rest of the force north-wards through Karamoja, hoping to arrive eventually at Lado, where he would make contact with Kitchener's gunboats, steaming up the Nile from Omdurman. After concluding treaties with the

[129] Emin further noted (pp. 296 and 415) that he himself had seen men from 'Bognia' and 'Lirem' who had come to Pajule 'to barter', and that the people of 'Lirem, the Aje division of the Lango tribe' had secured for him some 'splendid camels' from the 'Turkan' living further east. I was unable to record any specific recollection in Jie oral tradition that any 'barter' was being conducted as far afield as Pajule or that any camels were obtained from the Turkana to be traded to any peoples in the west.

under Wat-el-Mek sent eastwards from Baker's fort at Patiko does not appear to have actually reached 'Lobbohr' (S. W. Baker, *Ismailia* (London, 1874), ii, 117–9). In May 1874 Chaille-Long also mentioned 'Lobbohr', and noted that its people were feuding with an 'adjacent hostile people', probably the eastern Acoli kingdoms. This was most probably the beginning of the feud which culminated in the battle of Caicaon (C. Chaille-Long, *Central Africa* (London, 1876), pp. 67–8).

Karimojong on the Omanimani River, however, Macdonald was warned by them that the tribe which lived to the north, 'the Jiwe', were 'very hostile and treacherous',[130] and so he was very careful to skirt their country on his way northwards, although he did conclude additional treaties with the Dodos, north of Najie. Thus, while direct contacts and treaties were made with their chief rivals, the Karimojong and Dodos, as well as with some sections of the Turkana, the Jie themselves were completely ignored, and there is nothing in Jie tradition to show that they were at all aware of Macdonald's expedition.

Macdonald, and then Sir Harry Johnston, concerned by the amount of illegal ivory hunting and the uncertain boundary between the Abyssinian and British spheres as revealed by Macdonald's expedition, had urged the Protectorate Government to establish direct control over Karamoja. Limited resources, however, precluded such control, and except for the establishment of a station at Mbale, south of Karamoja, to issue hunting licences and to attempt a vague, long-distance control over the traffic in ivory, Karamoja was again almost totally ignored for the next twelve years. Apparently the only exception was a journey by Lt. C. E. Fishbourne from Nimule, via the Omanimani, to Mbale in 1907. Fishbourne's route took him through Labwor and Nyakwai, west and south-west of Najie, and at Omanimani he found that the Indian and Swahili traders who had maintained a depot there had withdrawn upon orders from the Government. His report painted a rather alarming picture of inter-tribal fighting and bands of Ethiopian raiders, but again no immediate action was taken.[131] By 1910, however, the Government of British East Africa finally undertook the administration of its own areas between the Turkwel River and Lake Rudolf, and the Government of the Uganda Protectorate realized that it must extend its administration into adjacent areas of its own north-eastern territory, Karamoja. Accordingly, two patrols, one under P. H. S. Tanner of the Uganda Police, and the other under Captain T. Grant, were sent to Karamoja in that year. The twelve years since Macdonald's

[130] Austin, op. cit., p. 144. For a detailed account of Macdonald's expedition see J. P. Barber 'The Macdonald Expedition to the Nile', *UJ* 28, 1 (1964); also his *Imperial Frontier*, Chapter 2. Macdonald's report on the treaties he conducted can be found in F.O.C.P. 7402 (paper no. 27); also his confidential report and a map (paper 30).

[131] Excerpts from Fishbourne's report appear in Moyes-Bartlett, op. cit., p. 234. He also described his journey in 'Lake Kioga (Ibrahim) Exploratory Survey, 1907–1908', *GJ* 33 (1909).

expedition had seen the spectacular rise of Loriang, and the arrival in Karamoja of Tanner and Grant corresponded closely to the pinnacle of Jie military successes.

Probably just before the arrival of Tanner and Grant, Karimojong oral tradition recalls that a patrol of K.A.R. *askaris*, led by one or two European officers, arrived in the Matani area of the Bokora country, and apparently for no other reason than to demonstrate their power to the Karimojong, clashed with them:

> Those people came here from the direction of the Kumama [Iteso, i.e. the west], and they were led by the European called *Apalokilorot*. I was a young boy at that time and I was living here on this spot at my father's homestead. The European came here with many K.A.R. *askaris*, as well as the chiefs of the Kumama. He camped there at Matani [about a mile from the interview site] and I saw all of what followed. The *askaris* were mostly Acoli. They wore caps with pieces of cloth hanging down in back and pieces of cloth wrapped around their legs. In the morning, the *askaris* began going out and taking people's cattle by force. They did that for no reason, as we had no quarrel with them. No one understood why they did that. Afterwards, the people realized that the European just wanted to show he was the ruler here. When the *askaris* reached Kayopath, the Karimojong attacked them, but the *askaris* shot them with their guns and many of our warriors were killed. The Karimojong were defeated, and then the European went away with our cattle.[132]

No official report appears to have been submitted by the officer(s) who commanded this patrol and so neither his identity nor his motives can be known. Despite this incident (or as Barber has implied, possibly *because* of it),[133] Grant and Tanner were well received by the Karimojong, and a horrified Grant was urged by anxious Karimojong elders to inspect the site of the recent Jie victory at Loreapabong. Grant duly reported to Entebbe that the 'Jiwe, Kamchuru [Acoli], Chimareng [an Acoli age-set, *Cunareng*], Taburu [Labwor], Ja-leno, Mugegenei, and Turkana of Tarash combined . . . and attacked Karamoja', adding that a large percentage of the attackers had guns and that hundreds of casualties had been inflicted on the Karimojong.[134]

---

[132] Longorio, BK 9. The incident was also mentioned by J 23, BK 6, 7, 8, and MTK 3, and by Barber, *Imperial Frontier*, pp. 126–7, who was told of it by Lopuko, a former government chief, who also witnessed the battle.

[133] Barber, ibid.

[134] Grant's Report, 13 Feb. 1911, E.A. 1049, Part II. Whether the Jie army did in fact include any 'Turkana or Tarash' seems very much in doubt, however. A number of Jie informants, including those of J 80, 81, 87, and 123, the

In the same report, Grant stated that he had been informed by
'Mr Tanfani, an Italian Trader' (one suspects that he may well have
been the tall man with the black beard who got on poorly with the
Acumpa recalled in Jie oral tradition) that 'the Jiwe are well armed . . .
about 90 per cent have rifles . . . Martini Henris and ·303 are supposed to have been traded by Swahilis; the Belgian rifles to have
come from the Congo through the Nile District and the French Gras
from Abyssinia'.[135] A year later, the Acting Provincial Commissioner
reported that a Mr. Johnson (not identified, but presumably an
ivory hunter) had told him that it was chiefly in the 'Jiwe' country
that gun-trading was taking place.[136] From these and other pieces
of indirect intelligence, the Jie came to be regarded as a belligerent
tribe whose military successes were mainly attributable to their being
very heavily armed with muskets and rifles. The picture implied by
the government reports has led Barber recently to conclude that:
'There were hundreds, perhaps thousands of firearms among
such tribes as the . . . Jie'.[137] To the vanguard of the Protectorate
Administration, however, the real villains were the Swahili and
Ethiopian hunters and traders, who were frequently pictured in the
reports as lawless bandits, primarily engaged in gun-running and
even slaving, and who often participated directly in inter-tribal
raids.[138]

However, the picture painted by these reports conflicts sharply
both with the oral tradition of the peoples of Karamoja and with the
only existing first-hand report of a European visitor to Najie before
1910. It is difficult to see the long-nosed individuals with the greasy
robes of Jie oral traditions as pillaging brigands, and every Jie informant who was asked emphatically denied that even a single Jie

[135] Grant, ibid.
[136] Letter of A. H. Watson to the Touring Officer, Karamoja, 16 Oct. 1911,
E.A. 2119.
[137] Barber, *Imperial Frontier*, p. 125.
[138] For a good idea of the picture built up by the government reports, see
J. P. Barber, 'Karamoja in 1910', *UJ*, 28, 1 (1964), and *Imperial Frontier*,
especially Chapters 9 and 10.

Karimojong informants of BK 2, and the Turkana informants of T 19 all
agreed that no 'Turkana of Tarash' were ever included in Loriang's army. The
Turkana informants of T 15 and T 16, however, stated that the Turkana knew
of and respected Loriang, and that occasionally some Turkana would join
with him. It would seem quite likely that Turkana who did join Loriang were
not very numerous and they were probably Turkana who were visiting or
trading in Najie at the time of a compaign rather than a force specially recruited from as far away as the Tarash.

was ever carried off into slavery by the traders, with the exception of the famine refugees sold by the Acoli for the muskets they used at Caicaon.[139] Except for the very early clash with the *Habaci* at Nalingaken, there was no hostility between the Jie and any of the traders in Najie, and the only instance of any armed conflict between the Jie and any traders outside Najie took place some years later when a Jie raiding party attacked a *Habaci* encampment near Kopos in Dodos and were driven off with heavy casualties.[140] On the contrary, the Jie appear to have had generally good relations with both the *Acumpa* and *Habaci*, and all the traditions still acknowledge the great debt owed to the traders for their having brought large numbers of healthy cattle to Najie after the great disasters. As to the general 'lawlessness' in Najie, it seems curious that even among the government reports is the statement made by the Government Touring Officer for Karamoja in 1911 that 'porters [i.e. traders] could go about by themselves there [in Najie] with no weapons but a stick and come to no harm'.[141] Moreover, Jie informants, who readily stated that Loriang's army was joined by Labwor and Acoli musketeers, universally denied that any of the traders ever participated in any Jie military activity, except for providing the very dubious service of spying: 'Those people never helped the Jie in their fights. Sometimes they acted as spies, informing us if they saw any Karimojong armies in the bush. But they used to tell the Karimojong if they saw any of our armies, as well.'[142]

As to the gun-trading activities of the *Acumpa* and *Habaci* and the number of fire-arms in the hands of Jie warriors, there is even a greater discrepancy. Loriang and his warriors, having witnessed the destruction by traditional weapons of a force of Acoli musketeers perhaps four times their size, had little reason to be at all impressed with the military capabilities of fire-arms. While Loriang eventually permitted the inclusion of Acoli and Labwor musketeers in his army, undoubtedly more to swell his numbers than to augment his armament, his policy towards the use of fire-arms by his own men was clear: 'Loriang bought no guns from the traders. He did not want them. His men fought with spears. Had not their spears defeated the

---

[139] As Barber has suggested (*Imperial Frontier*, pp. 103–4), most Ethiopian slaving activity was probably confined to the southern provinces of their own territory. My Dodos, and Labwor informants also denied that any of their people had ever been taken as slaves.

[140] The incident was described in J 21 and D 1.

[141] H. M. Tufnell's Report, 11 Sept. 1911, E.A. 2119.

[142] Amuk (Akitibuin), J 89.

Acoli guns [at Caicaon]? A few of the younger men bought guns but not many.'[143]

A few fire-arms were lent or given to Jie individuals willing to help them actively in hunting elephants after the great disasters by the *Habaci* and *Acumpa*, and while some of the hunters and traders did begin to arrive in Najie with rifles and muskets as part of their trade-goods during the first decade of the twentieth century, few of those guns were purchased by the Jie. Despite Mr. Tanfani's report that guns could be obtained for ivory or 'a few cows each',[144] most of the Jie regarded the prices of guns far higher than their potential value: 'The Jie never bought many guns. Only a very rich man could afford to buy one from the traders. The price of one gun was as many as ten oxen. Few could afford that . . . Here in Kanawat [territorial division] my own father owned one gun, and there were three others who had them as well. That was all. Only those four.'[145]

Moreover, in 1905, 'Karamoja' Bell could note that most of 'the firearms which were picked up by the Jiwe [from the Acoli.casualties after the victory at Caicaon] had since been traded off to Swahilis', in direct reversal of the picture suggested by the government reports, and that the Jie army relied on 'spears alone.'[146] This was further supported by both Jie and Labwor oral tradition, which stated that most of the Acoli muskets were either sold to the *Acumpa* or else to the Labwor:

> My father killed two Acoli at Caicaon and captured their guns. One he sold to his Labwor friend Apulobu for ten goats, and the other he sold to the *Acumpa*.[147]
> The Jie captured some guns from the Acoli [at Caicaon]. After the Labwor got some of those guns [from the Jie] we were able to drive the Acoli away [from the Labwor area].[148]

The Labwor, to whom adoption by the Jie army of large numbers of fire-arms would have seriously disrupted their own lucrative trade in traditional iron weapons, were themselves clearly unconcerned by

[143] Lobwal, J 34.
[144] Grant's Report, E.A. 1049, Part II.
[145] Inua (Lodweny), and others, J 128. Informants from other territorial divisions, including those of J 12, 15, 16, 22, 33, 40, 41, 111, 118, 120, and 123, indicated that correspondingly few guns were owned in their own divisions. From their collective testimonies it would seem that the maximum number of fire-arms of all varieties ever possessed by the Jie did not exceed more than about 100.
[146] Bell, *Wanderings of an Elephant Hunter*, p.63.
[147] Nakade (Peter), J 57; also J 125.
[148] Ogira (Jebedayo), Oceng, and Odiyo (Saul), L 4; also L 10.

the numbers of fire-arms that were being bought by Jie warriors: 'The Jie never bought many guns and there was still a great need for our spears. Even those few warriors who had a gun still continued to carry their spears as well.'[149]

In 1909, only a year before the battle of Loreapabong and Tan-fani's intelligence that 90 per cent of the Jie were armed with fire-arms, Bell could write an eye-witness report that although the Jie did still own a certain number of the muskets captured at Caicaon, as well as some additional ones captured in later raids, such arma-ment hardly played any great role in their military activities:

> ... the Jiwans thought that firearms made a big noise and a nasty smell ... Besides being the possessors of all these captured guns, they had ... executed raids on their softer Nile-Valley dwelling neigh-bours, thereby adding still more to their armament and wealth. But it was chiefly at their dances that they used the alien armament, and then only to produce noise ... It will thus be seen that they were in a very nasty state of ignorance of the potentialities of the modern firearm ...[150]

Bell went on to note that because of the success of their army, the Jie had by this time given up most of the ivory-hunting activities to which they had been forced to turn after the great disasters, thereby eliminating from their economy one of the two commodities which Tanfani claimed could be exchanged for guns. According to Bell, the Jie relied on their own military system, rather than the traders, to amass their great wealth:

> Indeed, the Jiwans generally show an indifference to, and a detach-ment from, the subject of [hunting] elephant not found among the poorer and less war-like tribes such as the Bukora, Dodinga, and Dobossa. And here it may be remarked that tribal interest in hunting methods for acquiring wealth varies in inverse ratio to fighting abilities.[151]

Even the enemies of the Jie, who bore the full brunt of Loriang's victories, were clearly aware that the Jie army did not depend on fire-arms for its successes, and that the guns employed against them were mainly in the hands of Loriang's Labwor and Acoli allies, and then only at the very end of the Jie offensive campaigns: 'The only time that any Jie ever used guns against us was at Loreapabong. In that battle the Jie themselves had a few guns, but their friends the

[149] Ibid.
[150] Bell, *Wanderings of an Elephant Hunter*, pp. 136–7.
[151] Ibid., p. 141.

Acoli and the Labwor had most of them. Before that battle, Jie armies had always come against us with only spears.'[152]

In all fairness to them, the Karimojong had quite probably tried to indicate to the European observers that it was not the Jie, but their western allies, who had most of the guns, as their meticulous listing of all the alien elements in the Jie army for Grant's benefit seems to show. However, the vanguard of the Protectorate Government either misunderstood, or else chose to ignore any such intelligence, and chose instead to credit the picture painted by Tanfani and Johnson, who may well have been in direct rivalry with the *Acumpa* and *Habaci* traders and hunters, and would have had every reason to resent the good relations which existed between them and the Jie. At any rate, Grant drew no distinction between the Acoli musketeers and Jie spearmen in Loriang's force, and was clearly oblivious of the efficient Jie military system forged by Loriang's own genius which was the true reason behind the Jie successes.

At any rate, Tanner was sent north with a patrol to investigate the stories of gun-running and lawlessness and thus became the first representative of the Protectorate Government to set foot in Najie. He must have passed through Najie very quickly, for although Jie traditions recall the patrol, it seems to have gone on to the north without an incident of any kind there. Most of Tanner's investigations were conducted at Tshudi-Tshudi (the site of present-day Kaabong township) in northern Dodos, where he found an important Ethiopian trading post, considerable gun-running activity, and a great deal of ivory which was being sent out of Karamoja, to Ethiopia.[153] On his return from Dodos, Jie traditions do recall that Tanner (*Topana* to them)[154] did stop off briefly in Najie where he left behind

[152] Nakong and Angela, BK 8; also MTK 2 and 3.

[153] It is most regrettable that the file (E.A. 71/1910) containing Tanner's report has 'disappeared' from the Entebbe Archives, possibly lost during a transfer of files from one room to another. A number of other potentially valuable files, including E.A. 64/1911, E.A. 1411, E.A. 1754, and 1294/06, have also disappeared, or have been re-classified as 'confidential'. Barber saw Tanner's report before its loss, and according to his account of the patrol (*Imperial Frontier*, p. 111), it does seem clear that all of Tanner's descriptions of gun-running and lawlessness referred to the Tshudi-Tshudi area of northern Dodos. Dodos oral tradition largely supports Tanner's account, and admits that they had 'many more guns than the other peoples of Karamoja' (D 7), and that the traders often combined with Dodos armies in battles. This was clearly a very different situation than in Najie.

[154] All the early European officers were given nicknames by the Jie (as well as by the other peoples of Karamoja). Often it is difficult to be certain which officer is being referred to by a given nickname. Tanner and Tufnell (and possibly Turpin), for example, were apparently known by the same nickname,

four porters, described in a subsequent report by Tufnell as 'too sick to travel',[155] to be cared for by the Jie. According to Jie traditions their 'sickness' had been caused by having the skin cut from the soles of their feet as a punishment either for lagging behind the patrol or for trying to desert.[156]

It was the next patrol, composed of a force of Uganda policemen under the command of H. M. Tufnell, who marched northwards in September 1911, that made the first real contacts with the Jie. Acting as his guides were Lokothowa, the Magos leader whose people had been driven out of their homeland to the southern parts of Karamoja perhaps thirty years before, and Nakinei, a Bokora battle-leader who had been one of the few Karimojong to offer brave resistance to the Jie army at Loreapabong. Both men had been employed by *Acumpa* traders at various times and their knowledge of Kiswahili and the ways of the world outside Karamoja had ensured that they would be paid considerable attention by the vanguard of the Protectorate Government. Both had related detailed stories of the atrocities committed by Jie armies and, undoubtedly recalling the fire-power of a similar patrol against their fellow Karimojong at Kayopath, had readily volunteered to guide Tufnell and his men to Najie.[157] On 6 September, Tufnell and his men arrived in Panyangara territorial division, and he immediately sent for 'Lorengamoy [Loriang] . . . said to be the organizer of all the raids', but Loriang, unused to being summoned by anyone, contented himself with sending some of his messengers to see what the strangers wanted.[158] Infuriated by Loriang's disdain, Tufnell, after waiting three days, took a detachment to his kraal and rounded up all of Loriang's cattle that he could find. After a thorough search through the houses of Loriang's settlement, the men returned with a total of thirty-seven rounds of

[155] Tufnell's Report, 2 Oct. 1911, E.A. 2119.
[156] Interviews including J 28, 40, 94, 114, 119, 120, 127, and 131.
[157] Interviews including J 28, 111, BK 7, 8, 9 and TK 1.
[158] Tufnell's Report, 11 Sept. 1911, E.A. 2119. A number of Jie informants gave descriptions of Tufnell's arrival which corresponds closely to his own account. Unknown to Tufnell, a party of Swahili traders were fleeing north, just ahead of his patrol. Although in a great hurry, Jie informents recalled that they took the time to stop off in Najie to warn them of the approach of the patrol and urged the Jie to exercise great caution in dealing with it.

Topana. Some informants stated that this was an attempt to say 'Governor', while others claim that it was an attempt to say the officer's name (possible for 'Tanner' and 'Turpin', but hardly likely for 'Tufnell'). Fortunately, Tufnell is frequently referred to as *Lokijukwa* ('the slow-moving one' because by Jie standards his patrols covered such short distances in a day's march), or as *Topana-Lokijukwa*.

ammunition and some gun-powder, but found no firearms. During the confiscation of the cattle, a total of five guns had been seen in the hands of Jie warriors who fell back before the detail (one of them had fired a round at Tufnell). Loriang, who had gone to another part of Najie with the arrival of the patrol, was soon surrounded by his battalions who, with typical efficiency, had begun to mobilize at the appearance of the strangers. Many of the warriors were irate over the confiscation of Loriang's cattle, and the men of the Ngikwei age-set of Ngikosowa, veterans who had served under Loriang in every battle since Tiira, clamoured to be allowed to crush these impudent strangers. A different course of action was urged by one Lopetum, however, a Rengen who had worked for the *Acumpa* after the great disasters and, in visiting areas outside Karamoja, had come to under-stand something of the strangers' potential power:

> The Europeans made their camp at Panyangara. The Jie had heard how the Bokora had attacked them at Akalale [Kayopath] and how the Europeans had killed many of the Bokora. The Europeans had black soldiers with them at Panyangara and they dug a deep hole all around their camp. But the Ngikwei were very brave warriors and they said, 'Let us go and slaughter these people like goats!'. But the man from Rengen [Lopetum] who knew the most about Europeans came and said, 'Brothers! Are you really going to kill these people? You can kill these few very easily, but I have been to the place they come from, and there they are as numerous as black ants! If you kill these, many, many more will come here, until they are enough to kill us all.' And so the Ngikwei, grumbling, went back to their homes and left the Europeans in peace.[159]

Loriang accepted Lopetum's advice, and the next morning ap-peared in Tufnell's camp to reclaim his cattle and to make peace with the strangers. In his previous dealings with the Acoli after Caicaon and the Nyakwai after the clash at Lolung, Loriang had demonstrated his diplomatic skill, and had shown that he would readily make peace if he considered it to be advantageous to the Jie. His offensive campaigns had secured every Jie frontier and had re-claimed all of the grazing lands, watering points, and salt-licks that the Jie had ever controlled. He had established excellent relations with the western neighbours of the Jie. Militarily, it could be argued that Loriang's offensives were already somewhat over-extended, and with his very clear understanding of strategy and tactics, it can be reasonably assumed that he himself was aware of it. Jie traditions

[159] Inua, Apalodokoro, and Lomongin (Julio), J 23.

recall that in their meeting, *Topana Lokijukwa* (Tufnell) 'spoke with a soft voice' and Tufnell himself reported that

> ... [the Jie] were told that the days of raiding must now come to an end. I told them that I did not want to go into past shauris [affairs] and that they could keep what they had captured but that the women and children taken [in raids] must be produced and returned to Bakora in my presence. This they agreed to do and the compact has been carried out.[160]

The peace talks appear to have been conducted with a certain amity on both sides, but the whole affair nearly ended in disaster when, some days later, Tufnell discovered that the four 'sick' porters left in Najie were dead. The Jie tried to explain that the porters, fearing to sleep inside a Jie homestead, had remained outside and were murdered by a small Bokora raiding party which came to Panyangara one night to steal cattle. Tufnell refused to believe them, and confiscated forty Jie cattle. According to Jie traditions, this was accomplished by Tufnell's first seizing a number of aged senior elders and roping them together by the necks, releasing them only when the forty cattle were paid in ransom. Again, the Jie army clamoured to attack the strangers, and again it was only by Loriang's extraordinary control that it was kept from doing so.[161]

Before leaving Najie, Tufnell presented Loriang with a *kanzu* and made him chief of the southern part of Najie, and appointed Lopetum chief of the northern part (Rengen), apparently for no better reason than his ability to speak Kiswahili and Acoli, acquired during his employment by the traders.[162] Except for the five guns seen during his raid on Loriang's kraal, Tufnell had apparently seen no other fire-arms in Najie, and having relied on the rather suspect and clearly exaggerated reports of Tanfani, Johnson, and others, he was obviously rather surprised, and somewhat lamely reported: 'It is difficult to get any idea as to the numbers of rifles these people have obtained as they are very cunning and pretend that they have none, or when asked about those that are by chance seen say they were captured from the Kamcuru [Acoli].'[163]

---

[160] Tufnell's Report, 11 Sept. 1911, E.A. 2119.

[161] It is notable that sixty years later, every Jie informant I asked about it was still adamant that the porters had in fact been murdered by the Bokora, and all were still very resentful towards *Topana Lokijukwa* for not believing them and subsequently mistreating the elders.

[162] Tufnell's reports of 11 Sept. and 4 Oct. 1911, E.A. 2119; interviews including J 23, 34, 36, 59, 90, 125, 131.

[163] Tufnell's Report, 11 Sept. 1911, E.A. 2119.

In the following year, when Tufnell made a systematic confiscation of Jie fire-arms, he managed to collect only twenty-two, including seven antiquated muzzle-loaders which were probably souvenirs of Caicaon. By the end of the year he was able to report that there were 'few guns left in the district'.[164] While the officers of the Uganda Protectorate had thus been mistaken concerning both the lawlessness and the numbers of firearms in Najie, the anxiety caused by exaggerated and misleading reports had been sufficient for the expansion of 'the Imperial Frontier' (to borrow Barber's term) northwards through Karamoja. Having taken the initial steps, the Protectorate Government found itself inexorably committed to the administration of Karamoja, for as Tanner led his patrol northwards in 1910, the Governor in Entebbe received intelligence that Dejaz Beru, the Ethiopian Ras of Maji, was preparing to establish permanent Ethiopian posts in Karamoja and Turkana.[165] The British realized that if they were to retain this north-eastern part of their sphere of influence, a discernible presence must be maintained in the area, and from 1911, Karamoja and the Jie came under military administration, with regular patrols, initially by the K.A.R., and then during the First World War by the Uganda police, operating throughout the district. Permanent outposts were established at Moroto, Moroto River, and Loyoro, and in addition to the appointed chiefs, each territorial division of Najie was to be governed by its own representative 'Atuk' (native council) selected by its own people, and directly responsible to the District Commissioner. By 1920 a 'Rest House' for the officers of visiting British patrols had been built in each territorial division and the boundaries of Jie County had been officially delimited to include all of the territory effectively under their control by the end of Loriang's campaigns.[166] In the following year, the military administration was replaced by a civil administration.

A few years after his encounter with Tufnell, Loriang died of an infected abscess on his leg. With him died the long era of conflict which had culminated in the recovery of their lost territories and had ensured, at least temporarily, the endurance of an independent and more closely integrated Jie community. With Loriang's death and the extension of the Protectorate Administration, some of Loriang's veterans bemoaned the passing of the era in which they had won so

[164] Barber, *Imperial Frontier*, pp. 142–3. Jie informants stated that after the collection of the guns, *Lokijukwa* burned them.
[165] The Dejaz Beru incident and the events which transpired are fully treated by Barber, *Imperial Frontier*, pp. 112–15.
[166] Chidlaw-Roberts, op. cit., pp. 1–3.

many great victories: 'When *Topana* and *Lokijukwa* and the other Europeans began coming here, they stopped the wars. There was no more real fighting after they came. After they came we who had been warriors were made like women.'[167]

To other Jie, however, the peace brought by the Administration was welcomed, and they accepted that a new era had dawned:

> Before *Lokijukwa* came here, we were constantly fighting. It is true that Loriang led us to many great victories, but many people were becoming tired of the wars. When *Lokijukwa* told us not to attack the Karimojong and Dodos anymore, we obeyed. He said that he who killed an enemy would himself be killed. We kept our country, and peace came. And the people were happy. Those were good days. Those were days of peace and rain.[168]

It would seem likely, then, that the expansion of the Jie had gone almost as far as possible (or at least desirable) by the time of the arrival of the British Administration; and, in retrospect, it is probable that peace between the Jie and their northern and southern rivals would have been concluded not long after Loreapabong, even if the Administration had not arrived. The Administration was first accepted and then even welcomed by many Jie who soon realized that it could and would ensure their right to the use of vital resources on the peripheries of their now officially delimited country.

What can never be known is how far the new-found military integration of the Jie community under Loriang would have been extended into peace-time if the Administration had not arrived at that moment in Jie history. With the return of peace, would Loriang and his hereditary successors have continued to exert a degree of centralized authority over all the Jie, or would the Ngikorwakol and Rengen fire-makers have re-emerged as the focal points for the separate identities of each of their respective major divisions? Or (and this must be regarded as unlikely) would the strongly segmentary system of the Lokorwakol territorial divisions which had prevailed before the nineteenth century have returned once again?

In the somewhat artificial environment brought about by the British and then the independent Ugandan administrations, the senior elders have retained a great deal of respect and a certain amount of authority within the context of the generation-set system, despite the imposition of a system of government-appointed chiefs. Among the Rengen, the fire-makers have remained as a certain focal

---

[167] Munu (Apaesiyai) and Apalokapel, J 33.
[168] Longok (Apacelem), Ekongor, and Lothike (Elawa), J 29.

point of unity and identity, but among the Ngikorwakol, the office
has apparently declined considerably from the importance it achieved
during the first half of the nineteenth century; twenty years have
elapsed since the death of the last Jimos fire-maker, Lotum, without
one of his several sons being chosen to replace him. During the
1950s and 1960s Atom, Loriang's grandson, made use of his office
of hereditary war-leader to attain considerable power and influence,
commanding well-organized and disciplined armies in huge raids
against the Karimojong, reminiscent of Loriang's great campaigns.
Since that time an increasingly vigorous presence by the Uganda
Army in Karamoja has precluded the mustering of large Jie forces,
and during recent conflicts with the Turkana, individual battle-
leaders with their own 'private companies' have again become
increasingly important, although Atom has remained a military
authority much respected and often consulted by both the
Ngikorwakol and the Rengen.

APPENDIX
Reasearch Assistance

JAMES LODUNGO—Age, about 30; Kanawat territorial division; initiated as part of first group of Ngitome initiates, 1963. His maternal uncle, Erisa Longok (informant of J 1, J 86), a former County Chief of Jie. Four years at Moroto High School, 1964–8. Research assistant Nov. 1969–Feb. 1970. Left my employment for career with Uganda Police.

ERNEST KOROBE—Age, about 23. Four years at Moroto High School, 1964–8. Very good English. From Komukuny territorial division. Father killed during Karimojong raid in 1950s; raised by his maternal great-uncle, Lothike Elawa (informant of J 29 and J 131) of Panyangara. Research assistant from Feb.–June 1970; Jan.–Feb. 1971. Left my employment temporarily to train as a health assistant.

MARIO LONGOK—Age, about 20. One year secondary schooling in Kampala. Much better English than his formal education might indicate. Son of Nameu, former County Chief of Jie who saw long service under Colonial Administration. Father died when Mario was still very young, raised by his maternal great-uncle, Teko Ekalam (informant of J 76) of Loser clan of Kotido. Research Assistant June 1970–Feb. 1971. Mother now resident in Labwor, and so helped make some contacts there.

PART-TIME JIE ASSISTANTS
PETER LOKIRU—Age, about 25. Initiated into first group of Ngitome, 1963. Four years at Moroto High School, 1964–8. A very popular young man throughout Jie and Labwor counties. Has strong political aspirations. Was training as prison officer during part of my stay in Najie. From Ngikalogwala clan, Nakapelimoru territorial division. Son of Loceng Natwanga (informant of J 16, J 83). Helped arrange interviews J 16 to J 22, and did some interpreting and translation. Had lived some years in Labwor and knows that dialect well, and so also helped with translations of some Labwor tapes.

JOHN PEIKAN—Age, about 20. Seven years of primary school education in Kotido. From Rengen major division. Helped to make contacts and arrange interviews in Rengen during early part of 1970.

MICHAEL LODIO—Age, about 23. Third-year student at Moroto High School. From Jimos clan of Losilang. Grandson of Lotum, the last

Jimos fire-maker. Helped to make contacts with members of fire-maker family and arranged J 53.

MODING—Age, about 30. Some primary education; very little English, but some Kiswahili. From Lokwor clan of Kotido. Initiated into first group of Ngitome, 1963. Helped make contacts in Kotiang and Kotido territorial divisions. Arranged J 38 and J 39. Took an active role in my own initiation.

PETER LOPADING—Age, about 20. Seven years primary schooling. Although a Jie, has lived much of life in Labwor with his mother and so has good knowledge of that dialect. Helped translate several Labwor tapes.

PART-TIME NON-JIE ASSISTANTS

MICHAEL NGOROK—Age, about 20. Fourth-year secondary school student in Kampala. A Labwor from the Jo-Kagot clan. Son of Ruben Okec (informant of L 1). Had helped Professor Webster of Makerere to gather historical information in Karamoja before my arrival in Uganda. Interpreter for Labwor interviews L 1 and L 3. Observed several Jie interviews late in 1969 and early in 1970.

JOHN OTTOO—Age, about 25. Eight years of primary schooling, working as health assistant in Southern Karamoja during my stay in Najie. A Labwor of the Jo-Kajimo clan. Son of Oceng (informant of L 4 and L 5). Interpreter for L 4.

MILTON OWOK—Age, about 23. Third-year student at Moroto High School. Younger brother of John Ottoo, above. Interpreter for L 4, 5, 6 and NY-1.

PAULINO OYNGI—Age, about 23. Second-year student at Moroto High School. A Labwor from Jo-Kakec clan. Son of John Ogwang (informant of L 8). Interpreter for L 7 to L 11, and NY 2.

PHILIP AKOL—Age, about 23. Four years at Moroto High School. A Matheniko Karimojong; clan, Katek. Grand-nephew of Lomongin (informant of MTK 4). Arranged a number of Karimojong interviews, and helped with several Jie and Turkana interviews. Interpreter for MOK 1, MTK 4, TK 1, and T 19.

LARGO LOMURIA—Age, about 20. An Eyan. A student at Moroto Teachers' College. Served as guide in Mt. Orom area and helped make contact with Ngieyan informants.

GABRAEL S/O SAMPSON—Age, about 20. A Dodos from the Poot clan. Student at Moroto Teachers' College. Helped with Dodos interviews, especially in Kopos area. Son of Sampson Adupa (informant of D 12).

Select Bibliography
and Bibliographical Notes

(A.) ARCHIVAL SOURCES AND HISTORICAL TEXTS

1. *Entebbe Archives.* More than thirty separate files were consulted, of which three: *E.A.-1049*, Part II; *E.A.-2119*, and *E.A.-4325*, Part I, were most relevant to research on Jie oral history.

2. *Foreign Office Confidential Prints.* About fifty confidential prints were examined. Most of the relevant material was duplicated in the Entebbe Archives.

3. *Historical Texts.* The series of 195 formal interviews or 'Historical Texts', conducted during 16 months in Karamoja and Turkana Districts was by far the single most important source of information used in writing this book.

Initially, it was hoped that a full list of informants, with relevant biographical information, could be included. However, space has precluded this. The reader's attention is directed back to my London Ph.D. Thesis, 'The Oral History of the Jie of Uganda', available at Senate House and S.O.A.S. Libraries at the University of London, in East Africa at Makerere and Nairobi Universities, and in the United States on microfilm from C.A.M.P. in Chicago, where such a list with biographical sketches can be found. Eventually, it is hoped that the historical texts themselves can be published, and of course biographical information on the informants would appear there, as well.

Jie informants were drawn from every territorial division, every major clan, and most of the minor clans. About two-thirds of the informants participated in a single formal interview, while the remaining one-third participated in from two to five interviews. Non-Jie informants were also drawn from as wide a range of territorial and kinship groups as possible.

With a very few exceptions, both Jie and non-Jie informants had had no formal education and most had not travelled or lived far outside their own district. However, a good proportion had seen some form of government service (often as porters) during the early decades of the twentieth century. Most of the older Jie informants had seen military service in Loriang's army. Very few informants were Christian converts and only one was a Muslim.

(B.) OTHER UNPUBLISHED SOURCES

ATKINSON, R., 'State Formation and Development in Western Acholi', seminar paper presented at Makerere University, 1971.
BLACKBURN, R. H., 'Okiek History', a manuscript awaiting publication

as Chapter I of the forthcoming volume, *Aspects of Pre-Colonial History of Kenya*, B.A. Ogot, ed.

CHIDLAW-ROBERTS, J. R., 'Sketch Map of the Northern Frontier District and Turkana', a blue print drawn by Lt. T. P. C. Stuttaford, 4th K.A.R., Dec., 1919. Scale 1:500,000. Copy at the Royal Geographical Society, London.

DESHLER, W., 'Factors Influencing the Present Population Distribution in Dodoso County of Karamoja District', paper presented for the East Africa Institute of Social Research, Kampala, 1954.

HERRING, R., 'The Origin and Development of the Nyakwai', seminar paper presented at Makerere University, 1971.

——,Production and Exchange in Labwor, Uganda', seminar paper presented at Dalhousie University, Canada, 1973.

JACOBS, A. H., 'The Traditional Political Organization of the Pastoral Maasai', D. Phil. Thesis, Oxford, 1965.

Jie County Census Figures, 1968, typewritten report compiled by County Chief's Office, Kotido, Karamoja District, Uganda, and on file in the office of the A.D.C., Kotido.

KING, A., 'The Development of Political Organisation on the Albert Nile: The Case of Koc-Ragem', seminar paper presented at Nairobi, 1970.

LAMPHEAR, J. E., 'The Oral History of the Jie of Uganda', Ph.D. Thesis, University of London, 1972.

LOGIRA, S. L., 'Calendar of Notable Events in Jie', a typewritten manuscript drawn up to aid census workers in 1968. A copy is on file in the A.D.C.'s office, Kotido.

MOYES-BARTLETT, H. (A file card index of the officers of the K.A.R.).

MURIUKI, G., 'A History of the Kikuyu to 1904', Ph.D. Thesis, London University, 1969.

NAGASHIMA, N., 'Historical Relations Among the Central Nilo-Hamites', conference paper presented to the Social Sciences Council, Makerere University, 1968.

ODADA, M., 'The Fusion of Lwo and Ateker—The Kuman', seminar paper presented at Makerere University, 1971.

OGWAL, R., 'History of Lango Clans', n.d., a typewritten manuscript; a copy is in the possession of the Department of History, Makerere University.

Records of Raids in Jie County, April 1969–October 1970, a typewritten report compiled by and filed at the Police Post, Kotido, Karamoja District.

ROBBINS, L. H., 'The Archaeology of Turkana District', seminar paper presented at Nairobi, 1970.

STEWART, FRANK, 'Fundementals of Age Set Systems', D. Phil. Thesis, Oxford, 1972.

TOSH, J. (A file card index of Lango clans, compiled during his fieldwork in Uganda in 1969).

——, 'The Background: Environment, Migration and Settlement', Chapter I of 'Political Authority among the Langi of Northern Uganda, circa 1800 to 1939', Ph.D. Thesis, University of London, 1973.

WEBSTER, J. B. (A series of seminar papers, all presented at Makerere University):

——, 'The Iteso During the Asonya', 1969.

——, 'State Formation and the Development of Political Institutions in Eastern Acholi', 1970

——, 'A Tentative Chronology of the Lwo', 1971

——, 'The Peopling of Agago', 1971
——, 'Lira Palwo—An Expanding Acholi State', 1971
(other unpublished papers):
——, 'State Formation and Fragmentation in Agago, Eastern Acholi', conference paper presented at Dar-es-Salaam University, 1970
——, 'Acholi Historical Texts', compiled at Makerere University, 1971
WILSON, J. G., 'Recent Archaeological Finds in Karamoja District, Uganda and Related Finds in Kenya', a typewritten manuscript written in 1970, currently awaiting publication.

(C.) PUBLISHED SOURCES

AUSTIN, H. H., *With Macdonald in Uganda* (London, 1903).
BAKER, S. W., *Ismailia*, vol. ii (London, 1874).
BARBER, J. P., *Imperial Frontier* (Nairobi, 1968).
——, 'Karamoja in 1910', *UJ* 28 (1964).
——, 'The Macdonald Expedition to the Nile', *UJ* 28 (1964).
BARTON, J., 'Notes on the Turkana Tribe (Part I)', *JAS*, 1921.
BEATON, A. C., 'The Bari Clan and Age-class Systems', *SNR* 19 (1936).
——, 'A Chapter in Bari History', *SNR* 17 (1934).
——, 'Record of the Toposa Tribe', *SNR* 31 (1950).
BELL, W. D. M., *Karamoja Safari* (London, 1949).
——, *Wanderings of an Elephant Hunter* (London, 1925).
BERE, R. M., 'An Outline of Acholi History', *UJ* 11 (1947).
CHAILLE-LONG, C., *Central Africa* (London, 1876).
CHIDLAW-ROBERTS, J. R., *Report on the Karamoja District of the Uganda Protectorate* (Government Printer, Entebbe, 1920).
CLARK, DORIS, 'Karamojong Age-Groups and Clans', *UJ* 14 (1950).
——, *Looking at East Africa* (B.C.M.S. Publications, London, 1953).
COHEN, D. W. *The Historical Tradition of the Busoga* (Oxford, 1972).
COLE, SONIA, *The Prehistory of East Africa* (New York, 1965).
COLLINS, R. O., 'The Turkana Patrol, 1918', *UJ* 25 (1961).
CRAZZOLARA, J. P., *The Lwoo*, vol. iii (Verona, 1954).
——, 'Notes on the Lango–Omiru and on the Labwor and Nyakwai', *Anthropos* 55 (1960).
DRIBERG, J. H., *The Lango* (London, 1923).
DUNDAS, K. R., 'Notes on the Tribes Inhabiting the Baringo District', *JRAI* 40 (1910).
——, 'The Wawanga and Other Tribes of the Elgon District', *JRAI* 43, (1913).
DYSON-HUDSON, N., *Karimojong Politics* (Oxford, 1966).
EHRET, CHRISTOPHER, *Southern Nilotic History* (Northwestern University Press, 1971).
EMLEY, E. D., 'The Turkana of Kolosia District', *JRAI* 57 (1927).
FISHBOURNE, C. E., 'Lake Kioga (Ibrahim) Exploratory Survey, 1907–1908', *GJ* 33 (1909).
FOSBROOKE, H. A., 'The Masai Age-group System as a Guide to Tribal Chronology', *African Studies* 15 (1956).
GIRLING, F. K., *The Acholi of Uganda* (London, 1960).
GRAY, J. M., 'Acholi History, 1860–1901 (Part I)', *UJ* 15 (1951).
GULLIVER, P. H., 'The Age Organisation of the Jie Tribe', *JRAI* 83 (1953).
——, *The Family Herds* (London, 1955).
——, 'Jie Agriculture', *UJ* 18 (1954).
——, 'The Jie of Uganda', in J. Gibbs (ed.), *Peoples of Africa* (Holt, Rinehart & Winston, 1963).

——, 'The Karamojong Cluster', *Africa* 22 (1952).

——, 'The Population of Karamoja', *UJ* 17 (1953).

——, *A Preliminary Survey of the Turkana* (University of Cape Town, 1951).

——, 'The Teso and the Karamojong Cluster', *UJ* 20 (1956).

——, 'Turkana Age Organization', *American Anthropologist* 60 (1958).

——, and Gulliver, Pamela, 'The Central Nilo-Hamites' (London, 1953).

HOHNEL, L. VON, *The Discovery of Lakes Rudolf and Stefanie*, vol. ii, (London, 1895.)

HOLLIS, A. C., *The Masai* (Oxford, 1905).

JACOBS, A. H., 'A Chronology of the Pastoral Masai', in B. A. Ogot (ed.), *Hadith I* (Nairobi, 1968).

KAGOLO, S. M., 'Tribal Names and Customs in Teso District', *UJ* 19 (1955).

Kenya Land Commission—Evidence and Memoranda, vol. ii (London, 1934).

LAMPHEAR, J. E., and WEBSTER, J. B., 'The Jie–Acholi War: Oral Evidence from Two Sides of the Battle Front', *UJ* 35 (1971).

LAWRANCE, J. C. D., 'A History of the Teso to 1937', *UJ* 19 (1955).

——, *The Iteso* (London, 1957).

——, 'The Karamojong Cluster: A Note', *Africa* 23 (1953).

LEEKE, R. H., 'The Northern Territories of the Uganda Protectorate', *GJ* 49 (1917).

MCKEAN, J. D., 'Northern Turkana History', report in *Kenya Land Commission—Evidence and Memoranda*, vol. ii (London, 1934).

MCMASTER, D. N., *A Subsistance Crop Geography of Uganda* (Bude, Cornwall, 1962).

MOYES-BARTLETT, H., *The King's African Rifles* (Aldershot, 1956).

NALDER, L. F. (ed.), *A Tribal Survey of Mongalla Province* (London, 1937).

NELSON, CHARLES, 'A Report on Archaeological Survey of the Kotido Area, April, 1970', a supplement to *Uganda Monuments Section Monthly Report* (April, 1970), Ministry of Culture and Community Development, Kampala.

OGOT, B. A., *History of the Southern Luo* (Nairobi, 1967).

PAGET-WILKS, H., *Lokong Tells His Story* (B.C.M.S. Publications, London, 1930).

PERISTIANY, J. G., 'The Age-Set System of the Pastoral Pokot', *Africa* 21 (1951).

RADCLIFFE-BROWN, A. R., and FORDE, D. (eds.), *African Systems of Kinship and Marriage* (London, 1950).

ROSCOE, J., *The Bakitara or Bunyoro* (Cambridge, 1923).

SASSOON, H., *Uganda Monuments Section Monthly Report* (April 1970), Ministry of Culture and Community Development, Kampala.

SCHWEINFURTH, G., *et al.,* (eds.), *Emin Pasha in Central Africa* (London, 1888).

SELIGMAN, C. G. and B. Z., *Pagan Tribes of the Nilotic Sudan* (London, 1932).

——, 'The Social Organization of the Lotuko', *SNR* 8 (1926).

SPENCER, PAUL, *Nomads in Allience* (London, 1973),

——*The Samburu* (London, 1963).

SUTTON, J. E. G., 'The Settlement of East Africa', in B. A. Ogot and J. A. Kieran (eds.), *Zamani* (Nairobi, 1968).

TARANTINO, A., 'Lango Clans', *UJ* 13 1 (1949).

——, 'Notes on the Lango', *UJ* 13 2 (1949).

THOMAS, ELIZABETH MARSHAL, *Warrior Herdsmen* (London, 1966).

THOMSON, JOSEPH, *Through Masailand* (London, 1883).

TUCKER, A. N., 'Fringe Cushitic', *S.O.A.S. Bulletin*, 30 3 (1967).

——, and BYRAN, M. A., *The Non-Bantu Languages of North Eastern Africa* (London, 1956).

TURNBULL, C. M., 'The Ik: Alias the Teuso', *UJ* 31 (1967).

TURPIN, C. A., 'The Occupation of the Turkwel River Area by the Karamojong Tribe', *UJ* 12 (1948).

VANSINA, J., *Oral Tradition* (London, 1965).

WALSHE, C. I., 'Notes on the Kumam', *UJ* 11 (1947).

WAYLAND, E. J., 'Notes on the Board Game known as "Mweso" in Uganda', *UJ* 4 (1936).

——, 'Preliminary Studies of the Tribes of Karamoja', *JRAI* 61 (1931).

WEATHERBY, J. M., 'Inter-Tribal Warfare on Mt. Elgon in the Nineteenth and Twentieth Centuries', *UJ* 26 (1962).

——, 'A Preliminary Note on the Sorat (Tepeth)', *UJ* 33 (1969).

——,'Pioneers of Teso', *Tarikh* 3 2 (1970).

WEBSTER, J. B., (ed.), *History of Uganda,* vol. i (East African Publishing House, Nairobi, Forthcoming).

WERE, G., *A History of the Abaluyia of Western Kenya* (Nairobi, 1967).

——, *Western Kenya Historical Texts* (Nairobi, 1967).

WHITEHEAD, G. O., 'Suppressed Classes Among the Bari", *SNR* 34 (1953).

WILLIAMS, F. L., 'Teso Clans', *UJ* 4 (1936).

WILSON, J. G., 'Preliminary Observations on the Oropom Peoples of Karamoja', *UJ* 34 (1970).

——, 'The Vegetation of Karamoja District, Northern Region, Uganda', in *Memoirs of the Research Division*, Uganda Department of Agriculture, Ser. 2, No. 5 (1962).

WRIGHT, A. C. A., 'Notes on the Iteso Social Organisation', *UJ* 9 (1942).

Index

All clans, territorial divisions, age- and generation-sets listed are Jie, except when designated, as follows: 'A', for Acoli; 'D', for Dodos; 'E', for Eyan; 'I', for Iteso; 'K', for Karimojong; 'L', for Labwor; 'N', for Nyakwai; 'S', for Samburu; 'T', for Turkana; 'Tp', for Toposa; and 'U', for groups of the same name existing in two or more socieites.

Ngikosowa—*cont.*
  as 'real' name of, 41–2; praise songs of, 41–2; date of opening of, 48–51; Ngikolimoru age-set of, 48; Ngidewa age-section of, 48, 158; Nginyamanyang age-set of, 48, 49 n.; Ngikwei age-section and age-set of, 48, 49–50, 229, 258; Ngingatunyo age-set of, 49–50; Ngilobai age-set of, 49; as informants, 53–5; as current 'senior elders', 154 and n.; Ngimoru age-set of, 158; as 'junior officers' in Loriang's army, 239

Ngikuliak, 64, 65 and n., 67, 100, 116, 141; magic and religion of, 65, 72 and n., 181 n.; language of, 65, 66 and n., 73 and n., 103; symbiotic relationship of, 66, 192; Jie attitudes towards, 66, 70, 192; connection of, with Lokwor clan, 66, 70, 216; settlements of, 67 (*see also* 'Maru Hill'); songs of, 67; pottery of, 67 and n.; rock-paintings of, 67–8; economy of, 68–70; pipes of, 68–9 and n.; domestic animals and, 69–70, 115–16; derivation of name, 69 n.; socio-political system of, 71–2; population of, 71 and n.; leaders of, *see* 'Awangaki', 'Lobeimoe', 'Loceno', 'Lolemutum', 'Lomare'; circumcision of, 72–3 and n., 76–7; impact on, of Jie, 115–16, 135, 192; at Kiruu cave, 148; iron-trade of, 192–3; assimilation of, 217; Jie take refuge with, 224

Ngimirio generation-set (D), 108; (K), 42 n.

Ngimis (or 'Ngimik') generation-set (T), 93 n., 109 n., 119

Ngimonia division (T), 91 ff., 107 n., 117–19, 130, 194, 216; clans of, 94 n.

Ngimoru generation-set (K), 42 n.

Ngimothingo generation-set (D), 229

Ngimugeto generation-set, 36 n., 40, 120; Ngikoria as 'real' name of, 42; praise song of, 42; Ngikakerekerei age-set of, 45 n.; date of opening of, 46–8, 50–1; as informants, 54–5; 'promotion' of, 154; ornaments of, 156

Ngingatunyo generation-set (K), 42 n., 200; Ngikadokori age-set of, 207

Nginute (or 'Ngisuguru') generation-set (T), 194

Ngipalajam generation-set, 93, 108 and n., 109, 114, 117–19; Ngimirio age-set of, 108, 133; as settlers of Najie, 131, 133, 140; Ngingatunyo age-set of, 133

Ngiputiro generation-set (D), 143; (T), 194

Ngiro. *See* 'Jie'

Ngisigari clan (K), 198

Ngisigari group, 195–6, 198; Kalenjin elements of, 195; dispersal of, 195–6, 198; migration of, to Apule, 196; Samburu elements of, 198. *See also* 'Moru Apalon'

Ngisir generation-set, 44 and n., 109 and n., 131 n.

Ngisiroi generation-set, 29, 44, 183, 186, 207, 209, 227; date of opening of, 51, 163; Ngimadanga age-set of, 163, 188; Ngiwapeto age-set of, 188; Ngiyarameri age-set of, 188, 209; in Poet war, 188, 202

ngitalia/etal ('clan observances'), 23–5, 28, 55, 82–4 and n., 136, 182; bushbucks (*akoloba*) in, 23, 82, 100 n.; squirrels (*loceleku*) in, 23, 82; *ekalungur* bridal aprons in, 23, 82, 83; gazelles in, 23, 82, 83; *lobunat* ceremony in, 23, 82, 83, 97 n.; *lokidori* ceremony in, 22, 83, 84; *lomalol* ceremony in, 82, 83, 97 n.; *ngadalai* bridal aprons in, 83, 84; *nyakaiya* bridal aprons in, 83. *See also* 'clans'

Ngitome generation-set, 35, 38, 40, 42, 44, 45 n., 56; date of opening of, 46; as informants, 55

Ngitukoi generation-set (K), 42 n.

Nile River, 3, 249

Nyakwai, 1, 71 n., 82 n., 103, 126 n., 217, 249, 250; interviews with, 60 n.; R. Herring's work with, 82 n., 88 n., 126 n., 147 n., 204 n., 236 n.; relations of, with Jie, 147; conflicts of, with Jie, 203–4 and n. (*see also* 'Lolung'); Loriang makes peace with, 236 and n., 258

Nyamdere. See 'famines and droughts'

Nyanga Peak, 166, 203

Nyangea, 64, 98 n., 100, 215 n.; J. Weatherby's work with, 143 n.; hills of, 141, 143, 145, 225

Odanga, 161 and n.

Oding, 128 n., 186–7, 230; as fire-maker, 121 ff.; as founder of Rengen, 123–4, 126, 127; moves from Daidai, 127–9; return of, to west, 138–9; 'fire-sticks of', 188

Okeo, Yonasan, 114 n.

Okiek, 65 n., 66 n.

Olemukan, 111, 112 n.

Omanimani River, 103, 250

Onyipo, 111

Opio, 114, 123, 139

Orom, Mt., 88–103 n. *passim*, 112, 148, 165, 183, 225

Oropom (or 'Iworopom'), 63–4,

100, 200; J. Wilson's work with, 60, 63–4, 199; economy of, 199; destruction of, 199–200

Orwakol, 65, 119 and n., 131–2; as fire-maker, 121 ff., 169; as founder of Lokorwakol, 122–3, 127, 130, 169, 170, 180; 'fire-sticks' of, 176

Otukei, Mt., 52, 89, 99, 103, 117, 159, 160, 161

Pader Kingdom (A), 236
Paibwor clan (A), 159
Paicam Kingdom (A), 159
Paimol Kingdom (A), 183 n., 190
Paiper Kingdom (A), 236
Pajimu clan (A), 162
Pajule Kingdom (A), 159, 248, 249
Paluo, 178 n.
Panyangara territorial division, 18, 29, 95 n., 112, 133, 138 n., 147, 163, 175, 219, 224; early settlements of, see 'Lokibuwo'; assimilations in, 135, 190 (see also 'Kadokini'); control over Toror iron, 166; conflicts of, with Karimojong, 203, 205, 207, 212–13 (see also 'Lokibuwo'); treaty of, with Bokora, 213; settlements of, at Kapuyon and Loputh, 218; warriors of, at Tiira, 228; battalion of, in Loriang's army, 231 and n., 235; Tufnell's camp at, 257, 258
Panyamenya clan (L), 95 n.
Patiko Kingdom (A), 126 n., 248 n.
Payira (or 'Payera') Kingdom (A), 100 n., 111 and n.
Pei section (K); 200 n., 204 n.; conflicts of, with Jie, 212, 213, 215, 237, 240, 247 (see also 'Nakaterot', 'Juuru', 'Namuget', 'Lokicar'); loss of territory by, 240, 244
Pelekec, Mt., 194
'people of the axe' (ngika-aep), 174 n., 191. See also 'Kathewok'
Pian section (K), 80, 200, 220; role of, in wars with Jie, 215
Poet clan, 27, 190–1; ngitalia of, 83; branches of, 190–1
Poet (or 'Poot') group, 71 n., 88, 95 n., 141; economy of, 81–2, 90, 183; migration of, from north, 89–90, 103, 139; at Kapeta River, 89, 103, 114, 139, 146, 183; language of, 99, 191; effect on, of Nyamdere, 112–14; encounter of, with western refugees, 114, 139; form Lokaato group, 124, 191; settlements of, near Najie, 139, 185, 191; allies of, 146; relations of, with Jie, 146, 185; occupation by, of Nyangea, 146–7; settle with Eyan, 147 n., 183; effect on, of Laparanat, 183; sojourn of, to

Acholi, 183, 185; relations of, with Dodos, 185; war of, with Jie, 185–92, 202, 207, 8; attacks on, by Dodos, 190; destruction of, 190, 202; as war-captives, 190, 216
Pokot (or 'Upe'), 64, 76, 156 n., 195, 247
Poot clan (D), 124; (E), 147 n. See also 'Poet group'
Potongo (A), 116 n.

Ratai clan, 186–7, 188; as Rengen fire-makers, 121, 124, 138, 159 (see also 'Oding')
Remokwori clan, 135 and n.
Rendille, 194
Rengen major division, 3, 17, 18 and n., 39, 97 n., 114, 119, 140, 159, 164, 183, 248–9; sacred animals of, 17 n., 128, 186; origin of, 30, 80, 112, 126–7 (see also 'Oding'); fire-makers of, 124 ff. (see also 'Kalolet clan', 'Ratai clan'); and concept of rwot, 125; pastoralism of, 129–30; north-western settlements of, 139, 146, 151, 183, 186, 210–11; and Kapeta watering-points, 146, 185, 210, 219; iron-trade of, with Eyan, 165; war of, with Poet, 185 ff.; conflicts of, with Bokora, 205, 211, 214–15; conflicts of, with Dodos, 210–11, 229 (see also 'Tiira'); during Apetai campaign, 214–15; battalion of, in Loriang's army, 238
research assistants, 56–7, 60, 263–4
Rikitai group, 225 n.
ritual groves, 22; Nayan, 39, 154, 180; Nakerwon, 44; Looi, 157, 174, 179, 219, 246; Lomukura, 172; Namoja, 186. See also 'Daidai', 'Moru Anamit', 'Moru Eker'
Rudolf, Lake, 3, 50 n., 76, 194, 195 and n., 196
rwot/rwodi, 100, 125, 178 n., 179; ceremonies and councils of, 125; concept of, as influence on office of fire-maker, 178
Rwot, Mt., 88, 111
Ryemarot, Rwot, 236

Salisbury, Lord, 249
Samburu (or 'Ngikor'), 75, 194–6; fire-ritual of, 121–2; P. Spencer's work with, 195. See also 'Ngisigari group'
Sebei, 199
Shilluk, 89
Sidok (or 'Kicok'), 76
Simotoi clan, 162
smallpox epidemic, 49, 224
'Sudan-Wila', 88
Swahili (Acumpa), 50, 221, 223, 225,